CULTURAL

POLITICS

AND SOCIAL

MOVEMENTS

☐

CULTURAL

POLITICS

edited by

AND SOCIAL

Marcy Darnovsky,

MOVEMENTS

Barbara Epstein,

and Richard Flacks

 Temple University Press

Philadelphia

Temple University Press, Philadelphia 19122
Copyright © 1995 by Temple University. All rights reserved
Published 1995
Printed in the United States of America

Text design by Nighthawk Design

Library of Congress Cataloging-in-Publication Data
Cultural politics and social movements / edited by Marcy Darnovsky, Barbara
    Epstein, and Richard Flacks.
        p.   cm.
    Includes bibliographical references and index.
    ISBN 1-56639-322-1 (cl : alk. paper). — ISBN 1-56639-323-X (pb : alk paper)
        1. Social movements—Congresses.   2. Group identity—Political aspects—
    Congresses.   I. Darnovsky, Marcy.   II. Epstein, Barbara Leslie, 1944–
    III. Flacks, Richard.
    HN28.C85   1995
    303.48′4—dc20   94-37908

Contents

Introduction

Like so much else about social movements, the meaning of the term is itself often hotly contested. For us, social movements are collective efforts by socially and politically subordinated people to challenge the conditions and assumptions of their lives. These efforts are a distinctive sort of social activity: collective action becomes a "movement" when participants refuse to accept the boundaries of established institutional rules and routinized roles. Single instances of such popular defiance don't make a movement; the term refers to persistent, patterned, and widely distributed collective challenges to the status quo.

While traditional definitions usually focus on movement challenges to political structures, economic arrangements, and institutional rules, social movements—perhaps especially contemporary ones—also take on established cultural categories and social identities. Accordingly, social movements appear to be simultaneously spontaneous and strategic, expressive (of emotion and need) and instrumental (seeking some concrete ends), unruly and organized, political and cultural. The seeming contradictoriness of movement activity therefore challenges not only political systems and cultural status quos but also many of our explanatory frameworks and analytic categories. When social movements are surging, both social order and social theory are called into question.[1]

Social Movements as a Field of Study

Intellectual discourse about social movements has always been tightly connected to theorists' attitudes toward democracy. At the most conservative pole have been those who, from at least the time of the French Revolution, saw the actions of unruly mobs as proof of the inherent danger of democracy and of the need for authoritative social control. At the liberal center has been the view that movements, although undesirable, are symptoms of institutional failure, and, therefore, that they signal the need for social reform, including reforms that would strengthen the legitimacy of established authority by granting the unruly certain rights of democratic citizenship. On the left have been those who interpreted popular movements as evidence of the illegitimacy of established institutions because they exposed the oppression and deceit inherent in the prevailing system. Those who believed in authentic democracy would, in this view, sympathize with popular movements and try to aid them.

Academic theorizing about movements has been grounded in such ideological preconceptions. Theories about the irrationality of the crowd and the vulnerability of masses to manipulation and authoritarian control shaped much of the work on social movements and mass society in the 1940s and 1950s. Analyses of social movements during that period emphasized the aberrational, the bizarre, and the potentially totalitarian and stressed what came to be called "collective behavior"—that is, the expressive, transgressive, and spontaneous facets of movement experience. The dominant understanding was that movements were to be taken seriously only as symptoms of social "strain" (disorder or disorganization), as symptoms of the breakdown of communal ties in "mass society," as a species of "deviant behavior," as phenomena needing to be treated or controlled. The contents of movements' beliefs, structures, and programs were rarely attended to for their own sake. Instead, movement beliefs were thought to typify mass tendencies to short-circuit rational considerations and institutional realities in an effort to find magical solutions to people's troubles.

Marxism offered an alternative to these "collective behavior/mass society" sorts of interpretation. For Marx, movements arose from the reality of subordination and exploitation and were best understood as authentic collective problem-solving efforts. Mass irrationality was expressed not in movements but in the traditional, culturally established "common sense" that deluded people about their conditions and their options. So he argued, for example, that religiously oriented movements should be understood as authentic expressions of the pain and hopes of oppressed people but that insofar as people sought religious solutions they could not overcome the real sources of their troubles. For Marx, the promise of movements rested on the possibility (indeed likelihood) that as people struggled collectively they would abandon religious, ethnic, and other irrational traditional belief frameworks and become increasingly ready for rational collective action. Such rationality would be found particularly in movements based on class organization and interest. If exploited workers would band together across the boundaries of religion, ethnicity, race, region, or gender, they would finally find the power to change their shared conditions. Moreover, if and when the working class movement fulfilled its aims, its victory would set the stage for the creation of the first rational society: a fully realized democracy.

Thus, for Marx, the purpose of studying movements was not to enable authorities to control them but instead to assist workers in learning from their collective experience and in achieving collective power. Marx shared with conservative intellectuals a desire to advance "reason." For him, however, the triumph of reason in human affairs depended not on the suppression of the popular will but on its fullest expression in a revolutionary social movement constituted by the oppressed majority.

In Western Europe, Marxism has long been an important element of intellectual work in the universities and outside them, and it has significantly shaped the discussion of social movements there. In the United States Marxism was hardly an influence in academic life prior to the 1960s. The principal alternatives to the pessimistic conservative perspective on social movements during that period were versions of liberal reformism—expressed, for example, in the work of labor historians. Rather than simply labeling social movements as irrational, reformist scholars studied movements to try to increase "understanding" of them among elites and publics. In this view, movements were seen as symptoms not of the breakdown of authoritative control but of the failure of the political system to be adequately inclusive. Reformists argued that support for "rational" and moderate leadership of movements and the provision of legitimate channels for expressing grievances and participating in institutional decision making would offset the irrationality of unruly mobs and the manipulations of demagogues. Such pragmatism encouraged the systematic study of movements so that their institutionalization and routinization would be fostered by rational elites and informed publics.

Interestingly, this sort of orientation to movements had certain similarities with the principal variants of Marxism that gained political and intellectual dominance in Europe. Both Leninism and social democracy shared deep doubts that workers would develop rational class consciousness out of their own direct movement experience. Like U.S. labor historians of the period, Leninists and social democrats regarded the spontaneous actions of the working class movement as hopelessly primitive. For both, the key to rational collective action was the formation of a party that would in effect supplant the fluidity and decentralization of movement organization with a centralized mode of coordination capable of strategically directing popular activity, educating members, and taking state power. Obviously, European communists and social democrats were fundamentally at war about the nature of the party and the struggle. Still, both streams contributed to a view of social movements as transitional precursors, indicators of the potential for working class mobilization, the mature vehicle of which would be a full-fledged, professionally run, long-term party structure. For both, the role of the intellectual was as a social scientist who would provide the data and the analysis that would enable such a party to operate with maximal effectiveness.[2]

The Impact of the Sixties on Social Movement Theory

The movement surge of the 1960s in the United States and Europe transformed both social reality and social theory. Indeed, none of the master interpretive frameworks survived the experience of the civil rights movement, the new left, the youth revolt, antiwar protest, women's liberation, and all that has come after.

The southern civil rights movement posed a fundamental challenge to the "collective behavior" framework. Here was a movement filled with expressive unruliness but hardly to be understood as an expression of irrational mobs or rootless masses imbued with magical belief and manipulated by demagogues. On the contrary, the civil rights movement compelled all observers to appreciate the rationality of disorder and disruption, the capacity for collective challenge inherent in cohesive communities, the intricate complexity of relations between leaders and followers, and the necessary interplay of spontaneity and organization.

The emergence and character of the student movement and the counterculture, and the new left activists within them, called into question Marxist class analysis. Here were movements whose class locations did not readily make Marxian sense and yet whose manifest content was explicitly socialistic if not socialist. Indeed, class analysis was challenged by most of the progressive upsurges of the 1960s and 1970s, and the question of class was made still more poignant when a large sector of organized labor lined up against these movements. In Europe, the parties based in the working class were at best cool to the protests of radical youth. Indeed, not only did Marxism seem unable to comprehend these developments theoretically, but the Marxian expectation that they would be subordinated to or controlled by the working class and its parties was deeply resisted by the new activists. Although some orthodox Marxists, in light of these realities, tried to dismiss the protests of students and women as various sorts of petit-bourgeois (or worse) phenomena, most left activists interpreted these movements as progressive even if they had no full-fledged theory from which to derive such a judgment.

The sixties movements also challenged the pragmatic, reformist, pluralist perspectives that underpinned much of the media treatment of protest and provided the defining framework for the various public commissions (Kerner, Eisenhower, Scranton) that formulated policy proposals for dealing with it. Pluralist depictions of power in the United States and liberal analyses of political dynamics confidently expected that political and economic elites would promote effective reform in response to the mobilized demands of the civil rights coalition. But policy reform could not fully address some of the deep cultural concerns raised by the movements and, in any case, the commission reports recommending substantive reform were not, for the most part, turned into public policy. Nor did those movement leaders who worked within the established institutional frameworks achieve much for their efforts. Indeed, the evidence seemed to grow that movements were more powerful when they refused to institutionalize.[3] Liberal reformism was unable to account for the considerable intractability of structures of power in polities assumed to be pluralist and did not anticipate the degree to which U.S. and European politics would shift to the right in the aftermath of the movement surge. Liberal social theory further suffered, after the 1960s, from the dwindling of government funding for social research—especially for the sort of research that promoted liberal social policies.

Academia after the Sixties

In the immediate aftermath of the sixties movement upsurge, academic theorists embarked on a far more systematic and broad-gauged effort to study social movements than had been the case prior to the decade. Many of the new scholars had themselves been movement activists and participants. The field of social movements was, moreover, deeply influenced by broader paradigmatic shifts occurring in the various social sciences and later in the humanities.

As a result of the radicalizing experience of the sixties, academics were less interested in orienting their work toward the need to enlighten elites or improve the effectiveness of social control, whether of an authoritarian or liberal sort. Functionalist modes of explanation, which emphasized the capacities for equilibrium in the established system and differentiated between the normal and the deviant, were largely discarded in favor of a more critical, if not cynical, scrutiny of established institutions and their claims. Marx was avidly reread. European traditions of critical theory (Frankfurtian, Gramscian, Althusserian), grounded in the Marxian paradigm, propelled a new wave in sociology and social psychology, while neo-Marxian conceptualizations in political economy helped revitalize and transform the macroanalysis of society. And as academic Marxism evolved in the 1970s, it became as much involved in the critical analysis of orthodox Marxian categories and propositions as in demolishing liberal theory. Meanwhile, non-Marxian and post-Marxian brands of critical and radical theory were also emerging. Varieties of feminist theory, anarchist influences, social constructionist perspectives, radical democratic approaches, and communitarian notions all entered the mix.

Despite their apparent diversity, critical academics who had come of political age during the 1960s shared a certain generational outlook: a readiness to challenge claims of established authority and the viability of established institutions and a generalized sympathy for social protest and movements. In the early 1970s, some actively sought to redefine professional roles so that engagement with movement goals would be as (or more) legitimate than the postures of academic neutrality claimed in an earlier period. Indeed, some argued that if intellectuals provided their skills for hire to established political bureaucracies and corporations, the very legitimacy of the academy as an open, pluralist terrain depended on the presence of some who would lend their skills to challengers and dissenters. A still broader philosophical foundation was provided by those who argued that the future of democracy was embodied in the stated hopes and aims of the major movements—for full social equality, for example—and that efforts to enhance the effectiveness of movements fulfilled the highest interests of all in the academy. In any case, post-sixties efforts to analyze movements were carried out in a climate that assumed the legitimacy of these movements and was hostile to claims that they were manifestations of the irrational.

Resource Mobilization Theory

As early as the mid-1970s, it had become evident that there was a decided new look in American sociology's approach to social movements. The term "resource mobilization" (RM) has come to be used as shorthand to define that perspective. RM's core assumption was that movements were to be understood not as aberrational or deviant phenomena, nor as "symptoms," but as deliberate, patterned frameworks of collective action. Their emergence was not to be explained by the levels of grievance, the beliefs, or other psychological conditions of participants but by the opportunities, benefits, and costs perceived by members to flow from collective action. In other words, movements were to be understood as similar in many ways to more established organizational structures. What was most interesting about them, from this view, was not simply their unruliness but their rationality, their strategic capacities, and the ways in which they were shaped by the resources and opportunities available to the organizations that operated to achieve movement goals.[4]

The RM perspective promised to be a major advance for both social movement academics and activists. For sociologists, RM theory refocused analysis away from efforts to understand why people protest (and the psychological condition of protesters) to the study of the conditions that promoted movement growth and political effectiveness. Accordingly, social movement research would now have to be historical and comparative. It would have to connect with macrostructural analysis. Indeed, the study of social movements was coming to be seen as a major theme in the study of society as such. At the same time, RM theory seemed to promise making academic research a resource for activist practice.

Resource mobilization perspectives triggered something of an explosion of research on social movements and stimulated sophisticated and systematic academic debate about theoretical issues arising from that work. Movements are now understood to be integral elements of social and political life and not the product of social or psychological pathology. We now have a far more nuanced grasp of the internal dynamics of movements: considerable knowledge about the complex interrelationships between leaders and followers and between spontaneity and organization. An important conclusion of this research emphasis has been that movements are, by and large, shaped more by opportunities available to members for expression and action than by the ideologies they profess to represent.

The Politics of Identity and Culture

Even as resource mobilization was coming to dominate academic understanding of social movements, the perspectives of movement activists were turning in a direction that has come to be known as "identity politics." The term summarizes movement activity and analysis that focuses on issues of social identity, especially identities defined by race, ethnicity, gender, and sexuality. Identity politics flow from insights of the black and women's liberation movements of the late 1960s and 1970s—insights condensed in the slogans "black is beautiful" and "the personal is political." Identity-oriented activists and academics were concerned with the political meanings of everyday life and interpersonal relations, sexuality and subjective experience, lifestyle and popular culture. The argument that these domains are actually crucial political battlegrounds, rather than private or apolitical realms, opened new areas of cultural and social life to political action and scholarly examination. The emergence of identity politics triggered strong campus demands for ethnic, women's, and, later, gay studies, as well as for recruiting faculty and students from underrepresented and excluded groups. People of color, feminists, and gays and lesbians in the academy pioneered cutting-edge approaches across the curriculum–in social science and perhaps even more in the humanities; in fields as diverse as sociology, history, psychology, literature, film studies, and communication; in work that transcended boundaries between disciplines.

In the discourse of movement activists, identity politics sometimes emphasized struggles to rescue ethnic, racial, gender, and other identities—characterized as being stable with fixed, shared attributes—from their distortion or erasure by dominant society and culture. Inside academia, such notions have often been criticized as essentialist. By the 1980s, social constructionist perspectives held sway among movement-oriented academics. These scholars, deeply influenced by structuralist, poststructuralist, and postmodernist approaches, sought to uncover the social and cultural processes by which meanings and identities are constructed. In recent years, the cultural turn in both movement practice and academia has called into question the earlier dominance of resource mobilization as the primary paradigm for interpreting movement dynamics.

New Social Movement Theory

During the same period that RM came to dominate the sociological study of social movements in the United States, a somewhat different approach was developing among European scholars. In Europe, what impressed theorists was not that movements could be understood as rational instruments of social change but that organized protest was emerging in social sectors and in forms and with a focus on issues that could not be explained by classical Marxian categories and predictions. Feminism, student protest, oppositional youth cultures, environmentalism, antimilitarism, and U.S.-style identity politics were hard to assimilate into conventional understandings of class as the primary framework for collective action. Moreover, these non-working-class movements were taking forms that were, in the European context, surprising: they appeared antiorganizational, disdainful of political parties, and indifferent to problems of state power and to the question of socialism.

In some European left and sociological circles, these developments were described as "new social movements" (NSM), whose social meaning and internal dynamics had to be understood in new ways. Just as these new movements challenged the primacy of the labor movement and socialism as frameworks of social progress, so "NSM theory" was seen as a lever within academia for dislodging Marxian theory as the master framework for interpreting contemporary society.

NSM theorists argued that movements have social meanings irrespective of their strictly political impacts. Feminism, environmentalism, and other movements that aim at reconstituting aspects of everyday life demonstrate that large-scale social change is accomplished in face-to-face relations, at the level of personal identity and consciousness, in the household and neighborhood, whether or not such change is enunciated in public policy and macro-level power relations. Like those activists and scholars associated with identity politics and cultural studies, NSM theorists stressed that social transformation is mediated through culture as well as politics narrowly defined—that the personal and the cultural are as politically real as, and are not reducible to, power struggles in the state and economy.

Theoretical Encounters

For some years, the resource mobilization and new social movement approaches developed without much overlap or cross-fertilization, in part because of the continental divide between the scholars most committed to each. Indeed it seemed clear by the beginning of the 1990s that neither RM nor NSM separately was an adequate frame for social movement research, but that some synthesis of the two might be an important next step in the effort to apprehend the richness and historical meanings of contemporary popular struggles.

The strength of new social movement theory has been in insisting on the salience of cultural concerns and examining their sources. But NSM theory has been more descriptive than analytic or strategic. And, not surprisingly, it has been unable to answer all the questions it raises: Why has culture become a

major focus of movement concern since the 1960s? What is the relationship between culture and politics in the new movements? What ought it to be? Like
the new movements themselves, NSM theory has tended to avoid examination of how cultural change and the transformation of social structures can be
brought together. It has all too often evaded issues of class, power, and policy
rather than rethinking them.

Meanwhile, leading resource mobilization–oriented scholars have come to
acknowledge that the RM framework has not been helpful for understanding
some important features of movement experience. The RM approach was well
suited for the study of relatively formalized movement organizations, such as
those in the civil rights and peace movements of the 1950s and 1960s and national environmental organizations of the recent period. But it tends not to
comprehend movements, or tendencies within movements, that want to
change cultural and social assumptions rather than challenge political and
economic policies and rules.[5]

RM analysis examines movements as vehicles of reform in institutional
structure and government policy. Movement success is measured in terms of
political outcomes; movement strategies and tactics are assessed in relation to
what might be called instrumental criteria. As RM theorists themselves have
recently been arguing, this angle of vision is too narrow to encompass the full
range of social and personal meanings that movements embody. Moreover,
an effort to see movements as instruments for the achievement of political
goals makes it hard to understand how intense and prolonged commitment
and self-sacrifice can regularly be mobilized. By itself, a strictly political framing of movements is too denatured, too limited in predictive and explanatory
power.

A fundamental problem in current academic work on movements is less
the particular theoretical perspective adopted than the academic tendency to
fall prey to what C. Wright Mills called "abstracted empiricism." Too often,
academic discussion (especially among social scientists) revolves around efforts to generate hypotheses and formulate empirical generalizations about an
increasingly reified entity called "social movements." The trouble with such
efforts is precisely that they are abstracted. The content of such work tends to
assume a movement so lacking connection to a particular time and place that
its existence may well be doubted. This movement *sui generis* tends to be scru-
tinized as if it can be understood without much reference to its particular social roots or its distinctive goals but instead by utilizing an array of generic
concepts. Movements are in danger of being treated in academia simply as
items for classification and comparative analysis, as grist for the researchers'
mill. This style of work, reminiscent of the scientism of the 1950s, is abstract
not only in its content but in its value for real-world practitioners. One might
almost become nostalgic for the time when the sociology of social movements
connected directly to the interests of agencies of social control, for at least such
connection meant that researchers were dealing with specific movements

with some effort at descriptive depth. In any event, the more systematic, the-oretical, and coherent the field of social movement research has become, the less it seems able to tell us much about what is happening in the world we ac-tually inhabit and the less able it is to offer systematic knowledge to those whose vocations are to promote or inhibit the growth of movements.

During the 1980s and 1990s, the gap between activists and academics seemed to widen.[6] In the immediate aftermath of the 1960s, numbers of young academics undoubtedly felt connected with and accountable to friends and associates who remained movement organizers, and activist/academic net-works of various kinds had considerable vitality. But such linkages became progressively more frayed as the years went on.

Reasons for the growing separation between movements and those who study them are numerous and complex. On the activist side of the gap lies a healthy suspicion of academic obscurantism and disinterestedness but also an unhelpful strain of anti-intellectualism. This anti-intellectualism often mani-fests itself as indifference to theory. Investigations of toxic contamination or the details of corporate structure, for example, may be considered worth-while, but theoretical speculation and systemic analyses are dismissed as ab-stract or irrelevant. Among the consequences is a dearth of self-reflexiveness: the proliferation of diverse activist scenes and networks is often seen only as a strength; the drawbacks of fragmentation are usually glossed over. Though many activists enact sophisticated approaches to culture and identity, they are too often indifferent to thinking through the strategic implications and broader meanings of their efforts.

But the widening gap between academics and activists has more to do with the character of academic roles and milieus than with the characteristics of movements or their participants. Here are at least some of the recent and on-going conditions of academic life that affect the willingness or ability of move-ment-oriented academics to sustain ties with activism:

1. Career pressures in an ever-tightening job market compel concentration of time and energy on one's "own work" that is, publishing and mundane role responsibilities. Many people—perhaps especially those who entered academia in the aftermath of the sixties—are undoubtedly surprised by how preoccupied they become with the quest for tenure and how that quest shapes their personal priorities (whatever their continuing belief about their beliefs). Leaving aside the vicissitudes of job markets and tenure pressures, academic culture seems to foster a degree of self-regard and status striving not comfortably compatible with participation in col-lective efforts.

2. The campus is itself a field of political struggle over efforts to build women's and ethnic studies programs, to advance or protect affirmative action, to challenge institutional priorities, to counsel and support minor-ity and women students and colleagues, to develop courses that would

contribute to raising student consciousness. All of these activities seem po-litically necessary and fulfilling, yet they undoubtedly shift attention and energy away from off-campus scenes.

3. Academic discourse is notoriously estranging. One may have hoped that the post-sixties recruits to academia would have challenged such es-trangement, would have struggled to make academic discourse more ac-cessible and relevant to wider publics. It is all the more astonishing, then, that the 1970s and 1980s witnessed a veritable explosion of jargon-ridden theorizing and esoteric discourse in the very academic circles that pro-fessed to be most closely linked to social movements.

4. Whether or not academic discourse is particularly esoteric, however, par-ticipation in it inevitably weakens one's links to movement activism. Aca-demic culture at its best—what Gouldner called the "culture of critical dis-course"—demands independence from all institutional and organizational shibboleths and claims, a capacity to distance oneself from one's own emo-tional ties, an ability to bring bad news to one's friends, to search for the limits and failings of one's cherished values. Such qualities and practices have immense social value: the more vital the culture of critical discourse (when it is practiced authentically), the more society's members have the chance to learn from their experience, question authority, and grasp rela-tions between intention and outcome. But the emotional distancing and practiced objectivity demanded in that culture quite obviously can deeply conflict with one's capacity to remain strongly tied to a movement, and—even more problematic—to specific movement organizations.

The Santa Cruz Conference

The essays in this book were originally prepared for a conference called Con-temporary Social Movements and Cultural Politics held at the University of California, Santa Cruz, in March of 1991. The conference was inspired and an-imated by several overlapping political and theoretical dilemmas that con-front both those who participate in contemporary social movements and those who study them: the tensions between activism and academia, between the new social movement and resource mobilization perspectives, and between the "cultural/poststructuralist/identity" and "political/Marxian/strategic" versions of social movement discourse. These tensions are not only theoreti-cal dilemmas but often also painful practical problems.

The conference was intended to provide an opportunity for deliberation and dialogue and that it would strengthen connections between academia and movements for social change. Thus, we tried to bring together different gen-erations of academics and activists, scholars and organizers, new social move-ment theorists (mostly from Europe), and resource mobilization scholars (mostly from the United States).

An unexpected theme emerged in the days just before and during the conference itself—the Gulf War. Many conference participants were actively involved in antiwar organizing and protest; the topic of the popular response to the war and its impact on prospects for opposition in the United States was a burning one. These concerns were expressed in much of the informal discussion at the conference, and several presentations tried to examine the experience of "Desert Storm" and the protest against it. Though this topicality may have somewhat deflected the conference from its originating themes, the Gulf War and popular reaction to it provided shared concrete reference points for many discussions.

So the Santa Cruz conference had an ambitious agenda. Whether or not that agenda was advanced during the days in Santa Cruz can best be assessed by participants; a conference's effects are most significant in the multiplicity of conversations and encounters that occur between the sessions and on the lawns. The present volume grows out of that conference but is not its record. Not all of the conference participants wrote papers. The public discussions and debates that occurred were not transcribed and are not found here. And most of the essays included in this anthology were significantly rewritten.

The activists and academics, sociologists and "humanists" included in this volume all confront, in one way or another, some of the main agonies those seeking democratic change now experience. From a variety of situations and stances, the contributors try to come to grips with a core issue: What are the historical meanings of popular movements when the frameworks of identity, ideology, and institution that sustained them have drastically shifted? What possibilities for solidarity and hope are opened, and what truncated, by the reconfigurations of the cultural maps, personal anchors, and social organizations that fueled and structured movements at an earlier time? If "fragmentation" and "decentering" accurately describe contemporary social movements, how can they construct common meaning, unifying vision, and coherent strategy in behalf of democratic political, cultural, and social change?

Activists and Academics

One crucial step in answering these questions is to find ways to connect academic and movement discourses about social and cultural change. Three chapters address this topic. Each in somewhat different ways argues that academics, however "radical" their critique, cannot fulfill public roles adequately, or even formulate adequate theory, without deep connection to movements. Barbara Epstein raises the question of whether a cultural politics located in the university may not be reduced to a counterculture lacking concern for social change. She suggests, provocatively, that the much-publicized "culture wars" on campus cannot be viewed as an adequate framework for political engagement by academic leftists. Jeffrey Escoffier, focusing on the gay movement and AIDS activism, examines the tensions between community and academic intellectuals. He shows how the AIDS awareness movement has affected the research agenda of academically based science and the social practice of other professionals and suggests that, notwithstanding the "cultural authority" of university intellectuals, the intellectual vitality of society depends on the front-line activity of movement intellectuals. Noël Sturgeon argues that the new social movements transform the relationship between theory and practice. Movements embody implicit theories about power; these are constructed and tested in the direct experience of mobilization and conflict.

Both Escoffier and Sturgeon are suggesting that efforts to interpret social reality from the privileged sanctuary of the academy miss the ways in which movement intellectuals and activists are themselves significant contributors to social knowledge. These papers shed new light on the question of the role of intellectuals in social change, suggesting that the claims to cultural authority of academic intellectuals may actually limit their capacity to be effective knowledge producers.

Cultural Politics after the Counterculture

"The Sixties" is by now a perennial topic, but the writers in this volume make it fresh by examining its meanings both for society as a whole and for individual lives. Sympathetic reevaluations of that period have been hampered by the neoconservative insistence that the upheavals of the sixties represent a destructive force, shredding the cultural fabric necessary for social stability and human decency.

Osha Neumann unflinchingly examines the destructive side of the countercultural experiments sparked by the new left. His essay is remarkable for its insights into the ways in which the cultural revolt expressed (rather than created) the anomie and cultural dislocation already felt by large numbers of youth. Despite Neumann's justified dismay and disillusionment with much that he experienced, he affirms possibilities for liberatory culture. Presumably such possibilities depend on succeeding generations' awareness of the dangers inherent in cultural transgression and on their capacity to confront these with open honesty.

Rebecca Klatch, in an essay drawn from a larger project that compares the experience of left- and right-wing sixties activists, shows that the right-wing youth were hardly immune to the seductions of sex, drugs, and rock and roll. The countercultural experience of student conservatives led some toward libertarian rather than authoritarian politics. One of the ironies embedded in her study is that the counterculture aided the emergence of a new breed of right-wing intellectuals.

Craig Reinarman suggests that the cultural dislocations of the sixties were an important catalyst for new, grassroots efforts at self-recovery, most notably the explosive growth of the "twelve-step movement." Alice Echols shows that post-sixties feminism was not simply a reaction against the male-dominated new left but in a number of ways a continuation of the new left's quest for political and cultural transformation. Each of these chapters offers significant clues toward an interpretation of the sixties cultural revolution that is neither apologetic nor nostalgic nor condemnatory but instead sees that experience as a moment in a longer process of cultural reformulation.

Identity Politics and Activist Projects

For all its confusions and contradictions, the sixties counterculture was described by participants, critics, and observers as a coherent phenomenon and depicted as a response to what all assumed to be a coherent dominant culture. By the 1980s, efforts to define clear-cut oppositions and polarization in culture and politics seemed increasingly artificial. A number of essays written for this volume explore the fragmentation of politics, ideology, and collective identity that seems now to be the mark of our times. Instead of sixties optimism about emergent political and cultural alternatives, we are faced with a situation that permits no easy expectations.

Arlene Stein begins her chapter by looking back twenty years to a time when radical feminism and the lesbian movement seemed to embody a unitary character, and she contrasts that era with a present in which identities, agendas, and perspectives seem to multiply endlessly. As L. A. Kauffman argues, fragmentation is now characteristic of radical politics and oppositional cultural efforts generally. This situation is dismaying to some older veterans of the movements, but both writers eloquently suggest that the breakdown of "totalized" identities and ideologies opens new possibilities for democratic action.

An illustration of the role of identity politics in activist mobilization is provided by Mindy Spatt's report on antiwar protest in San Francisco during the Gulf crisis. Lesbians provided the backbone of antiwar activism during that period; Spatt suggests that the kind of identity politics they practice may be seen to have socialized a new generation of politically aware activists. Some of them are able to take leadership in other movement contexts—neither abandoning their identities nor being politically confined by them. In a somewhat similar vein, Ilene Feinman suggests that feminist perspectives, particularly ecofeminism, provide images and insights that can "re-weave" the culture. Exploring a tendency in feminism that is often castigated for "essentializing women," Feinman shows how it contributes not just to an understanding of gender but to a general analysis of the Gulf War and of militarism.

Howard Winant suggests that the fragmentation and decentering of the post-sixties era ought to be understood as a transitional condition and foresees the emergence of a new "hegemony." Winant argues that the current fragmentation of discourse about race, and the multiplication of what he calls "racial projects," may be a prelude to a new consolidation. The terms of this new hegemony have not been set and depend very much on how the relationship between race and class is configured in popular consciousness.

Cynthia Hamilton explores the ways in which environmental concerns have emerged as a focus for movements rooted in racial and sexual inequality. She argues that the critique of capitalist development expressed by people of color represents an expanded definition of environmentalism, one rooted in cultural as well as political critique. Unless environmentalism challenges the largely Western systems of meaning and value that undergird the structures of power set in place by the industrial revolution, Hamilton writes, a mildly greener capitalism will be the likely outcome.

Marcy Darnovsky and Andrew Szasz discuss movement strategies in relation to the mass media. Both argue with conventional activist assumptions: that information alone can be depended upon to spur action or that the biases of the mass media make them irrevocably closed to movement messages. In somewhat different ways, both insightfully probe the nature of mass media images to find ways they can be turned against dominant ideological frameworks.

Dilemmas of Activist Strategy

The essays in this section are efforts to contribute to the strategic thinking of movement participants; to bring together the results of participation in activist projects and academically grounded research and theorizing; and to bolster the capacity of contemporary social movements to act in strategic, goal-oriented, politically effective ways. Most assume the desirability of some shared programs, strategies, and visions among movement activists, now that the ideological structures that once sustained the left are gone for good.

The first two chapters in this section, one by Frances Piven and Richard Cloward, the other by Dick Flacks, explore the relationship between movements and electoral politics. The authors agree that efforts by movements to act simply as pressure groups within the framework of the two-party system are likely to enjoy limited success. Piven and Cloward suggest that an important political accomplishment of movements is to break apart established majoritarian electoral consensus so that potentials for politics of reform can be opened up. Instead of joining existing coalitions, movements seeking to influence national politics need to force their realignment. Flacks suggests that the mass political party can no longer be the primary vehicle for the political aspirations of disadvantaged sectors. What is now necessary and possible is for movements to be more directly empowered at a community and institutional level, and he notes that such empowerment could be the basis for a national political program.

The next two contributions, by deeply reflective European analysts of social movements, serve both to inspire and chasten. Bronislaw Misztal, pondering the unfolding process of change in Eastern Europe, warns of the large chasm between the hopes of activists when they initiate social transformation and their capacities to make the world new once they have overturned the old. Misztal's observations confirm how much more straightforward it is to overthrow oppression than it is to promote full-scale democratization.

To this rather pessimistic view of the possibilities before us Italian theorist Alberto Melucci provides a kind of antidote. The meaning of social movements should not, he argues, be measured by their immediate political impacts. What is fundamental is that the "internal landscapes" of human beings are in process of transformation. Movements are both the expression of new human possibilities and the means of their fulfillment. Democratization requires a new politics: but, says Melucci, that in turn requires human beings capable of democratic understanding and feeling.

Margit Mayer and Roland Roth argue that the cultural and political dislocation of recent years results from the disintegration of a particular "accumulation regime" of postwar capitalist societies, an arrangement that has become known as Fordism. Mayer and Roth are among those who believe that a post-Fordist integration is on the horizon. Again, its terms have not been set, but Mayer and Roth show how social movements are influencing its development.

Allen Hunter argues that the impulse to drop "revolution" from the vocabulary of contemporary social movements and from the conceptual frameworks for understanding them underestimates their radicalism. He suggests that the new movements are attempting social changes that involve not only reforms of specific institutions but also broad—indeed revolutionary—transformation of the rules of the game as a whole. It seems fitting to conclude the anthology on this note of qualified optimism about the prospects for radical and democratic social change.

ACKNOWLEDGMENTS

Many people helped us bring this anthology to fruition. Funding for the Santa Cruz conference was generously provided by the Humanities Research Institute at the University of California, Irvine; the Center for Cultural Studies at the University of California, Santa Cruz; and the Rockefeller Foundation. Mark Rose and Jim Clifford were key in making the conference possible. We would also like to thank Michael Ames and Jennifer French at Temple University Press, and Elizabeth Johns for her thorough and engaged copyediting.

NOTES

1. In this collection, we focus primarily on "progressive" social movements—that is, organized efforts toward a more egalitarian society. The term "social movement" can also be applied to collective action seeking to preserve societal inequalities or pursuing right-wing agendas. Some observers expand the meaning of "social movement" even further, using the term to refer to groups that are dedicated to self-help and self-improvement. Two pieces in this collection—those by Rebecca Klatch and Craig Reinarman—treat movements of these sorts. These groups, as well as the proliferation of loose but identifiable subcultures, raise new questions about how to define the term "social movement." Is there a "New Age" social movement? Do waves of cultural expression like hip-hop constitute social movements? Our emphasis on a definition of social movements that stresses efforts toward a more equitable society, and that distinguishes groups with social change agendas, rests on the assumption that movements opposed to established hierarchical arrangements have characteristics that differ from other sorts of collective action with conservative or restricted social agendas.

2. Chantal Mouffe and Ernesto Laclau, *Hegemony and Socialist Strategy* (London: Verso, 1985). A contemporary intellectual/activist who privileged mass action rather than the party was Rosa Luxembourg (see *Rosa Luxembourg Speaks* [New York: Pathfinder Press, 1970]).

3. Frances Piven and Richard Cloward, *Poor People's Movements* (New York: Vintage Books, 1979).

4. For reviews of the development of resource mobilization perspectives, see Doug McAdam, John McCarthy, and Mayer N. Zald, "Social Movements," in *Handbook of Sociology*, ed. Neil Smelser (Newbury Park, Calif.: Sage, 1988); Craig Jenkins, "Resource Mobilization Theory and the Study of Social Movements," *Annual Review of Sociology* 9:527–53.

5. See Aldon Morris and Carol Mueller, *Frontiers in Social Movement Theory* (New Haven: Yale University Press, 1992), for an excellent compilation of recent critical assessments from within the resource mobilization perspective.

6. The most comprehensive statement about this issue is Russell Jacoby's *The Last Intellectuals* (New York: Basic Books, 1987).

PART ONE

ACTIVISTS
AND ACADEMICS

□

CHAPTER I

"Political Correctness"
and Collective Powerlessness

Barbara Epstein

□   □   □   □   □   □   □   □   □   □   □   □

For nearly a year the U.S. media have been preoccupied with the question of "political correctness" and the threat that it supposedly poses to free speech and other accepted liberal values. The attack on "political correctness" has been directed at a number of intersecting targets within the universities: affirmative action; curricular concerns around multiculturalism, feminism, and gay rights; the intellectual/cultural arena of what is loosely called postmodernism or poststructuralism, located mainly in the humanities; and the field of cultural studies, in which concerns with race, gender, and sexuality intersect with interest in postmodernism and poststructuralism. It is remarkable how long interest in this topic has been sustained; the U.S. public does not usually find accounts of developments within academia, or the left, particularly riveting. But the articles keep appearing: In 1991, "political correctness" was the theme of the cover story in the January 21 issue of *New York*, the entire February 18 issue of *The New Republic*, Dinesh D'Souza's article in the March issue of *The Atlantic Monthly*,[1] and innumerable articles elsewhere in the mainstream media. The issue of "political correctness" fascinates the intelligentsia as well: It has been a continuing theme in *The New York Review of Books*, from John Searle's "The Storm over the University" to C. Vann Woodward's review of Dinesh D'Souza's *Illiberal Education*.[2]

The response to the attack has not been nearly as effective as the attack itself. There have been articles in *The Chronicle of Higher Education*, based on interviews with feminist faculty and faculty of color, defending efforts to include multicultural, feminist, and gay perspectives in university curricula; there have been critical reviews of neoconservative books on higher education (see, for instance, Roger Rosenblatt's review of Roger Kimball's *Tenured Rad-*

This chapter is reprinted from an article of the same title in *Socialist Review* 21, nos. 3/4 (1991):14–35, by permission of the *Socialist Review*.

icals in *The New York Review of Books*).[3] Still, the neoconservatives have had the upper hand in this debate, partly because the media have highlighted their charges, not the response to them. But there is another reason as well, which is that the responses, which mostly consist of matter-of-fact defenses of multicultural programs and arguments that such programs are necessary in an increasingly diverse society, fail to address the social concerns to which the attack speaks. I suspect that the public attention to the "political correctness" debate reflects not only fears—especially among whites and men—about the impact of affirmative action, but also less easily articulated fears that U.S. culture is coming apart, that it is disintegrating into a series of disconnected and potentially warring fragments.

The neoconservatives are attacking university radicals for intellectual and cultural developments that are far beyond the control of the left, inside or outside the university. The attack is intellectually sloppy: It labels people as radicals who do not deserve to be so described, and it distorts the broadly progressive, or critical, academic culture that it is attacking. Nevertheless the attack raises some uncomfortable issues for the left, and for the much broader critical culture that the neoconservatives confuse with the left. It seems to me that confronting these issues is part of the process of addressing the broader issue of how we would envision a more inclusive, egalitarian, and humane culture. It is a pity that the neoconservatives have initiated, and set the terms for, a debate bout the transformation of culture; it would have been better if this discussion had been begun by the left. Part of the problem is that—contrary to the fears of the neoconservatives—the left barely exists anymore; it has been largely replaced by a collection of progressive forces with particular, limited concerns. Taking on the issue of the direction of U.S. culture as a whole is understandably not high on the agendas of any of these groups. So the discussion has to begin with the neoconservative attack.

The media's obsession with "political correctness" began in October 1990, when the Western Humanities Conference held what it called an interdisciplinary forum, entitled "'Political Correctness' and Cultural Studies," at the University of California–Berkeley. The conference, organized by people who have promoted the inclusion of multicultural and feminist perspectives in the humanities, was intended to provide a forum for looking at the impacts, both positive and negative, of explicit political agendas in scholarship. Richard Bernstein, a writer for *The New York Times* with neoconservative sympathies, attended the conference and reported on it. In his telling of the story, the conference turned into a Twentieth Congress of the U.S. academic left, a collective acknowledgment of former student radicals, now in positions of academic power, that under their influence the universities have come under the sway of a new orthodoxy from the left. He asserted that

> a cluster of opinions about race, ecology, feminism, culture and foreign policy defines a kind of "correct" attitude toward the problems of the world, a

sort of unofficial ideology of the university. . . . "Politically correct" has become a sarcastic jibe used by those, conservatives and classical liberals alike, to describe what they see as a growing intolerance, a closing of debate, a pressure to conform to a radical program or risk being accused of a commonly reiterated trio of thought crimes: sexism, racism and homophobia. . . . The dubious implications of a politically correct orthodoxy have fallen under some scrutiny by the left, and that is what the conference last weekend at Berkeley was about.[4]

Bernstein went on to argue that in spite of such good intentions, the conference had actually been more an illustration than an examination of the problems of politically correct orthodoxy. He quoted one conference participant—Leon Botstein, president of Bard College—who, according to Bernstein, argued that "the universities are being polarized into two intolerant factions. The idea of candor and the deeper idea of civil discourse is dead. The victims are the students."

Contrary to Bernstein's melodramatic account of debate over a threat to free speech in the universities, judging by the program the conference seems to have been a relatively low-key examination of the role of politics in literary scholarship, with panels on such topics as "The Politics of Establishing Revisionary Literary Canons" and "Some Missing Considerations in Current Cultural Studies." Though Bernstein acknowledged that the term "politically correct" has been used on the left for some time as an ironic, self-deprecatory joke his account of conservatives, "classical liberals," and a few guilt-stricken radicals courageously standing up to the new "politically correct" orthodoxy entirely missed this point.

Bernstein's attack on "political correctness" set off a flurry of similar pieces in the press, many of them written either by neoconservatives or by journalists who largely echoed the neoconservative view that a new breed of academics has come to power in the universities, or at least in large areas of the universities, who give precedence to politics over the traditional value of scholarly objectivity. The attack on free speech by "tenured radicals" (a reference frequently made in these articles to neoconservative Kimball's book by the same name) is, according to these accounts, reinforced by "politically correct" students who denounce and harass faculty or other students caught using disapproved language or otherwise violating the "code" of political correctness.

Neoconservative Fears

The most obvious thing wrong with the neoconservative discussion of "political correctness" is that it is an attempt to undermine much-needed efforts to introduce the voices and experiences of those who have been excluded from academic curricula and intellectual discourse more generally. Though none of the neoconservative pieces that I have seen explicitly calls for restricting scholarship to that which is by or about white heterosexual men, in fact the attack on "political correctness" proceeds from the assumption that any attempt at greater diversity is driven by a suspect ideology. The sharpest edge of the attack is directed toward the effort to construct a multicultural curriculum, and the effort to address questions of racism in the universities. The February 18 [1991] issue of *The New Republic* is devoted to a series of articles attacking multiculturalism. The introduction to these pieces describes multiculturalism as an attempt to displace the Western canon, and equates multiculturalism with anti-intellectualism by assuming that the Western canon defines intellectual excellence. In other articles on "political correctness," efforts to introduce the perspectives of women and homosexuals are dismissed in the same terms. This argument suggests that the Western canon is static, and more or less rules out possibilities of extending, enriching, or criticizing it.

Though the neoconservative attack on "political correctness" is put forward as an attack on the academic left, in a sense it is less about radicalism than it is about the rejection of what the neoconservatives call "classical liberalism." What one senses, on reading these articles, is a group of men who are terrified that their world is falling apart, that their worldview is being rejected. Their fury over this collapse seems to blind them to the differences among the various critics of "classical liberalism" and leads them to attack all such critics as radicals and enemies of civilization. In these accounts, the coalition consists of multiculturalists, feminists, gays and lesbians, and poststructuralists (sometimes referred to as postmodernists or deconstrictionists)—with the latter category leading the pack. A *Newsweek* article on "The New McCarthyism," for instance, argues that PC is Marxist in origin but is currently more closely associated with deconstruction, which the authors describe as

> a theory of literary criticism associated with the French thinker Jacques Derrida. This accounts for the concentration of PC thought in such seemingly unlikely disciplines as comparative literature. Deconstruction is a famously obscure theory, but one of its implications is a rejection of the notion of "hierarchy." It is impossible in deconstructionist terms to say that one text is superior to another. PC thinkers have embraced this conceit with a vengeance. . . . The rejection of hierarchy underlies another key PC tenet, "multiculturalism." This is an attack on the primacy of the Western intellectual tradition, as handed down through centuries of "great books."[5]

Other articles on "political correctness" equate criticisms of classical liberalism with the rejection of objectivity, which is in turn equated with an abandonment of scholarship in favor of politics. John Taylor, in an article in *New York* magazine entitled "Are You Politically Correct?," calls PC "the new fundamentalism." He argues that this fundamentalism is based on a rejection of individualism and the concept of objective truth. Rejecting objectivity, Taylor argues, leads to a power struggle within the university, because "to the politically correct, everything is political. And nothing is more political, in their view, than the humanities, where much of the current controversy has centered."[6]

This argument assumes that politics are only now being introduced into a previously apolitical academy. Framing the debate in the humanities as a contest between those concerned with the disinterested pursuit of truth and those who are bent on politicizing the academy is a misleading rhetorical strategy on a number of counts. It implies that there is only one version of truth, namely the tradition of liberal (or perhaps more accurately, conservative) thought; it implies that the neoconservatives are the current representatives of this tradition, and that those who see things differently are therefore opponents of the truth. This way of framing the debate ignores the fact that there have always been conflicts over what counts as truth, and which truths are more or less important. It subsumes all critiques of "objectivity" under the heading of anti-intellectual political radicalism, thus obscuring important differences among the various critics of objectivity and including under a general rubric of radicalism many who would more accurately be described as critics of traditional liberal thought, in particular its equation between truth and objectivity.

In fact there are at least two critiques of the concept of objectivity. There is the argument, associated with Marxism and other forms of social radicalism, that claims to objectivity mask the power relations in which all ideologies are rooted. And there is poststructuralist rejection of objectivity, flowing from the insistence upon the socially situated nature of all perspectives, the rejection of even the attempt to approach any ultimate truth, and the denial of the desirability of universally shared values or standards of judgment. Although these two critiques of objectivity overlap, they are not the same. According to the Marxist view, all perspectives are socially situated, but they are not therefore of equal moral or intellectual worth. The perspective of an entrenched ruling class is shaped by narrow self-interest, by that class's impulses to preserve its power. If an oppressed class organizes itself against the prevailing system, it may construct a worldview that is not narrowly self-interested but points toward a better society for other oppressed classes as well. The impulse to defend the existing system is likely to constrain the development of new ideas, while the critical impulse of those in opposition is likely to encourage intellectual development.

The Marxist approach differs from the radical relativism, the rejection of any search for universal truths or values, that appears in much of poststructural theory. Many feminists, and to some extent other radicals as well, are attracted to the poststructuralist suspicion of statements put forward as truth. Yet divisions also exist. There are many radicals who keep their distance from poststructuralism because of its tendencies toward cynicism and elitism, and there are many poststructuralists whose interest in social change is limited.

Putting all those who question the concept of objectivity into the camp of those who would politicize the university, or who place politics above scholarship, not only distorts the debate taking place in the humanities (placing the neoconservatives at the center of a debate in which they are actually marginal), but also makes the category of academic radicals appear much larger than it is. In reality, faculty members who are committed to joining politics and scholarship are few in number and concentrated in small departments with little institutional power or resources, such as women's studies, ethnic studies, gay and lesbian studies, or peace and conflict studies. This way of framing the debate also masks the political agenda of the neoconservatives, which I believe is not so much to undermine the already quite feeble left, but to pull the liberal-conservative middle—which actually dominates the world of universities, foundations, and publishing houses—toward the right. The neoconservatives, it appears, hope to accomplish this by portraying the left as a threat to the values that sustain intellectual life.

Moralism on the Left

Clearly there is a lot wrong with the neoconservative attack. Nevertheless, under the rubric of "political correctness" the conservatives are describing trends in the academic left that I believe are real and quite disturbing, and that should be of concern to progressives. I hesitate to take the term "political correctness" out of quotation marks because I have never heard it used on the left except in a joking way; as far as I know it is not used to refer to a politics that anyone actually endorses. Also, I hesitate to adopt a term that carries the right-wing agenda of the neoconservatives. But the term does get at what seems to me to be a troubling atmosphere on the left, having to do with the intersection of identity politics and moralism. The neoconservatives describe "politically correct" students and faculty denouncing and intimidating liberals, and clearly there are instances of this—but what I am more aware of is a process of self-intimidation in the name of sensitivity to racism, sexism, and homophobia, which tends to close down discussion and make communication more difficult. John Taylor, in his article on PC in *New York* magazine, claims that the guiding principle of PC is "Watch what you say."[7] People are being denounced, he writes, for speaking of Indians rather than Native Americans or blacks rather than African-Americans, or for using the word "girl" rather than "woman"—even when the person in question is a teenager. One can object that we *should* watch what we say: that this is what is required to criticize, and ideally transform, a culture that is deeply imbued with racism, sexism, and homophobia. Still, there is a difference between maintaining a critical awareness of the assumptions behind our language and creating a subculture in which everyone is on edge, waiting to be charged with bias or looking for opportunities to accuse others of it.

I frequently find myself in discussions that seem to be dominated by a collective fear of saying something wrong: fear of betraying a racist, sexist, or homophobic attitude, or criticizing a movement made up of women, people of color, or homosexuals. I find this atmosphere of self-intimidation among students, among faculty, and in progressive circles outside the university. A few examples: I teach in the History of Consciousness Board at the University of California at Santa Cruz. For years I have used Clayborne Carson's book, *In Struggle: SNCC and the Black Awakening of the 1960s*,[8] in my course on social movements. It has become more and more difficult for me to induce what are always predominantly white classes to discuss this book, which asks how SNCC moved from a nonviolent politics with a broad appeal to a more sectarian politics with a much narrower base. The students read it, I can tell from their papers that they learn from it, but discussion is halting at best. The last time this happened students acknowledged—under my prodding—that they could not talk about the book without entertaining criticisms of a black movement, which would raise the possibility of racism.

I have also had a hard time, though of a different sort, with discussions of Alice Echols' *Daring to Be Bad: Radical Feminism in America, 1967–1975*,[9] an account of radical feminism in the late sixties and early seventies, which includes accounts of the ideological rigidities and personal attacks that took place under the slogan of "the personal is political." Echols' book is dedicated to the goals of radical feminism, just as Carson's is to the goals of the civil rights movement. But both books include candid accounts of problems. My class, which was predominantly female and strongly feminist, was not silenced by this book, but the tone of the discussion was disapproving. Students' comments implied that an account that placed women, especially feminists, in a bad light was sexist. Some students argued that even if early feminists had made some mistakes, to write about them was to give ammunition to the enemy.

This kind of attitude is by no means limited to students. I attended a meeting of feminists of my own generation—some academics, some activists—held to discuss Echols' book. Most of the women who had not been directly involved in this history (which in this case mostly meant the women more identified with academia) argued that Echols must be wrong, that these things could not have happened, that if they had happened surely they had not been very important and should not be emphasized in an account of the history of feminism. Several women who had been closer to the movement (including one former leading radical feminist, whose role—and mistakes—were described at length in the book) argued that these things *had* happened, that they were in fact an important part of the history of the women's movement, and that if we wanted to build another movement we had better look carefully at these problems, because similar things could happen again. The point I am trying to make is not that Echols', or Carson's accounts are unchallengeable—but that challenging them by suggesting that it is racist or sexist to criticize SNCC or radical feminism (or that such criticism should be avoided because it makes the movement vulnerable to its enemies) only makes it more difficult to think about these histories.

The two stories about discussions of Echols' book are stories about fears of sexism getting in the way of discussions among feminists. Self-intimidation also gets in the way of people talking with one another across divisions of race, gender, or ethnicity. For example, a coalition of student groups, calling itself the Student Antiwar Coalition, played a major role in quite an impressive antiwar mobilization on the Santa Cruz campus in the spring of 1991. One of the member groups was a progressive Jewish student organization. Several weeks into the war members of this organization became uncertain that they could continue to oppose the war; their representatives reported this to the coalition. The coalition, instead of regretting the departure of this group, decided to abandon the name "antiwar coalition" and entered a period of crisis about its own identity and role. Evidently the fear of being seen as anti-Semitic overrode the desire to maintain clear opposition to the war. In the faculty antiwar organization, the issue that we never managed to discuss was the Israel-Palestine question—out of the fear that there might be conflict, and I think out of a deeper fear that positions might be expressed that might be interpreted as anti-Semitic.

The problem is not just self-censorship. There are also overt attempts to define certain areas as off-limits for discussion. Many people in the organized Jewish community have habitually equated criticisms of Israel with anti-Semitism and have been ready to call any Jewish person who consistently makes such criticisms a self-hating Jew. This has been a problem not only for Jews who are critical of Israel and do not want to be written out of the Jewish community, but for the peace movement as a whole. The mainstream peace organizations were caught off guard by the Gulf War—partly because these organizations have tended to avoid addressing the question of the Middle East, out of a fear of being called anti-Semitic for taking stands at variance with those of the mainstream Jewish organizations. Sensitivity to anti-Semitism is legitimate: Anti-Semitism is very much alive, and the war was an occasion for widespread expressions of it. But it does not help the fight against anti-Semitism when charges of it are used to silence one side of a legitimate debate. And even when what is at stake is actual bias, silencing discussion doesn't help. To use the example of anti-Semitism again: There seems to have been a lot more progress toward its elimination in West Germany, where it has been an open topic of discussion, than in Eastern Europe, where it was driven underground by being made a crime—and simply continued to fester.

From CP to PC?

This is certainly not the first time that the fear of saying something wrong has stifled discussion in progressive movements. In the Communist Party we called it "correct lineism." Unfortunately the tendency to use ideology as a weapon against others in the same movement has not been limited to Communists or other Marxist-Leninists. Virtually every sector of the radical movement was overcome by this dynamic in the late sixties. In the antiwar movement it was accepted practice for leading activists (mostly men) to browbeat other activists (often women) by wielding what they regarded as a superior political line. Nor was this behavior limited to white men. The same dynamic was replicated within the women's movement and the black movement, as well as in the interactions among all these movements.

"Political correctness"—or, more generally, the tendency to use ideology as a bludgeon—is always a danger for a social movement. It can appear in movements with very different aims and ideologies; it can appear in movements that are strong as well as those that are weak. It takes different forms under different circumstances. The "correct lineism" of the Marxist tradition involved a humorless, single-minded focus on results; it meant putting a particular objective ahead of everything, including democratic discussion that might go against pursuing this objective. Today's "political correctness" comes out of a movement, or a political atmosphere, that is dominated by identity politics. It is more oriented toward moral than strategic thinking; it often seems more concerned with what language is used than with what changes are made in the social structure. The danger is not so much regimentation as preachiness, a search for moral self-justification, the assigning of moral status in terms of exclusion or subordination, and the use of moral judgments as clubs against ourselves and others.

Perhaps today's "political correctness" bears some relation to the peculiar situation in which progressives find ourselves in the eighties and nineties: We have considerable cultural influence, at least in some arenas (notably the university and intellectual circles), but virtually no political clout. This state of affairs can lead to frustration, cynicism about the possibility of political effectiveness, and a temptation to focus on berating each other rather than finding grounds for unity.

The appeal of identity politics is no doubt partly due to the fact that the identities that have become the main basis for radical discourse are often uncertain or fragile—especially for young people. Enormous numbers of people of color in the United States are racially mixed: One parent may be white, or the two parents may come from different groups of color. This is probably more the case for younger generations than older ones, and particularly true among the young people of color of relatively privileged class backgrounds; thus it is an issue for many students of color. Lesbian and gay identities can also be fragile: A student who defines him or herself as homosexual today may adopt a different definition tomorrow. Adopting a political identity as a Jew is—for many Jews—problematic, given the political positions that it connotes, and also given the long history of Jewish involvement in a more broadly defined left. Self-definition as a woman is stable, but its meaning may be very different for different women, and for the same woman at different points in her life. In any event the women's movement does not have the same vitality on today's campuses as movements of gays, lesbians, and people of color.

A politics based on identity encounters not only the problem of the fragility of particular categories of identity, but the fact that everyone occupies various categories at once. One may be female but white, or black but male; virtually everyone is vulnerable to some charge of privilege. The language of "political correctness" is saturated in guilt—from which no one is immune. In a world of shifting identities, emphasizing one's difference from others can give organizations, and people, a sense of security. But it can also get in the way of efforts to find common ground for action. I am not arguing that we should soften our opposition to racist, sexist, and homophobic language. I am arguing that a politics that is organized around defending identities based on race, gender, or sexuality forces people's experience into categories that are too narrow and also makes it difficult for us to speak to one another across the boundaries of these identities—let alone create the coalitions needed to build a movement for progressive change.

The left moralism that I am describing flourishes in an atmosphere in which identity by race, gender, or sexuality has become the main basis for politics. I think that basing politics primarily on identity creates several problems. First, in the name of opposing objectification, I think identity politics can actually reinforce it. Identity politics is dominated by categories that are easily absorbed into highly moralized terms. For instance, I am a woman and a Jew; but I am also a product of the left, in particular the Old Left, and an intellectual. These latter terms are also important parts of my identity—and of my experience of objectification, in a society not particularly fond of either Communists or intellectuals. But these terms do not easily fit into a moral framework. A political language that does not know how to incorporate aspects of identity such as these, but tries to fold all experience into categories of race, sexuality, and gender, compounds the objectification. It also makes it more difficult for people to understand their own experience in a complex way, to understand that different aspects of identity can take on different meanings at different times or can be more or less important at different points in people's lives.

Postmodernism/Poststructuralism

Thus far I have focused on the connections between identity politics and the variety of moralism that the neoconservatives call "political correctness." This leaves out the question of poststructuralism/postmodernism, which the neoconservatives regard as the intellectual source of the political culture that they deplore. The problem with this claim is that poststructuralism challenges any assertions of essential or fixed identity; it argues that all identities are shifting, unstable, socially constructed, and therefore always open to change. Poststructuralism would thus appear to reject the fundamental basis of identity politics. Nevertheless, identity politics and the postmodern/poststructural sensibility do come together in the field of cultural studies, and, more broadly, in constituting the academic and intellectual arena that defines itself as radical; there is considerable overlap and mutual intellectual/political influence between the two. It seems worth asking what the basis for affinity is, and what impact this affinity has on current definitions of radical politics and thought.

I use the awkward term "poststructural/postmodern sensibility" to suggest the ambiguity of this arena. "Poststructuralism" refers to the collection of theories that have challenged modernist conceptions of rationality and of inherent unity, order, and direction in the individual and in history; these theories have stressed the role of language in the construction of experience, and they tend toward a denial of, or at least agnosticism about, the possibility of any underlying, independent reality. In the realm of social analysis, a poststructural perspective implies a view of social actors—such as classes—as having no inherent character or set of interests, but rather as being defined through the process of social interaction, a process which is not governed by any set of fixed rules and which has no trajectory that can be predicted with any confidence. The term "poststructuralism" suggests the names of Lacan, Derrida, Foucault, and dozens of others who, even if they would not entirely agree with each of the above statements, nevertheless have followed this general approach. Probably the most important attempt to develop the implications of this theoretical approach for radical politics is Ernesto Laclau and Chantal Mouffe's *Hegemony and Socialist Strategy*.[10]

The term "postmodernism" has related but broader connotations. It was at first a term used in architecture and the arts to refer to a style that departed radically from high modernism and which rejected modernism's assumptions of universally valid standards and values, its understanding of art as a separate and privileged realm, its search for logic and order. By extension, "postmodernism" came to connote the aspects of late twentieth-century culture that appeared to fit this description: the loss of a sense of connection between past, present, and future; the rejection of universal values and, more generally, the loss of a sense of meaning; the breakdown of traditional cultural values and expectations; the emergence of a bewildering array of cultural forms and social actors; the rejection of any attempt to impose either analytic framework or moral judgment; a fascination with style, language, symbolism, theater.

What is confusing about the term "postmodernism" is that it can mean many things: a style of architecture and art that breaks with modernism; a rejection of modernist culture and thought as a whole; the strands within popular culture that emphasize spectacle and lean toward a kind of avant-garde cynicism and self-mockery; the diverse, disjointed, unstable qualities of late twentieth-century Western culture. A "postmodernist" can be someone who participates in this culture, someone who endorses it and tries to promote it, or someone who argues that we are inhabiting this culture and believes that we must understand it if we want to go beyond it. (The latter is the stance that Fredric Jameson, for instance, takes in his article "Postmodernism, or the Cultural Logic of Late Capitalism," in *New Left Review.*[11] This article could be described as postmodernist, Marxist, or both.) Given the specificity of the term "poststructuralism" and the vagueness of "postmodernism," I have resorted to the awkward couplet "poststructuralism/postmodernism" to refer to the intellectual culture that has grown up around poststructural theory.

There are some intellectual affinities between poststructuralism/postmodernism and identity politics. They are both at least in part responses to insecurity and instability. Identity politics provides a basis for building communities in a chaotic environment; poststructuralism/postmodernism describes that chaos—and on the whole applauds it, and looks for opportunities for creativity within it. Identity politics, at least in its current expression in this country, shares the poststructuralist/postmodern rejection of the idea that there is any leading social actor or any guiding historical law; in its current form it also shares the poststructuralist/postmodern fascination with language and symbolism. In any form, identity politics, like nationalism, revolves around a concern with naming, with defining boundaries, with constructing a usable language and tradition, and thus has appeal for a theory with similar concerns.

Nevertheless, it seems to me that to see postmodernism as the contemporary theory of radicalism—whether or not one views such a connection as desirable—is wrong. Granted, poststructuralism/postmodernism has a good deal to contribute to a theory and culture of social change. It encourages an appreciation of the importance of culture and ideology as aspects of domination and as components of a radical politics, an understanding that there is no automatic connection between a particular social position and a particular politics; it provides tools for analyzing the construction of gender, sexuality, and race. But cultural analysis is not a theory of social change, nor is it in itself a basis for strategy. The aim of poststructuralism, as I understand it, is to undermine the belief that there are established or discoverable absolute truths and to insist that reality is constructed through social discourse. This is a radical theory in the sense that it changes familiar ways of thinking. But discrediting existing paradigms does not necessarily lead to radical social change, or even to a radical social critique. It may instead lead to nihilism, which in turn may produce an apolitical, elitist aestheticism, or even a cynical endorsement of authoritarianism.

Poststructuralism/postmodernism often brings with it a hegemonizing impulse; it tends to go beyond merely presenting a set of tools for cultural analysis to suggesting that cultural analysis and theory are superior to other intellectual enterprises. It also often contains the suggestion that theory is an end in itself and that its value lies in its elegance, not in its ability to explain social facts. This skews poststructuralism away from concerns relevant to social change.

The poststructuralist denial that there is any basis for universal human discourse easily translates into lack of interest in communication beyond the narrowest of spheres—and often into contempt for clear writing. Though postmodernism/poststructuralism revolves around the analysis of discourse, most postmodernist/poststructuralist writers employ a language that makes dialogue difficult. It is not oriented toward the presentation of arguments that might be criticized or developed further; what matters is not so much the persuasiveness of a claim as the aesthetic appeal of the presentation. The obscurity of postmodernist/poststructuralist language, its tendency toward a self-enclosed, self-referential discourse, is a clue to its orientation away from concern with social change. I am not arguing that there is no place for technical terms or that all writing should be immediately transparent. Intellectual precision often calls for a specialized vocabulary; intellectual creativity often involves an unfamiliar or jarring use of language. Sometimes the language of poststructuralism/postmodernism makes for a more finely tuned cultural analysis than would otherwise be possible; sometimes it allows for leaps of intuitive insight. But too often the obscurity of poststructural/postmodern language appears to be valued precisely for its incomprehensibility, for its ability to create a self-contained circle of insiders.

Poststructuralism has encouraged close attention to the relation between language and power. To cite one example, feminists in particular have been receptive to Carol Cohn's analysis of the seductive power of the discourse of nuclear strategy. In her article "Sex and Death in the Rational World of Defense Intellectuals," Cohn recounts her experience of entering the world of defense analysis and learning to speak the language of nuclear strategy.[12] She writes that gaining fluency gave her the pleasure of feeling smart because she could engage in discussions that few outside the inner circle could understand. But in speaking this language, she found herself seduced into assuming an elitist perspective and set of values that on a deeper level she found repellent. I would like to suggest that a similar analysis could be applied to the appeal of poststructural/postmodern language; that, on a quite different plane, it also fosters a sense of superiority and power, and that it entails a danger of further weakening the already tenuous connections between intellectuals and the public.

Many of the ideas that are accepted within the world of postmodernism/poststructuralism are important correctives to traditional left ways of thinking. Insisting that no historical trajectory is given, no social class has a prescribed role, helps unstick left teleologies about the inevitability of socialism. But rejecting any connection between social position and politics, any connection between past, present, and future, makes strategic thinking difficult or impossible.

In thinking about the relationship of poststructuralism to the left, I find the analogy of psychoanalysis helpful. Poststructuralism challenges ingrained assumptions in much the same way that psychoanalysis did around the turn of the century. When psychoanalysis was new, people tended to dismiss it on grounds that it was an elite fad of no importance to people outside of certain rarefied circles. It is clear that this rejection was wrong: Psychoanalysis was an intellectual contribution of enormous importance. Although I am not convinced that poststructuralism/postmodernism will turn out to have anything like the same significance, I think it is misguided to dismiss it on grounds that it is located mainly in the literature and philosophy departments of elite universities. The analogy can be carried further. Some of its proponents have tried to put psychoanalysis forward as a substitute for Marxism or for social analysis; these efforts generally trivialize psychoanalysis and needlessly undermine its credibility. Adherents of poststructuralism at times display a similar and equally annoying aspiration to intellectual hegemony, as well as the same tendency that adherents of psychoanalysis have often shown to sneer at anyone who remains unconvinced. Using the categories of one's own intellectual tradition to undercut criticisms of the assumptions that underlie that tradition is not fair play. Psychoanalysis counters dissent by calling it "resistance"; poststructuralism dismisses opposing perspectives as "essentialist" or "totalizing" and invites rewriting debates of the past into contests between the (bad) essentialists and the (good) precursors of an enlightened social constructionism, regardless of the actual concerns of the protagonists. Not that the Marxist left has been immune from this: The concept of "false consciousness" has often been used to dismiss dissent or to avoid confronting evidence that history is deviating from its expected trajectory. Leaving aside the question of whether an overarching theory will ever be possible, no one has it yet, and intellectual modesty is still called for. One of the strengths of poststructuralism is its celebration of particularity and difference; at the same time, unfortunately, the competitive dynamics of intellectual discourse (and academic politics) encourage the impulse to undercut any perspective that appears to compete with one's own.

To return to the question of where the affinity between poststructuralism/postmodernism and identity politics lies: While one can find points of intellectual connection, I think the alliance between the two has more to do with the dynamics of the university and the intellectual world. The neoconservative claim that the universities, or at least the humanities, are dominated by former student radicals who now have tenure collapses two histories that are linked but not identical: the university radicalism of the sixties and early seventies, and the emergence of a critical academic and intellectual culture during the eighties. Most student activists of the sixties and early seventies did not go on to graduate school and do not have academic jobs today. Although many present-day faculty members who were students in the sixties supported and were to some degree involved in the antiwar and other movements of that time, it was very difficult to participate fully in these movements and stay on the academic track. Some people stepped off that track with the expectation that they could return whenever they wanted, but the academic job market closed down in the mid-seventies. Many of those who did manage to return to academia found themselves teaching a course here and a course there, or occupying non-tenure-track positions, or teaching in marginal departments. Radical thought continued to flourish on many campuses: People who got jobs in the seventies, even if they had not been activists, had in many cases been deeply influenced by the movements of their student years and by the intellectual currents that followed these movements, especially feminism, radical political economy, and Althusserian structuralism. But these currents were increasingly divorced from the aim of building a movement for social change.

In the sixties and early seventies, the centers of campus radicalism were the sociology departments, and to a lesser degree the other social sciences, because that was where most students interested in social change, or revolution, thought they should be. The critical currents of the eighties and nineties have been concentrated in departments of literature, art and art history, and philosophy because poststructuralism/postmodernism is rooted in artistic radicalism and radical literary criticism. Poststructuralism/postmodernism's influence in politically radical circles stems partly from a growing appreciation among radicals that cultural change is a crucial component of social change as a whole. The shift of focus from social analysis and political economy to cultural analysis also probably has to do with a sense that for the time being we have little chance of directing the course of social change as a whole, but we might have some chance of affecting the culture we live in, or at least our corner of it.

The most important factor in understanding the history of radicalism in the United States over the last twenty years or so, or the history of radical or critical thought, is the defeat of the left in the mid-seventies. In the eighties and nineties some universities have found themselves providing enclaves for what remains of a radical culture, by this time more critical than radical, if the word radical is taken to mean oriented toward social change. Over the last ten years or so, poststructuralism/postmodernism has been making a bid for intellectual hegemony within the academy and in the intellectual arena more generally. Under these circumstances an affiliation with insurgent movements can be an asset. The danger is that a rising intellectual movement can appropriate the cachet of radicalism while remaining more interested in intellectual and cultural criticism than in social change. It can harbor a certain contempt for the radical movements with which it is ostensibly allying itself, for their spirit of activist commitment which stands as an implicit criticism of its distanced, ironic stance. It is crucial that radical movements take cultural criticism seriously; but an uncritical alliance between postmodernism/poststructuralism and a disoriented and fragmented set of progressive movements poses dangers for the latter.

The defeat of the U.S. left in the mid-seventies is the context not only for the shift from social analysis to cultural studies and the affiliation between radicalism and poststructuralism/postmodernism, but also for the emergence of the particular kind of moralism that the neoconservatives call "political correctness." Poststructuralism and "political correctness" can coexist, and to some degree intertwine, because despite their differences they both flourish in a setting that is extraordinarily protected and at the same time represents a deep disappointment for many people. The language of "political correctness" takes on different tones among different groups of people. Many students see identity politics as their only point of leverage in a society with shrinking resources. Faculty members who find the language of "political correctness" compelling are more often drawn to it by an uneasiness about privilege combined with a sense of powerlessness. There is no denying our privilege: Faculty members at least have stable, interesting jobs, secure incomes, and opportunities for status and prestige. But on a deeper level, for those of us who were students in the sixties and either took part in or identified with the movements of that time, the experience of being incorporated into academia has involved a profound defeat.

We were part of, or powerfully influenced by, a movement that criticized the university for serving the corporations and the military, for reproducing within itself the competition and alienation of capitalist society. This is of course one of the reasons why many activists did not continue in academia. Those of us who did hoped that we could begin to transform the universities from within, as well as provide intellectual resources that would help sustain a broader radical movement. Academia has changed in certain ways: There is more room for women and people of color than there was twenty years ago. There is also room for feminist and multicultural curricula. But the university as a whole has not changed, either in its internal structure and values or in its relation to society. The university remains rigidly hierarchical. It promotes individualism and competition, and military research continues. The University of California, where I work, continues to sponsor the production of nuclear weapons.

For those of us who hoped for something better, this situation produces various combinations of guilt and alienation. I think that a sense of collective powerlessness has something to do with the appeal of a relativism that often borders on nihilism. It also has something to do with the aridity of much left and feminist theoretical discourse, the widespread use of a vocabulary that makes it virtually impossible to speak with passion, the attraction to a language largely inaccessible to outsiders. It helps explain the appeal of a moralistic form of politics. The right's ascendance to power in the late seventies has left us with a poor set of options. The current progressive academic culture is shaped by the odd situation of being a radicalized generation caught both in an era dominated by the right and in an institution in which the possibility of radical transformation has come to seem remote. In this sense "political correctness" is a substitute for radical politics, a wish for a radical community that we don't have, and for the ability to make changes that seem beyond our reach.

NOTES

Acknowledgments: I would like to thank Jeffrey Escoffier and the members of the *Socialist Review* Bay Area collective for their comments on this article.

1. Dinesh D'Souza, "Illiberal Education," *The Atlantic Monthly*, vol. 267, no. 3 (March 1991), pp. 52–79.
2. John Searle, "The Storm Over the University," *The New York Review of Books*, December 6, 1990, pp. 34–38; C. Vann Woodward, "Illiberal Education," *The New York Review of Books*, July 18, 1991, pp. 32–37.
3. Roger Rosenblatt, "The Universities: A Bitter Attack," *The New York Review of Books*, April 22, 1990, pp. 3–4.
4. Richard Bernstein, "The Rising Hegemony of the Politically Correct," *The New York Times*, October 25, 1990, pp. 3–4.
5. Jerry Adler, with Mark Starr, Farai Chideya, Lynda Wright, Pat Wingert, and Linda Haac, "Taking Offense," *Newsweek*, December 24, 1990, pp. 48–54.
6. John Taylor, "Are You Politically Correct?" *New York*, January 21, 1991, pp. 32–40.
7. Ibid. On p. 37, Taylor says that "making people watch what they say is the central preoccupation of politically correct students."
8. Clayborne Carson, *In Struggle: SNCC and the Black Awakening of the 1960s* (Cambridge: Harvard University Press, 1981).
9. Alice Echols, *Daring to be Bad: Radical Feminism in America, 1967–1975* (Minneapolis: University of Minnesota Press, 1989).
10. Ernesto Laclau and Chantal Mouffe, *Hegemony and Socialist Strategy: Toward a Radical Democratic Politics* (London: Verso, 1985).
11. Fredric Jameson, "Postmodernism, or the Cultural Logic of Late Capitalism," *New Left Review*, no. 146 (1984), pp. 53–83.
12. Carol Cohn, "Sex and Death in the Rational World of Defense Intellectuals," *Signs: Journal of Women in Culture and Society*, vol. 12, no. 4 (1987), pp. 687–718.

CHAPTER 2

Community and Academic Intellectuals: The Contest for Cultural Authority in Identity Politics

Jeffrey Escoffier

□   □   □   □   □   □   □   □   □   □   □   □

Tensions and differences between intellectuals based primarily in the community and intellectuals working within the university are a persistent feature in the cultural life of the lesbian and gay male communities. Similar tensions also haunt the activists and intellectuals of other movements and communities—for example, feminists, African Americans, Chicanos.

The production of culture and the definition of identity is absolutely crucial to the formation and collective action of the new identity movements that have become an important feature of American political life.[1] It is a politics constituted by construction of shared knowledge and ethical norms, one that nurtures a new affirmative sense of self. The personal and collective identities enabled by these social movements are constructed through discourse and other social interactions. A combined sense of self and group membership is created in reaction to and relative to those outside the shared practices and knowledge of the group. Identity and otherness are established simultaneously.[2]

Intellectuals—and I mean intellectuals in the broadest sense of the term as people who formulate programs, strategies, and interpretations of their activities—are central to this process of articulating collective identities and forging a sense of group loyalty, both for already established groups that are seeking social recognition as well as groups in the process of becoming established. But the important role that intellectuals play is complicated by the divergent pull exercised on the cultural production of these communities by two of the dominant institutions of cultural legitimacy in our society: the university and the mass media. Each of these hegemonic institutional systems exercises a powerful sway over the framing and transmission of the minority discourses that help to establish and maintain these identities and communities.

Each kind of intellectual starts out with a different relation to the production of the collective representations of their community. Since the identities represented by these new social movements are not accepted by the society at large, many of the intellectuals who embark on the project of enunciating new collective representations operate outside the established institutions of cultural legitimation. In identity politics, as in nationalism, there is a strong emphasis on inventing a new language, a new vocabulary, and defining new bodies of knowledge. These new languages and knowledges are developed in order to replace the institutionalized forms of knowledge that oppress certain communities or social groups. And it is by this means that identity politics provides social and symbolic resources for individuals to articulate the link between self-knowledge and the formation of social identities.[3]

While the possibility of collective action hinges on the construction of shared knowledge and beliefs, social and political movements are also often the source of new scientific theories and new academic fields, as well as of political and social identities.[4] Likewise the lesbian and gay movements have provoked the reformulation of theories of sexual development and identity: the theory of discursive sexual identity formation, developed in part by participants of the gay and lesbian movements, has challenged traditional psychoanalytic theories of homosexuality.

It is this interplay between social movements, the construction of new knowledges, and cultural politics that sets the stage for the complicated tensions between activists and intellectuals within the social movements, on the one hand, and the intellectuals of the university who are also participants in their communities' political life, on the other. I will explore this charged terrain by examining the differential political effects created by the production of knowledge and culture of lesbian and gay life, both in the community and within universities.

Cultural Politics and the Uses of Authority

Tensions between social movements and the university take many forms, but a number of them involve contestation over the forms of knowledge that are produced in the university and their value to social movements and communities. For example, one concern of many activists in the gay and lesbian movement is the validity of research, and the character of knowledge, on the causes of homosexuality. Research on the genetic basis of homosexuality might be interpreted as a fairly traditional form of disciplinary knowledge. But community intellectuals (as well as many academic intellectuals) are passionately divided between those who believe in the political value of homosexuality-as-genetic (because it removes homosexuality from the realm of a moral or lifestyle choice) and those concerned about the potential eugenic implications of such research—that genetic engineering or selective genetic counseling could then be used to reduce the births of homosexual children.[5] These tensions are produced by differing judgments of the value of the knowledge that is generated in the course of everyday life, community organizing, and political discussions.

While the validity (what might be called "the truth effect," in Foucault's terms) of knowledge is certainly one of the key concerns of both scholars and political activists, one fundamental issue typically dividing activist intellectuals from those in the university is the political effects (or "power effects," for Foucault) of different forms of knowledge that are relevant (or potentially relevant) in the understanding and representation of those communities, movements, or political issues.[6] By the power effects of different forms of knowledge I mean not only the impact of the legitimacy and validity of that knowledge in the social and political development of those communities or movements, but also their effects on the political and intellectual leadership of the movements and their strategic implications. The power effects of knowledge are important because they confer authority—different forms of knowledge legitimate different activities—on those who use that knowledge in their representations and interpretations of the communities, movements, or issues in the course of political or social life.

The tensions between academic intellectuals and community intellectuals also reflect differences in material resources. Academics usually earn salaries greater than those of activists and writers, they have access to the benefits and privileges of the university (such as insurance, office space, photocopiers, a teaching year of nine months, and so forth). Within the academy scholars pursuing ethnic studies, women's studies, lesbian and gay studies, or leftist research face indifference if not outright hostility, and they often work in underfunded programs. Inequalities between mainstream and committed academics result from differences in status, within the institutional hierarchy of the university or within the society at large, of the academic research that these scholars have chosen to pursue. All the while many such academics, particularly those who are younger teachers and who do not have tenure, are under pressure to teach large classes and publish an enormous number of papers in order to keep their jobs or remain in their profession.

As intellectuals and political activists, our intellectual commitments (our basic cognitive predispositions) determine not only the kinds of conduct we consider right and wrong but the kinds of phenomena that we regard as puzzling or self-explanatory, what frameworks or interpretative schemas we use to understand our experience, and what kinds of intellectual arguments we consider cogent and plausible. And since we live in society with many different historical and cultural milieus, we are faced with the question: What authority can be claimed and by whom and in what social sphere or community?

The different social value accorded disciplinary knowledge based in the university compared to the vernacular knowledge of community intellectuals yields unequal degrees of cultural authority or symbolic capital. And those differences in symbolic capital have distinct power effects. Community intellectuals engage in the production of knowledge as part of a project to create solidarity within their community, while academic intellectuals are engaged in the creation of intellectual legitimacy (sanctioned by the institution that is the primary source of intellectual authority in our society).[7] These highly charged differences create tensions between the different kinds of intellectuals most often identified as "academics" and "activists." We might characterize this conflict as one between disciplinary intellectuals who have an "epistemic" authority of the university and community intellectuals who have the "charismatic" authority of everyday community experience.[8]

Intellectuals and the Epistemology of the Closet

The identity politics of the lesbian and gay communities is shaped by a deeply entrenched syndrome of invisibility, self-knowledge, institutionalized ignorance that affects the personal and social development of homosexuals. Homosexuals are not born or raised in a community that recognizes our affectional and sexual interests. Instead lesbian and gay identities are established—as adults or by conscious choice—much later than in our consciousness of gender, ethnic, or racial identities. While many of us do not experience our homoerotic desires as something we choose (in fact, we grow up finding no positive reinforcement in the culture or community for homoerotic desires), we do, however, usually choose whether to come out and whether to participate in the lesbian or gay communities. Thus in the life of lesbians and gay men both vernacular and formal disciplinary knowledges play an important role (and perhaps a greater role than among many other movements or communities). First of all, the closet is an institutionalized form of ignorance; it is a silence that surrounds any young person's homoerotic desire.[9] Further, this institutionalized form of ignorance is reinforced by institutionalized forms of knowledge like sex education, psychiatry, and medicine; institutionalized religion; and the electronic media and movies (through silence and stereotypes). Thus coming out and the formation of gay and lesbian identities are very frequently contingent on cultural and intellectual developments. An individual's struggle to come out often relies heavily on new ideas and critical reading, and most importantly on a rejection of the vernacular knowledge of the heterosexual world as it is embodied in stereotypes and normative expectations, in forms of disciplinary knowledge like medicine, psychiatry, and religion, and in the portrayal of homosexuality in literature, the movies, and on television. When other lesbians and gay men are encountered either through sexual relations, love affairs, or political activities, the critical (discursive) evaluation of stereotypes, misinformation, and social norms is one of the most significant results. Out of this process a sense of community is created. This is one of the reasons why writers, journalists, librarians, booksellers, and other intellectuals are particularly important in lesbian and gay life.

Gay and lesbian communities, however, did not always exist. Like all communities they are historical creations, imagined in the process of speaking, writing, and public communication. Political activists, journalists, artists, and other community intellectuals articulate the vernacular knowledge of communal beliefs, practices, and norms. Like all vernacular knowledge, it is produced in the course of political and everyday social activity. As a form of knowledge it is usually practical, it is very dependent upon the social context and cannot be easily formalized (it is a form of personal knowledge), and it is transmitted casually to new members of the community. It is most rigorously tested by public discussion.

Two examples of vernacular knowledge are the camp sensibility and the idea of safe sex. Camp originated among homosexuals many decades ago. It was widely appreciated by gay men as a form of ironic commentary and broad humor that plays with the situation of a man being sexually attracted to another man. ("Is a man attracted to another really a woman?") It uses the irony of a male adopting feminine mannerisms and sometimes dressing as a woman to comment on male homosexual life. In a fundamental way, it builds on the idea that gender is a role. Camp was thus a very important form of vernacular knowledge (about the representation of gender, sexuality, and cultural coding) and cultural criticism in the gay and lesbian communities. The subsequent career of our society's knowledge of camp also provides a perfect illustration of the differential power and truth effects it carries as a form of vernacular knowledge and as disciplinary knowledge.

Although it received frequent expression in certain literary works, camp as a form of humor and as an aesthetic sensibility existed for a long time before intellectuals attempted to give a formal and coherent account of it.[10] Two influential accounts of camp that were published for audiences outside the gay community were those of Susan Sontag and Esther Newton.[11] Sontag's essay on camp treated it as an aesthetic sensibility that made a contribution to the intellectual climate of the early sixties. She saw camp as the forerunner of a new "erotics of art" that downplayed art as a representation of external reality and promoted a theory of art as subjective expression. Esther Newton's work on camp was an essay in the urban ethnography of contemporary America. Newton's study explored the life of female impersonators and the central importance of camp in their lives. For Newton camp was, in part, a profound vernacular commentary on the social construction of gender and sexual roles. In the translation of camp as a body of vernacular observations and practices into other intellectual frameworks, both Sontag and Newton formalized different "truths." And through their translations camp moved out into other spheres of American society. Each became an "authority" on camp, and camp as an aesthetic sensibility and as a commentary on gender roles and sexuality had an impact outside the gay community. Camp entered the realms of disciplinary knowledge among literary intellectuals and anthropologists. However, the power effects of camp as a form of vernacular knowledge indigeneous to the gay male community and camp as loosely formalized in literary criticism and anthropology are quite different.[12] Sontag and Newton became authorities on camp to those outside the world of drag queens and other practitioners of camp, while drag queens remained authorities only in their own communities.

When the social conditions that gave camp its existential punch changed with the emergence of a lesbian and gay movement that emphasized coming out of the closet and insisted upon the social construction of gender and sexual roles, camp lost some of its critical edge. Yet the disciplinary syntheses of camp forged by Sontag and Newton have proved useful to later generations of lesbians and gay men who never personally experienced anything like the camp culture of the fifties. Thus, camp still exists—sustained by vernacular cultural traditions and the public disciplinary formulations of intellectuals like Newton and Sontag—and is currently being reinterpreted by a younger generation of gay men and lesbians.[13]

The idea of safe sex originated in the early days of the AIDS epidemic. Even before the virus was discovered, early epidemiological information suggested that AIDS was transmitted during sexual activity or by direct contact with the bloodstream. Most doctors recommended that gay men stop having sex altogether except for those in monogamous couples. Many men in the community felt, for both personal and political reasons, that the sexual freedom achieved during the seventies would be difficult to give up. Moreover, many gay men thought it was unrealistic to limit the spread of AIDS by calling for sexual abstinence. In 1982, the Sisters of Perpetual Indulgence, a group of gay men in San Francisco who originally dressed in nun's habits to protest the Catholic Church's position on homosexuality, began working with other activists to develop a list of prevalent sexual practices and to classify which ones carried a high risk, which were moderately risky, and which were probably safe.[14] This was an important synthesis of vernacular knowledge and the available epidemiological information. The discovery of the human immunodeficiency virus in 1983 confirmed the reliability of most of the classifications in the early guidelines. Safe-sex guidelines are the basis for AIDS education and stopping the spread of HIV. And of course the sexual practices of the gay male community have been undergoing a process of social reconstruction.[15] The vernacular knowledge of sexual behavior, drawn upon by community intellectuals like the Sisters of Perpetual Indulgence or Michael Callen and Richard Berkowitz (see note 14), has contributed to the development of many important AIDS-education strategies which have then undergone translation and reformulation into the disciplinary frameworks of medicine, health education, cultural criticism, and sociology.[16]

The development of the camp sensibility and the idea of safe sex are powerful examples of the role of community intellectuals. But shifts in the forms of knowledge of camp and safe sex also demonstrate that the cultural authority of vernacular knowledge is very unstable and limited. This is due in part to the economic fragility and limited lifespan of the institutions that communicate that knowledge to the community (for example, the drag bars that were one of the bases for camp) and that provide the support for the work of community intellectuals. Contemporary examples include community newspapers and magazines (such as *The Advocate*), art or drama collectives (groups like Gran Fury and the Sisters of Perpetual Indulgence), history projects, civil rights law firms (the National Center for Lesbian Rights and Lambda Legal Defense Fund), community-based AIDS research initiatives (the Treatment Issues Committee of ACT UP, the Community Research Initiative, *AIDS Treatment News*, or Project Inform) and political organizations (like ACT UP, Queer Nation, and the lesbian and gay Democratic clubs).

But another limitation originates in the belief that vernacular knowledge is spontaneous, that it emerges from the community almost directly. This "essentialism" belies the conflict that often surrounds the development of vernacular knowledge. Vernacular knowledge is deeply embedded in the political and moral conflicts of the community. Because of that its authority relies heavily upon social pressure and often serves as the basis of moralistic criticism of behavior and institutions that appear to transgress community norms. It is precisely the context-dependence and the normative priorities of vernacular knowledge that severely limit the power it can have outside the community. (This should not be taken to imply that disciplinary knowledge is without its own normative priorities.) Thus, community intellectuals, as the producers of vernacular knowledge, do not usually have much authority outside their own communities.

One interesting consequence of the political struggle over the AIDS epidemic is that, contrary to the usual tendencies, gay intellectuals have earned some authority outside the gay community. Gay AIDS activists have created important social service and educational institutions and have had a major effect on AIDS policy.[17]

The power to articulate a collective identity, as in every other form of discourse, is based on the use of cultural capital. The power of inculcating in other minds a vision, a sense of self, and the recognition of new social possibilities depends on the social authority acquired in previous struggles. Cultural or symbolic capital is like credit; only those who have obtained significant recognition can legitimately demand recognition. Representatives of a community or movement can only be chosen at the end of a long process of institutionalization because a group gives its representatives the power to shape the group. Cultural authority or symbolic capital cannot be fabricated by fiat; it can never be practically effective if a social movement's vision of history is not based on actually existing social forces and developments.[18]

University Intellectuals and Identity Politics

The university as one of the major institutions that produces and legitimates knowledge in our society gives lesbian and gay academics a different relationship to the production of knowledge and culture than that experienced by intellectuals and activists in the community.[19] Alvin Gouldner has characterized the culture of the university as "the culture of critical discourse."[20] The culture of critical discourse is relatively less dependent on context, more theoretical, and more explicit about its underlying assumptions. And Gouldner argues that this cultural style is also a form of cultural capital—that is, it is a set of skills and achievements that are economically rewarded within the professional and academic milieu. In addition, the social organization of universities shapes the forms of knowledge and their social usefulness. The disciplinary knowledge produced at the university is formal and regulated by the intellectual norms of already-established disciplines, by the requirements of university curriculums, and by the power structure of educational institutions integrated within the larger society.[21] It is this institutional context that differentiates academic intellectuals from community-based intellectuals.

Lesbian and gay academics who are working to establish lesbian and gay studies as a legitimate field of teaching and research face enormous challenges. They must not only contend with the pervasive blatant and subtle effects of the homophobia within academia but must also produce work that satisfies the norms of the culture of critical discourse. Lesbian and gay academic intellectuals acquire disciplinary identities that are determined both by their specialty's status within the hierarchy of academic fields and departments and by the fact that the field of lesbian and gay studies is only one distinct element of an eclectic curriculum that is not integrated into a coherent program.[22] The process of constructing knowledge within the disciplinary boundaries governs the choice of methodologies, canonical texts, and acceptable research programs. To succeed in giving lesbian and gay studies legitimacy, the intellectual work of the new field must satisfy the conventions and norms that various scientific or humanistic disciplines use to determine whether a particular intellectual contribution is legitimate and reliable knowledge. Whatever cannot satisfy those norms and conventions—for example, some forms of the lesbian or gay community's vernacular knowledge—is marginalized and excluded.

However, even the construction of acceptable disciplinary knowledge will not guarantee the incorporation of lesbian and gay studies into the university curriculum. The university is currently the battleground between rival political philosophies of education that specifically cite lesbian and gay studies (along with African American studies, women's studies, and ethnic studies) as subjects of debate. The recent controversies over curriculum, the debate on the canon, is more than a battle over reading lists and great books: it is a conflict between different conceptions of social order.[23] Each conception of education implies different "academic identities." Classical curriculums like the Great Books Program or ones that emphasize the supposed coherence of Western civilization aim to develop individuals who do not have strong loyalties to any particular discipline, while the eclectic curriculums of most universities in the United States tend to encourage a strong subject loyalty that can serve as the basis for a professional identity. Thus the debate over the canon in the humanities represents a challenge by communities or movements outside the university—African American, lesbian and gay, Latino, and women's, for example—to the ideological basis of education in the humanities, which has been communicated via strongly defined boundaries of subject matter. This "secular humanist" educational ideology is one that incorporates new fields of knowledge and new intellectual identities by means of an open-ended eclectic curriculum with no coherent educational philosophy. Meanwhile those on the right like Allan Bloom, William Bennett, and the *New Criterion* have exploited the canon debate to try to establish a coherent educational philosophy and enforce closure against the inclusion of new disciplines in the curriculum. The conservative educational ideology definitively excludes those who they believe contribute to the "cultural decline of Western, male-dominated, family-based, capitalist civilization."[24]

Academic intellectuals who are politically committed to the left or who are members of the lesbian and gay communities, like the scholars who are members of any oppositional, ethnic, racial, or oppressed group, must work within the structure of the university system. They must negotiate the overlapping demands of academic life and their political and social commitments. To some extent the identities of academic intellectuals are shaped by the academic hierarchy of disciplines and the university—that is, as one get older one knows more and more about less and less, or one become increasingly different from everyone else. In the university, one's intellectual (or disciplinary) identity is clearly marked and bounded. This environment can insulate university intellectuals from their communities. In the end, lesbian and gay academic intellectuals must address much of their intellectual work to other members of their academic disciplines in order to guarantee the work's intellectual credibility. Thus lesbian and gay academics may do intellectual work that is potentially interesting to the community at large, but its disciplinary form inhibits their ability to communicate directly with a nonacademic lesbian or gay audience.[25]

The intellectual autonomy of academic disciplines that the American university encourages gives academic intellectuals a great deal of authority independent of their community. Their authority rests ultimately on the status and resources of the university in our society.[26] Community institutions cannot offer comparable conditions for carrying out intellectual work, nor can they do much in the way of transmitting articulated and developed knowledge to new generations. Very few if any representatives of institutions within communities are able to address the larger society with the authority that a professor or even an assistant professor at Harvard, Stanford, or the University of California can.

Solidarity and Legitimation: Intellectuals and Authority in the Public Sphere

Cultural politics become hegemonic through the slow building up of authority; the university, along with the mass media, is potentially one of the most powerful instruments of cultural legitimation. In contemporary American society a great deal of our cultural politics originate in the struggle for recognition and empowerment of communities forging and reconstructing collective identities. These political struggles require both vernacular and disciplinary knowledges—both solidarity *and* legitimation. This is most forcefully illustrated by the battle against AIDS. Efforts to limit the transmission of HIV can only be effective if the vernacular knowledge of the particular community affected is articulated and available—say, for example, the practices and beliefs of a community of intravenous drug users—and combined with the disciplinary knowledge of epidemiology and medicine.

The legitimation that accrues to disciplinary knowledge of a minority or stigmatized community's life contributes to the social acceptance of that community. But academic intellectuals who are committed to that community depend on the collective representations of community intellectuals and activists to articulate the new meanings and values, the new relationships, and the new practices that are continually being created.

What is at stake in the tensions between academics and activist intellectuals is control of the very grounds on which knowledge is produced and legitimated. The question of cultural authority is also the question of *who* gets to represent the community politically and intellectually. Community and academic intellectuals often have different orientations toward theory and need to acknowledge those differences. Among community intellectuals resistance to theory originates in recognition of the context-dependence of vernacular knowledge, but theory, as academics often insist, is nevertheless necessary to make very explicit the links between social and political institutions and interpretative strategies. While community and activist intellectuals often have greater access to the community public sphere—performance and gallery spaces, cabarets, local gay press, national magazines, theater companies, and film festivals—academic intellectuals have the potential backing of one of our society's major institutions of cultural legitimacy as well as greater access to institutional security. From the university lesbian and gay academics can often speak with greater authority to the rest of society.

Currently there is hardly any kind of institutional framework that encompasses both community and academic intellectuals.[27] In the United States the lesbian and gay community does have a relatively diverse and lively public sphere, but there is much greater paucity in the number of public forums for academic research: an annual series of lesbian and gay studies conferences (which have taken place at Yale, Harvard, and Rutgers); one established journal, the *Journal of Homosexuality*, a new one on the way, *GLQ*, and a growing number of mainstream academic publications (such as the *Journal of the History of Sexuality*) that will publish research on homosexuality; and a number of lesbian and gay studies centers that sponsor seminars, panels, and conferences. Despite the lack of interlocking public spheres, there are rarely any efforts to exclude members of either category from participation in the activities of both arenas. Yet lesbian and gay scholars' investments in the academic cultural capital (that is, the privileges of the university) have led Eve Sedgwick to caution that "the extreme difficulty, not at all to say impossibility, of doing or thinking coalition politics at more than a superficial level" may be reinforced by the fact that "relative privilege in our mode of labor is inevitably going to oppose to most of our investment of real creativity, courage, and steadfastness."[28]

It is only through the creation of some form of interlocking public spheres (what Nancy Fraser calls "interpublic discursive interaction") that the psychological investments and academic privileges of the scholars and the charismatic authority of community intellectuals and activists can be modified in order to produce knowledge that draws from both vernacular and disciplinary sources.[29] The validity (the truth effects) and eventually the authority (the power effects) of each kind of knowledge must be tested by debate, analysis, and social experimentation. Without a mutual encounter in public life both forms of knowledge are trivialized and socially limited. Whether in academia or the community knowledge is a product of collective debate. This is evident in the evolution of safe-sex guidelines, the post-movement therapeutic understanding of lesbian and gay relationships, and the widespread recognition of the social construction of identity. The creation of such an institutional framework requires the establishment and support of cultural intermediaries like publishing houses, journals, and conferences (the international AIDS conferences are good examples), which must exist so that dialogue and negotiation can take place between the community and academia.

According to Michel Foucault and many others, the universal intellectual who spoke for a universal and abstract idea of human rights is no longer a politically acceptable role. Rather Foucault has argued that the specific intellectual is the appropriate example for our time, a conception that most closely resembles what I have spoken of here as the academic or disciplinary intellectual who uses the specialized knowledge of his or her research for social purposes.[30] By contrast, the community intellectual most resembles Antonio Gramsci's organic intellectual.[31] Without the creation of a real institutional framework of interlocking public spheres along the lines suggested by Nancy Fraser, all of these models of intellectual activity are either limited or inadequate.

The first step in creating a dialogue between the university and the community is the mutual testing and debate by intellectuals in the university and the community of both vernacular and disciplinary knowledges. As intellectuals we live within a set of complex loyalties to overlapping identities of gender, generation, political orientation, ethnicity, and so on. The cultural authority of specific intellectuals or organic intellectuals is open to question. Therefore we must adopt a new role, one that is deeply hybridized by the multiple sources of knowledge and authority in cultural life. This is the responsibility of intellectuals in contemporary society, the responsibility of public intellectuals.

NOTES

Acknowledgments: An earlier version of this paper was originally delivered at the conference Contemporary Social Movements and Cultural Politics, the University of California, Santa Cruz, in March 1991.

1. Two writers have explored this subject very suggestively: Mary Douglas, *How Institutions Think* (Syracuse, N.Y.: Syracuse University Press, 1986) and, in many essays, Pierre Bourdieu. See in particular Bourdieu's "The Social Space and the Genesis of Groups," *Theory and Society* 14, no. 6 (November 1985):723–44.

2. See Jeffrey Escoffier, "Sexual Revolution and the Politics of Identity," *Socialist Review* no. 82–83, vol. 15, nos. 4–5 (July–October 1985):119–53; Carlos Muñoz, Jr., *Youth, Identity, Power: The Chicano Movement* (London: Verso, 1989).

3. For discussions of nationalism and its cultural politics, see Benedict Anderson, *Imagined Communities: Reflections of the Origin and Spread of Nationalism* (London: Verso, 1983); and the essays in Homi K. Bhabha, ed., *Nation and Narration* (New York: Routledge, 1990).

4. For example, the environmental movement has stimulated new conceptions of the interdependence between human life and nature in scientific disciplines. It has also stimulated the elaboration of new forms of spirituality such as "deep ecology" with its religious conception of human responsibility to nature or the belief in Gaia as the spiritual unity of nature. See Will Wright, *Wild Knowledge: Science, Language, and Social Life in a Fragile Environment* (Minneapolis: University of Minnesota Press, 1992), for an examination of some of these issues.

5. For a discussion of one recent study see Chris Bull, "Mom's Fault," *The Advocate: The National Gay and Lesbian Newsmagazine*, August 24, 1993, 30–33.

6. I have adapted these terms, somewhat loosely, from Foucault. The terms "power effects" and "truth effects" are the double effects of any discursive operation by which power/knowledge is constituted. See in particular Michel Foucault, "Truth and Power," in *Power/Knowledge: Selected Interviews and Other Writings, 1972–1977* (New York: Pantheon, 1980), 108–33. Barry Smart discusses the relation between Foucault's conception of power/knowledge and

Gramsci's concept of hegemony in "The Politics of Truth and the Problem of Hegemony" in David Couzens Hoy, ed., *Foucault: A Reader* (Oxford: Basil Blackwell, 1986), 157–74.

7. This distinction was suggested by a similar one made by Richard Rorty in "Solidarity or Objectivity?" in his collected essays *Objectivity, Relativism, and Truth* (Cambridge: Cambridge University Press, 1991), 21–34. I do not, however, mean to equate "legitimacy" with "objectivity."

8. We have few sociological discussions of authority. There are, of course, the classic contributions by Max Weber in his essays on bureaucracy and charisma. See *From Max Weber: Essays in Sociology*, ed. Hans H. Gerth and C. Wright Mills (New York: Oxford University Press, 1946). For more recent discussions see Richard T. De George, *The Nature and Limits of Authority* (Lawrence: University of Kansas Press, 1985), and Robert Dahl, *After the Revolution? Authority in a Good Society*, rev. ed. (New Haven: Yale University Press, 1990).

9. See Eve Kosofsky Sedgwick, *The Epistemology of the Closet* (Berkeley: University of California Press, 1990), and Michelangelo Signorile, *Queer in America: Sex, Media, and the Closets of Power* (New York: Random House, 1993).

10. For example, literary works that are deeply rooted in the camp sensibility are the plays of Oscar Wilde and the poetry of Frank O'Hara. On the latter, see Bruce Boone, "Gay Language as Political Praxis: The Poetry of Frank O'Hara," *Social Text* no. 1 (Winter 1979): 59–92; and Rudy Kikel, "The Gay Frank O'Hara," in *Frank O'Hara: To Be True to a City*, ed. Jim Elledge (Ann Arbor: University of Michigan Press, 1990).

11. See Escoffier, "Sexual Revolution," 140–41; Susan Sontag, "Notes on Camp," in *Against Interpretation* (New York: Farrar Straus Giroux, 1966); and Esther Newton, *Mother Camp: Female Impersonators in America* (Englewood Cliffs, N.J.: Prentice-Hall, 1972). One early discussion of camp as an indigeneous form of vernacular commentary appeared in Christopher Isherwood's novel *The World in the Evening* (New York: Noonday Books, 1954).

12. For an exploration of the ways in which vernacular knowledge is translated into the disciplinary knowledge of anthropology, see the essays in James Clifford and George E. Marcus, eds., *Writing Culture: The Poetics and Politics of Ethnography* (Berkeley and Los Angeles: University of California Press, 1986).

13. David Bergman, "Strategic Camp: The Art of Gay Rhetoric," in his *Gaiety Transfigured: Gay Self-Representation in American Literature* (Madison: University of Wisconsin Press, 1991), 103–21.

14. In New York Michael Callen and Richard Berkowitz also drew on their vernacular knowledge of gay men's sexuality to propose new forms of safer sex in a series of pieces published in a New York gay newspaper ("We Know Who We Are," the *New York Native*, November 8–21, 1992) and as pamphlets: "How To Have Sex in an Epidemic" (New York: From the Front Publications, 1983).

15. Steven Epstein, "Nature vs. Nurture and the Politics of AIDS Organizing,"

OUT/LOOK: National Lesbian and Gay Quarterly (Fall 1988): 46–53. See also Cindy Patton's book *Inventing AIDS* (New York: Routledge, 1991).

16. Michael Callen's book *Surviving AIDS* (New York: HarperCollins, 1990) is a survey of the vernacular knowledge regarding the long-term survival of people with AIDS. Cindy Patton's book *Inventing AIDS* is a study of power and truth effects in the construction of AIDS knowledges.

17. For documentation of the impact of AIDS activists and community intellectuals on medical research and federal policy see Bruce Nussbaum, *Good Intentions: How Big Business and the Medical Establishment Are Corrupting the Fight against AIDS* (New York: Atlantic Monthly Press, 1990); Robert M. Wachter, *The Fragile Coalition: Scientists, Activists, and AIDS* (New York: St. Martin's Press, 1991); and Steven Epstein, "Democratic Science? AIDS Activism and the Contested Construction of Knowledge," *Socialist Review,* 21, no. 2 (April–June 1991). For an exploration of the impact of activist artists on AIDS education and political mobilization, see Douglas Crimp with Adam Rolston, *AIDS Demo Graphics* (Seattle: Bay Press, 1990).

18. Pierre Bourdieu, "Social Space and Symbolic Power," *In Other Words: Essays Towards a Reflexive Sociology* (Stanford, Calif.: Stanford University Press, 1990), especially pp. 134–39.

19. For a detailed discussion of the relationship between the university as an institution of cultural legitimation and intellectuals outside the university see Pierre Bourdieu, "The Market of Symbolic Goods," in *Poetics* 14 (April 1985):13–44.

20. Alvin Gouldner, *The Future of Intellectuals and the Rise of the New Class* (New York: Oxford University Press, 1979); see especially pp. 28–43.

21. See, for example, a number of the interviews and lectures in Michel Foucault's *Power/Knowledge* and also Basil Bernstein, *Class, Codes, and Control: Theoretical Studies Towards a Sociology of Language* (New York: Schocken Books, 1975).

22. The work of Basil Bernstein offers an illuminating exploration of disciplinary knowledge, particularly "On the Classification and Framing of Educational Knowledge," "Class and Pedagogies: Visible and Invisible," and other essays in part 2 of *Class, Codes and Control:* Volume 3, *Towards a Theory of Educational Transmissions* (London: Routledge and Kegan Paul, 1975).

23. See the excellent book on this topic by John Guillory, *Cultural Capital: The Problem of Literary Canon Formation* (Chicago: University of Chicago Press, 1993).

24. See Jerry Herron, *Universities and the Myth of Cultural Decline* (Detroit: Wayne State University Press, 1988); and the essays in Darryl J. Gless and Barbara Herrnstein Smith, eds., *The Politics of Liberal Education* (Durham, N.C.: Duke University Press, 1992), particularly the essay by Eve Kosofsky Sedgwick, "Pedagogy in the Context of an Antihomophobic Project."

25. For a discussion of these issues see Jeffrey Escoffier, "Inside the Ivory Closet," *OUT/LOOK* no. 10 (Fall 1990):40–48; and Jeffrey Escoffier, "Generations and Paradigms: Mainstreams in Lesbian and Gay Studies," in Henry Minton, ed., *Gay and Lesbian Studies* (New York: Harrington Park Press, 1992), 7–26. See also

John D'Emilio, "Part Two: Remaking the University," in *Making Trouble: Essays on Gay History, Politics, and the University* (New York: Routledge, 1992), 117–78.

26. For another take on the relation between lesbian and gay studies and the university's power/knowledge regime, see Eve Sedgwick's discussion of the university's representational economy in "Gender Criticism" in Stephen Greenblatt and Giles Gunn, eds., *Redrawing the Boundaries: The Transformation of English and American Literary Studies* (New York: Modern Language Association of America, 1992), 294–98.

27. See my discussion of the exclusion of community intellectuals from mainstream public spheres in Jeffrey Escoffier, "Pessimism of the Mind: Intellectuals, Universities and the Left," *Socialist Review* 18, no. 1 (January–March 1988).

28. Sedgwick, "Gender Criticism," pp. 297–98.

29. "Rethinking the Public Sphere: A Contribution to the Critique of Actually Existing Democracy," in Craig Calhoun, ed., *Habermas and the Public Sphere* (Cambridge, Mass.: MIT Press, 1992), 109–42.

30. See Foucault, *Power/Knowledge*. Disciplinary intellectuals and community intellectuals sometimes work within different intellectual paradigms. The disciplinary intellectual working within the intellectual norms of disciplines like cultural studies and the social sciences is usually committed to the theory of social construction of identity, while the community intellectual (who may often be an autodidact and working outside the university) frequently thinks in terms of authenticity and an essentialist concept of identity. For a partial explanation see Steven Epstein, "Gay Politics, Ethnic Identity: The Limits of Social Constructionism," *Socialist Review* nos. 93–94 (May–August 1987):9–54.

31. Antonio Gramsci, "Formation of the Intellectuals," *Selections from the Prison Notebooks* (New York: International Publishers, 1971), 5–14.

CHAPTER 3

Theorizing Movements:
Direct Action and Direct Theory

Noël Sturgeon

□   □   □   □   □   □   □   □   □   □   □

The "nonviolent direct action movement" is my name for a combination of extra-institutional political practices and organizational structures that have been regularly used since the middle 1970s in opposition to nuclear power plants, nuclear weapons, American intervention in Central America, and the war in the Persian Gulf.[1] The importance of these particular targets to the movement supports a general characterization of it as antimilitarist. Intermittently, however, these practices and organizational forms have been used for actions organized by gay and lesbian groups, by the homeless, by anti-apartheid groups, and others. The identifying characteristics of this movement are the use of affinity groups (decentralized small groups that independently decide the nature of their participation in an action), consensus process (a participatory democratic decision-making method), nonviolent direct action often involving civil disobedience, and a multifaceted radical democratic politics that combines the analyses of previous American left movements, particularly those of the sixties. Thus, the politics of this movement figure militarism as the apex of interlocking systems of dominance that include racism, sexism, environmental degradation, hierarchy, and economic exploitation.[2] The closing of the Cold War era may mark the end of this particular movement configuration, but I believe this is still an open question.

While the radical democratic politics of the movement were explicitly theorized by many direct actionists, many participants seemed hardly aware of this multifaceted political analysis or were openly hostile to one or another of its aspects. Further, there was rarely any explicit discussion of the political theory of the movement within hundreds of meetings usually overwhelmingly focused on logistical details and strategies. During my many years of participation in and observation of this movement, I began to realize that the movement's political theory was to a great extent expressed through its organizational structures and political practices, giving many participants the same general understanding of why they proceeded as they did but not requiring an identical, explicit ideology from every participant. To analyze this theory, therefore, I learned to read the movement's practices and structures as a form of theorizing through practice, a praxis I call "direct theory," a lived analysis of contemporary domination and resistance. With the term "direct theory" I try to make visible and keep in view the constant interaction between theory and practice that I think is one of the primary characteristics of this movement. But I do not intend this term to obscure the fact that I am involved in a second-order interpretation of the political theory of the movement, one that can be contradicted and contested by other participant observers.

Most attempts to analyze the nonviolent direct action movement have either uncritically celebrated it or critiqued its "ineffectiveness," its organizational instability, or its lack of an overall strategy.[3] My approach assumes this critique but looks past it to explore the reasons for the movement's particular organizational form and political strategies. The repeated choice of such problematic organizational structures as decentralized affinity groups, time-consuming decision-making procedures like consensus process, and the politics-as-spectacle of nonviolent civil disobedience should be understood as a form of political theorizing about certain political problems within the complex societies of industrialized Western liberal democracies. It seems novel to understand a movement as engaged in political theorizing *through its practice* because of the long Western tradition of separating thought and object, theory and practice, which has enabled the constitution of political theory as an academic discipline. Because we think of movements as engaged in practical action, with strategizing as perhaps the main kind of thinking going on, it seems as though they are far apart from the practice of political theorizing, which we imagine involves a single (traditionally male) thinker who, in order to reflect on politics, is necessarily separate from political action itself. But in reality, political theorists are always inside the political relations they simultaneously analyze and critique; they are participant observers themselves. Further, political theory is meant to affect those political relations. Political theory is both critical and creative, just as movements are both oppositional and prefigurative. The direct action movement's structures and practices both critique and describe the political formation "militarism." At the same time, they create and prescribe an alternative political vision.[4]

To make the movement's "direct theory" visible, I use a form of "thick description":[5] an interpretive layering of practices, symbols, actions, and social structures that sculpts the processes of the social construction of reality so that they can be "seen" and understood. My method can also be called "critical hermeneutics": an interpretation that seeks a "deeper" meaning but considers that meaning as partially constructed by my interpretation and thus always open to further interrogation.

Taking this approach to the movement allows me to explain the choice of particular organizational structures and political strategies as a form of theorizing about political problems of consent, authority, the construction of knowledge and identities, and the processes of social change. The political theory of the movement is not just a reflection of, and resistance to, contemporary structures of power but also a continuance and critique of the American radical democratic tradition, particularly the sixties movements that are the direct action movement's most immediate ancestors. Thus, the organizational structures and political practices of the direct action movement serve several functions: as practical frameworks to accomplish immediate and specific movement goals, such as forcing the closure of a specific military facility; as methods of radicalization of internal consciousness-raising for participants; as efforts to change public opinion on certain issues, or external consciousness-raising; as critical commentaries on the American tradition of radical social movements; and finally, as forms of prefiguring an alternative political vision. The theoretical assumptions involved in each of these levels can be analyzed both synchronically and diachronically—in other words, as arising from and aimed toward both the operative configurations of power and the historical conditions of radical opposition in the United States. Ultimately this analytical separation of the functions of the movement's structures and practices intends to redefine "effectiveness" away from a limited notion of instrumentality and toward a more comprehensive understanding of how movements act as important promulgators of new forms of "commonsense" apprehension of political realities and thus serve as critical intervenors in the ongoing process of the construction of hegemonic relations.

Theories of Movements and Movements of Theory

I am not interested here in proving that the movement succeeds on its own terms in all of the areas mentioned above but rather in promoting a more complex notion of "effectiveness," a wider understanding of the processes of social and political change, than is generally found in American schools of social movement theory. The dominant model in the United States, resource mobilization theory, is generally ill equipped to understand, or even to see, the nonviolent direct action movement.[6] Given its emphasis on the need for elite resources, stable movement leadership, and hierarchical movement organizations, resource mobilization theory leaves decentralized, antihierarchical movements like the direct action movement invisible or by definition pronounces them failures. Thus, resource mobilization theory cannot account for the continual reappearance of the direct action movement in the period between 1976 and 1990 or for its attraction for large numbers of Americans, diverse in almost every aspect except race (which is a large limitation on diversity, indeed).[7] Generally, resource mobilization posits a process of social change in which excluded groups form social movements, which then become interest groups that serve as the vehicles for including the previously excluded group in the institutionalized political process. Movements that eschew interest group formation, or are directed away from gaining fixed relations with state political institutions, are seen as completely marginalized in relation to political and social change.

This model, therefore, maintains a narrow focus on change in institutional political structures, particularly those shifts necessary to accommodate newly included groups. While based on an elite model of politics, resource mobilization thus reveals a repressed pluralist belief system: that "out" groups can be included in the political system without major structural change. Resource mobilization cannot thoroughly account for movements that attempt political change through direct changes in what are seen as "private" social relations, or through a complex contestation with various other social forces over the discursive construction of a range of political and economic developments whose political implications are ambiguous.

Such a notion of change as taking place through a Gramscian "war of position," engaging the strategic contest of power in political institutional structures only indirectly or secondarily, is better suited for analysis by the mainly Western European "new social movement" theories.[8] Particularly useful for analyzing the direct action movement is the theory developed by Alberto Melucci, which analyzes the meanings produced by "the way in which the visible action of contemporary movements depends upon the production of new cultural codes within submerged networks."[9] On the other hand, these contemporary Western European social movement theories, while better able to analyze this movement and other contemporary movements like it, cannot do so with useful specificity unless they see movements as constructing "direct theory" and unless they include an analysis of gender relations.

Affinity Groups: Decentralizing Identities

Affinity groups provide an example of "direct theory" and enable one focus on the kinds of political problems I think this movement is constructed to address. First, several cautions: I am not arguing that every participant subscribes to the political positions I outline here, nor am I saying that the movement lives up to all of these alternative political visions, nor that there is nothing problematic in the movement's structures and practices. I am engaged in a reading, or a critical hermeneutics, of the theoretical implications of these structures and practices, an interpretation that remains an interested and contestable story of my own.[10]

Affinity groups are small groups of people, on the average about ten, that serve as the primary organizational structure of the movement. Affinity groups autonomously decide the nature and extent of their participation in a direct action. They also provide material, emotional, and sometimes legal support for themselves, resulting in the creation of a relatively self-sufficient unit of the whole action. In actions that include civil disobedience, each affinity group consists of people willing to risk arrest (or planning to be arrested) and those who will provide support and assistance but will not risk arrest.

The affinity groups in a given direct action form a decentralized organizational structure that minimizes bureaucracy and formal leadership, consistent with the antihierarchical and antibureaucratic proclivities of the movement. Though sometimes formed of previous acquaintances, the members of the affinity group construct an obligation to each other that is based only on their participation in consensus process and their mutual political action. It is not a tie of kinship, economics, or circumstance but a nonutilitarian arrangement of political commitment, obligation, and action. The circle of the affinity group, like the circle of a consensus process meeting, serves as a symbol of an alternative political order intended to be placed against the straight lines and hierarchical structures of police barricades and military facilities. The alternative political order temporarily (and imperfectly) created by the affinity group structure is radically democratic, collective yet individualistic, and symbolized by new names of resistance that constitute a constructed community.

Affinity groups in the movement often name themselves with an ironic, humorous flair: for instance, "the Communist Dupes," "No Nukes of the North," "The Anti-Rockettes," "Barrier Method," "The Post-Mod Squad," or "Mutant Sponges." Affinity group names express an aspect of a common identity among members of the group, which might be geographic (the "Downwinders" came from a portion of Utah downwind from the nuclear test zone at the Nevada Test Site), religious ("Epiphany Plowshares"), or occupational ("Gardeners for a Nuclear Free Future"). Affinity group names are frequently specific to a particular action goal ("Bay Area Peace Test") or a broader political goal ("Women Opposed to Nuclear Technology" or "Just Us"). In a large action, participants commonly identify themselves as being from a particular affinity group when they speak; frequently, this takes the form of using the affinity group name as a last name ("Tim Infinity" or "Marge of the Surrogate Others").

The ironic and funny names of affinity groups that seem to be preferred make these new constructed "families" playful ones in their inception. Rather than signifying a rigid sense of loyalty to one group, or the biologistic qualities of "nuclear" family membership, the humorous names allow a certain distancing from the act of association involved in joining an affinity group. The moment of humor is also the moment of theory, the ironic distance of participant observation. Yet the obligation to an affinity group is still a serious commitment, even though many affinity groups only stay together for the time surrounding the organizing of a civil disobedience action.

The importance of the name of the affinity group is demonstrated by the lengthy debates involved in choosing them. Nonviolence preparers, who do a large part of the organizing for actions, know that giving a group the task of choosing its affinity group name is a sure way to get the group to set another meeting time for more discussion. The attention paid by the group to this task points to the way the action of self-naming is felt to be an act of "empowerment" for participants, a recognition of the way dominant power is understood to work through naming and categorizing.

This process of renaming becomes a form of direct action involving the creation of a personal political identity. The use of affinity group names as new last names produces a constructed "family" that is nonpatriarchal and nonbiological. Organizational roles, such as facilitator, within the affinity group are consciously nonsexist and ideally unfixed to particular persons or genders (though in practice some people become more skilled than others at facilitating). In this way, the creation of identities through the formation of affinity groups works against the dominant ideological assumption of the naturalness and necessity of the heterosexual, male-dominated family as the origin of the individual. The affinity group name supplants the patriarchal last name, the name used as the first source of identification in institutionalized systems of surveillance and control.

That this is a way of creating a subject who will not (at least not automatically) respond to the interpellation of dominant ideology can be seen in the way in which affinity group membership is deployed within the legal/jail apparatus. For example, in actions at the Seabrook (1976) and Diablo Canyon (1981) nuclear power plants, Vandenberg Air Force Base (1983), and Livermore Laboratories nuclear weapons design facility (1983, 1984), part of the jail solidarity agreements constructed by affinity groups was a demand that affinity groups be arraigned together, or in some cases, be housed together. In all of these actions, the legal/jail authorities were forced to accede at least partially to these demands by the noncooperative actions of the jailed participants. Many other examples of jailed participants insisting on the recognition by guards, prosecutors, and judges of the importance of their affinity group membership speak to the perception by the movement that the affinity group serves as an alternative, resistant locus of a new politicized identity.

Yet affinity group identities are of a different kind from those constructed by the identity politics of other movements. Indeed, the use of affinity groups constitutes a connection with and a retheorization of sixties-style identity politics, recognizing both the necessity and the problematic nature of such a politics. The politicized identities of an affinity group are not simply collective (that is, identifying as an individual member of a broad-based group: black, woman, gay) but localized in the affinity group and individual as well; they are fluid and nonessential, as people may be members of many different affinity groups in the course of their participation in the movement.

The affinity groups thus allow for the expression of various politics of identity but without requiring that one identity be taken on, or privileged, by everyone in the movement. Like most movements of the sixties, the direct-action movement has been made up of many different kinds of people. But instead of searching for the "correct" revolutionary subject to follow, the direct action movement has proliferated revolutionary subjectivities. Affinity groups of gay people, or of organic gardeners; of students, or of women; of Marxists, or of witches; of "disabled" people, or of collective housemates, create many different kinds of politicized identities. They may work together within the safe space of the affinity group, but they must also work with, and learn from, other groups' political positionings. Thus, important analyses of racism, classism, sexism, and heterosexism (as well as other political-economic-environmental-cultural-pyschological-spiritual analyses that circulate among the groups via the construction of political identities) can be articulated throughout the movement without isolating or essentializing those who do or do not fit the ascriptions. Even if these analyses may be less coherent or confrontational than in particular sixties movements, people have the opportunity to identify with more than one of these politics of identity rather than face the constricting logic of certain separatist tendencies in the earlier movements. Conversely, people are challenged to decide whether they do or do not fit within a variety of politicized identities as they come in contact with many different kinds of affinity groups.[11]

Finally, the fluid character of these various politics of identity requires the movement to provide a framework for the connection of these political analyses within one movement. The political theory of the direct action movement thus attempts what Chantal Mouffe calls "a chain of equivalencies" between the democratic demands of differently located subjects.[12] Thus, for instance, the movement takes on the responsibility of analyzing the military's dependence on racism and constructs an antiracist stance, even while remaining primarily white.[13] The movement's politics breaks the link between an essentialized subject and the epistemology of sixties radical politics (that is, that one can only know the complexity of a given oppression when one is the oppressed subject). Instead, the movement relies for its radical analysis upon the continually contested collective construction of knowledge produced by consensus process and the carnivalesque direct actions.

The novel political subjects constructed within affinity groups are both less and more than new actors in contemporary complex societies. A movement participant has membership in concentric collectivities of affinity groups, spokescouncils, clusters, organizing groups, and regional affiliations—alternative political associations existing alongside but unconnected with the legitimized dominant institutions of party politics. These networks of participation, responsibility, and obligation are meant to serve as an operative alternative political society for the period of time surrounding an action, as well as a prefiguration of an alternative political formation. Affinity groups thus construct political subjects who, at least temporarily, are able to make political decisions themselves, to disobey fixed and undemocratic authority, and to maintain ties of mutual obligation based on a foundation of democratic participation. Consent within a democratic polity is thus redefined as requiring participation, in contradistinction to liberal political theory which assesses nonparticipation as consent. Thus, like other movements in what Flacks calls "the tradition of the left,"[14] the movement is centrally involved in the project of teaching people how to struggle for themselves, how to work collectively, and how to theoretically reinterpret the discourse of liberal rights in an effort to enlarge the meaning of democracy and expand the arenas subject to their control. Further, the movement's challenging of social roles that are gendered, raced, and classed (even if this challenge is uneven) signals its intention to change social relations as well as particular military policies.

Theorizing the Direct Action Movement

The effects of teaching a radically democratic citizenship to large numbers of people in almost all areas of the United States over a period of more than fifteen years are practically immeasurable by the tools of resource mobilization theories. For instance, through its public actions and its process of organization, the direct action movement articulated an ethical and alternative political vision that drew widespread support in the 1980s and helped transform the elite assessment of the necessity of nuclear weapons (without necessarily changing their negative opinion of the movement itself). This impact on social and political change is not measurable in the same way as one can, for example, count the number of congressional votes for and against a nuclear freeze initiative (although the two phenomena are clearly connected).

Neither can the constituency of the direct action movement be completely characterized as an excluded group (often a requirement in the resource mobilization model) since many of its participants are not without socioeconomic privilege and some participate as well in institutional politics. Rather, the movement goal of disarmament, particularly because it is connected to the redistribution of social resources from militarization to human services, has been an *excluded politics*. In the arena of institutionalized politics, it was not recognized as a viable political vision, let alone a legitimate political discourse, until the early 1990s.[15] Understanding movement action as about an excluded politics rather than dismissing it because it is not about an excluded group points away from certain tenets of resource mobilization theory that presuppose that the creation of interest groups is the only viable goal of a movement.

The oppositional discourse of the direct action movement has not aimed at becoming part of institutional politics but rather intends to engage the discursive frameworks within which those institutions function and are legitimated. While supporting more mainstream groups (and in many ways making their discourse appear more reasonable to the dominant political structures), the direct action movement remained far more marginalized. The nature of the direct action movement's structures and practices is different from that of more mainstream groups. It has a different aim and a different assessment of power and its operation. Its aim is not inclusion but the articulation of an oppositional political theory. I use "articulation" here in its double sense: the movement both speaks a silenced politics and connects various forms of inequality and injustice to concrete practices of the state and corporations. This intervention into the maintenance and construction of consent has an effect on the ability of political actors (both dominant and marginal) to envision and act on different political goals. From the middle 1970s to the early 1990s, the direct action movement sought to articulate the commonsense understanding of the military and its importance to political and economic formations leftward toward a conception of "militarism."[16]

Thus, examining the oppositional discourse of the movement using the tools of new social movement theory does more than simply bring to light practices and organizational structures that have generally been ignored by resource mobilization scholarship; it also provides a different angle on the discursive practices that support the "security state."[17] It challenges the uncritical acceptance of the metaphor of "inclusion-exclusion" that is preferred by elite theories of power and emphasizes the concrete effects of the movement's intervention on the terrain of hegemonic contestation over political meanings. The movement's "effectiveness"—because it is imbedded in a process of theoretical practice, of "direct theory" or praxis that is directed both internally (within the movement and within political consciousnesses) and externally (against state and corporate practices)—cannot be assessed or measured by an "empirical" perspective that separates culture from politics, or theory from practice, or everyday life from history.

What is immeasurable, however, is not untheorizable, and new social movement theory, which pays attention to the decentralist, discursive, and antihierarchical tendencies of "new" movements, sees them as a form of organization reflective of developments in areas central to the restructuring of political and economic structures, areas such as militarization, consumerism, bureaucracy, and technology.[18] New social movement theories argue that, especially in moments of political or economic crisis, or intensive restructuring, movements are involved in articulating the questions around which struggle over political and economic change takes place. Similarly, the direct action movement identifies conceptions of consent and authority as crucial to the hegemonic relations of Western industrialized democracies. The movement thus attempts to articulate radical democratic notions of participation, consent, authority, and equality as a strategy for opposing domination, resisting the state, and changing social relations. The movement's theory of power assumes that within the political structures of liberal democracy, this strategy is effective because it is the process of constructing consent that is crucial to the maintenance of these specific relations of power. In these polities, according to Hall's useful gloss of Gramsci's theory:

Mastery is not simply imposed or dominative in character. Effectively, it results from winning a substantial degree of popular consent. It thus represents the installation of a profound measure of social and moral authority, not simply over its immediate supporters, but across society as a whole. It is this "authority," and the range and the diversity of sites on which "leadership" is exercised, which makes possible the "propagation," for a time, of an intellectual, moral, political and economic collective will throughout society.[19]

Toward New Theories of New Social Movements

Understanding the direct action movement using the concept of direct theory can also illuminate several problems with new social movement approaches. First, while some theorists see the important ways in which movements are producing meanings through their "action systems," to use Melucci's terminology, most new social movement analyses tend to remain synchronic, or in other words only to analyze movements as oppositional to a particular contemporary political, economic, or cultural formation. However, taking the construction of meaning as a serious function of movements means keeping in mind that movements are also social movement theorists. That is, movements construct their "action systems" and organizational structures as critiques, as well as continuations, of earlier movements (whose history is generally obscured by those in power). For instance, the choice of affinity groups has to do not just with resistance to the centralization and bureaucratization of the dominant political structures but also with a critique of the essentialized identity politics of the sixties movements. Conceptualizing the action of social movements as direct theory allows a historical dimension sometimes missing from new social movement analyses.

Secondly, while many new social movement theorists point to the importance of changes in the family, the commodification of domestic production signaled by the expansion of the service sector, the "collapse" of public and private realms, and so forth, they rarely acknowledge that shifts in gender relations are crucial causes and effects of these broad structural changes. The women's movement appears in most of these theories as just one among many other movements, and women's struggles are often conceived as centered around "new identities," rather than issues of knowledge, power, and economics. The theorizing emerging from women's movements is not recognized as affecting issues outside a narrowly conceived women's sphere.[20]

As a result of this narrow conceptualization of feminism, most new social movement theorists do not use feminist theories (which arise from, but are not the same as, the women's movement) to analyze the various elements said to be characteristic of the "new" movements: the self-reflexivity regarding the construction of social identities, the centrality of the body as a location for political discourse, the emphasis on changing personal relations as a method for revising social relations, the expansion of the political arena into previously "private" areas, the critique of immediatist (and masculinist) theories of revolution and the preference for transformational models of social change, and the supposed expressiveness rather than instrumentality of new movements. All of these areas have been important loci of feminist theorizing.

Nor are feminist theories used to analyze the elements said to differentiate the "post-Fordist society" from previous historical periods. For example, Melucci examines the lack of fixed social identities, increased bureaucratization, new reproductive technologies, the ambiguous status of nature in contemporary political discourse, new attention to the liberation and purity of the body, and new definitions of sexuality, without any reference to the wealth of feminist theory on these subjects.[21]

To take one instance, while new social movement theory sees movements as challenging the distinction between public and private,[22] they do not theorize the way in which this distinction is a central one for the creation and maintenance of unequal gender relations and gendered subjectivities, and vice versa. Many new social movement theorists make the assumption that state intrusion into "private" areas results in increased social control, using a model of the state that is problematic and one that has been challenged by feminists.[23] It assumes a relative autonomy from the state of previously private areas of life that operated in a "quasi-natural" way, as Hirsch puts it.[24] The logic of describing the development of the Fordist and post-Fordist state as a process of "stratification of society," as Hirsch does, implies that the previous arrangement was more free and the present less and less so. This does not account for power in civil society or the complex and ambiguous ways in which the discourses of the helping and policing services, the educational apparatus, and other social agencies are productive of particular political consciousness and identities, as well as repressive of certain desires and choices, a process that does not have simply the effects of control or invasion. The ambiguity of the political consequences of the stratification of society means that these are arenas worth struggling over for movements, not simply in terms of defense or resistance but in terms of prefiguration and empowerment. Without feminist analyses of the patriarchal nature of the contemporary capitalist state, the particularity of the ground on which movements struggle against and within the state goes untheorized.

In addition, the pervasiveness in many movements of organizational forms and political practices developed especially by feminists is not fully explained by new social movement theories. For example, the feminist development of, and emphasis on, the process of consciousness raising as an important practice of movements, as well an important metaphor for theory, argues the necessary interaction between the recognition of the social construction of identity, resisting expert discourses, and struggling against the interpellation of dominant ideologies that occurs when the private trangresses the public. Another example is the way in which the feminist critique of the masculinist turn to violence in the black power movement and in the New Left, as well as a feminist analysis of the way in which militant confrontation and the expression of anger are wholly compatible with nonviolence, undergirds the persistent choice of nonviolence in the direct action movement. The confusion in the direct action movement between feminism and nonviolence, feminism and antihierarchical politics, and feminism and consensus process (sometimes called "feminist process") speaks to the ways in which feminist explanations gain currency in the context of deep shifts in gender relations.

Such an introduction of feminist analysis into new social movement theory would help prevent the recurrence of the economic as the primary explanatory tool (frequently expressed in new social movement theory in terms of its reliance on the economic assumptions of the regulation school)[25] and perhaps allow us to begin to rethink the nature of class as well. As Stuart Hall suggests, class must be (re)theorized as embedded in relations of gender and race. Without the use of feminist theories, new social movement theory will only return to the repressed economism that it has sought to banish, leaving important aspects of both societal restructuring processes, and contemporary social movements, unexplained.

NOTES

1. See Noël Sturgeon, "Direct Theory and Political Action: The Political Theory of the U.S. Nonviolent Direct Action Movement" (Ph.D. diss., University of California, Santa Cruz, 1991). This study was based on several years of participant observation, interviews with movement participants, and reviews of movement literature. I thank the University of California Institute for the Study of Global Conflict and Cooperation for support that enabled a great portion of my field research.

2. I date the beginning of the nonviolent direct action movement in 1976, during the anti–nuclear power actions against the Seabrook, New Hampshire, nuclear power plant. Other important direct actions during the movement's history have been those at the Diablo Canyon nuclear power plant, Vandenberg Air Force Base, Livermore Laboratories nuclear weapons design facilities, Concord Naval Station (all in California), the Seneca Women's Encampment (in upstate New York), the Rocky Flats nuclear weapons facility (in Colorado), and the Nevada Test Site. There have been a multitude of smaller actions around the country from 1976 to the present. See Sturgeon, "Direct Theory," chapter one; and, for a more detailed history, Barbara Epstein, *Political Protest and Cultural Revolution: Nonviolent Direct Action in the Seventies and Eighties* (Berkeley: University of California Press, 1991).

3. Treatments of the nonviolent direct action movement have not generally seen it as a movement in itself but have examined a part of this movement as belonging to other movements. In treating it as one movement, I do not mean to

obscure the chaotic, argumentative, and factional nature of its groups and actions. For excellent accounts of those, see Barbara Epstein, *Political Protest*. For examinations of direct action groups as part of the anti–nuclear power movement, see Richard S. Lewis, *The Nuclear Power Rebellion* (New York: Viking Press, 1972); Harvey Wasserman, *Energy War: Notes from the Front* (Westport, Conn.: L. Hill, 1979); Jerome Price, *The Antinuclear Movement* (Boston: G. K. Hall, 1982); Anna Gyorgy and Friends, *No Nukes: Everyone's Guide to Nuclear Power* (Boston: South End Press, 1979); Marty Jezer, "Who's on First What's On Second? A Grass-Roots Political Perspective on the Anti-Nuclear Movement," *WIN*, October 12, 1978: 5–12; Steven E. Barkan, "Strategic, Tactical, and Organizational Dilemmas of the Protest Movement against Nuclear Power," *Social Problems* 27, no. 1 (1979); Stephen Vogel, "The Limits of Protest: A Critique of the Anti-Nuclear Movement," *Socialist Review* 10, no. 6 (1980): 19–37; Liv Smith, "Labor and the No-Nukes Movement," *Socialist Review* 10, no. 6 (1980): 135–49; Lynn E. Dwyer, "Structure and Strategy in the Antinuclear Movement," in Jo Freeman, ed., *Social Movements of the Sixties and Seventies* (New York: Longman, 1983). For examinations of direct action groups as part of the peace movement, see Jackie Cabasso and Susan Moon, *Risking Peace: Why We Sat in the Road* (Berkeley: Open Books, 1985); Samuel Day, Jr., "The New Resistance," *The Progressive* 47, no. 4 (1983): 22–30; and Barbara Epstein, "The Culture of Direct Action," *Socialist Review* 15, nos. 4–5 (1985): 31–61. For articles concerning feminism and direct action groups, primarily in the peace movement, see the collection edited by Pam McAllister, *Reweaving the Web of Life: Feminism and Nonviolence* (Philadelphia: New Society Publishers, 1982); Ynestra King, "All Is Connectedness: Scenes from the Women's Pentagon Action USA," in Lynne Jones, ed., *Keeping the Peace* (London: Women's Press, 1983); Participants of the Puget Sound Women's Peace Camp, *We Are Ordinary Women: A Chronicle of the Puget Sound Women's Peace Camp* (Seattle: Seal Press, 1985); Johanna Brenner, "Beyond Essentialism: Feminist Theory and Strategy in the Peace Movement," in Mike Davis and Michael Sprinker, eds., *Reshaping the U.S. Left: Popular Struggles in the 1980s* (London and New York: Verso, 1988); and Noël Sturgeon, "Positional Feminism, Ecofeminism and Radical Feminism Revisited," *APA Newsletter on Feminism and Philosophy* 93:1 (Spring 1994). For treatments of direct action as a movement ranging over several issues, see the section "Making Connections: Disarmament, Equality, and a Healthy Environment" in Robert Cooney and Helen Michalowski, *The Power of the People* (Philadelphia: New Society Publishers, 1987), and Barbara Epstein, "The Politics of Prefigurative Community: The Non-violent Direct Action Movement," in Davis and Sprinker, eds., *Reshaping the U.S. Left*. Espteín's important book, *Political Protest*, backs away from considering it as one movement; rather, she characterizes her approach as studying the "direct action wing" of several different movements.

4. I am not ready to claim that all social movements are involved in "direct theorizing," at least not to the extent that I think such praxis is important to the

direct action movement. It may be that this emphasis is more of a characteristic of movements in the post–World War II period, sometimes called "new social movements." But this discussion cannot be taken up here.

5. The term is Clifford Geertz's. See "Notes on the Balinese Cockfight" in his *The Interpretation of Cultures* (New York: Basic Books, 1973).

6. For an early statement of the resource mobilization position, see John McCarthy and Mayer Zald, *The Tend of Social Movements in America: Professionalization and Resource Mobilization* (Morristown, N.J.: General Learning Press, 1973). The classic resource mobilization texts are Charles Tilly, *From Mobilization to Revolution* (Reading, Mass.: Addison-Wesley, 1978) and John McCarthy and Mayer Zald, eds., *The Dynamic of Social Movements* (Cambridge, Mass.: Winthrop, 1979). Jo Freeman's important early study of the women's movement, *The Politics of Women's Liberation* (New York: Longman, 1975), develops a position much like that of resource mobilization without using that name. Also see Freeman, ed., *Social Movements of the 60s and 70s,* for good examples of the approach used for several different movements and J. Craig Jenkins, *The Politics of Insurgency: The Farmworkers Movement in the 1960s* (New York: Columbia University Press, 1985) for an important book-length study using the approach. For a concise summary of the approach, see J. Craig Jenkins, "Resource Mobilization Theory and the Study of Social Movements," *Annual Review of Sociology* 9 (1983): 527–53.

7. My own and others' demographic analysis of the movement indicates that participants tend to be predominantly white and female, to have some college education, and to work in the service sectors of the economy. Other than these delimitations, participants vary widely in their age, geographic location, socioeconomic class, and political, religious, and sexual orientations. See Epstein, *Political Protest,* and James Jaspers and Evelyn P. Waters, "Mobilization for Protest: Values and Activities in the Movement against Nuclear Power" (unpublished ms., Dept. of Sociology, University of California, Berkeley, 1985).

8. Theorists associated with this school include Alain Touraine, *The Voice and the Eye* (New York: Cambridge University Press, 1981); Joachim Hirsch, "The Fordist Security State and New Social Movements," *Kapitalistate* 10–11 (1983): 195–230; Claus Offe, "New Social Movements: Challenging the Boundaries of Institutional Politics," *Social Research* 52, 4 (1985): 817–68; Jean Cohen, "Rethinking Social Movements," *Berkeley Journal of Sociology* 28 (1985): 97–113; Ernesto Laclau and Chantal Mouffe, *Hegemony and Socialist Strategy: Towards a Radical Democratic Politics* (London: Verso, 1985); Carl Boggs, *Social Movements and Political Power* (Philadelphia: Temple University Press, 1986); and Alberto Melucci, *Nomads of the Present: Social Movements and Individual Needs in Contemporary Society* (Philadelphia: Temple University Press, 1989). Important anthologies of new social movement theories are Dieter Rucht, ed., *Research on Social Movements* (Frankfurt/Boulder: Campus/Westview Press, 1990); Russell J. Dalton and Manfred Kuechler, *Challenging the Political Order: New Social*

and Political Movements in Western Democracies (New York: Oxford University Press, 1990); and Margit Mayer, ed., *New Social Movements in Europe and the U.S.* (London: Routledge, forthcoming). Some of those cited above would not necessarily call themselves "new social movement" theorists. For a recent discussion of the usefulness of new social movement theory for American movements, see Barbara Epstein, "Rethinking Social Movement Theory," *Socialist Review* 20, no. 1 (1990): 35–66.

9. Melucci, *Nomads*, 44.

10. Although it is an account deeply indebted to the theoretical work and political practice of many other people, I wish particularly to thank Barbara Epstein, Donna Haraway, Ilene Rose Feinman, T. V. Reed, and Donald Beggs as critical readers and co-affinites. In my larger study, I also examine in a similar fashion consensus process; the occupation of land and facilities during direct actions; the practice of civil disobedience; movement feminism(s), including ecofeminism; and nonviolence.

11. Once again, by making this argument, I don't mean to present the movement as achieving this dispersed but relational politics of identity in a noncontested manner. The movement has been frequently riven by conflicts between different identity constituencies. But because this process has been difficult and incomplete, it does not follow that the construction of these identities by the affinity group structure does not have the theoretical meaning I attribute to it.

12. See Mouffe, "Hegemony and New Political Subjects: Toward a New Concept of Democracy," in Cary Nelson and Lawrence Grossberg, eds., *Marxism and the Interpretation of Culture* (Chicago: University of Illinois Press, 1988).

13. There certainly are very serious problems with racism in the movement in that its whiteness creates a difficult atmosphere for participants of color. But it is definitely a "post-sixties" politics that can imply, as the movement's antiracist stance does, that it is important for white people to take on the responsibility of analyzing and combating racist structures without first requiring the presence of people of color to ensure that this activity will take place.

14. Richard Flacks, *Making History: The American Left and the American Mind* (New York: Columbia University Press, 1988).

15. I am not simply arguing here that if the movement uses noninstitutionalized tactics, it must involve an "excluded politics." Many groups (such as unions) use "noninstitutionalized" tactics for political purposes deemed quite acceptable to the institutional arena.

16. That the meaning of political and economic changes can be articulated to the left or to the right is cogently argued by Stuart Hall, "The Toad in the Garden: Thatcherism among the Theorists," in Lawrence Grossberg and Cary Nelson, eds., *Marxism and the Interpretation of Culture* (Chicago: University of Illinois Press, 1988), 35–74.

17. The term is Joachim Hirsch's, "The Fordist Security State," esp. 78–79.

18. For discussions of these processes of "restructuring" and their relation to "new social movements," see Joachim Hirsch, "The Apparatus of the State, the Re-

production of Capital, and Urban Conflicts," in Allen Scott, ed., *Urbanization and Urban Planning in Capitalist Society* (New York: Methuen, 1981); Manuel Castells, *The City and the Grassroots: A Cross-Cultural Theory of Urban Social Movements* (Berkeley: University of California Press, 1983); Timothy Luke, "Power and Resistance in Post-Industrial Society" (paper presented at the 3d International Social Philosophy Conference, 1987); and Roland Roth, "Fordism and New Social Movements," in Mayer, *New Social Movements in Europe and the U.S.*

19. Stuart Hall, "Gramsci's Relevance for the Study of Race and Ethnicity," *Journal of Communication Inquiry*, 10, no. 2 (1986): 15.
20. Exceptions to this are Timothy Luke, "Power and Resistance," and Joyce Gelb, "Feminism and Political Action," in Dalton and Keuchler, *Challenging the Political Order*, 137–55.
21. See Melucci, *Nomads*, esp. 92, 63, and 178. I will not attempt to list an entire, wide-ranging, and complex discipline in one footnote. Elsewhere, I detail the usefulness of many feminist sources for analyzing the direct action movement; see Sturgeon, "Direct Theory." A few examples here will have to suffice. On "nature" in political discourse, see Donna Haraway, "The Promises of Monsters: A Regenerative Politics for Inappropriate/d Others," in Lawrence Grossberg, Cary Nelson, and Paula Treichler, eds., *Cultural Studies* (New York: Routledge, 1992), 295–337; and Hilary Klein, "Marxism, Psychoanalysis and Mother Nature," *Feminist Studies* 15, no. 2 (1989): 255–78. On the lack of fixed social identities, see Chela Sandoval, "Feminism and Racism: A Report on the 1981 NWSA Conference," in Gloria Anzaldúa, ed., *Making Face, Making Soul: Haciendo Caras* (San Francisco: Aunt Lute, 1990); Gloria Anzaldúa, *Borderlands/La Frontera: The New Mestiza* (San Francisco: Spinsters/Aunt Lute, 1987); and Deborah King, "Multiple Jeopardy, Multiple Consciousness: The Context of a Black Feminist Ideology," in Micheline Malson et al., eds., *Feminist Theory in Process and Practice* (Chicago: University of Chicago Press, 1986, 1989). On the ambiguous relation of women to the state, see Irene Diamond, ed., *Families, Politics, and Public Policy* (New York: Longman, 1983). On the relation between bureaucratization and gender, see Kathy Ferguson, *The Feminist Case against Bureaucracy* (Philadelphia: Temple University Press, 1984). On the body as site for "liberation" and "purity," see Ann Snitow, Christine Stansell, and Sharon Thompson, eds., *Powers of Desire* (New York: Monthly Review Press, 1983), and Donna Haraway, "The Bio-Politics of Postmodern Bodies," in *differences* 1, no. 1 (1989). On the relation between changing gender roles and the expanding military economy, see Cynthia Enloe, *Does Khaki Become You? The Militarization of Women's Lives* (Boston: South End Press, 1983). On feminist activism in many different movement contexts, see Ann Bookman and Sandra Morgen, eds., *Women and the Politics of Empowerment* (Philadelphia: Temple University Press, 1988). On the limits of nonfeminist social and political theory, see Nancy Fraser, *Unruly Practices: Power, Discourse and Gender in Contemporary Social Theory* (Minneapolis: University of Minnesota Press, 1989).

22. See, for one example, Claus Offe, "New Social Movements."
23. See, for one example, Zillah Eisenstein, *The Female Body and the Law* (Berkeley: University of California Press, 1988).
24. Hirsch, "The Fordist Security State," 78.
25. See Michel Aglietta, *A Theory of Capitalist Regulation: The U.S. Experience* (London: NLB, 1979).

PART TWO

CULTURAL POLITICS AFTER
THE COUNTERCULTURE

□

CHAPTER 4

Motherfuckers Then and Now: My Sixties Problem

Osha Neumann

□   □   □   □   □   □   □   □   □   □   □   □

In the sixties I was part of a group called the Motherfuckers, short for Up Against the Wall Motherfuckers. That's my sixties problem in a nutshell.

□ □ □

The Motherfuckers were a small group of hippie activists that operated on the Lower East side of New York between 1966 and 1969. The Lower East Side is a predominantly Puerto Rican ghetto. Before the Puerto Ricans there were Jews, who worked in the shirt- and cigar-manufacturing establishments on Cooper Union Square. I arrived in 1962, having dropped out of the graduate history department at Yale to become a painter. By the time of my arrival the Jews had moved on, leaving a few good delicatessens. Old Ukrainians sat on the benches of Tompkins Square Park, or, when they got hungry, they wandered over to the Odessa Restaurant to eat beet soup with two slices of dark bread for thirty-five cents.

In the summer the streets smelled of rotting garbage, flaking paint, and the brightly colored sweet syrups the pushcart vendors poured on cones of shaved ice. In the winter the ghetto turned gray with sooty snow and wind-blown trash.

My arrival coincided with a new wave of immigrants. Their passage to the Lower East Side reversed the route of their predecessors. They came to the ghetto fleeing America, not trying to gain entrance. They were escaping from the emotional dust bowl of their families, their schools, their hometowns, their jobs. They came because rent was cheap and no one would tell them to cut their hair or get a job. Stoned at night, they would stare in the windows of some corner *bodega* and watch the mice scurrying over piles of green plantains and sweet potatoes. They knew they were not in Great Neck, or Glens Falls, or Peoria, and they breathed a collective sigh of relief. The newspapers called them "hippies."

I didn't come to the Lower East Side to become a Motherfucker. As a painter, I lived a fairly isolated life, worked at various odd jobs, and studied at the Brooklyn Museum School of Fine Arts. I painted in the kitchen of my railroad flat, went to demonstrations against the war, but was not part of any organization. The hippie influx started in earnest a year or two after I arrived. Their presence tugged me out of my isolation, accelerated my dissatisfaction with the role of isolated artist. I began writing an extended essay about the end of avant garde art, about art eating itself up, lost in a meaningless play with limits that no one cared about any longer. Art's promise of liberation was now to be achieved in the total imaginative transformation of reality. I never finished the essay.

□ □ □

My plunge into countercultural politics began in 1966, when I participated in a disruption of a mass at St. Patrick's Cathedral to protest Cardinal Francis Spellman's support for the war effort. Twenty-three of us smuggled posters of napalmed children into the church. Each picture had above it the Fifth Commandment, "Thou shalt not kill," and below it the word "Vietnam"—very tasteful. We stood up in unison and began to unfurl our posters. Unfortunately the cops had been tipped off, and we quickly found ourselves surrounded by plainclothes officers and hustled off to jail. There someone began chanting, "Hare Krishna, Hare Krishna." We all joined in, and as we chanted I began to relax. I felt an enormous peacefulness, and the light in the jail cell seemed to change, to brighten and clarify.

The demonstration was the culmination of Angry Arts Week, a week of protest art, street theater, and demonstrations organized by artists from the Lower East Side. The Motherfuckers grew out of organizing around Angry Arts Week: We just kept meeting when the week ended. Our name derived from an Amiri Baraka (then LeRoi Jones) poem about the riots in Newark in which cops yell "Up against the wall, motherfuckers" at the black men they stop. If they threw the epithet at us, we would fling it back at them. We would be their worst nightmare; we would break their most sacred taboos. Our very name could not be said. Thus we were protected from co-option. Ours would not be an Abbie Hoffman–style media revolution. Someone called us "a street gang with an analysis."

We wore dark, dirty leather jackets and carried folding knives that we practiced clicking open with one hand. We appointed ourselves the defenders and organizers of the drop-out freak counterculture. Our street-gang analysis was simple: The flower children were vulnerable. Their naive faith in love and good vibes would not suit them for survival on the mean streets. They needed protection. Love needed to arm itself. We were, as one of our flyers said, flower children with thorns.

In the counterculture, which talked of love as if it were some disembodied fluid turning hippie culture into a lukewarm hot tub, we talked of rage—its reality in us and the dangerous rage of society against us.

One of our first actions was a bit of street theater aimed at Lincoln Center for the Performing Arts, the vast multimillion-dollar arts complex on Manhattan's Upper West Side.

The Lower East Side was in the grip of a garbage strike, and the streets were ripe. Great heaps of plastic bags filled with uncollected refuse piled up on the sidewalks. Rats were having a field day. Our action was simple. We collected bags of garbage, marched through the streets with them, took them on the subway to the Upper West Side, and deposited them on the impeccably clean marble steps of Lincoln Center. I composed my first Motherfucker flyer for the event:

WE PROPOSE A CULTURE EXCHANGE:
(garbage for garbage)

AMERICA TURNS THE WORLD INTO GARBAGE
IT TURNS ITS GHETTOS INTO GARBAGE
IT TURNS VIETNAM INTO GARBAGE

IN THE NAME OF UNIVERSAL PRINCIPLES (DEMOCRACY, HUMAN
RIGHTS)
IN THE NAME OF THE FATHERLAND (COLLIE DOGS, NEW
ENGLAND CHURCHS)
IN THE NAME OF MAN   IN THE NAME OF ART
IN THE NAME OF MONEY

AMERICA TAKES
ALL THAT IS EDIBLE, EXCHANGEABLE, INVESTABLE,
AND LEAVES THE REST

THE WORLD IS OUR GARBAGE, WE SHALL NOT WANT. WE LIE
DOWN IN GREEN PASTURES. THE REST LIE DOWN IN GARBAGE

AND WE PLAY AS WE MAKE OUR GARBAGE
BEETHOVEN BACH MOZART SHAKESPEARE
TO COVER THE SOUND OF OUR GARBAGE MAKING

AND WE EXCLUDE THE GARBAGE FROM OUR PALACES OF
CULTURE
AND WE WILL NOT ALLOW IT TO MARRY OUR DAUGHTER
AND WE WILL NOT NEGOTIATE WITH IT OR LET IT TAKE OUR
SHIPS

BUT WE ARE FACED WITH A REVOLT OF THE GARBAGE

A CULTURAL REVOLUTION
GARBAGE FERTILIZES
DISCOVERS ITSELF

AND WE OF THE LOWER EAST SIDE HAVE DECIDED TO BRING
THIS CULTURAL REVOLUTION TO LINCOLN CENTER—IN BAGS

IS NOT LINCOLN CENTER WHERE IT BELONGS?

The Lincoln Center action was followed by many others. We threw bags of cow's blood at Secretary of State Dean Rusk and his high-society guests. We participated in the Columbia University uprising. We were in the forefront of the battle with lines of jocks and frat heads who attempted to blockade "occupied" university buildings to prevent food from getting through. We went to the levitating of the Pentagon in 1967 and charged inside to be beaten back by guards. We were in Chicago in '68. On the Lower East Side we ran free stores and crash pads and organized community feasts in the courtyard of St. Mark's Church. We confronted Bill Graham, demanding community access to his Fillmore East concert hall. A Puerto Rican street kid with us hit him with a chain when he attempted to block an entrance, and we won a series of wild free nights for the community, where the MC 5, the White Panther rock group with John Sinclair, and the Living Theater played to an anarchic crowd. We put out hundreds of flyers on cranky mimeograph machines, and we fought with the police for turf, marching on the Ninth Precinct, running from the Tactical Patrol Force, throwing rocks through the windows of the bank on St. Mark's Place and Second Avenue opposite Gem's Spa.

□ □ □

As a long-haired, bearded, dirty Motherfucker I could look in the mirror and see, with some satisfaction, my mother's nightmare.

My parents were part of a circle of Jewish left intellectuals who fled Germany in the late thirties. We spent the war years in Washington, where my father and his colleagues worked in the OSS, the predecessor of the CIA, doing intelligence on Germany. After the war he got a job as a professor of political science at Columbia University. We lived on the upper west side of the Bronx in a comfortable two-story suburban house. On the opposite side of the street was the Nip Nichen Tennis Club, which, it was rumored, excluded Jews and blacks.

We lived on a quiet hill far above the gritty noise of the elevated subway and the bustle of commerce. My home was an enclave of intellect. My parents understood, I thought, everything. I acquired my fundamental commitment to antifascism listening to their dinner-table conversation. The world, I learned, was divided in a great war, a Manichean struggle, between the forces of fascism and antifascism. Fascism was a great upsurging of irrationality accompanied by a collapse of restraints, a loosening of all urges from the bounds of moderation and reason. It was a triumph of stupidity and conformity. The struggle against fascism was the struggle of the oppressed against the oppressor and of reason against irrationality. To be antifascist, I decided, was to be committed to reason. Passion, chaos, muscularity were all suspect. This was tough for a little kid.

The surface tranquility of our bourgeois family life was broken by fearsome conflict between me and my mother. We fought about the disorder I created, dirt, untidiness, my losing things. These terrible fights would end with her crying. I didn't know what I had done. My younger brother kept out of the line of fire, and learned to be "good" in all the ways that I was not. My father sought refuge in his book-lined study. Sitting on the couch, he would spend hours lost in the *New York Times* crossword puzzle. I would retreat to my room, feeling that I was out of control. All my bodily impulses were bad. I nurtured a secret sense of personal vileness. I was the damned spot in my clean and reasonable house that would not be cleansed. If antifascism was a battle of reason against unreason, I was unreason.

Only later did I realize that my parents' marriage was not a happy one. I have no memories of physical affection between them, and they slept in separate beds. My mother was ten years younger than my father, a strong, opinionated woman relegated to child rearing and the role of faculty wife and wanting to do it right in her new country.

I grew up lost in the contemplation of my own misery, reading Dostoyevsky at a precocious age, imagining myself the underground man reveling in his subversive sinfulness. As a teenager I was guilty about masturbation, self-obsessed, running regularly to look in the mirror at a glorious array of pimples. Walking home one evening when I was fourteen, I found a page turn from a pornographic magazine. It contained a portion of a black and white photo of a naked woman chained to a post. At the sight of it, I was completely consumed with sexual excitement. It was as if the picture was a radioactive isotope irradiating my entire body. I carried it home and hid it in a hole in the bottom of my bookcase. To my great shame, my fantasies became sadomasochistic. At times I would beat myself with a hairbrush, finding relief in physical pain from the psychological torture of my relationship with my mother. Across the street there was a Jewish family with two boys, like ours. The father was a surgeon who worked nights at one of the big city hospitals. He had hairy arms and knuckles and punished his children by spanking them. I wished I had a father like that. All of this I mention because it seems as relevant to the life of a Motherfucker as the conditions in a Bolivian tin mine are to the guerrilla movements of Bolivia.

When I was thirteen a series of catastrophes befell me that transformed my family situation, revealing what previously had been hidden like an earthquake that uncovers a hidden room in a house you'd lived in unsuspectingly for years. I lived on the top floor of our house in a room with slanting walls below the roof. One night I was awakened by the sound of my mother crying downstairs. The next day she informed me that my father and she were separating. My father had run off, she told me, with another woman, a graduate student of his. I was completely dumbfounded, not the least by this sudden revelation of my father's sexuality. I had thought of him as a eunuch—fat, passive, asexual, hard of hearing, balding, nearsighted. At the time of my mother's announcement, my father was on an extended trip traveling and lecturing in Europe. A few months passed and one morning my mother asked me to come down to the kitchen; she had something important to tell me. She asked me to sit down on a stool and offered me a glass of milk. Then she told me that my father was dead. A car in which he had been riding had gone off the road in Switzerland and plunged over the edge of a mountain. Everyone in it was killed. No one knew the cause of the accident. My father had been in the back seat.

I remember thinking I should feel something; in fact I seemed to feel nothing. But some weeks later, while doing my homework, I suddenly burst into tears. The tears surprised me. I had not even been conscious of thinking about my father at the time.

During the years my mother and father lived together in the Bronx, we shared our house with an old friend of the family whose wife had died of cancer. In what seemed to me no time after my father's death, my mother announced that she and this boarder were going to marry. They informed me that he had discussed it with my father before his death and he approved. It was all very civilized. No one told me until years later that they had been lovers for years, their affair beginning before he had moved into the house and continuing uninterrupted thereafter. I never found out if my father knew or did not know. Things had not been what they seemed.

In 1957 I graduated from high school and went to Swarthmore, a small Quaker college located near Philadelphia. The campus was famous for its rhododendrons, but I wandered about largely oblivious to its beauty, obsessed and self-absorbed and isolated from the world like a turtle in a beautiful terrarium. There was no student movement. Mine was the last apolitical class, wallowing in its alienation. I graduated in 1961. The following year the student movement was to shake the campus, and the tranquil botanical garden became a hotbed of agitation. I missed it and went on disconsolately to graduate school of Yale. More interested in doodling than studying, I left after a year. Nothing that happened in college or graduate school touched my sense of isolation, the sense of being unable to connect with anything but my own internal life.

□ □ □

The Motherfuckers allowed me to rant and rave as I never had before. The anger at the war and all the other manifestations of the evils of the system was real. But the rage was, partly at least, the expression of a very personal suffering.

As a Motherfucker, I broke out of my painful introversion. I thrust out of the circle of my self-consciousness. I stretched. I clawed through—I thought—to something real. I wanted to touch and taste reality; I wanted to be free of self-consciousness. All my life I have wanted that. The problem was to cut through façades, to unveil, to tear apart, to penetrate. If society is feminine then the metaphors I used, unconsciously and sometimes consciously, were often of rape. I wrote in my journal after the disruption at St. Patrick's Cathedral:

> I imagine Cardinal Spellman stripped naked in front of his congregation, beaten, defiled, shit upon, forced to kneel down in a circle of raw bleeding ass holes of the sodomized choir boys and be fahrted upon, forced to eat the flesh of burnt children, forced to shiver in icy puke for all eternity.
>
> His congregation will observe this spectacle while submitting themselves to a number of tortures. Their clothes will be taken away from them and they will be made to beat each other with whips. Their children will be brought to them and before their eyes married to dope addicted negro prostitutes. The marriages will be consummated in the aisles.

And after the Lincoln Center action:

LINCOLN CENTER IS
>   Jacqueline Kennedy's panties without the
blood stains,
hairdressers plastic high snot art.
Mod art, snatsy surfaces, frunky patterned,
fits into LINCOLN Center
like a hand into Jacqueline Kennedy's drawers,
the hand of her hairdresser.

The rage I felt inside now found some physical release in action. Fearful and excited, I thrilled to the sound of breaking glass. I ran in the streets, fought with the police, was chased and arrested. I felt free, even or perhaps especially when I ended up in jail.

The Motherfuckers was never a large group. There may have been about fifteen or twenty of us at the core. We came from various class backgrounds. Apart from some Puerto Rican street kids who attached themselves to us, and Alfonso Texador, a Puerto Rican poet with legs crippled by polio, we were all white. Women played a distinctly ancillary role in all matters. There were no couples with children, with the notable exception of Charlie and Mama Carol and Mama Carol's baby, Cha Cha. Mama Carol was famous for once having whipped open her shirt on the corner of Second Avenue and St. Marks Place and squirted the beat cop with breast milk. Crazy Bernadette briefly formed a women's auxiliary called the Father Rapers, but it was short lived and existed more as her personal joke than as a real organization. The vicissitudes of male emotional life dominated the group almost untouched by feminine intervention.

Our charismatic leader was Ben Morea, an Italian street kid and an ex-junkie. He was short and wiry, with intense, challenging eyes and tight, bottled-up energy that made you pay attention. He walked with a slight swagger and had a way of cocking his head and hitching himself up when preparing for a confrontation that would have seemed ridiculous in anyone else. But people took Ben seriously. Ben projected danger, risk, the commitment to turn rhetoric into real action. The style of the group became, under his influence, one of intense confrontation. Ben demanded unconditional loyalty. One couldn't simply attend meetings; one had to be a Motherfucker night and day. Ben rewarded us with the promise to protect us with his life. He could be withering about our weaknesses, taunt us with our cowardice, but if we measured up he would reward us with a look of intense affection that became the most valued currency of the group.

Out style was improvisatory, surreal, anarchistic. When Valerie Solanis shot Andy Warhol, Ben leafleted the uptown galleries in her support. I collected donations for our storefront by carrying an empty toilet bowl up and down St. Marks Place shouting "America shits money. Shit here," till an enraged cop beat the toilet bowl to death with his nightstick. We were not college students given to intellectual discussion of theory. We joined Students for a Democratic Society (SDS) not to argue ideology but to disrupt and chastise suitably impressed students for their lack of daring. At one SDS meeting, I seized the microphone during an interminable debate with the Progressive Labor faction, dropped my pants, and with my penis flapping in the wind condemned intellectual masturbation. On another occasion, we left a meeting that had become boring, found a flock of caged pigeons from a psychology laboratory down the hall, and returned to send them wheeling through the auditorium, a concrete symbol of liberation.

The Motherfuckers were comparatively short lived. The season of love and rage and extravagant expectations was over before we knew it. The cultural weather changed. By 1969, hard drugs began replacing LSD on the streets of the Lower East Side. The young dropouts had a nervous, jagged edge. There were biker gangs on Third Street. Ben had a confrontation with one of their leaders, pulled a knife, but ended up shaking hands, mutual respect having been established. We remained a tiny grouplet, easily targeted by the police. Scruffy undercover cops with black leather shoes who said "Right on!" a lot would sidle up to us in coffeehouses and line up for free food at our community feeds. We opened up our free store as a place for street people to sleep, and it would fill with drunks who'd wake in the middle of the night, still drunk, and go after each other with broken wine bottles. The emotional tone of the Motherfuckers darkened. We seemed to attract craziness. Optimism was giving way to a tight-lipped struggle for survival. I felt the balance in the group tip. New recruits were often tough guys from the street, drawn by our rhetoric of violence.

That violence to me was still a costume, a figure of speech. At one of my court appearances a judge called me a "mixture of Rap Brown and Hitler." Me? How could he not see that beneath the mask of Motherfucker I was still a nice Jewish boy?

I did not realize that the movement whose project it was to tear off all masks had itself become a mask. Hidden beneath the mask of bravado and violence was a world of fears, the longing to preserve the self, to reclaim security. The relation between mask and reality was reversed. In the rhetoric of the movement, the bourgeois values of America masked its barbarism. For me, committed Motherfucker, the barbaric exterior masked a commitment to bourgeois values.

Precisely the split that I had railed against in myself and attempted to cure in radical politics, I incorporated into my life as a strategy for self-preservation. I built it structurally into my life when I began a relationship with Leslie, a woman who had no connection with the Motherfuckers. She lived in a nice apartment in a building with an elevator, overlooking a quiet churchyard on Tenth Street. She worked as a community organizer for an antipoverty agency on the Lower East Side.

My previous relations with women had been brooding, guilt-ridden, sexually dysfunctional affairs or occasional anonymous one-night stands. Now a sexual relationship with a real woman appeared as a possibility but in polar opposition to the fantasy world of violence that went with the identity of Motherfucker. I would lie in Leslie's bed worrying that I was missing something out on St. Mark's Place.

I was split, hedging my bets. I would hand out flyers filled with inflamed rhetoric, taunt the police, proclaim the liberation of fantasy, but run from that fantasy into the arms of a woman. Once safe, I immediately feared imprisonment. This woman was Delilah, ready with her shears. I feared I would become a timid, trapped thing, isolated by her in a pleasant little apartment in the West Village where we would sit at the kitchen table, dipping pieces of croissant in our coffee cup, languidly turning the pages of the Sunday *Times*. Out in the street, I played the role of cultural terrorist, prophet of instinctual release, vengeful, relentless. I'd return from raging in the streets to find myself impotent in bed. Leslie would lie with me, coax sexuality out of me, quieting me, gently ridiculing my fears.

This divided life lasted for some months, but in the end, the neat compartments collapsed. A fire destroyed two Motherfucker crash pads on Fourth

Street, and the next week the Motherfuckers invaded Leslie's apartment. They simply moved in, tore down the art prints, and spray-painted slogans on the wall. Day after day the street people would ride the elevator to the apartment, watched disapprovingly by the Puerto Rican superintendent charged with the maintenance of the building. Apparently, over time, words were exchanged, and the superintendent became more and more upset about the invasion of his building. I was told later that he lay in wait one evening, and, when a group of these street kids entered the elevator, he took a bottle of lye and attempted to throw it in their faces. In return, they grabbed him at the entrance to the building the next day and stabbed him to death.

We had shouted "Off the pig!" but the first person to die was a Puerto Rican superintendent. The killing never made the papers, no one was ever arrested, and none of us was even questioned by the police. Within the group, at least in my presence, the matter was not discussed. My tentative inquiries were met with curt impatience: It was necessary; you cannot live on the streets and allow yourself to be attacked without defending yourself.

We continued to swagger in the street, but I was not the only one who felt the circle closing in on us. We had mined a thin vein that was giving out, leaving us deep underground, unsure of the strength of the supports shoring up the roof of the mineshaft. The little canary was beginning to cough and wheeze. It was time to get out.

Ben engineered the escape. There was to be a gathering of hippie tribes in New Mexico, and we would attend. With the help of the Hog Farm, a hippie commune, Ben procured an old school bus, and the Motherfuckers packed their belongings, such as they were, and set out across the country, shoplifting as they went. Leslie and I, following somewhat later in our own car, joined the group in New Mexico. Using his revolutionary credentials, Ben had secured free lodging for us in Canjilón, a little town in the northwest corner of the state.

Canjilón had been a center of Reies Tijerina's Alianza, a movement to reclaim ownership of the old Spanish and Mexican land grants from the Anglos. On June 6, 1967, Tijerina and a group of his men had stormed the courthouse in Tierra Amarilla in a daring Zapatista-style raid that they hoped would spark an uprising. They freed prisoners, shot a policeman and a jailer, and fled with a reporter and a deputy sheriff as hostages. During the manhunt that followed, Canjilón was occupied by the National Guard. Tijerina was captured, stood trial, and eventually went to prison. The residents of Canjilón returned to eking out a living surrounded by the national forest they considered stolen from them by the U.S. government.

This clearly was the place for us. We made trips to Española to sign up for food stamps, bought guns, hunted for deer in the woods, acquired a couple of goats, and rustled a cow when we got hungry for meat. We dug a kiva in the backyard, read *Black Elk Speaks,* and started turning ourselves into Indians. But the truth of the matter was we were isolated and self-destructing. Barry

Motherfucker was killed ripping off some dope deal in Albuquerque. Rick Motherfucker went to live by himself, injured his foot, got gangrene, and died. None of us did anything to earn a living.

After a year, Leslie got hepatitis and left to recover with her sister in La Jolla. I visited her. We made love. She became pregnant. She announced she was not going back to the Motherfuckers. I would have to choose—her or them. I chose her.

□ □ □

My sixties problem is to come to grips with the Motherfuckers, their strengths and terrible weaknesses. I think it is worthwhile to try to understand the split, uncertain, and troubled subjectivity that fueled the political rage and love of the period. I want to avoid the nostalgia that taints so much recollection of that time.

The reflections that follow largely derive from my personal experience, that of an uncomfortable white man who came from a background of material privilege. I cannot judge to what degree they apply to the experience of others with different backgrounds.

□ □ □

It felt liberating to be in the Motherfuckers, but what was liberated? In 1968, French students on the barricades chanted "All power to the imagination." But imagination does not discriminate. Did I really wish to liberate my angry sexualized sadomasochistic fantasy? "All power to the pornographic imagination?"—would that be a revolutionary slogan? And what of the guilt, the fear of—or longing for—punishment that comes with these imaginings? Charles Manson acted out the fantasies I confined to paper. Bernadine Dohrn, at one Weathermen gathering, waved three fingers in the air as a salute to the fork stuck in the bellies of the victims of the Tate-LaBianca murders. If society was an obscenity, what relation had my obscene fantasy to its obscenity? Vietnam was a rape. What of my rape fantasies?

□ □ □

There were conflicting strains in the hippie counterculture of the sixties. At one extreme, the Motherfuckers espoused a politics of rage and tribal bonding, flower power with thorns. We saw ourselves in ideological combat with those who were unwilling to differentiate between us and them, who extolled an amorphous, all-inclusive being, a soft swooning dissolution of the ego. They called it "love." This love they offered to the soldier with the bayonet, thrusting flowers in his gun barrel. They told the cop they loved him as the baton descended on their heads. This love they portrayed as the true alternative to all the warring unhappiness of the dominant culture. They danced its praise with loose long hair and flowing garments. They invited all those straight square folks with button-down personalities to join the dance. We Motherfuckers liked the dance but worried that the dancers were weak and didn't know it. They would not be able to organize an alternative space within the culture. They would be repressed and co-opted.

Little is left of that strain of hippie counterculture. It melted away, leaving only a residue of trivial curiosities—tie-dyed shirts, psychedelic posters, aging rock stars—hardly an impressive legacy. The Motherfucker strain fared little better. We quickly self-destructed, victims of our own rhetoric, hurtling toward death with such obvious relish that all but the most suicidal potential converts kept their distance.

□ □ □

We had a slogan: "The personal is political." Under a banner emblazoned with that slogan we whipped ourselves forward toward ever more encompassing commitment. We strove to break down the barriers between our personal and political life, with the paradoxical effect that the personal was made visible at the same time that it tended to disappear into the politics. We were all aware that the emotions we poured into our politics were derived in part from our personal histories. We were driven as much by private need as by moral imperative. But we did not care to dwell on that distinction for fear of creating a separation that would leave our politics without the fuel of passion and our personal lives without the possibility of transformation.

"The personal is political" was an invitation to politicize the most intimate details of daily life. Old living arrangements were obstacles to the revolution. We experimented with new ones. Communes formed; campaigns were launched to smash monogamy, "coupelism," heterosexism, the family. We encouraged a destruction of privacy, a totalitarian intrusion of the movement into personal life. Everything was opened up for public scrutiny, from the way we brushed our teeth to the way we fucked.

But in all of this examination, secrets were kept. And in those secret places we preserved from view—our own and others—impermissible contradictions. Proclaiming that we were giving ourselves unreservedly to the tides of revolution, we hid the anchors that bound us to the past. Proclaiming we were collectivizing all we possessed, we planted in private gardens the seeds of later reversion. And when our secrets became too many and the hold of ideology waned, people quietly left to take up deferred personal agendas, to marry, to have kids.

I live now in Berkeley, the postrevolutionary suburb. Martin Luther King's picture hangs from lampposts on Martin Luther King Jr. Way. City government offices are housed in the Martin Luther King Jr. Center, next to Martin Luther King Jr. Park. My daughter can go to Malcolm X Elementary School if she likes. ("The chickens have come home to roost," Malcolm commented when Kennedy was gunned down, but neither that slogan, nor any other, adorns the façade of the school named in his honor. There is a limit.) Apart from a few crusty anachronisms, well hidden in the wealthy hills, we here regularly vote our opposition to nuclear war, intervention in Central America, the bloating of the defense budget. Meanwhile property values continue to rise. The houses on either side of me were bought a few years back by young professional couples who jog by and have produced numerous offspring in no time at all. Here most of the ghettos are gourmet. Down on Sacramento Street, Sugar's Den and the Monkey Shine shoe parlor have been boarded up to make way for urban renewal. Here, while the media still blathers about "the People's Republic of Berkeley," the sixties lives on like a spayed cat, happily lounging in the sun, licking its fur, scratching the occasional flea.

□ □ □

The crisis of the sixties was experienced differently in different sectors of society. For white America it expressed itself as a children's revolt that tore the culture apart along generational lines.

Adolescence is traditionally a time of aching awareness of the gulf between the self and society's expectations. A sixteen-year-old I know lies in her bed, her sheets a mess, her room filled with clutter; she responds to her father's intrusions with disdain. When he asks her to do something she moves with exaggerated slowness, ready for a fight if he objects. She projects a cosmic distaste not just for his intrusions into her reverie but for all demands, all interruptions.

Societies depend for their continued stability on containing the turmoil of adolescence, on limiting the arc of the discontent. In the sixties that arc became abnormally extended. Children saw the family as the modular cell out of which the whole oppressive body politic was constructed.

Adolescents rebelled in droves. They rejected the menu of socially acceptable adult roles: cannon fodder, housewife, flunky in some menial and depressing job. It was not a time of scarcity: Fear of poverty was an insufficient whip to keep them on the path. Singing "Hell no, we won't go," they announced, en masse, an ultimatum: they would change what it meant to grow up or they would not grow up at all.

I did not experience the system as oppressive because I was materially deprived. I was not driven to revolt by rage at the privilege of others, or pangs of hunger or cold or blows to the flesh. Pain, cold, and hunger remind one of the body. The body in pain knows its reality and the reality of what causes it pain. I experienced my oppression as an inability to grasp anything real beyond my own subjectivity. Nothing outside myself had substance or impact, everything was denatured.

This unreality threatened to engulf me, to isolate me, to immure me in a soundless unreflecting room. I experienced in myself, and the world I encountered, a lack of connection between surface and interior. I lived in a world of masks. In the suburbs of my childhood, distance swallowed connection. I was isolated in my family. Our house stood in splendid isolation from the neighbors, protected by its moat of well-clipped lawn. There was none of the enforced proximity of poverty. And just as the surface of my family did not reflect its inner life, so the prosperous suburb floated in splendid isolation above a dimly sensed other world, a Third World of poverty and color and violence. White America was cut off from the depredations it practiced in the Third World and its own ghettos. Living with these separations, I believe, contributed to the diminished sense of the reality of my own being, which in turn decorporealized all that I perceived, desiccating the apple sitting on the plate, bleaching the sunset, sucking the juices and substance from things.

In revolt against the experience of unreality, I, like others of America's privileged white children, drifted into rebellion, determined to provide the system to reveal its real self, to transform its emptiness into a concrete fullness of brutality—to manifest itself as a policeman's club, the iron bars of a cell—to bring the war home. (As a child I had fantasized a strong father who beat me, imagining that beating as a pleasure in comparison to the psychological torture of my relationship with my mother.) I wrote in my journal during the Motherfucker period:

We live in an unreproducible zero, surrounded by husks of representation. The unreality is held together by its images. The less substantial it becomes in itself, the more images are required to hold it together.

The essence of America is that it is zero. It has already been wiped out. The war is over. By going into the streets and fighting cops we create our enemy. We make something to fight against. We call it into existence. As long as America doesn't exist it is invincible. We will have won when we have fully created our enemy, when we have forced him into a body. And we seem to be able to do this only by totally encircling him with violence. And the same with us. Violence gives us for the first time a body. And that body fills in the present by being beaten. Experience must be attached to a body that is being beaten or feels itself as potentially beaten.

We were the wrecking ball, punching through façades that concealed a destructive pestilent reality. Families presented to the world masks of respectability that concealed real nastiness within. The everyday lawful intercourse of civil society hid the brutal exercise of force on which it depended. Its victims were hidden, its worst depredations practiced overseas. We would "bring the war home," forcing the truth down the throats of the hypocrites.

Common sense was a façade. Nothing common made sense. We attempted to break through habits of perception using drugs as explosive propellants to hurl us into quite uncommon spaces (hidden as the subatomic world of the physicist is hidden from the macroscopic world of the senses).

We were immersed in unreality like a fetus in the amniotic sac. We needed to break through the façades to be born, again, out of the "belly of the beast." We were the children of that beast turning on our mother and destroying her, ripping her apart in the process of our birth. We, Motherfuckers, were fucking her from inside out. One current of the counterculture was about blissed-out being. The Motherfuckers were about penetration, the penetration of the prisoner through the wall of his cell, the penetration of the birthing infant through the vagina, the penetration of the rapist, angry and violent. Revolution as sex crime.

In the Third World, and in the ghettos of the First, the enemy that attacks the body of the family is also the enemy that attacks the body politic. The colonial power is the enemy of the motherland and of the mother. The revolutionary in the Third World fights for the right to grow up, to become a man or a woman, to inherit the home. The invader is the defiler of the home, who defiles the motherland. He comes from outside to rape and pillage. He leaves behind a crowd of bastards to do his bidding and to wreak revenge on those who revolt.

In Central America, revolutionaries love their mothers. The Sandinistas published posters showing a revolutionary fighter embracing his mother and urging respect for the mothers of the revolution. The Mothers of the Disappeared, the Mothers of Revolutionary Martyrs, are given the highest place in the revolutionary pantheon. Guerrillas underground, hiding in safe houses or clinging to the sides of volcanoes, long for their mothers and their deepest wish is to embrace them once again. The beating heart of maternal love is a drum rallying the children against the heartlessness of imperialism, against the vileness of dictatorships.

Central American revolutionaries defend the mother. We, the white American male hippie radicals of the sixties, sought to destroy her. They are strengthened by her love and saved by it from guilt at defying the paternal authority of the dictator. We rebelled against her and were burdened by an enormous sense of guilt. We birthed ourselves in fearful infantile rage. As we sought to destroy her, we longed for the maternal embrace. How could I explain in revolutionary Nicaragua or in a refugee camp in Gaza that the political group I belonged to was called the Motherfuckers?

The core of traditional revolutionary movements is a revolt against expropriation, against a taking away. These movements have defined for us the imagery of revolution. They are the movements of the poor all over the world, fueled by material scarcity. But the hippie counterculture was a product of material abundance. Motherfuckers were part of a movement of those who revolted against that with which they were stuffed. It was a revolt against "having" rather than the "not having." It was sparked by the oppressiveness of consumption rather than the conditions of production, the oppressiveness of a comparative material abundance. The scarcity hippies revolted against was not a material scarcity. It was an emptiness in the midst of plenty, a starvation of the spirit. Their hunger for nourishment differed from the hunger of Ethiopians but was hunger nevertheless.

□ □ □

The politicized counterculture that developed in the youth ghettos of the sixties was built on a set of correlations by which we oriented that culture's opposition. That portion of ourselves that society sought to *repress* we identified with those whom society *oppressed*. Blacks in the rural and urban slums, Vietnamese in their rice fields, Cubans among their sugar cane fields were real; we were struggling to become real. The unconscious became identified with the ghetto; one's personal vileness with the dirt of the ghetto streets; the violence of one's rages against one's parents with the violence of those streets; our rage with the rage of the oppressed.

Among the oppressed, we imagined, one's identity was clear. For us, revolt was a continual process of trying to externalize our oppression, to cough it up, to get it out of our system.

Despite our assertions of solidarity with the oppressed around the world, the qualitative differences in our struggles remained. We gagged on our piece of pie while others still struggled to get to the table. We dropped out; others were never offered the opportunity to "drop in." Our commitment to revolution seemed a matter of choice; theirs, a necessity.

No one would say of the blacks or the Vietnamese or the bearded Cubans in the Sierra Maestra that their struggle was "only a stage." But that charge was continually leveled against us. Our aberrant existence was seen as only some bright larval stage of development that would inevitably be exchanged for the drab conformist plumage of the adult of the species. We vehemently denied that our revolt was any bit less authentic than that of the colonized peoples with whom we declared our solidarity, but how could we defend ourselves against this accusation?

In some ways, we thought, our radicalism trumped theirs. The poor and the dispossessed struggled against deprivations. They were famished. It was not for them to elaborate a critique of the cuisine that was not on their plates. That critique was our job.

This was true and not true. The dominant culture penetrates everywhere and everywhere generates resistance. From corrugated tin roofs in favelas and ghettos and refugee camps in Asia and Africa and Latin America sprout television aerials. Inside, in the gloom, the TV blinks and the poor can see images of wealth, families with upholstered couches and doorbells, maids, cars, lawns, newly pressed jeans, deodorants, bathrooms with tile and soft towels. Outdoors time may move slowly and coherently, the village may breathe as a unit. But the music videos jump in frenzied fragmentation, loud, glitzy, sexual pumping. In the Third World, those who are exploited as producers are courted as consumers. Commodities are advertised on walls next to which donkeys browse and pigs root. The West sucks products from the Third World and sends back addicting images of an unobtainable lifestyle. One form that resistance takes is fundamentalism, a critique of what passes as progress, modernization, "Western" rationality. It is the cultural critique of the haves by the have nots. The self-critique of the haves as seen in the cultural revolt of the sixties also contained a critique of past reason and progress. But while fundamentalists in the Third World can extol a return to traditional values, for the hippies there was nothing to return to. We tried to build an ersatz counter-culture on the spot, with mixed results. We searched in other cultures for forms to copy. We imagined ourselves as twentieth-century Indians, creating tribal life from bits of reading and our own explorations. We were moving resolutely back to the future. With drugs we went spelunking into the caves of our consciousness, searching for origins, discovering extraordinary formations, tunnels that opened onto new landscapes. And sometimes we got lost and fell from rooftops.

□ □ □

"Freedom Now!"

The political culture of the sixties insisted that liberation was not to be deferred. Freedom would not come as the result of a long struggle during which people were unfree. Freedom had to be part of the struggle, an experience that one could grab now. The movement would grow by its shining example.

The key tactic for incorporating the experience of freedom into the struggle for liberation was civil disobedience. The act of disobeying the authority of the state allows there to come briefly into existence a zone of genuine freedom. In everyday life the forces of repression are omnipresent but veiled. Civil disobedience is the reagent that precipitates those repressive forces out of the formless fluidity of our humdrum existence. It compels them to array themselves against us and in so doing to take up a definable space. Once that space was defined, we could stand outside it. Where one stands at the moment of confrontation (the segregated lunch counter; the road to the recruiting center; facing the snapping dogs, the cops thumping their nightsticks, the curses) is liberated territory. Freedom blossoms at the point of confrontation because there the forces of repression take off their mask.

In jail, behind bars, we felt peace, we felt real. Singing freedom songs as the handcuffs were placed on our wrists, we felt community, we felt joy. The moment had an undeniable self-evident rightness. It was addictive.

The power of this experience of freedom created the civil rights movement and inspired the antiwar movement. Its discovery was a gift. But it was a deceptively simple gift, an insight that would unravel. A movement could not offer people such moments of freedom without a means for fulfilling their larger promise. One could not convince people to settle for less. The thirst for liberation gave energy but undermined form. Few structures and organizations have survived from the sixties. We never developed a strategy, a political culture, or an organization that could preserve the promise of those moments. The genuine achievement of liberation would require a "long march through the institutions." It would have to defer some promises while retaining its intransigent core. We have not yet created a movement that can bridge the gap—a gap perhaps of generations—between the experience of a moment of freedom and the realization of the promise of that moment. Such a movement cannot be built overnight. We have yet to create a political culture that can retain the promise of freedom while tempering it, insisting on the sublimation of the desire for freedom while retaining its fulfillment as the measure of any success. We cannot simultaneously shout "freedom now" and "freedom not quite yet."

The white antiwar movement, like the civil rights movement, drew converts to its cause by the promise of immediate liberation. The movement was a liberated zone within which one could be transformed. Liberation meant liberation from the old, despised self. It meant the possibility of taking on a new identity, of stepping out of one's old self as a butterfly from its cocoon or a snake from its old skin. The image of personal transformation came from a variety of sources. The southern civil rights movement was certainly one; the guerrilla movements of Latin America were another. Che and Fidel had taken to the mountains, leaving behind the comforts of home. In the mountains a "new man" was forged and tempered in battle. When they came down out of the mountains, bearded, cigar smoking, they looked different and they were different.

In strange amalgam, these political images of transformation fused with acid-fueled visions of the power to leap out of history. "Better living through chemistry," proclaimed a tongue-in-cheek poster of the time. LSD would dissolve the old self and allow a radical new being to emerge. A new frontier opened up for us. In a peculiar mutation of typical American hubris, we believed we could be anybody: Zen monk, Mexican *brujo,* Sioux medicine man. We were revolutionary Horatio Alger heroes. Horatio Alger's heroes pulled themselves up from rags to riches by their own bootstraps. We thought we could transform ourselves by pulling in the opposite direction—down from the heights of privilege, away from its constraints, and into the future. All that was required was the willingness to take off on the adventure.

The movement's emphasis on the transformation of personal life was charismatic, but at the same time it limited participation. Not everyone was ready for an intrusive political movement that accepted only total commitment. Not everyone was prepared to have their bedroom and bathroom transformed into a terrain of political struggle. The more global and universal the definition of the revolutionary project, the fewer, ultimately, were those who could or would meet its stringent demands. The perfect revolutionary cadres were young rootless dropouts with lots of time and no commitments. The movement became the whole of life for those who participated, a life increasingly cut off from the daily realities of ordinary working people with jobs, families, and children.

As we expanded the definition of what was political, we simultaneously narrowed the area of what we considered legitimate political action. All those activities that were not total, that did not call into question the very existence of those who participated, were illegitimate. Any act that lacked the element of ultimate risk was hopelessly compromised. Electoral politics, letter writing, peaceful demonstrations confined within the barricades set up by the police were worse than worthless. Civil disobedience became progressively less civil.

Only a total transformation of society would do. And the only group worthy of allegiance was one committed to that total transformation and one that required from its members a corresponding total commitment. These groups tended to become sectarian cults, tense pressure cookers, isolating their members from the ordinary intercourse of society.

□ □ □

Infantile rage is a fuel that is easily exhausted. It will not sustain a lifetime of commitment. Only structure—in the personality, in the organization of the movement—allows growth over time. We need organizations that are capable of exercising some authority but that avoid reproducing the authoritarian modes of the dominant society. We need organizations that can link generations, providing a way for revolutionary Peter Pans to grow up. Otherwise "growing up" will continue to seem an inevitable conspiracy of biology with the forces of reaction.

The movements of the sixties broadened the zone of political activity in all directions—inward into the personal and outward a critique of daily life. Everything was linked to everything else. The system was an integrated totality that subordinated all aspects of experience to its destructive purposes. The transformation of that system would transform the deep structure of society and of consciousness. The false smile of commodities would be extinguished. The real face of the world would emerge, washed in possibilities. The vision was intoxicating. It attracted craziness as shiny baubles attract magpies, as the open flame attracts moths and butterflies.

Seeing all the revolutionary moths crashing into the flame, we become frightened. The tendency since the sixties has been to douse the flame, to protect those delicate little beauties with their fragile wings. We have purged as an infantile aberration the inflamed imagination of possibilities. But the vision doesn't really die. The possibilities imagined by the counterculture of the sixties are real. The demand for their fulfillment will remain charismatic.

CHAPTER 5

The Counterculture, the New Left, and the New Right

Rebecca E. Klatch

□   □   □   □   □   □   □   □   □   □   □   □

In the last few years there has been a resurgence of interest in "the sixties."[1] Although this new literature offers fresh insights into the organization, influences on, and effects of the social movements of that era, the majority of these analyses fail to understand two fundamental aspects of the 1960s. First, the focus of these commentaries—and the popular conception of the 1960s—associates the decade solely with the politics of the left, with the civil rights, antiwar, and women's movements. Yet my previous research,[2] which focused on women in the New Right, found that many of today's conservative activists also came of age during the 1960s. Many New Right women and men first became active during their college years through participation in Young Americans for Freedom (YAF), a youth organization formed at the estate of William F. Buckley in Sharon, Connecticut, in 1960. YAF was founded in the same year as Students for a Democratic Society (SDS), one of the primary organizations of the New Left. Both were youth groups that grew out of older organizations of the right and left. Both issued founding principles: for YAF the Sharon Statement was adopted in 1960; for SDS the Port Huron Statement was issued in June of 1962. Ironically, both also had explosive national conventions in 1969. Yet little attention has been paid to the origins of the New Right within the context of the 1960s.

To be fair, in terms of both visibility and adherents, the New Left was more prominent. At its peak, from around 1967 to 1969, SDS membership is estimated to have been as high as a hundred thousand,[3] while YAF membership in 1969 was about fifty-one thousand.[4] Also, by the late 1960s mass student opinion was more in line with SDS than with YAF. Even so, we need to reassess the 1960s as fostering not only the politics of the New Left but also as

A version of this chapter also appeared in *Qualitative Sociology* 17, no. 3 (Fall 1994): 199–214. © 1994 Human Sciences Press.

the incubation stage for today's conservative movement. As one prophetic YAF activist commented during the 1960s: "We want to create a training ground now for articulate and effective conservative leaders. No matter what SDS says, it's not the kids who rule the world, it's the adults. . . . We're thinking of the future; and what we're doing now won't be felt for another five years. But we're going to be felt and we're going to be felt strong."[5] In fact, as I will discuss below, many former YAF activists hold positions of political power today.

The second shortcoming of much of the literature on the 1960s is its failure to consider adequately the influence of culture on political activism, although recent accounts have taken seriously the role of the counterculture and its relation to movements of the 1960s. Doug McAdam persuasively shows the ways in which Freedom Summer was an important moment in the development of the counterculture.[6] Both Gitlin and Breines view the counterculture as prefigurative, the embodiment of the "new society."[7] Flacks discusses the importance of the counterculture in sustaining activism, solidifying individual commitment to the group; music, for instance, helped symbolize the collective identity of the left.[8] Burns, on the other hand, concludes that the counterculture never really served as a culture for the left in the same way that the black church sustained black commitment to the civil rights movement.[9]

Although these accounts are important in their focus on culture, none gives sufficient attention to the possibility of culture as an essential aspect of activism, that is, to the ways in which the counterculture fostered social protest. While "new cultural historians" have taken up the question of the interplay between culture and politics,[10] surprisingly little attention has been paid to this issue within the sociological literature on social movements in general. Despite Swidler's call for analysis of historical contexts in which action is made possible through new cultural complexes,[11] few studies examine culture as an active ingredient in *creating* social change.

This paper is based on a research project that compares women and men who were active in SDS and YAF during the 1960s.[12] In 1989–91 I conducted seventy-four in-depth interviews with former activists across the country and examined archival materials of SDS and YAF.[13] Although there is no doubt that fundamental differences divide the left and right, I am concerned here with whether a generational impulse intersects the worldviews of left- and right-wing activists of the 1960s. What are the common grounds between YAF and SDS? What is the variation in interpretation and meaning by activists in these two groups as they experienced the social movements and changes of the 1960s?

The counterculture serves as a meeting ground in understanding the varying interests and overlapping impulses of what I term "the divided generation." The preliminary findings of this study indicate that the counterculture provided a means of reformulation of belief, provoking radicalization and serving to mobilize particular actors during the 1960s. Thus, this research suggests that culture plays an important role not only in sustaining or cementing commitment to a cause but also in *fomenting* political activism. After discussing the varying responses to the counterculture among former YAF and SDS activists, I will consider the implications of these findings in understanding the theory and politics of social movements.

The use of the term "counterculture" here specifically refers to the dress, music, drugs, sexuality, and "alternative lifestyles" associated with the cultural changes of the 1960s.[14] These lifestyles also signified a renunciation of conventional values, for example, of conventional manners and morals for an emphasis on spontaneity and self-expression; the replacement of traditional attitudes toward career, success, and money with a devaluing of materialism and a search for jobs that emphasized self-expression and social contribution; and an emphasis on naturalness expressed by the rejection of cosmetics, perfumes, and deodorants and the embrace of nudity.[15]

Thus, the counterculture implies not a single, unified entity; rather, it incorporated a range of beliefs and practices. For instance, the counterculture embraced diverse and even contradictory values. It encompassed both an urge toward individual expression and self-gratification and one toward collectivism and community. It is, indeed, this diversity of beliefs and practices that allowed people of varying backgrounds and ideologies to identify with an oppositional culture.[16]

Although cultural radicalism has accompanied leftist protest movements of the past, [17] the counterculture was able to reach a much larger audience due to the middle-class affluence of postwar America. A rise in the discretionary income of teenagers created an economic base for youth culture. This was closely linked to the expansion of the leisure and fashion industries directed at a "teenage market." The ability of the mass media (radio, television, records, movies) to promote and disseminate this youth culture further accelerated the collective identity of this generation.[18]

Given the growth of the youth culture of the 1960s, what variation of responses did members of SDS and YAF have to these alternative lifestyles? While issues of culture and meaning were a fundamental part of the New Left as a whole, how these issues got defined and specifically how different members of the left—and the right—related to these alternative lifestyles and values is what is decisive. Did activists embrace the counterculture? Or was apathy or disdain the more predominant attitude?

The preliminary findings of my research indicate there was a split within both SDS and YAF over activists' relationship to the counterculture. In brief, within SDS there is a division in attitude, with the pattern corresponding to year of entry into activism. There is a notable difference between the hostility expressed by the early activists (1960–64) and the more accepting embrace of the counterculture by later activists (1965–69).[19] For instance, one woman active early in the sixties said:

I was less into the cultural aspects than the political aspects. . . . Some of that may have been a question of age; by the time the counterculture really hit strong, I was already in my mid-twenties. . . . I had grown up in the fifties. . . . I look[ed] at some of [the counterculture] as kind of silly, self-indulgent. . . . I was . . . antagonistic to some aspects of it. . . . I just didn't really identify with it in a strong way.[20]

Another early SDSer, male, said:

I was always annoyed at people who thought that the counterculture was in and of itself the revolution and that all we needed to do was all get high and listen to rock music. Drugs had become kind of a metaphor of revolution, and I felt that really was wrong. That saying change your head, that wasn't a revolution.[21]

The social base of SDS shifted during the mid-to-late sixties. In contrast to the early activists, later SDSers were from outside the East and tended to be non-Jewish and nonurban; they were from a nonprofessional class and often lacked a family tradition of political involvement.[22] So, too, the attitude toward the counterculture shifted. Rather than rejecting the counterculture as a diversion from politics, the later activists I interviewed generally embraced the counterculture, seeing it not only as a valid part of 1960s activism but as an essential part of the political movement.

One woman of the later generation of activists said:

I really felt . . . that we were going to create a culture that really worked. . . . the counterculture and the political movement were the same; if you asked people what they belonged to, they belonged to everything . . . It was a very, very open time. . . . I really don't think [the history of the sixties] has been written yet. Until people can get a sense of what it was like to sit in a T-Group and talk about what you really think but you have not been saying because you didn't want anybody to know; or you could sit in a women's liberation group and say "my husband has never done a dish in his life and he's never going to" . . . I don't think people want to remember it because it really does challenge a person to be real.[23]

Another of the later activists said:

We were *very* involved in the counterculture. There was a lot of drugs in SDS, psychedelic drugs, not hard drugs. And it wasn't until '69 that SDS came out against drugs because the counterculture stuff was so strong in SDS that it was a long time before the black perspective gained dominance. . . . The counterculture was great but it was a very youth culture . . . what you did between the ages of fourteen and twenty-five.[24]

What is more surprising is the deep lines of division among YAF activists regarding the counterculture. Basically, the division follows the ideological split that characterized YAF throughout the 1960s and remains one of the central splits in the conservative movement today, that is, the conflict between traditionalists and libertarians. Surveys within YAF indicate that about a quarter of the membership identified as a type of libertarian.[25] A common joke around YAF in the 1960s was that traditionalists wore colorless ties, sat straight, and prayed while liberatarians wore necklaces and slurped their soup. Not surprisingly, the traditionalists abhorred the counterculture, seeing it as immoral and destructive.

One woman who became active early in the 1960s, a traditionalist, discusses the counterculture as being imposed on people of the 1960s: "We all had to suffer through it. . . . I feel it was a very damaging time because of drugs. I know there were drugs before . . . but never were they combined with the self-righteousness of the antiwar movement and the music. . . . That was a very rotten combination of events that came together all at one time."[26]

A male activist who helped found YAF responded: "I was critical of the counterculture. I thought it was hedonistic, self-centered, disruptive." This YAFer was part of the countercounterculture; he worked with Ed Butler in forming the square movement in the late 1960s. Declaring "Square power is on the rise,"[27] they started a magazine called *Square*, put on square conferences, and had a television show with square writers and square entertainers like John Wayne. In his words, "It was very consciously against the counterculture."[28]

Libertarians in YAF, on the other hand, not only were less critical of the counterculture but often embraced it in their own lifestyles. One libertarian woman commented:

> I absolutely identified [with the counterculture]. I was living in San Francisco at the height of hippiedom. I can remember going down to Haight-Ashbury, thinking that this was neat. . . . I saw it as people just being what they wanted to be. That was to me the essence of the counterculture. . . . On all these aspects of conventionality, where the conservatives were so stuffy, and I said, "What's the big deal?" Long-haired hippies? Who cares what length somebody's hair is? Like big deal—what does that have to do with a person's worth?[29]

A libertarian male YAFer put it was way:

> [We did] identify with the counterculture . . . we were in our raggedy blue-jeans and listening to rock music and wearing worker shirts and growing our hair longer. . . . The libertarians in YAF really identified with the freedom that was being expressed by the Woodstock generation. . . . I saw more of a free-spirit philosophy being expressed—and that attracted me a lot.[30]

This division within YAF was also played out in a fascinating debate that took place in *New Guard*, the YAF monthly magazine, in commentary on the movie *Easy Rider*. A 1969 review by Stanford YAF chair Harvey Hukari applauded *Easy Rider* as dealing with "the quest for freedom from societal restraints, the task of finding one's self and difficulty of being an individual in an indifferent or hostile atmosphere." The movie shows us "an America where individuals with long hair are treated as outcasts, where redneck southerners deal harshly with those who choose to be different and where most of the 'straight' people are mindless, drab and bigoted."[31]

In another positive review, *Easy Rider* is labeled a "remarkable commentary on America" that presents an "America that excuses its collective bigotry by hiding or legitimizing it in the name of democracy."[32] These words are striking because they could as easily have been uttered by someone on the left.

In response to Hukari's review, David Brudnoy called the movie "implicitly subversive of important values. . . . it's cool porn, subtly subverting, cleverly luring the. . . . uncorrupted to worship at the shrine of Our Lady of Grass." Brudnoy objects to the message of the movie, which he sees as "what's wrong with America is 'straight' America," that "hippieism . . . always drug accompanied, is great stuff," and that "straights are . . . simple wits at best, at worst savages."[33] Supporting this view, one person wrote a letter to the editor deploring *Easy Rider* as "a cheap representation of drugs, sex and filth with no responsibility to God, family or country."[34]

Clearly, what is being played out here is not only a divergence of opinion regarding the counterculture but also a battle over the meaning of America, a struggle over who and what is responsible for the problems ripping apart the nation.

What is also evident is how the libertarian embrace of the counterculture overlaps with a segment of the New Left. There is a common ideological impulse between the libertarian right and the countercultural New Left. In particular these sectors shared a common hostility toward the state, a strong impulse toward personal freedom, and a call for decentralization and local control of neighborhoods, schools, and the police.

The Vietnam war and the counterculture were the two most significant factors in bringing together these sectors of the left and right. By the late 1960s the war was creating ideological strain within YAF. Although most YAF members opposed conscription, libertarians grew more and more hostile to the state drafting individuals as well as to American involvement in an illegal war. In 1969 YAFer Ron Kimberling declared he was "opposed to the U.S. imperialist venture in Vietnam, which is being conducted in a manner that seriously undermines freedom for the Vietnamese and for citizens in our own country, who are being subjected to fascism in the name of freedom." He encouraged students to participate in the Vietnam Moratorium.[35] In fact, many libertarians began taking part in antiwar demonstrations and teach-ins.

But it was not just Vietnam that drew together the right and left. The counterculture became a common currency between these two political worlds. One specific way the counterculture created grounds for common cause was through drugs. As Paul Willis points out, during the 1960s drugs were important in uniting individuals in opposition to straight society.[36] It was both the actual experience of taking drugs as well as run-ins with the state resulting from drug use that brought together the worlds of the right and left.

The radicalization evident in one libertarian man's story is typical. Having been active in YAF for five years, he was in the top leadership of the California branch. Enamored with the music of the times, one day in the spring of 1967 he heard Jim Morrison sing "Light My Fire" and knew *then* that he was going to smoke dope. Reflecting on this he says:

> The whole drug thing really impressed me and gave me literally a new way of thinking. And it changed the rules: suddenly I was an enemy of the state. I was doing something illegal, and the government could come down and bite my ass. I didn't like having to be put in that position for doing something I thought was absolutely none of their business and was exercising my personal freedom.

He claims to have become the Johnny Appleseed of YAF, turning on others ripe for change. This counterculture experience brought him to realization of common grounds with the left:

> Timothy Leary and reading Baba Ram Dass . . . was just amazing. It wasn't right or left. It was "Be Here Now." . . . It was a different lifestyle. The counterculture was a great common ground. We had all these common values— love and peace, freedom from government interference and personal growth. . . . I was an enemy of the state. . . . Drugs and the war were the catalyst. . . . And the lifestyle that Nixon and his gang didn't approve of.[37]

A parallel statement was made by an SDS member who said, "There were common grounds with the right. They were against Big Brother, against narcs on campus. There were common grounds when it came to getting Big Brother off your back."[38]

Thus, government repression and the delegitimation of authority forged a link between the left and right. One libertarian YAFer discusses what radicalized him:

> When you see the way the administration responded to opposition to the war and the kinds of things that were going on—domestic surveillance, the efforts to control personal behavior, the drug laws that were being passed. . . . I reacted very, very negatively to the way government was responding to protest. . . . They were opposed to dissent. . . . The government responded

in a fascist way. . . . I never could understand why other people in YAF didn't see that association.[39]

Typically, this view of the U.S. government created a gap that libertarians experienced as they felt more and more alienated from the conservative movement. The late 1960s witnessed accusations by liberatarians charging YAF with being run by reactionaries and bigots. The right was accused of being a "wasteland of authoritarianism" bordering on fascism. Karl Hess, a former speechwriter for Barry Goldwater who later turned libertarian, put it this way: "To really love this land, you must first learn to loathe this nation and the system for which it stands."[40] The parallel to the language of the New Left is striking.

Interestingly, 1969 proved to be pivotal for both groups. The 1969 SDS convention resulted in the splintering of the organization and the demise of SDS. The 1969 YAF convention erupted in intense verbal and even physical confrontation between traditionalists and libertarians. When one young libertarian burned his draft card on the convention floor, the convention turned into an angry mob. A resolution was passed expelling the card-burner; ultimately, all libertarians were purged from YAF. One libertarian faction stormed out of the meeting, denouncing "domestic fascism" and calling for resistance to the Vietnam War, legalization of marijuana, and unity with SDS.

□ □ □

What can we say about such a radical turn of events? Certainly, a portion of this divided generation of the 1960s spoke a common language, if only for a brief moment in time. This language was formed in part through the counterculture. I want to conclude by stepping back from this historical moment to consider the implications of the counterculture for social movement theory.

First, we need to understand how the counterculture served as a reservoir of meaning. For those who embraced it, did the counterculture mean the same things to activists on the right and left? As an oppositional culture, did the dress, music, drugs, and alternative lifestyles of the 1960s act to subvert the dominant culture for people in both camps? While it is certainly true that people with different ideologies brought separate values and interests to the counterculture, what is evident is that experiences within the counterculture provided a means for shared interpretations of reality. Both identity in the counterculture (as being outside of mainstream society) and external responses to alternative lifestyles brought sectors of the left and right into conversation with each other. The counterculture became a means of communication between travelers in foreign countries. The stigmatization suffered by those adopting a "hippie" or "freak" lifestyle further solidified the bonds between these sectors of the left and right.[41]

For the libertarian right, the counterculture did *not* represent merely a lifestyle change; rather, participation in counter-institutions and lifestyles led to direct run-ins with state authority and a requestioning of belief. Flacks argues that the climate fostered by the music, marijuana, and bohemianism of the counterculture encouraged youth to challenge conventional cultural repression, hierarchical authority, and forms of bureaucratic rationalization. This cultural climate made mass protest possible by creating a shared ethical framework of resistance and solidarity of youth.[42] While Flacks is speaking here of youth on the left, this cultural climate drew in libertarian activists on the right as well. One of the unintended consequences of the counterculture, then, was the conversion of libertarians within YAF to a more radical perspective. The oppositional culture of the 1960s unified the interests of sectors of the left and right through convergence of belief around individual expression and revolt against the state. This unity extended to shared participation in protest against the government.

What this points out for social movement theory is the importance of understanding the changing nature of participation. As the 1960s progressed, libertarians were drawn into different circles and mobilized on issues distinct from those deemed important to their traditionalist allies. This exemplifies the point made by Snow et al. that participation in social movements is not static, that decisions to participate are subject to reassessment and renegotiation as people realign their interpretive frames.[43] This is certainly true of the libertarian right's experience, and this dynamic even gave rise to a new party, the Libertarian Party, born in 1971, which many of the libertarians purged from YAF helped found.

The 1960s experience further challenges social movement theory by suggesting that culture may play a key role in fostering political protest and prompting new beliefs or actions. The few analyses that discuss the culture of social movements speak of culture in terms of sustaining activism, as providing support and solidarity to keep up "the spirit of the movement." But given the effects on libertarian activists of the right, the counterculture acted not only to regenerate the movement but also became the locus for mobilization and even radicalization. The music, drugs, and lifestyle of the 1960s became an access point both to bring in new members and to educate people into a critical ideology.

This case of the 1960s provides an empirical example that confirms Swidler's analysis. She argues that bursts of ideological activism occur during periods of social transformation in which competing ways of organizing action are contending for dominance. Culture plays an essential role during such unsettled periods, acting as a toolkit or repertoire from which people construct new strategies of action.[44] The 1960s case demonstrates how certain types of oppositional culture, particularly when they are attached to larger political movements, evoke feelings and experiences that in themselves stimulate the reassessment of political belief and commitment. In short, we must give more weight to the cultural aspects of social movements, whether their results are intentional or not.

Finally, we must evaluate the impact of cultural aspects of social movements. How do we measure the cultural changes induced by social movements of the 1960s for the 1990s? The essential question is whether the counterculture was co-opted, losing its critical edge as it was absorbed by the dominant culture, or whether the counterculture made its mark in important and pervasive, although less visible, ways.

On the one hand, on could argue that the only lasting effects of the counterculture evident today are the songs and symbols of the 1960s used to sell more products to Baby Boomers. The Beatles now sing for Nike, "Born to be Wild" is used to sell motorcycles; the words "natural" and "whole grain" decorate General Mills cereals; and every Wendy's and McDonald's offers a salad bar. What is termed "New Age consciousness" has even seeped into corporate America as human-potential programs, meditation and visualization, crystals and Eastern mysticism are used to transform managers and to create happy workers and higher profits. Apparently even one president made decisions after consultation with astrologers.

Several commentators interpret trends such as these as representing the absorption and commodification of countercultural symbols and styles into mainstream America. Whalen and Flacks see an inherent contradiction between the counterculture and politics.[45] By viewing the counterculture solely in terms of self-expression, individual liberation, and personal retreatism, they pose the counterculture as conflictual with the commitment and social responsibility demanded by "the movement." In a culture upholding individualism and liberty, it is no surprise that those elements of the 1960s that emphasized self-expression and personal liberation survive.

Hall et al. cynically view the commodification and mainstreaming of countercultural styles as pioneering new social forms that better fit the needs of the system. Capitalism required not thrift but consumption, style not sobriety, immediate satisfaction of needs, not postponed gratification. Thus, they conclude: "In many aspects, the revolutions in 'lifestyle' were a pure, simple, raging, commercial success."[46]

Although it is important to recognize the co-optation of countercultural styles by dominant society, there is another side to the story. As Joe Gusfield puts it, to understand the impact of social movements we need to examine the redefinition of everyday meanings of things.[47] In this way we must understand the social changes of the 1960s not just in terms of organizational goals or structural change, but rather we must look at the broader impact, the ways that the movements—and the counterculture—opened up new ideas and actions that were previously unthinkable. The counterculture transmitted a new vocabulary by which to live, literally in the shift from "Negroes" to "blacks," from "homosexuals" to "gays and lesbians," from "girls" to "women." But also figuratively the counterculture created a shift in vocabulary. We might say that in contrast to the 1950s, the 1960s gave birth to a new idea of the possible. And for many youth, it was the culture of the 1960s that brought them awareness of these new possibilities.

Those participating in the counterculture continued to struggle over choice of lifestyle into the 1970s and 1980s, refusing to settle down or to resign themselves solely to material comfort. The libertarian right, like those in the New Left, followed a more circuitous life course, exploring experimental routes, tentatively feeling their way toward adult life.[48] Many remained mobile both geographically and vocationally into their thirties. While many libertarians spent months or even years traveling or wandering between jobs and locations, unclear about their direction, none of the traditionalists reported similar paths. Comparing the career trajectories of traditionalists and libertarians in YAF, traditionalists typically moved from one political job to another, following a course that brought many of them to positions of political importance today.

There is a marked difference in the current occupations of the two groups. Among the libertarians I interviewed, over half presently have jobs related to education, including two professors, a high school teacher, a college vice president, a director of a libertarian public affairs institute, and one activist who works in computer management at a university. Among the remaining libertarians in the sample are two lawyers, both of whom work in their own companies which are not oriented to politics. Other interviewees include an engineer, a controller, a technical writer, a political consultant, and a congressman; interestingly, this latter activist has become more traditionalist in recent years.

In contrast, many more traditionalists are currently in positions with direct political affiliations: seven own or work in political consulting firms that do fund-raising, marketing, and campaigning for conservative candidates; two are editors of conservative journals; one is president of a nonprofit public-policy organization devoted to defense issues; and one is a high-level government appointee. The remaining traditionalists holding "nonpolitical" jobs include a managing editor of a major magazine, a vice president at a leading pharmaceutical company, a lawyer, a business owner, an activist working in desktop publishing, and a woman who works at night in a lab. Interestingly, over half of the traditionalist women are full-time homemakers, a position not held by any of the libertarian women.

The libertarian activists' occupations more closely resemble those jobs held by SDS activists. Overall among the SDS sample, there are presently seven college faculty, four therapists, four directors of social service agencies, three people working in nonprofit organizations (related to the environment, the homeless, and Central American policy), three lawyers, a judge, a journalist, a freelance writer, a filmmaker, a nurse, a surgeon, a public school teacher, and an owner of a counterculture health-foods restaurant. Other activists own a manufacturing company, do telemarketing consulting, are in graduate school, or are unemployed, and one is temporarily a full-time homemaker. The majority, then, are concentrated in educational fields and social service occupations.

In terms of lifestyle, there are also differences between traditionalists and libertarians. While three-quarters of the traditionalists in the sample are married, about one-quarter are divorced, and *none* never married, among libertarians equal proportions (39 percent) are married or are divorced (39 percent), and nearly one-quarter never married. Compare this to SDS in which over half (55 percent) of the sample is married, nearly one-third remain never married,[49] and only 14 percent are divorced.

Further, the mean number of children between traditionalists and libertarians is 2.24 and 1.23 respectively. Interestingly, the libertarians are more nontraditional than SDS, whose mean number of children is 1.5. Further, while eight of the traditionalist activists have four or more children, none of the libertarian activists have this number (while two SDS activists do). Thus, in styles of life libertarians, like New Leftists, have followed less conventional paths than traditionalists.

Such decisions about jobs, about whether to marry or how to spend leisure time, are private individual decisions that, when socially patterned, take on public, historical meaning. Given the differences in participation in the counterculture, these configurations of individual lives represent a renegotiation of the terms and conditions of everyday life.[50]

For the population at large, as well, the counterculture fundamentally altered many aspects of life. Natural cereal produced by General Mills doesn't create political change, but the deep, critical questioning that took place in the context of the sixties culture opened the doors for changing relations between the races, between women and men, between children and parents, between the gay and straight worlds. All of a sudden the essential question of "What shall we do and how shall we live"[51] was reevaluated. What was formerly taken for granted was replaced by the questioning of assumptions.

Whalen and Flacks admit to the widespread dimensions of changes sparked by the 1960s: regarding sexuality and gender relations, childrearing and household organization, aesthetic taste and personal morality, spirituality and psychotherapy. Even Hall et al. concede that as much as the counterculture fit capitalism's needs, this did not exhaust its oppositional content. At the simplest level the emergence of the counterculture marked the failure of the dominant culture to win over the attachment of some of its brightest and best members. Their widespread disaffiliation from the goals, structures, and institutions of straight society provided an opening that contained subversive elements.[52]

Flacks concludes that the 1960s produced an unparalleled range of alternatives for identity, an unprecedented richness of resources for self-development, and a degree of freedom for self-expression that brought us closer to the ideal of liberty than ever before. Thus, the culture of the 1960s was essential in sustaining an adversarial thread to counterbalance society's push toward conformity. This collective capacity to innovate culturally is a primary resource of political power.[53]

To understand the impact of the counterculture of the 1960s we need, therefore, to take account of both the public *and* and the private domain, of both in-

stitutional structures *and* individual interaction and meaning. To measure social change we must focus not on the obvious splashes of color on the canvas
but on the simple strokes and on the small details of everyday life.

NOTES

1. See, for example, Wini Breines, *Community Organization in the New Left,
   1962–1968: The Great Refusal* (New York: J.F. Bergin, 1982); Stewart Burns, *Social Movements of the 1960s: Searching for Democracy* (Boston: Twayne Publishers, 1990); Michael X. Delli Carpini, *Stability and Change in American Politics:
   The Coming of Age of the Generation of the 1960s* (New York: New York University Press, 1986); Todd Gitlin, *The Sixties: Years of Hope, Days of Rage* (New York:
   Bantam, 1987); Doug McAdam, *Freedom Summer* (New York: Oxford University Press, 1988); James Miller, *Democracy Is in the Streets: From Port Huron to
   the Siege of Chicago* (New York: Simon and Schuster, 1987); Jack Whalen and
   Richard Flacks, *Beyond the Barricades: The Sixties Generation Grows Up* (Philadelphia: Temple University Press, 1989); Nancy Zaroulis and Gerald Sullivan,
   Who Spoke Up? American Protest against the War in Vietnam (New York: Holt,
   Rinehart and Winston, 1984).
2. Rebecca E. Klatch, *Women of the New Right* (Philadelphia: Temple University
   Press, 1987).
3. Kirkpatrick Sale, *SDS* (New York: Vintage Books, 1973), p. 664.
4. "Unrest Spurs Growth of Conservative Student Groups," *New York Times*, October 12, 1969.
5. Pat Korten, quoted in "Unrest Spurs Growth of Conservative Student
   Groups," *New York Times*, October 12, 1969.
6. McAdam, *Freedom Summer*.
7. Gitlin, *The Sixties*, 354; Breines, *Community Organization in the New Left*.
8. Richard Flacks, *Making History: The American Left and the American Mind* (New
   York: Columbia University Press, 1988).
9. Burns, *Social Movements of the 1960s*, 100.
10. See, for example, Lynn Hunt, ed., *The New Cultural History* (Berkeley: Univer-
    sity of California Press, 1989).
11. Ann Swidler, "Culture in Action: Symbols and Strategies," *American Sociolog-
    ical Review* 51 (April 1986): 273–86.
12. Richard Braungart and Margaret Braungart are two of the few researchers
    who have also compared SDS and YAF. See, for example, Richard G. Braun-
    gart, "Parental Identification and Student Politics," *Sociology of Education* 44
    (Fall 1971): 463–75; Margaret M. Braungart and Richard G. Braungart, "The
    Life-Course Development of Left- and Right-Wing Youth Activist Leaders
    from the 1960s" (paper presented at the 199th Annual Scientific Meeting of the
    International Society of Political Psychology, Secaucus, N.J., July 1–5, 1988);
    Richard G. Braungart and Margaret M. Braungart, "Reference Group, Social
    Judgment and Student Politics," *Adolescence* 53, no. 14 (Spring 1979): 135–57.

Also see David L. Westby and Richard G. Braungart, "Class and Politics in the Family Backgrounds of Student Political Activists," *American Sociological Review* 31 (1966): 690–92.

13. All people chosen for this study were active for at least two years in SDS and/or YAF. The final sample of 74 activists contains 34 female activists, equally divided between SDS and YAF, and 40 male activists, 19 from SDS and 21 from YAF. Although a serious attempt was made to diversify the sample, because both organizations were primarily composed of whites all activists interviewed are white except for three black activists in SDS and one black activist in YAF. In SDS the sample contains 24 rank-and-file members and 12 people who were part of the national leadership and/or were at the Port Huron conference, 6 of whom were women (50 percent); the YAF sample consists of 23 rank-and-file members and 15 who held national office and/or were at the founding Sharon conference of YAF, 2 of whom were women (13 percent). However, among the rank-and-file activists in the sample some were leaders of local chapters.

The sample was also chosen to reflect the ideological differences within each organization. YAF activists include 25 traditionalists and 13 members who defined themselves as libertarian. The SDS sample includes 5 Progressive Labor members or sympathizers, 5 Weathermen members or sympathizers, and 2 Revolutionary Youth Movement II members of sympathizers; the majority of SDS interviewees were either unaffiliated with any faction during the 1969 splits (12 activists) or were uninvolved in SDS politics by 1969 (12 activists).

Further, given previous research on the New Left that indicates differences in background and upbringing between those who became active in the early 1960s, as opposed to those who were drawn in during the mid-to-late 1960s (e.g., Milton Mankoff and Richard Flacks, "The Changing Social Base of the American Student Movement," *Annals of the American Academy of Political and Social Science* 395 [May 1971]: 54–67), the SDS sample also contains a mixture of activists who joined from 1960 through 1964 (17 people) and those who were drawn in from 1965 through 1968 (19 people).

The interviews focused on four sets of issues: (1) Background and upbringing (questions on the demographic backgrounds of activists and their parents, parents' political and religious beliefs, family dynamics, and early political and sex-role socialization); (2) political involvement and organizational experiences (questions on how and why individuals became involved, the experiences of men and women in YAF and SDS, and the development of ideology); (3) interpretations of key events of the 1960s including the 1964 and 1968 elections, the assassinations of John F. Kennedy, Robert Kennedy, and Martin Luther King, the civil rights movement, the Vietnam war, and the counterculture; (4) post-1960s lives (questions on changes in lifestyle—occupation, religion, marriage, children—as well as any shifts in political beliefs during the past twenty years).

Archival materials examined include papers, newsletters, pamphlets, correspondence, and other documents of SDS and YAF.

14. To my knowledge, the first use of the term "counterculture" was by an academic, Theodore Roszak, in his book *The Making of a Counterculture: Reflections on the Technocratic Society and Its Youthful Opposition* (Garden City, N.Y.: Anchor Books, 1969). The phrase is identified primarily with the white New Left. Other forms of counterculture, particularly incorporating elements of cultural nationalism, were aspects of black and Chicano political activism.

15. For discussion of the values embodied in the counterculture see Lauren Langman, Richard L. Block, and Ineke Cunningham, "Countercultural Values at a Catholic University," *Social Problems* 20, no. 4 (Spring 1973): 521–33; also see D. Lawrence Wieder and Don H. Zimmerman, "Generational Experience and the Development of Freak Culture," *Journal of Social Issues* 30, no. 2 (1974): 137–61.

16. Langman et al. found widespread diffusion of countercultural values even among students at a conservative Jesuit university in the ten days following the killings at Kent State, May 4–14, 1970. See Langman et al., "Countercultural Values at a Catholic University."

17. See Flacks, *Making History,* for discussion of the history of cultural radicalism in social movements of the left.

18. Stuart Hall et al. make this argument in regard to postwar Britain; see Stuart Hall et al., "Subcultures, Cultures and Class," in *Resistance through Rituals: Youth Subcultures in Post-War Britain,* ed. Stuart Hall and Tony Jefferson (London: Hutchinson and Company, 1976), 9–74. Also see Wieder and Zimmerman, "Generational Experience and the Development of Freak Culture."

19. The exception to this pattern is activists who ended up joining the Progressive Labor faction of SDS. As a Marxist-Leninist group based on democratic centralism, the party line in PL viewed the counterculture as "bourgeois decadence." Thus, membership in PL cut across year of activism in creating opposition to the counterculture.

20. Interview with anonymous former SDS activist, July 26, 1989.

21. Interview with anonymous former SDS activist, July 24, 1989.

22. Sale, *SDS,* 204. Also see Mankoff and Flacks, "The Changing Social Base of the American Student Movement," fn. 16.

23. Interview with anonymous former SDS activist, July 25, 1989. A T-Group is a therapy group in which people collectively analyze their feelings and experiences.

24. Interview with anonymous former SDS activist, March 6, 1990. This interviewee refers to the antidrug stance adopted by many black activists in the movement.

25. See, for example, "Young Americans for Freedom: A Philosophical and Political Profile," *New Guard* 10, no. 1 (January 1970): 21–22

26. Interview with anonymous former YAF activist, July 10, 1989.

27. "Nixon's Unsilent Supporters," *Time,* November 21, 1969.

28. Interview with anonymous former YAF activist, July 11, 1989.

29. Interview with anonymous former YAF activist, February 7, 1990.

30. Interview with anonymous former YAF activist, March 15, 1990.

31. Harvey H. Hukari, Jr., "Review: Odyssey 69: Freedom on a Bike?" *New Guard* 9, no. 8 (October 1969): 23–24.

32. This comment was taken from a local college paper published by YAF. See Doris Pfeiffer and Scott Harris, "Where Is America?" *The Davis Arena* (University of California, Davis) 1, no. 2 (November 3, 1969).

33. David Brudnoy, "Re-Review: Hot Pornool Porn—and Propaganda," *New Guard* 10, no. 1 (January 1970): 31–32.

34. James D. Hartwell in letter to the editor, *New Guard* 9, no. 10 (December 1969).

35. Ron Kimberling, "Vietnam: A Libertarian View," in *The Forty Niner,* October 15, 1969. *The Forty Niner* was published by YAF at Cal State–Long Beach.

36. Paul Willis, "The Cultural Meaning of Drug Use" in *Resistance through Rituals: Youth Subcultures in Post-War Britain,* ed. Stuart Hall and Tony Jefferson (London: Hutchinson and Company, 1976), 106–18.

37. Interview with anonymous former YAF activist, February 6, 1990.

38. Interview with anonymous former SDS activist, May 18, 1988.

39. Interview with Dave Schumacher, September 1, 1989.

40. Quoted in J. M. Cobb, "Young Authoritarians for Freedom," *The Libertarian Connection,* February 1970. Also see William F. Buckley, Jr., "Convervatism Revisited," *New Guard* 10, no. 7 (September 1970): 14.

41. For discussion of the role of group stigmatization in the creation of solidarity, see John Clarke, "Style," in Hall and Jefferson, eds., *Resistance through Rituals,* 175–91.

42. Richard Flacks, *Making History,* 184.

43. David A. Snow et al., "Frame Alignment Processes, Micromobilization, and Movement Participation," *American Sociological Review* 51, no. 4 (August, 1986): 464–81.

44. Swidler, "Culture in Action."

45. Whalen and Flacks, *Beyond the Barricades.*

46. Hall et al., "Subcultures, Cultures and Class," 66.

47. Joseph Gusfield, "Social Movements and Social Change: Perspectives on Linearity and Fluidity," in *Research in Social Movements, Conflicts, and Change,* vol. 4 (Greenwich, Conn: JAI Press), 317–39.

48. For a detailed and fascinating account of the life trajectories of one small sample of New Leftists, see Whalen and Flacks, *Beyond the Barricades.*

49. Of the never married in the SDS sample, eight are women and only three are men. Included in this group are two lesbians and one gay man. This difference in gender supports Doug McAdam's finding regarding Freedom Summer volunteers. See McAdam, *Freedom Summer.*

50. See Flacks, *Making History,* chapter 3.

51. Max Weber, "Science as a Vocation," in *From Max Weber: Essays in Sociology,* trans. and ed. H. H. Gerth and C. Wright Mills (New York: Oxford University Press, 1946), 143.

52. Stuart Hall et al., *Resistance through Rituals.*

53. See Flacks, *Making History,* pp. 7, 186.

CHAPTER 6

The Twelve-Step Movement and Advanced Capitalist Culture: The Politics of Self-Control in Postmodernity

Craig Reinarman

□   □   □   □   □   □   □   □   □   □   □   □

The largest and longest-running social movement in nineteenth century America was the temperance movement. This movement has been read as a peculiarly Protestant American response to the wrenching change wrought by industrialization, urbanization, and immigration.[1] But whatever its structural, class, or ethnic underpinnings, the temperance movement took the phenomenological form of a struggle against booze—specifically against the loss of self-control attributed to drink. Because self-control was central to both the Protestant ethic and the spirit of capitalism, its loss was especially feared by nineteenth century Americans, who therefore blamed all manner of personal and social problems on alcohol.

Nearly two centuries after the temperance crusade began and three-quarters of a century after national Prohibition, something strangely similar is afoot. As the end of the twentieth century approaches, the largest movement in America may well be the twelve-step movement based on Alcoholics Anonymous (AA). The current movement differs in many ways from the earlier temperance movement. For example, while the temperance movement was in important respects a collective political movement for social change, albeit one focused on alcohol's putative effects on individuals, the current twelve-step movement is predominantly individualist and therapeutic in focus. But there are also some historical parallels between the two. Just as temperance depicted drink as the source of most social problems and was linked to broader reform efforts, so, too, the modern twelve-step movement has been broadened far beyond booze, other drugs, and their attendant problems to encompass a staggering array of human troubles. Moreover, the core problematic shared by each of the groups in this burgeoning movement remains the loss of self-control.

In this chapter I first describe the origins and organizational logic of AA, the model for all other twelve-step groups. Second, I summarize the extraordinary proliferation of non-drug-related twelve-step groups. Third, I offer a beginning interpretation of the remarkable resonance of twelve-step ideology in terms of the postmodern condition. Specifically, I argue that the collapse of traditional communities and cosmologies said to characterize postmodernity has left millions of people without the sustaining cultures and stable identities that help regulate desire. In such a state, they are especially torn by the contradiction between the need for self-control (temperance culture) and increasing incentives for indulgence (the culture of mass consumption). In this context, "addiction" comes to serve as the meta-metaphor for all manner of human troubles, and the twelve-step movement provides the identity, community, and cosmology that are said to be as problematic in postmodern society as they are necessary for a self-regulating daily life.

Beyond its remarkable size and scope, there are several reasons why it is important to understand the twelve-step movement. First, many social movement theorists and activists have remarked upon the centrality of culture and identity in other so-called new social movements.[2] It may be that older, class-interest–based social movements do not speak as clearly as the twelve-step movement to the identity interests that many people seem to find increasingly compelling under postmodern conditions.[3] Second, while the other so-called new social movements are still ultimately concerned with changing social conditions, twelve-step groups define themselves in terms of "self-help" and eschew social change in favor of individual change. Yet, the twelve-step movement is composed of people who often have in the past and might again participate in movements for social change. If my interpretation of the rapid growth of the twelve-step movement has merit, it may shed some new light on those features of our culture and epoch that are pushing millions of people toward changing the self rather than changing the world.

Alcoholics Anonymous and the Birth of the Twelve-Step Movement

After national Prohibition was repealed in 1933, a movement arose that began to redefine alcohol problems in terms of disease. Proponents of repeal had made drinking officially acceptable. The evils of drink could no longer be situated in the bottle, as if the substance itself was inherently addicting. Over time, the founders of Alcoholics Anonymous, along with the public-relations experts and scientists who began the alcoholism movement, reconceptualized alcohol problems as existing in the person—that is, as a person-specific "disease."[4] A temperance and Prohibition discourse of moral condemnation began to give way to one of disease, science, and treatment.

Alcoholics Anonymous arose in this context (in 1935) and played a major role in forging it. In 1939, the founders of AA published "Twelve Suggested Steps of Recovery" in the so-called "Big Book" of accounts of recovery from alcoholism. The only explicit requirement for membership was and still is "the desire to stop drinking." The twelve steps were originally offered as a sort of formula that was a direct distillation of the first hundred members' experiences with alcohol problems and recovery.

The first step was admitting both that one was "powerless" over alcohol and that one's life "had become unmanageable" because of it. This was followed by an assertion that "we came to believe that a Power greater than ourselves . . . could restore us to sanity" and by a "decision to turn our will and our lives over to the care of God as we understood him." Subsequent steps included taking a "fearless moral inventory," admitting wrongs, being "ready to have God remove all these defects of character," making amends to all persons harmed, and so on, up to the final, twelfth step—a "spiritual awakening" that included practicing these principles and carrying the "message to others."

AA is organized to remain responsible principally to local communities. Its primary unit is the "group," which retains autonomy and can differentiate itself over a broad range of membership characteristics (for example, there are specific groups for nonsmokers, Hispanics, lesbians, and longshoremen). Groups also vary with respect to their affiliation with one another at the local level as well as with the main New York office. The overall comportment of AA groups is guided by the Twelve Traditions, which clarify AA's public-relations policy with respect to the "outside" world. Cooperation rather than affiliation is the rule when groups deal with outside issues or parties. The stated purpose of all AA members and activities is to help the "still-suffering alcoholic." Unlike the for-profit, professional treatment industry, none of this takes the commodity form. There is an explicit proscription against the organization accumulating money, property, or prestige. Anonymity in the non-AA world is the rule. Unlike professional alcohol counselors or psychiatrists, AA members have always believed that only a "drunk" can truly understand and help another drunk.

There are no formal, centralized mechanisms in AA to control members and the ways they "work" their "program." The national and regional bodies above the group level are conceived as service structures that represent the wisdom of the mass of members or the "conscience" of the groups. The decision-making process within groups is based on consensus after lengthy egalitarian debates over any contentious issue; "politicking" is discouraged. National and regional offices publish pamphlets and flyers that are "conference approved," but they do not delegate or legislate to local groups or the "fellowship" at large. Leadership of all local groups and service structures rotates.[5]

Attending meetings is the primary activity of all AA members, the purpose of which is to "carry the message to the still-suffering alcoholic." Meetings consist mostly of members' talk about their "experience, strength and hope." Criticism or debate ("crosstalk") about what others say or believe is not tolerated; members hold that all contributions to group discourse have prima facie validity. The result is a group process in which learning results from sharing candid stories, reactions, and commonsense strategies for achieving and maintaining sobriety. These shared accounts provide the basis for comparing one's own situation and ways of coping with those of others; further, they stimulate self-examination, deconstruct the "former self," and inculcate a new epistemology.

For many, this process of "recovery" is a spiritual quest for a new way of life and a new consciousness sharply different from those one had during active drinking. The member's life is reconceptualized in terms of "addiction." Members come to believe that this concept explains their past and orders their future.[6] They learn that abstention is the first and most crucial step in a long process of personal development. At each meeting members affirm their own recovery and sobriety by working to get others to do the same. Thus, while one often hears twelve-step groups referred to as "self-help" groups, organizationally and therapeutically they might also be seen as mutual-help groups. Nonetheless, responsibility is always assigned to the individual; members believe that belonging to a group, participating in meetings, and giving "service" to fellow alcoholics result in "the program's" real essence: spiritual recovery of the self by means of adherence to a clear moral order.[7]

Members have long insisted that terms such as "God," "Him," "His Wisdom," and "Higher Power," which permeate AA discourse, do not make it a "religious" organization. In my view, it is deeply religious, albeit nondenominational. AA's founders came out of and drew directly upon a religious organization (the Oxford Group), and AA's "steps" have always made reference to God or a Higher Power, although always in ecumenical terms ("God as we understand Him"). They insist that they are a "spiritual" rather than a religious organization, but members are encouraged to pray, and fully half of the twelve steps mention "God" or a "higher power."[8] In the post-repeal era, AA's founders struggled to remain secular and nonpartisan to avoid the religious and moralistic connotations of temperance and Prohibition discourse. They walked a fine line: seeking to recast alcohol problems in the quasi-medical terms of disease that were seen as progressive at the time, and maintaining an original vision of recovery that was clearly modeled on religious conversion.

The practices of AA and its newer offshoots remain in some sense evangelical.[9] However, as Harry G. Levine has argued, this evangelicalism was different from virtually all other forms of Protestant evangelicalism in that it included no Victorian proscription of sexual pleasure. It may be that this nod to modern sensibilities helps account for the appeal of AA-based groups and the recent proliferation of membership. Twelve-step groups not only offer real help for pressing personal problems but they do so in a way that speaks to broader spiritual needs—all without asking for sexual abstinence or old-fashioned moral perfection.[10]

AA was never merely religious, however. Its evangelical side was from the start married to a rational, pragmatic psychology that drew on early cognitive psychologists such as William James. Its founder and chief proponent, Bill Wilson, rhetorically recrafted words such as "sin" and "retribution" into "character defects" and "amends" that resonated with modern, anticlerical, and "wet" (post-Prohibition) sensibilities.[11]

This scientific side of AA is the source of its views of the nature of addiction. Alcoholism (and, later, other substance-abuse problems and compulsive behaviors) is seen as a "progressive disease" that can never be cured, only managed by absolute abstention. If the drinker does not stop drinking, the disease results in death. The defining feature of this disease is "loss of control" over drinking. (Paradoxically, the road to recovery, to regaining control,[12] passes first through an admission of powerlessness and then to turning oneself over to one's "Higher Power"). The notion that "loss of control" was the quintessential feature of the disease constituted a stroke of genius by AA's founders, for it absolved drunkards of moral culpability—or at least for their behavior prior to joining and recognizing their disease.[13] They were no longer immoral but sick, not deviant but diseased. This post-temperance conception added to AA's allure by not only allowing alcoholics to reconstruct positive selves but also to argue for public policies supporting treatment.

This scientific side of the twelve-step movement is, however, a narrowly psychological one. Addictions or compulsions are not conceptualized as linked to social circumstances. Rather, in keeping with its Protestant roots, AA and its progenitors locate responsibility exclusively within the individual. Any social-structural factors that might be thought of as predisposing people to abuse or addiction are explicitly excluded from the twelve-step worldview.

Members generally do not refer to social context, social causes, or social responsibility. AA members proudly proclaim that their ideology is stringently apolitical. Even comments about politics that are not used to account for personal behavior are defined as "outside issues" and excluded from the discourse of group meetings. Neophyte members who mention, say, race, class, gender, poverty, marital or job stress in their accounts of their drinking are quickly taught that all such factors are irrelevant because they lie outside the corporeal self. Moreover, to invoke such social factors as having something to do with one's personal problems is often interpreted by members as prima facie evidence of "denial." In the twelve-step "lexicon of recovery," any attributions of addiction to forces outside the self are regarded as false rationalizations ("denial") and therefore manifestations of the disease.[14] According to twelve-step ideology, in order to recover members must stop invoking such "excuses" and accept "life on life's terms," difficult though those terms may well be.[15]

There is in all group meetings an unremitting focus on "personal recovery." Even awareness of social conditions is actively shunned, along with any mentalities, modes of discourse, or actual efforts to change social reality. The individual is pathologized anew within the disease model of alcoholism. There is a "we" mentality in twelve-step groups that seems to stem from the mutual help and "united we stand" values. Yet there is no systematic analysis or ideology reaching beyond the self. Through the lens of twelve-step ideology, the locus of every problem of every member in every meeting is the individual—not poverty, injustice, skin color, stress, or any other external factors.

Addiction as Meta-Metaphor: The Proliferation of the Twelve-Step Movement

As early as 1840 Tocqueville noted America's penchant for voluntary associations, but even he might be struck by the exponential growth of twelve-step groups since the 1960s. In 1969, AA estimated its membership at 225,911 in nearly thirteen thousand groups across the United States. Twenty years later estimated U.S. membership had swelled to nearly a million (978,982) active members in 38,276 official groups, a 300 percent increase. These estimates are considered conservative because members remain anonymous and no official need authorize the start of any new group. In fact, a recent federally funded national survey of a representative sample of U.S. households by the Alcohol Research Group found that one in ten adult males and one in twelve adult females had attended at least one AA meeting in their lives (nearly two-thirds of them for a drinking problem other than their own).[16]

Perhaps more important, other types of twelve-step groups based upon but not started by AA have proliferated at an even more rapid clip and now outnumber AA groups. The Alcohol Research Group's national survey found that 13.3 percent of the adult population reported having attended at least one twelve-step meeting in their lifetimes, 5.3 percent in the past year.[17] This is a higher percentage than attended any non-twelve-step form of group therapy for all other nonalcohol problems.[18]

The first offshoot was Al-Anon family groups for family members of alcoholics, which Lois Wilson, the wife of AA founder Bill Wilson, took charge of in the early 1950s. Here the "addiction" at issue was not to a substance but was a "process addiction." Al-Anon's founders saw wives, for example, as being addicted to their alcoholic husbands' dependence on them, such that they engaged in behavior that facilitated or covered up for their husbands' drinking problems and was thus unhealthy for both partners. BY 1980, Al-Anon estimated that nearly twelve thousand such groups existed in the United States. In the 1970s, Alateen was formed for teenagers similarly affected by "alcoholic homes."

Perhaps the most explosive growth in the twelve-step movement has occurred in groups for Adult Children of Alcoholics. ACA began in the late 1970s and ten years later had thousands of chapters nationwide. According to ACA doctrine, most of the life troubles and personality problems faced by children of alcoholics are the consequences of growing up in "alcoholic homes." For example, with a parent drinking abusively, they had to suppress their own concerns to "cover" for them and / or felt pressured to be "good" all the time. In the ACA lexicon, they were forced by their parent's disease to be "self-denying" and / or "people pleasing"—unhealthy traits according to ACA ideology. The result, adherents claim, is that ACAs are not as happy as they would like to be; they suffer from "stunted emotional development," hence their self-donned label "adult children." The ACA model, in turn, has been generalized into an even broader type of group called Co-Dependents Anonymous—people for whom no substance need be abused by anyone but whose "addiction" is an "unhealthy dependence" on another person caused by "dysfunctional families."[19]

A cornucopia of other twelve-step spin-offs have also proliferated. Some of these groups are for people who claim to be addicted to a drug (Narcotics Anonymous, Cocaine Anonymous, Smokers Anonymous, Chemically Dependent Anonymous, and even Marijuana Anonymous). Other groups of more recent vintage grapple with "process addictions" that involve no substances: Women Who Love Too Much, Sex and Love Addicts Anonymous, Couples Anonymous, Parents Anonymous, Prostitutes Anonymous, Overeaters Anonymous, Gamblers Anonymous, Debtors Anonymous, Credit Abusers Anonymous, Artists Recovering in the Twelve Steps (ARTS), Workaholics Anonymous, CFIDS (Chronic Fatigue Immune Dysfunction Syndrome) Anonymous, Emotions Anonymous, Incest Survivors Anonymous, Sexaholics Anonymous, Racism and Bigotry Anonymous, Survivors of Societal Abuse, Obsessive-Compulsive Anonymous, Shame Addiction Anonymous, and Shopaholics. Now even trichotillomaniacs (people who pull their hair too much) have a twelve-step recovery group. As Room and Greenfield summarized all this, "It is hard to conceive of a problem which a psychotherapist might deal [with] which would not fall within the scope of one or another twelve-step organization.[20]

This proliferation has generated an astonishing array of "recovery literature," including a number of runaway bestsellers, that occupies several shelves in the "Health" or "Recovery" sections of most bookstores. Moreover, there are separate "recovery stores" that carry this material exclusively. I visited one such store in an affluent San Francisco neighborhood and found, in addition to literature about all of the above groups, books such as these: *Overcoming Religious Addiction and Religious Abuse; From Uptight to Alright: A 12-Step Program for Stress Prevention; Grandchildren of Alcoholics: Another Generation of Co-Dependency* (apparently for children of Adult Children of Alcoholics); *The Addictive Organization: Why We Overwork, Cover Up, Pick Up the Pieces, Please the Boss, and Perpetuate Sick Organizations;* and *A**hole No More: A Self-Help Guide for Recovering A**holes—and Their Victims* (written by a proctologist). Nor is the merchandise in recovery stores limited to books. They also carry movement buttons, T-shirts, sweatshirts, jewelry, videotapes, posters, bumper stickers, and talking teddy bears.

Newsweek estimates that the number of such twelve-step offshoots quadrupled in the 1980s, with total twelve-step membership now totaling 15 million. The official archivist at AA's national office reports that over 140 twelve-step spin-offs have formally asked to call themselves "anonymous" groups and to adapt the twelve-step model. He believes this may well be an underestimate because scores of groups use some or all of the AA "program" without ever contacting its guardians for permission.[21]

The proliferation of all these new twelve-step groups has so stretched and gerrymandered the concept of addictive disease that it has now been applied to almost every imaginable personal problem in the modern world. It does not seem too much of an exaggeration to say that addiction, the defining feature of which is "loss of control" has become the reigning metaphor—or metametaphor—for human troubles in *fin de millénium* America.[22]

□ □ □

In the remainder of this chapter, I offer a beginning sociological interpretation of this proliferation and the reasons it occurred when it did. AA has been around since 1935 and the essential characteristics of its model have remained the same. Thus, it is curious that the twelve-step model expanded exponentially only in the 1980s.

I want to suggest that understanding the timing of this proliferation may deepen our understanding of recent developments in other social movements and cultural politics. First, as I mentioned at the outset, at a historical moment when more traditional social movements seem on the wane, twelve-step groups have attracted millions of people from all walks of life. Like other movements, twelve-step participation entails time away from private life, discipline, sacrifice, and even evening meetings. Thus it may be useful to explore what it is about the current context that gives twelve-step groups a resonance that other movement groups may lack. If twelve-step groups, say, speak to personal problems, provide meaningful identities, or feed some spiritual hunger, then we may learn something about our times that will help us interpret the fate of other social movements.

Second, the twelve-step movement is unlike other social movements in that it makes no overt attempts to change the conditions under which people live. As noted above, even the mention of such conditions is ritually eschewed in twelve-step discourse. The twelve-step movement thus appears to invert C. Wrights Mill's sociological imagination: Rather than transforming private troubles into public issues or at least linking the two, twelve-step ideology tends to sever this link or to transform what might be understood as public issues into private troubles.[23] To the extent that this individualist movement competes with or even impedes other collectivist movements, then movement activists and analysts alike may find it useful to ponder its proliferation.

Third, however, it may be that the twelve-step movement can still find common ground with other movements. Like many cultural practices, members can turn twelve-step ideology to a wide range of purposes. Robin Room has argued that twelve-step ideology may not be inherently individualistic or a diversion from movements for social-structural change. For example, he analyzed articles and letters from a San Francisco area twelve-step newsletter, *Recovery,* and showed that many members used the ideology to challenge America's actions in the Gulf War. Twelve-Steppers wrote of the U.S. government's tendency to be "a power and control addict" due to its "institutionalized dependence" on Middle East oil or its "codependent denial" about "economic deprivation." Another contributor to the newsletter argued that because twelve-step programs stress "process not product," and "equality, not hierarchy," they are "our best hope for healing ourselves and our planet."[24]

Such sentiments may add up to little more than a projection outward of the addictive disease paradigm. And Room correctly cautions that such sentiments may reflect the leftist traditions of the 1960s and 1970s that still hold meaning for the membership base in the San Francisco area. But it is worth remembering that the temperance movement, while focused on demon drink, was also about broader social reform. Room holds out the possibility that "a more outwardly oriented facet of the twelve-step movement might emerge, critical of the excesses of market-driven consumerism, and with a generally ecological, feminist, pacifist, and community-building orientation."[25]

One of my AA informants, Susan B., noted similarly that twelve-step groups may "indirectly" encourage social change. AA sees alcoholics as having "moved out of the mainstream of social life" into the isolation of their "disease," so the twelve-step recovery process can be read as a "rebirth" that returns people to this mainstream and thus potentially to other civic involvements. If these alternative readings of the politics of the twelve-step movement are plausible, then it seems important to understand the allure of the twelve-step movement because it may work either against the sorts of social change other movements seek or in concert with them.

In what follows I attempt to interpret the growing appeal of the twelve-step model first in terms of the general condition of postmodernity, and secondly in terms of several historically and culturally specific features of American society.

Cosmology, Community, and Identity in Postmodernity

There does not seem to be any agreement on the precise periodization of modernity and postmodernity, and I have neither the space nor the expertise to settle the question here. I will instead summarize some of the core features of lived experience in the trajectory between these overlapping epochs on which there does seem to be agreement and suggest how these features feed the growth of the twelve-step movement.

Marshall Berman's book *All That Is Solid Melts into Air* is a useful place to start, for as a classic defense of the value of modernity it helped define the debate about postmodernity. In his first chapter, Berman cites Rousseau as proclaiming that European society was "at the edge of the abyss" and that daily life in the cities was experienced as "*le tourbillon social*," a whirlwind. In Rousseau's romantic novel *The New Eloise* (1761), for example, the young protagonist moves, as millions of others would, from his ancestral village to the bustling metropolis. There he finds himself awash in "a perpetual clash of groups and cabals, a continual flux and reflux of prejudices and conflicting opinions." Through this hero's eyes the clatter of constant change that was early modernity offered "a multitude of new experiences." In his letters to his lover the excited and bewildered hero wrote that he had to be "pliable" and "ready to change his principles with his audience." He wrote of feeling "dizzy" in "the drunkenness that this agitated, tumultuous life plunges you into." All this made him "forget what I am and who I belong to." He longed "desperately for something solid to cling to" but found only "phantoms."[26]

Nearly a century deeper into modernity, Marx's description of the industrial capitalist engine that was driving all this change suggests why Rousseau's hero and all who followed him into modern urban life felt dizzy and looked in vain for solidity: "Constant revolutionizing of production, uninterrupted disturbance of all social relations, everlasting uncertainty and agitation, distinguish the bourgeois epoch from all earlier ones.... All fixed, fast-frozen relations, with their train of ancient and venerable prejudices and opinions, are swept away, all new-formed ones become antiquated before they can ossify. All that is solid melts into air."[27]

This fundamental change animated all the classical social theorists. While Marx wrote of alienation, Durkheim worried about the anomie and pathological individualism he saw arising from the new "organic" division of labor in industrial society. Weber wrote of the disenchantment that followed in the wake of science, rationalization, and bureaucratization. Simmel noted that only by screening out the rush of complex stimuli that is modernity can we tolerate it.

As modern industrial capitalism continued its march toward the twentieth century, Nietzsche, the archetypal voice of philosophical modernity, wrote of the collapse of Christian cosmology and the "advent of nihilism." Despite the opening up of a cornucopia of once-unimagined possibilities, or perhaps because of them, culture imploded.[28] Values were either absent or empty, "communal formulas" no longer existed, and myriad "egoisms" clashed to such a degree that they were "unable to find any limitation."[29]

If I may jump (in postmodernist fashion) to the beginnings of postmodernity in the 1970s, one finds further lamentations of the same sort. Daniel Bell, for example, complains that modernism has seduced us into hedonism, brought disunity to culture, and destroyed the discipline and rationality of the bourgeois cosmology. The irony for Bell is that capitalism gave rise to modernism, which resulted in the "dissolution" of the very "shared moral order" on which capitalism's success was based.[30]

From a different vantage point, Habermas reaches similar descriptive conclusions. He finds that "radicalized consciousness of modernity" has "freed itself from all specific historical ties." In its "forward gropings" modernism has exalted the present well beyond merely expressing the "experience of mobility in society, acceleration in history, and *discontinuity in everyday life.*" Thus the celebration of "the transitory, the elusive and the ephemeral" over tradition. In "blowing up the continuum of history," he writes, modernity comes to live "on the experience of rebelling against all that is normative." Habermas finds that capitalist growth and state expansion have led modernism to penetrate "deeper and deeper into previous forms of human existence." The result, he argues, is that "life worlds" are so subordinated to system imperatives that "the communicative infrastructure of everyday life" is deeply disturbed.[31]

David Harvey begins his monumental study *The Condition of Postmodernity* with one novelist's celebratory account of modern urban life, which allows escape from the traps of traditional community. Here, identity can become "soft, fluid, endlessly open." In this view, the city is an "emporium of styles" in which "all sense of hierarchy or even homogeneity of values was in the course of dissolution"; a theater in which individuals performed "a multiplicity of roles"; a labyrinthine encyclopedia of subjectivities in which people were free to become whomever they chose.

But if this plasticity is liberatory, Harvey demonstrates, it also makes people vulnerable, for the very "malleability of appearances and surfaces" that freed personality also gave it a certain depthlessness. What Baudelaire saw as the defining characteristics of modernity—"the transient, the fleeting, the contingent"—have become exponentially so of postmodernity. Harvey concludes with other analysts of postmodernity that the result is unstable subjectivities, fragmented selves, decentered identities. When historical continuity is gone, so is the biographical continuity of the self. Just as collage and pastiche are the leitmotivs of postmodern art and architecture, so are all manner of identity fragments jumbled together in the postmodern character.[32]

I have detoured into this literature in order to suggest that however great the liberatory propensities of modernity and postmodernity, sustaining cultures and stable identities has become increasingly problematic.[33] While it is fair to say that identity has always been achieved rather than ascribed—constructed from lived experience rather than given at birth—analysts of postmodernity seem to share the view that this achievement process has become a more complex and self-conscious one in advanced capitalist societies.[34] The logic of profit maximization and capital accumulation from early twentieth-century Fordism on requires the constant cultivation of new needs, the satisfaction of which is channeled into the commodity form.[35] Indeed, not only the hardware of social life like food, clothing, and shelter, but increasingly the software of the self—excitement, entertainment, eroticism—become grist for the promotion of wants to be satisfied in commodity consumption. Moreover, under the pressure of advertising, language itself is sufficiently commodified that the bond between signifier and signified is shattered, thus further eroding structures of meaning.[36] As Harvey observed, one key characteristic of postmodernity is the increasing "impossibility of representing the world in a single language."[37] In short, postmodern theorists suggest that because the fundaments of culture and identity have been incessantly colonized by the hyperconsumerism of late capitalism, more people find it necessary to search for meaning and community.

This, I submit, is precisely the sort of world in which people crave membership in social groups that help them still all the ceaseless swirling said to characterize the postmodern condition. To this general portrait I will now add specific features of American history and culture that I think add special appeal to twelve-step groups in modern America.

America as a Temperance Culture

American society has long been characterized as the land of the "self-made man." As Levine has argued, in such a society self-control assumes extraordinary importance. Indeed, for the middle-class Protestants who settled and defined the United States, self-control was both the characterological sine qua non of economic survival and success and the principal form of social control that held society together.[38] In contrast, older European industrial democracies have deeper normative traditions and more external forms of social control such as the church and state.

With Levine, I suggest that in a culture in which self control is inordinately important, the experience of "loss of control" often becomes the object of obsession and inordinate fear. This is one reason why, of all industrialized societies, the United States is uniquely worried about consciousness-altering substances. This is why, when drunkenness was a problem almost everywhere in the industrialized world, the temperence movement arose first, was most passionately expressed, and has lasted longest in the United States. And this is why temperence sentiment persists and periodically reappears here in the form of antidrug crusades.[39]

All this was visible at the close of the eighteenth century when drink was first problematized and "addiction" discovered. What has happened since is even more relevant to the proliferation of the twelve-step movement. As suggested above, the onset of Fordist accumulation strategies in the 1920s has led American capitalism toward an increasing dependence on hyperconsumption. In their different interpretations of the consequences of this phenomenon, Herbert Marcuse and Daniel Bell both conclude that the United States has become a mass-consumption culture characterized by a genius for producing new "needs" that can be satisfied by the consumption of commodities. Both suggest that the Protestant work ethic and denial of gratification may still be sanctioned in the sphere of production, but immediate gratification and indulgence reign supreme in culture, leisure, and daily life.[40]

For purposes of understanding the rise of so many new twelve-step groups, the point is that the combination of mass consumption and its indulgence ethic have created a culture in which growing numbers of people perceive an increasing number of ways to *lose control*. At the same time, the forms of social control that might offer some counterweight—religion, tradition, community, extended families—have been eroded by mass-consumption culture's constant trumpeting of the new.

In sum, one part of the explanation for the extraordinary resonance of twelve-step ideology is the contradictory demands placed on the postmodern self: On the foundation of a temperance culture in which self-control has been traditionally and uniquely important, advanced capitalism has built a culture of mass consumption that produces more and more things over which the self might lose control, while simultaneously eroding more and more countervailing social controls.

American Culture, 1960–1990: Pleasure and Postmodernity

The 1960s saw two rather different "revolutions" that together form another piece of the puzzle of the proliferation of the twelve-step movement. First, in the late 1950s there was a pharmaceutical revolution. Modern medicinal miracles brought with them the idea that technology could be applied to human consciousness. Psychiatrists and pharmaceutical companies popularized the notion that pills could improve our moods and fix what ails us. Second, in the 1960s many affluent children born amidst the postwar consumers' bazaar, the first "television generation," rebelled against the residues of the Protestant ethic and Victorian morality in what some called a cultural revolution. This rebellion included subcultural practices that removed drugs from the exclusive control of the medical and pharmaceutical industries. (Young drug users even turned DuPont's corporate slogan, "better living through chemistry," to new satirical ends.) The so-called counterculture popularized the use of drugs solely for "mind expansion" and pleasure. The word "pleasure" is important, for whether one likes it or laments it, one fact of postmodernity is that the captains of commerce who created mass-consumption culture helped establish pleasure as a standard vocabulary of motive.[41]

The guardians of the dominant moral and political order launched a drug scare, but in the charged atmosphere of the 1960s, antidrug warnings were perceived as hysterical, counterfactual, moralistic, and thus "political." Moreover, such warnings carried as their subtext the Protestant ethic of the temperance culture, which cut squarely against the grain of the pleasure ethic of mass-consumption culture. The result was that the warnings were dismissed as one more imposition of ideology by the "establishment." Thus, for purposes of understanding the coming proliferation of the twelve-step movement, I suggest that the 1960s left America with a popular culture in which drug use for pleasure became widespread and warnings about the risks thereof were neutralized.[42] It seems important to add here that most of those who now attend the new, non-alcohol-related twelve-step groups are of this generation.[43]

As the movements of the 1960s faded, the optimism implicit in the notion that the world could be changed for the better seemed to give way to a more pessimistic awareness of threat in the 1970s. This threat took many forms. The post–World War II "American century" of economic dominance turned out to be the American quarter century; the affluence that we had been told was our birthright foundered on the shoals of European and Japanese competition, oil price shocks, and inflation. The Pentagon Papers and Watergate scandals took their toll on political legitimacy. Medical research daily discovered more health threats stemming from the sedentary lifestyles of an affluent, service-based, postindustrial society. New environmental hazards proliferated and new forms of cancer appeared. There was a heightening of Cold War tensions and talk from the highest levels of the Reagan administration about the United States "winning" or "prevailing" in a nuclear war. The list went on. In a word, the world seemed more and more out of control.

One characteristic response to the fading collective passions and optimism of the 1960s and to the threats of the new decade was an inward turn. If not society, at least the self might be controlled for the better. Of course, the so-called narcissism of the "me-decade" had firm roots in the traditional individualism of American culture, which had only been deepened by the celebration of self-indulgence in mass consumption. But it seems fair to add that the spread of jogging, Jazzercise, and Jane Fonda workouts, along with the rise of growth industries in diet centers, exercise spas, and therapy, were all part of a broader health consciousness.[44] And this health consciousness took the form of specific practices centered on individual responsibility—work, discipline, abstention, renunciation. Such practices are in harmony with the twelve-step movement.[45]

Thus, even before Reaganism and a renascent right made self-control central to public policy, it was already extant, already high on the agendas of even those who voted against him. When Reagan moved to replace welfare-state supports with individual self-control, he was on firm cultural ground. Even his "war on drugs" was to some extent facilitated by the broader war for wellness being waged by aging hippies cum yuppies with the weapon of self-control. Individualism was a general ideological theme under the Reagan regime. While selfishness was sanctified("Greed is good") for the middle and upper classes, working-class living standards were reduced, Republican economic policy demanded "belt tightening," and the poor were told that the solution to all their worsening problems was greater self-control. In this sense, the turn to conservatism, too, provided fertile ideological soil for the growth of the twelve-step movement.

Conclusions

At the dawn of modernity in 1761, Rousseau described the decentered identity of his community-less hero. If life then was fragmented, fleeting, and in flux, and if all these phenomena have only intensified in the mass-consumption culture of postmodernity, then there should be little wonder that people look for things like twelve simple steps with which to organize their lives and selves. In this sense, the remarkable growth of such groups may be read as an attempt to retrieve the certainty of a premodern lifeworld as a means of coping with the postmodern one they face, a groping for a way to stop all that is solid from melting into air.

At its simplest, my argument is that twelve-step groups have spread far and fast in recent years because they offer participants two crucial components of a meaningful way of life that seem increasingly difficult to find in advanced capitalist culture. First, twelve-step groups offer participants a clear *cosmology*—a system of commonsense beliefs about how the world works, a sense of one's place in it, a vocabulary or discourse within which one can construct a positive self, answers to unanswerable questions, and a basic strategy for self-control that provides concrete solutions to personal problems. Second, twelve-step groups provide participants with a caring *community*—a fellowship of people who welcome them, know them by name, share their language, have experienced their troubles, listen to their tellings, support their struggles, and care about their general well-being. In short, the twelve-step movement provides a new sort of kinship network to replace far-flung, fragmented families.

In my view, a commonsense cosmology and a caring community are prerequisites for sustaining cultures and stable identities. To the extent that the twelve-step movement provides these prerequisites, its proliferation in the 1980s is no mystery. At bottom, twelve-step groups offer a defense against the rudderless drift toward psychic implosion that postmodernists claim is characteristic of our world. If this interpretation has merit, then it may also help explain why other social movements that fail to provide such personal ballast against the churning currents of postmodernity seem to have lost some of their appeal in the 1980s.

NOTES

Acknowledgments: Parts of this chapter were presented at the conference Contemporary Social Movements and Cultural Politics at the Center for Cultural Studies, Univeristy of California, Santa Cruz, March 22–24, 1991, and at the nineteenth annual Alcohol Epidemiology Symposium, Akademia Medyczna, Kraków, Poland, June 10, 1993. I am grateful particularly to Mary Dana Phillips and Harry Gene Levine for teaching me about the twelve-step movement. I also thank Robin Room, Joseph Gusfield, Richard Cloward, Wini Breines, Susan Murray, Ruth Thibodeau Gendron, Ethan Nadelmann, Joké Haafkens, John Lofland, Mark Traugott, Alexandra Goulding, and the editors of this volume for helpful comments on an earlier draft, even though I have heeded none of them adequately.

1. Joseph R. Gusfield, *Symbolic Crusade: Status Politics and the American Temperance Movement* (Urbana: University of Illinois Press, 1966); Harry G. Levine, "The Discovery of Addiction: Changing Conceptions of Habitual Drunkenness in American History," *Journal of Studies on Alcohol* 39 (1978): 143–67; Levine, "The Alcohol Problem in America: From Temperance to Alcoholism," *British Journal of Addiction* 79 (1984): 109–119; and Levine, "Temperance Cultures: Concern about Alcohol Problems in Nordic and English-Speaking Countries," in *The Nature of Alcohol and Drug-Related Problems,* G. Edwards, M. Lader, and C. Drummond, eds. (Oxford: Oxford University Press, 1992).

2. See, for example, Barbara Epstein, "Rethinking Social Movement Theory," *Socialist Review* 90 (1990): 35–66; L. A. Kauffman, "The Anti-Politics of Identity, *Socialist Review* 90 (1990): 67–80; Richard Flacks, *Making History: The Radical Tradition in American Life* (New York: Columbia University Press, 1988).

3. The notion of identity interest is developed in Craig Reinarman, *American States of Mind: Political Beliefs and Behavior among Private and Public Workers* (New Haven: Yale University Press, 1987).

4. See Levine, "The Discovery of Addiction."

5. Mary Dana Phillips, "How It Works: A Discussion of AA from a Social Learning Theory Perspective" (working paper, Alchohol Research Group, Berkeley, Calif., 1990).

6. I draw here on John Rice's insightful analysis of how such groups, particularly a new AA offshoot, Codependents Anonymous, remake the self. He shows how group practices function to induce members to "select [codependency] as a narrative of their lives to acquire a new and more satisfying sense of identity." See Rice, "Discursive Formation, Life Stories, and the Emergence of Co-Dependency: 'Power/Knowledge' and the Search for Identity," *Sociological Quarterly* 33 (1192): 337–64, 338; also see Rice, *A Disease of One's Own: Therapy, Addiction, and Co-Dependency* (Princeton: Princeton University Press, forthcoming).

7. See M. E. Donovan, "A Sociological Analysis of Commitment Generation in Alcoholics Anonymous" (*British Journal of Addiction* 79 [1984]: 411–18), on the elements of commitment in AA: sacrifice, investment, renunciation, communion, mortification, and transcendence.

8. The definitive history of AA is Ernest Kurtz, *Not God: A History of Alcoholics Anonymous* (Center City, Minn.: Hazelden Educational Services, 1979).

9. Note the parallels between the twelve-step recovery process and Juster's description of the "central event" in late eighteenth- and early nineteenth-century evangelical conversion: "awakening the sinner to the true nature of his or her depraved state and the final regeneration of the soul through a process of self-abasement and unconditional surrender to the will of a gracious God" (Susan Juster, "'In a Different Voice': Male and Female Narratives of Religious Conversion in Post-Revolutionary America," *American Quarterly* 41 [1989]: 34–62, 34).

10. I should note that AA folklore, if not its formal Steps and Traditions, advises against entering a new relationship or marriage during one's first year "in recovery" or "sobriety." This is routinely suggested to members by other members, although routinely ignored. Moreover, it should be noted that AA has never proscribed pleasures such as food or tobacco, although the taking of "moral inventories" is a central part of "the program." However, these points do not, in my view, detract from the importance of Levine's observation.

11. Robin Room, "The Party Ends for the Wet Generation: Alcoholics Anonymous in U.S. Films, 1940–1965," *Journal of Studies on Alcohol* 50 (1989): 1–50; Mary Dana Phillips, "Breaking the Code: Toward a Lexicon of Recovery" (paper presented at the Kettil Bruun Society Alcohol Epidemiological Meetings, Budapest, June 1990).

12. AA and other twelve-step adherents are taught to refrain from using the word "control" because they believe it to be illusory. Indeed, Kurtz's classic history of AA opens with an epigraph from the core AA text, "First of all we had to quit playing God" (*Not God,* vii), which he correctly notes is what AA members are taught about the foolishness of trying to control their drinking. I use the term in spite of this because I think that, functionally, control is precisely what they are talking about. On the latter point, see Herbert Fingarette, *Heavy Drinking: The Myth of Alcoholism as Disease* (Berkeley: University of California Press, 1988); and Stanton Peele, *Diseasing of America: Addiction Treatment out of Control* (Lexington, Mass.: Lexington Books, 1989).

13. As Levine shows in "The Discovery of Addiction," Dr. Benjamin Rush invented the disease concept in the late eighteenth century and spoke in similar terms about the drunkard's inability to control "his" drinking. The founders of AA, however, perfected and promulgated this notion.

14. In some of the newer, specialized AA groups, this is less true. While it remains controversial, feminist or women's AA groups sometimes employ gender discrimination, exploitation, or domination in understanding drinking problems. Similarly, AA groups in the gay community sometimes cite "external" factors as contributing to problem drinking; for example, homophobia was one important reason why a gay bar subculture became so central to the gay and lesbian community.

15. Phillips, "Breaking the Code."

16. Alcoholics Anonymous World Survey, "Analysis of the 1989 Survey of the Membership of AA," (New York: Alcoholics Anonymous, 1990); Alcohol Research Group, National Institute of Alcohol Abuse and Alcoholism, National Survey of Drinking Practices and Problems, unpublished (Berkeley, 1990).

17. Ibid.; Robin Room, "Alcoholics Anonymous as a Social Movement" (Toronto: Addiction Research Foundation, 1992).

18. Robin Room and Tom Greenfield, "Alcoholics Anonymous, Other 12-Step Movements and Psychotherapy in the U.S. Population, 1990," (Berkeley, Calif.: Alcohol Research Group, 1991).

19. See Rice, "Discursive Formation" and *A Disease of One's Own.*

20. Room and Greenfield, "Alcoholics Anonymous," 4.

21. *Newsweek,* "Afflicted? Addicted? Support Groups Are the Answer for 15 Million," February 5, 1990. Interview with the AA archivist conducted by Mary Dana Phillips, 1991, personal communication.

22. One pop feminist-psychologist gives new meaning to the plasticity of the concept of addiction by claiming that society itself is an addict: Ann W. Schaef, *When Society Becomes an Addict* (San Francisco: Harper and Row, 1987).

23. C. Wright Mills, *The Sociological Imagination* (New York: Oxford University Press, 1959). For this reason, the twelve-step movement probably is not a social movement in the traditional sense of the term, that is, a collective effort by relatively powerless people to alter the conditions under which they must live. See Richard Flacks, *Making History.*

24. Room, "Alcoholics Anonymous as a Social Movement," 18.

25. Ibid.

26. Cited in Marshall Berman, *All That Is Solid Melts into Air: The Experience of Modernity* (New York: Penguin, 1982), 17–18.

27. Karl Marx, *The Communist Manifesto* in *Political Writings,* vol. 1 of *The Revolutions of 1848,* ed. D. Fernbach (New York: Vintage, 1974), 70.

28. A similar point was made more poetically by Yeats in the famous line from his "The Second Coming": Things fall apart; the centre cannot hold."

29. Quotes from Nietzsche appear in Berman, *All That Is Solid Melts into Air,* 22.

30. Daniel Bell, *The Cultural Contradictions of Capitalism* (New York: Basic Books, 1978), xxvii. Although Bell understands that the impulses to which modernism has given rise have been channeled into commodity consumption, he nonetheless causally privileges avant-garde culture over capitalism (e.g., "culture has taken the initiative in promoting change, and the economy has been geared to meeting these new wants" [xxv]).

31. Jürgen Habermas, "Modernity versus Postmodernity," *New German Critique* 22 (1981): 3–14, 4–8; emphasis added.

32. David Harvey, *The Condition of Postmodernity* (Oxford: Basil Blackwell, 1989); quotes are from Chaps. 1–4. Gitlin's review essay on postmodernity is also an eloquent summary of many of the same features: "The . . . subject is fragmented, unstable, even decomposed . . . finally nothing more than a crosshatch of discourses . . . . Modernism tore up unity and postmodernism has been en-

joying the shreds. . . . [In a] homeless world political economy . . . there is no here here, because historical continuity is shattered by the permanent revolution that is capitalism" (Todd Gitlin, "Postmodernism: Roots and Politics," *Dissent* [Winter 1989]: 101–3).

33. See Douglas Kellner's important comparative analysis of the fixed identities of traditional societies versus the "mobile" and "multiple" ones of postmodern societies: "Popular Culture and the Construction of Postmodern Identities" in *Modernity and Identity*, Scott Lash and Jonathan Friedman, eds. (Oxford: Basil Blackwell, 1992), 141–77.

34. I should note that many postmodernists (e.g., Derrida, Lyotard) argue that postmodernity is other than or at least not reducible to advanced capitalist culture. Other postmodern theorists, however, argue that postmodernity is a phase of advanced capitalism (e.g., Jameson, Harvey). While this debate has little bearing on the core concerns here, for purposes of this chapter my argument follows those of Jameson and Harvey.

35: See Richard Lichtman, *The Production of Desire* (New York: Free Press, 1982); Herbert Marcuse, *One Dimensional Man* (Boston: Beacon Press, 1964); Jean Baudrillard, *La Société de consummation* (Paris: Gallimard, 1970); Stuart Ewen, *Captains of Consciousness: Advertising and the Social Roots of the Consumer Culture* (New York: McGraw Hill, 1976); Daniel Bell, *The Cultural Contradictions of Capitalism*; David Harvey, *The Condition of Postmodernity*.

36. Jean Baudrillard, *Selected Writings*, Marc Poster, ed. (Stanford, Calif.: Stanford University Press, 1988).

37. Harvey, *The Condition of Postmodernity*, 30.

38. Levine, "The Discovery of Addiction" and Levine, "Temperance Cultures."

39. Craig Reinarman and Harry G. Levine, "Crack in Context: Politics and Media in the Making of a Drug Scare," *Contemporary Drug Problems* 16 (1989): 535–77.

40. Marcuse, *One-Dimensional Man*; Daniel Bell, *The Cultural Contradictions of Capitalism*.

41. C. Wright Mills, "Situated Actions and Vocabularies of Motive," *American Sociological Review* 5 (1940): 904–13; Stephen Mugford and Phil Cohen, *Drug Use, Social Relations, and Commodity Consumption: Report to the National Campaign against Drug Use* (Canberra: Australian National University, 1988).

42. Gitlin "Postmodernism: Roots and Politics" offers an important related point: "The cultural upwellings and wildness of the sixties kicked out the props of a teetering moral structure, but the new house has not been built" (104).

43. Room and Greenfield, "Alcoholics Anonymous, Other 12-Step Movements and Psychotherapy in the U.S. Population, 1990."

44. This would include reductions in the incidence and prevalence of drug taking, a decline in distilled spirits consumption in favor of white wine, less red meat and more chicken and fish, and the rise of a strong antismoking movement. All these trends were especially pronounced among aging baby boomers who had come of age in the 1960s but now faced mortgages, children, and stressful careers.

45. Crawford offers an insightful analysis of the rise of "health as self-control" in what many saw as the "toxic society" of the 1970s: "[T]hroughout the 1970s, numerous health disasters, a multitude of health warnings . . . had transformed our sense of safety. . . . When the macro conditions that affect health appear to be out of control, self-control over the considerable range of personal behaviors that also affect health is an only remaining option. Particularly in a conservative political climate, when both political and corporate leaders repeatedly warn that our jobs are dependent on giving business a free hand." Robert Crawford, "A Cultural Account of 'Health,'" in J. B. McKinlay, ed., *Issues in the Political Economy of Health Care* (London: Tavistock, 1984); 74. The author is grateful to Brandy Britton for pointing out Crawford's work.

CHAPTER 7

"We Gotta Get Out of This Place": Notes toward a Remapping of the Sixties

Alice Echols

□   □   □   □   □   □   □   □   □   □   □   □

The past, as historians have observed, offers us the opportunity to glimpse other possibilities, to see that the world needn't be as it is now.[1] No period in recent U.S. history stands in greater contrast to the present, or seems to have held more possibilities for radical transformation, than the sixties. This is no doubt why the sixties remains the site of intense ideological contestation more than thirty years after it all began. While liberals have typically reacted to the sixties as an enormous embarrassment, conservatives have used the period to great political effect, deploying a version of the sixties that emphasizes disorder, permissiveness, and black as well as female assertiveness in such a way that accelerating poverty, crime, drug use, and even AIDS can be laid at the decade's doorstep. The right's vilification of the period has, of course, served the strategic function of obscuring the connection between the catastrophe that is the United States in the late twentieth century and the policies of the Reagan and Bush administrations.

But if the right's version of the sixties has prevailed in the realm of formal politics, it has been a different story in the cultural and intellectual arenas of American life. Here we find rap musicians like Public Enemy disrupting the mainstream construction of the black freedom movement as a "friendly crusade for racial integration" by claiming for Malcolm X a critical role in that struggle.[2] Documentary films such as *Berkeley in the Sixties*, and two television series, *Eyes on the Prize* and *Making Sense of the Sixties*, chronicle the achievements (and, to a lesser extent, the missteps) of various sixties movements in a largely unrepentant manner.

This chapter is reprinted with revisions from an article of the same title in *Socialist Review* 22, no. 2 (1992): 9–34, by permission of the *Socialist Review*.

Predictably, Hollywood's record is more mixed. But certainly Oliver Stone, who has directed four films on various aspects of the sixties (*Platoon, The Doors, Born on the Fourth of July,* and *JFK*), has offered audiences cynical appraisals of the government and sympathetic depictions of the antiwar and youth movements. Finally, within publishing the sixties has become a kind of growth industry as intellectuals and former activists have produced a host of memoirs, histories, and anthologies, most of which affirm the democratic and egalitarian vision of the sixties movements.

However, women often play a larger role in the conservatives' demonizing scripts of the sixties—predictably, as welfare cheats or selfish feminists—than in progressive accounts of the period. Most egregious of all are Oliver Stone's sixties films, in which citizenship, principled protest, and rock 'n' roll genius are assumed to be the unique preserve of men.[3] Stone's masculinist formulations of the period are particularly disturbing because he has become a kind of de facto historian of the sixties.[4] But even *Eyes on the Prize,* which in many ways is a model of documentary filmmaking, devotes little attention to the pivotal role of women in the civil rights movement or to that critical figure, Ella Baker. Especially troubling to me as a historian of the women's liberation movement is that virtually all recently published books about the sixties fail effectively to integrate that movement into their reconstructions of the period.[5] In fact, much of this work replicates the position of women in the male-dominated Movement—that is, the women's liberation movement remains on the periphery, far from the core of the narrative. Curiously, through their narrative containment of women these writers have managed to marginalize women more effectively than could the movements they write about, because, of course, women did succeed in taking center stage by the end of the decade.

In this essay I criticize how "the sixties" has been mapped in the many books that purport to tell its story, and I offer some thoughts on how we might remap it. My criticisms will center not only on the failure to embed women and the women's liberation movement within the history of the sixties, but also on the failure to engender the New Left—the focus, after all, of most of these sixties books. The remapping I envision would make the women's liberation movement an integral part of the sixties by demonstrating its considerable philosophical connections to the New Left and the black freedom movement, without, of course, denying its originality. This remapping should be understood as a political intervention, one that seeks to disrupt the accepted version of the sixties, which too often depicts the women's liberation movement and the New Left, in particular, as philosophically opposed. I am concerned that people understand that conflicts between the New Left and the women's liberation movement were a consequence of specific historical circumstances and not, as most sixties books (and many feminist accounts) would have it, the result of some inevitable and chronic antagonism—an interpretation that makes all feminist and left collaborations seem doomed. In this sense, the revisioning I call for shares much with Ellen DuBois's recent

work challenging the idea that in the early twentieth century the woman suffrage movement and socialism were fundamentally and irreconcilably antagonistic.[6]

My remapping also involves locating sixties radicalism in the postwar period and exploring the ways that both the white New Left and the white
women's liberation movement represented a rebellion against the dominant
gender constructions of the ultradomestic fifties.[7] I contend that future studies would benefit from exploring the contested terrain of masculinity in postwar America and its relation to sixties radicalism. I suggest that counterhegemonic constructions of masculinity, especially those advanced by Beats and
rock 'n' rollers, may not only have inspired white male New Leftists but, in
their appropriation of a "black" style, may also have helped destabilize racial
boundaries in the United States.

□ □ □

The marginalization of the women's liberation movement in sixties books has
several sources, but it has been facilitated by the scarcity of memoirs or autobiographies by women's liberation activists. While it sometimes seems as if
every male leader of Students for a Democratic Society has either written a
memoir or is in the process of writing one (the latest being Mark Rudd), only
Mary King, Angela Davis, and Jane Alpert have published book-length memoirs about their movement experiences. Moreover, neither King nor Davis was
active in the women's liberation movement, while Alpert, as a cultural feminist, presents her conversion to feminism as following from her rejection of
the left.[8] (It is also distressing that there have been few recent autobiographies
by African American men or women active in the radical black freedom struggle. James Forman's, Cleveland Sellers's and Anne Moody's compelling
memoirs are more than twenty years old. [9])

Not unrelated to this fact is that books by white male New Leftists stand as
representative of "the sixties." Their experiences are presented as universal,
as defining the era, whereas the experiences of women and people of color
(two overlapping categories, of course) are constructed as particularistic.
There is a depressingly familiar metonymy at work here. For instance, Todd
Gitlin's and Tom Hayden's books claim to be about "the sixties," and despite
the incompleteness of their accounts most reviewers have agreed. Yet had
Carlos Muñoz, the author of Youth Identity, Power: The Chicano Movement, used
"The Sixties" as the subtitle of his book and still focused primarily on Chicanos, as Gitlin and Hayden do on white men, most reviewers would have
thought it odd at the very least.[10]

I suspect the textual subordination of women's liberation also reflects a certain reluctance to part with what has become the conventional sixties storyline whereby radicalism emerges on February 1, 1960, with the Greensboro
lunch-counter sit-in, and ends with the February 1970 Greenwich Village

townhouse explosion or the Kent State killings later that year. If one's narrative is conceptualized around the idea that radicalism was simply played out by the decade's end, then there really is only token narrative space available for women's liberation (or for the Chicano, Native American, or gay and lesbian movements). Thus, most sixties books, while they do note the problem of sexism on the left and acknowledge the considerable achievements of the women's liberation movement, fail to provide any substantive discussion of that movement, including they ways in which it carried on and extended the radicalism of the era. The film *Berkeley in the Sixties*, for instance, devotes astonishingly little time to the women's liberation movement. Indeed, by ignoring or downplaying the connections between the women's liberation movement and the New Left and the black freedom movements, these accounts create the impression that the women's liberation movement was a breed apart.

But if women's liberation generally constitutes an interruption in the narrative flow, it is nonetheless presented as a significant interlude in two very important retrospectives of the sixties, Todd Gitlin's often brilliant *The Sixties: Years of Hope, Days of Rage* and Tom Hayden's wonderfully evocative *Reunion: A Memoir*.[11] In both books women's liberation is associated with the male-dominated Movement's unraveling and with each man's personal pain and turmoil.[12] In his brief chapter on women's liberation, for example, Gitlin analyzes with great perceptiveness the emotional divide separating left men and women in the late sixties. He observes that men who were not a part of hardline sects "were miserable with the crumbling of their onetime movement, [while] women were riding high." But he doesn't discuss the source of women's "high" in any depth. In fact, while his discussions of the New Left are marked by analytic rigor, his observations about the women's liberation movement are glib, if not diminishing—as in "there were a myriad of ways to be 'in the movement,' from sexual experimentation as 'political lesbians' . . . to journal-keeping à la Anais Nin."[13] (Of course, as anyone with even the most glancing knowledge of lesbian feminism knows, sexual experimentation was not exactly its driving force.) After this obligatory chapter on the women's liberation movement, Gitlin returns to the tale of the left's continued collapse and his own personal pain, much of it apparently caused by the women's movement.

Tom Hayden, too, associates women's liberation with the fragmentation of sixties radicalism. In fact, Hayden characterizes the period when black power and women's liberation were in ascent as a "Dostoyevskian nightmare."[14] For him, feminism's rise (and black power's as well) is inseparable from the disintegration of the "beloved community" and his own personal anguish. The lengthiest passage on the women's movement concerns the men's consciousness-raising group to which Hayden belonged and what he calls the "torture sessions" he and the others endured in an effort to undo their sexism.[15] (Although both Hayden and Gitlin were living in the Bay Area at the time, they apparently were not in the same group, since Gitlin remembers his men's group degenerating into gripe sessions about women rather than attacks on male members.[16]

It is true that the emergence of the women's liberation movement coincided with the disintegration of much of the New Left and SDS in particular. I would go even further and suggest that the rise of women's liberation is related to the collapse of the left as a national movement. The New Left's repudiation of prefigurative politics, which had emphasized creating in the present the desired community of the future, and its reversion to a tired Old Left politic not only guaranteed its irrelevance to most people in the United States but also contributed to the development of feminist consciousness. [17] But that isn't the point either of these authors are making. For Hayden and Gitlin (although Gitlin is more self-reflexive), women's liberation is the final nail in the coffin of the "beloved community" and it is remembered with sadness and not a little petulance. This attitude plays a role, I believe, in the diminished narrative status accorded the women's liberation movement in sixties books.

As Wini Breines has pointed out, a lot of sixties books (including these two) dichotomize the era into the "good" and "bad" sixties.[18] In the case of SDS, of course, it seems justified: After all, SDS did self-destruct in a spectacularly awful way. But this demonizing of the late sixties confuses SDS with all of sixties radicalism, which was recombining in some interesting and constructive ways at that time, as the case of women's liberation demonstrates.[19] My point is that when the sixties is recast so that the New Left no longer occupies the privileged narrative core, the record of the late sixties is somewhat more mixed than the reigning interpretation of destructive disintegration would suggest.[20]

This formulation of the "good" and "bad" sixties has something to do with the writers' own positions as SDS "heavies"—the sixties equivalents of what Josephine Herbst derisively termed "the head boys" to describe the male luminaries of the thirties literary left.[21] This conflation of the sixties and SDS confuses the fortunes of the Movement with these writers' own status, which, as Breines points out, was in serious decline by the late sixties. Inattention to their own circumstances is a factor as well in Gitlin and Hayden's failure to interrogate the ways in which the New Left was gendered, and in particular how masculinity was constructed in SDS. No one, with the exception of Barbara Epstein, has really grappled with SDS's androcentrism, except perhaps to suggest that it reflected the chasm separating the New from the Old Left, which, it is explained, at least acknowledged male chauvinism as a problem.[22] It is as though SDS's androcentrism requires acknowledgment and a few mea culpas, but no serious engagement.

My reading of the New Left suggests that while it failed to problematize gender inequality, it did call into question at least some of the prevailing cultural assumptions about masculinity. Indeed, I see the androcentrism of the New Left as, in part, a response to the domesticated, attenuated sort of masculinity critiqued by William Whyte in his book *The Organization Man.* Anxiety about masculinity was not confined to New Leftists. Pop culture abounded with images of "small dads." Social critics expounded on the dangers of the Organization Man and the "other-directed personality," attributing this new and untraditional form of masculinity to the expanding white-collar, corporate work world and sometimes to suburban matriarchs as well.[23] (As an aside, it's interesting how fears of emasculation figure in the radicalism of both the sixties and the thirties. While sixties white male radicals were rebelling against a spiritually depleted masculinity, male literary radicals in the thirties were outraged by the way in which masculinity had become physically depleted. As Paula Rabinowitz points out, the image of the male body diminished by hunger and unemployment was central to the radical iconography of the thirties.)[24]

By advancing an untamed masculinity, one that took risks and dared to gamble, the New Left was in some sense promoting a counterhegemonic (though not feminist) understanding of masculinity.[25] I suspect male New Leftists' admiration for the radical sociologist C. Wright Mills had as much to do with his leather jacket and BMW motorcycle and their evocation of an unfettered, unmanaged masculinity as it did with his excoriation of the white-collar world and his trenchant critiques of functionalism and anticommunism.[26] Similarly, this factor may explain why what Maurice Isserman has called the "tired heroism" of those Old Leftists associated with the journal *Dissent* had so little appeal to most New Leftists.[27] Gitlin notes Mills's maverick appeal and mentions in passing that Hayden's master's thesis on Mills was subtitled "Radical Nomad."[28] Hayden notes that his own father seemed the embodiment of Mills's white-collar worker.[29] But neither of them (nor James Miller, who spends considerable time on Mills in his book *Democracy Is in the Streets*) discusses the relation of Mills and masculinity to the politics they themselves forged and the lives they led.

The dissatisfaction of white New Left men with domesticated masculinity led them to identify with those on the margins of white U.S. culture, particularly African American men, or what they imagined African American men to be.[30] Todd Gitlin has written that in spheres of both music and justice, "white America was drawing its juice from blacks."[31] But for white male radicals (and perhaps others too) the attraction went well beyond music and justice to include masculinity and sexuality. White leftist men's admiration of African American men seems related to their romanticized view of these men as unencumbered by domestic constraints and therefore somehow more authentically masculine. This dynamic was at work in community-organizing projects such as SDS's Economic Research and Action Projects (ERAP), where white New Left men tried to cop a "black" or a white Appalachian style, depending upon the neighborhood.

Writing in 1970, Gitlin observed that ERAPers like himself romanticized the poor, whom they saw as "involuntarily insulated from the treadmill consumerism of the middle classes from which the organizers had come."[32] But while most ERAPers shared an antimaterialist stance and a desire to transcend their class through downward mobility, the very different responses of New Left men and women to the poor communities they entered suggest that these communities may have held different attractions for men than for women. According to Sara Evans's *Personal Politics,* former ERAPers agree that New Left women made significant progress in organizing poor women, while their male counterparts made little headway because they spent most of their time hanging out in bars and on streetcorners trying to emulate (or compete with) the most marginal men in the community. While ERAP women were attracted to the self-sufficiency and assertiveness of neighborhood women, the men were often drawn to the renegade and antidomestic masculinity of the most marginal men. Rennie Davis recalls that in order to be accepted by the gang in his neighborhood, he spent his whole first week drunk and, in what must have been one especially drunken moment, boasted that he would "beat every mean son of a bitch" in the local bar.[33] Steve Max remembers the ideologically inclined men "always kind of hanging back . . . trying to develop southern accents."[34]

Sara Evans has suggested that the macho posturing of ERAP men was compensatory. She contends "their commitment to the movement and their identification with the very poor required a break with the traditional avenues of success—money, prestigious jobs, respectability." Denied these avenues for "proving their 'manhood,'" they turned to the avenues provided by community organizing, including sexual conquest.[35] But it strikes me that this "break" Evans speaks of was fundamental rather than incidental to their radicalism. While they were undoubtedly committed to the poor and to the Movement, they were also committed to seeking alternatives to the prevailing model of domesticated masculinity in which men were ostensibly prisoners of their wives, their jobs, and the American Dream of achieving the good life through consumption.

□ □ □

If New Left men have produced a problematic rendering of the sixties, so have women's liberationists. Feminist recollections often formulate the relationship between the women's liberation movement and the larger Movement in entirely negative terms. Although there are exceptions, what emerges from many feminist recollections, especially from about 1973 onward, is not the way in which the Movement empowered women (however unintentionally) but the ways in which it exploited them.[36] The idea that women might have learned anything from their Movement experience, except, of course, a well-developed cynicism about leftist men, is disallowed. In many such accounts New Left men appear as possibly even more cretinous and patriarchal than the men they sought to supplant. For example, Robin Morgan, editor of the best-selling anthology *Sisterhood Is Powerful* (and a recent editor of *Ms.* magazine), denounced the "ejaculatory politics" of the New Left.[37] And Andrea Dworkin has written that what distinguished New Left men from others was that they "wanted to wield penises, not guns, as emblems of manhood."[38]

Although I disagree with these assessments, feminist cynicism was not unwarranted. The male-dominated New Left was almost willfully blind to sexism. After all, this was a movement where slogans like "Girls Say Yes to Guys Who Say No" went uncontested.[39] This was a movement where some men reportedly said "the movement hangs together on the head of a penis."[40] In other words, this was a movement where gender inequality was seen, as in the larger culture, as unremarkable. As feminists pointed out at the time, in this respect the Movement mirrored the larger culture all too accurately. But if it offered young white middle-class men a different version of masculinity than was available in the dominant culture, it offered different possibilities for their female counterparts as well. The Movement both was and wasn't the larger culture for white women. As Sara Evans has shown, it was in the New Left and the black freedom movement that white women acquired the skills, confidence, and political savvy necessary to discern the disjuncture between those movements' egalitarian rhetoric and their own subordination. It was here that they encountered black women whose self-reliance and assertiveness were at odds with the "feminine mystique." It was here, in the Movement, not in the larger culture. Although some feminist memoirs, especially those by Ellen Willis, Elinor Langer, and Kathie Sarachild, acknowledge this complicated history,[41] most depict the New Left in particular as unremittingly sexist.[42]

I don't dispute that the women's liberation movement caused many male leftists pain or that the New Left resisted feminism. But too many left and feminist reconstructions of the sixties misremember the past by treating the antagonism between these movements as somehow inevitable. Initially, even radical feminists, who were at the time often wrongly accused of being antileft, saw feminism as involving an expansion rather than a rejection of left analysis. They imagined themselves building a feminist radicalism and continuing to work on both left and feminist political projects.[43] Had the New Left not been in retreat from prefigurative politics, the relationship between these two movements might have developed very differently.

But the relentlessness of the war machine in Vietnam, the government's all-out war against black radicalism, and growing feelings of impotence among white radicals exiled from the black movement and unable or unprepared to fight white racism where it lived, led white New Leftists toward a politics of desperation.[44] This politics took different forms as some, embracing the (only recently) repudiated labor metaphysic, took jobs in factories in order to organize the white working class while others cast themselves as auxiliaries to the Black Panther Party or hoped to ignite a youth revolt. What all of these strategies shared was the conviction that authentic radicalism could not emerge among middle-class white students from college campuses. The idea that genuine radicalism (as opposed to mere liberalism) involved acknowledging and fighting one's own oppression, not struggling exclusively on behalf of other more downtrodden groups, was discredited just at the moment when women, empowered by that idea, were raising the issue of male dominance.[45] New Leftists dismissed the idea that women (much less the white middle-class women in the ranks of the New Left) were oppressed. New Leftists' trivialization and derogation of women's liberation as bourgeois and/or diversionary resulted not only from a desire to hold onto male privilege but also from the way in which class and race were now enshrined as the privileged categories. Women's liberationists responded by appropriating critiques of colonialism and the logic of black power to describe women's oppression and legitimate their struggle. Over time, and with the ascendance of cultural feminism—a strand that grew out of radical feminism but diverged from it in significant ways—anger at the left often solidified into an antileft politics. Under these circumstances a feminist radicalism simply could not grow.

Leftist and feminist constructions of this period not only fail to historicize the conflict between women's liberation and the New Left but also obscure what these two movements had in common, including the historical moment they shared. If New Left men were rebelling against the domesticated masculinity of their postwar fathers, women's liberationists were rebelling against the domesticated femininity of their mothers. If New Left men were drawn to C. Wright Mills, women's liberationists were drawn to Simone de Beauvoir, most obviously because of *The Second Sex* but also because of the independent female characters in her fiction and her own unconventional relationship with Sartre.[46] New Left men and women were in flight from both the nuclear family and the gender conventions of their day. What neither could know was that the "breadwinner/homemaker nuclear family" was an "aberrant and highly fragile" family system, one "already passing from the scene" by the late sixties, as Judith Stacey and Deborah Rosenfelt have argued.[47]

Feminist and leftist accounts of the period also elide other connections between women's liberation and the larger Movement. Although it is true that the women's movement has persisted (albeit in weakened form) while much of the U.S. New Left burned up and out in a spectacular fashion, often leaving little trace of itself in the larger culture, the two experienced many of the same dilemmas. Both movements discovered that creating group structures that were at once democratic and efficient was no mean feat. Both tended to conflate reform and reformism, a move that resulted in a too-total rejection of all reform. Nor was either able to acknowledge difference or own up to the inequalities that existed, whether in the "beloved community" or the "sisterhood." And, finally, both found it difficult not to succumb to the idea that somebody *else* out there—African Americans, the working class, or lesbians—must be the revolutionary agent of change.

More importantly, it is difficult to imagine women's liberation establishing itself as a radical force *without* the philosophical breakthroughs made by New Leftists and black radicals. While the left was often antagonistic to feminism, it nevertheless gave women considerable intellectual ammunition in building their own movement. This is, of course, the paradox at the core of the relationship between these two movements. The conviction that radicalism involved fighting one's own oppression, the commitment to both prefigurative politics and participatory democracy, the genesis of identity politics, and most importantly, the idea that the "personal is political"—all originated in the New Left and the civil rights movement.

While the women's liberation movement popularized the slogan "the personal is political," the idea that there exists a political dimension to personal life was first embraced by early SDSers who encountered the idea in C. Wright Mills's work. Rebelling against a social order whose public and private spheres were highly differentiated, New Leftists called for a reintegration of the two. They reconceptualized personal problems, specifically the alienation and powerlessness they felt, as political problems. Thus SDS's founding Port Huron Statement of 1962 declared that a New Left "must give form to . . . feelings of helplessness and indifference, so that people may see the political, social, and economic sources of their private troubles and organize to change society."[48] Theirs was a more expansive understanding of what constitutes politics than what prevailed in the Old Left. Power was conceptualized as relational, not reducible to formal power. As a consequence their focus was not on "class-based economic oppression" (at least not until the decade's end) but rather, as Ellen Kay Trimberger has argued, on "how late capitalist society creates mechanisms of psychological and cultural domination over *everyone*" (emphasis mine).[49] In the hands of New Left men, the idea that the personal is political remained rather abstract, suggesting the search for greater meaning and connectedness to others. It certainly didn't lead New Left men to explore the ways in which social relations are gendered. But by expanding political discourse to include personal relations, New Leftists unintentionally paved the way for feminists to criticize marriage, the family, and normative heterosexuality.

The idea, however, also suggested its converse—that the political is personal. It was not enough simply to sign your name to a leaflet or participate in a march because politics was meant to radically transform personal life. The challenge was to discover underneath all the layers of social conditioning the "real" self unburdened by social obligations and conventions. It is no exaggeration to say that the *individual* became a site of political activity in the sixties. In the black movement the task was to uncover the black inside the "Negro," and in the women's liberation movement it took the form of transgressing the taboos against female self-assertion or "daring to be bad." It seems that for New Left men the goal was to eliminate all vestiges of their dad's gray-flannel masculinity.

Much of what made sixties radicalism distinct from the Old Left, and so compelling, was that it promised to transform everyday life. The individual would be fulfilled, not subordinated, through politics. But "the personal is political" was one of those ideas whose rhetorical power sometimes seemed to work against its explication. It was an idea put to different and sometimes questionable uses. It was often deployed to suggest that politics is entirely a question of personal transformation. In fact, as early as 1965 Richard Flacks warned that this kind of politics could lead to "a search for personally satisfying modes of life while abandoning the possibility of helping others change theirs."[50]

The idea that "the personal is political" was also interpreted to mean that one's personal life should conform to some abstract notion of "political correctness."[51] Interpreted in this fashion it could, ironically, lead activists to embrace an asceticism that sacrificed personal needs and desires to political imperatives. In both the New Left and the women's liberation movement this tendency encouraged the practice of downward mobility or "self-proletarianization—steady diets of peanut-butter-and-jelly sandwiches, the apparent renunciation of the material world, and posturing as one of "the people."[52] Although these weren't exactly pernicious practices, neither did they help bring into the Movement working-class and poor people, who most likely viewed such behavior as a new version of slumming.

But "the personal is political" was not so innocuous an idea when applied to sexuality, as it frequently was. In the New Left, women in particular had mixed experiences with "sexual liberation." (Ellen Willis has observed that most early radical feminists—many of whom came out of the New Left—"felt about the sexual revolution what Gandhi reputedly thought of Western civilization—that it would be a good idea.")[53] And yet New Left women could not critique the coercive form sex sometimes took in that period without seeming hopelessly tied to bourgeois norms. Later, when the slogan "smash monogamy" became policy in certain sectors of the left, couples who didn't embrace the new standard enthusiastically were sometimes treated like lapsed revolutionaries.

In the women's liberation movement the idea that personal life is a reflection of political commitment was held in check for a very brief time by the insistence of some leaders that there were no real personal solutions to women's oppression, only collective solutions. But over time, credentialing within the movement came to hinge on such things as clothing, the shortness of one's hair, whether one was single or married, and whom one slept with (or, more accurately, didn't sleep with). This often led to sort of a political and personal recklessness where activists, to quote a line from a novel about the sixties, "made bombs of their lives."[54] It certainly gave new meaning to the slogan, "put your body on the line." (Parenthetically, I wonder if young women's current unwillingness to identify with feminism is related in part to this dynamic—their sense that feminism necessarily involves a narrowing, rather than an expansion of choices, specifically an eschewal of marriage, the traditional family, and heterosexuality. If so it would be ironic given that feminism was itself a response to women's lack of choices.) Of course, the two uses or deployments of "the personal is political" I've described are not necessarily mutually exclusive, for what is one person's duty is another's pleasure, or "self-realization," in the jargon of the day. This is especially true of sex, where there might be a confluence of political and erotic imperatives in, say, the practice of "smashing monogamy" or lesbianism.

While the idea that "the personal is political" could be put to problematic uses within the movement, the notion brought about a sea change in society—an overwhelmingly positive one. Usually discussions of the legacy of sixties radicalism focus on the ending of Jim Crow and black disenfranchisement and the amassing of the largest antiwar movement in the nation's history. But equally important is that our understanding of what is political has changed as a consequence of the sixties and more particularly of the women's movement. Thus, marital rape and domestic violence, which were once considered personal issues, are now conceptualized as political.

□ □ □

The remapping of the sixties that I envision would involve a narrative decentering of the New Left. It would acknowledge the women's liberation movement as a quintessentially sixties movement and would emphasize just how significant its redefinition of the political has been in the larger culture. It would be exciting to see histories of the sixties written in what Elsa Barkley Brown calls a "multivocal" style, so that we understand more about the variety of sixties radical movements and their often interrelated histories.[55] Finally, any remapping must necessarily involve a greater effort to locate sixties radicalism within the postwar United States. Resource mobilization theorists were perhaps the first to pursue this path.[56] But I would like to see more attention paid to official and oppositional discourses and the popular culture of the postwar period. For instance, recently it has been argued persuasively that the discourse of the Cold War, with its strategic rhetoric of democracy, may have unintentionally helped ignite the civil rights movement.[57] As I've already suggested, I think we could also benefit from an exploration into the ways that, for young white people in the United States, the sixties represented a gendered generational revolt against the ultradomestic fifties.

As others have pointed out, masculinity became a contested terrain in the postwar United States as the breadwinner ethic came under attack from a variety of sources.[58] I would expand the typical list of rebels to include fifties rock 'n' rollers and sixties New Leftists. I am struck by the way in which the domesticated masculinity of the postwar period is challenged repeatedly by the Beats, rock 'n' roll culture, and white New Leftists. Disaffected white men in all these examples come to identify, I think, with those forced to live on the margins of America, especially African American men. (Think, for instance, of the centrality and recurrence of the phrase "rolling stone(s)" to the sixties. It was the old proverb "a rolling stone gathers no moss" that inspired blues singer Muddy Waters to first use the phrase as the title of one of his songs, which was how the phrase came to be appropriated by the Rolling Stones. On this side of the Atlantic, Bob Dylan had his first top-forty hit with "Like a Rolling Stone." Finally, the aboveground magazine that best reflected the sixties was, of course, called *Rolling Stone*.) [59]

What interests me here is the way in which these revolts against domesticated masculinity did sometimes call into question racial categories. (The Organization Man and the white-collar worker were both radically marked concepts.) One can certainly see this in relation to rock 'n' roll, where what is most threatening about the genre is the way in which it is perceived by much of white America as disrupting racial boundaries, by not only bringing different racial groups into contact with one another but in promoting "jungle rhythms." [60] Rock changes the meaning of "whiteness" as white men, especially, strive to emulate a "black" musical style and stance, thereby challenging the cultural devaluation of "black" music. This is why Elvis, the "Hillbilly Cat" with his pomaded, dyed hair and "black"-inspired dress, moves, and vocal style, was so revolutionary—he violated and confounded the racial boundaries of the fifties. [61] (Of course, it was business as usual in the sense that once again a white person was reaping the profits from this appropriation of "black" music.)

What I want to suggest is that white rock 'n' rollers' revolt against domesticated masculinity, by leading them to identify with black men whom they perceived as both unencumbered by domesticity and having (in the words of the writer Claude Brown) "masculinity to spare" (or "the juice," as Gitlin put it), may have contributed to a shift in America's color line. Over twenty years ago, in *Soul on Ice,* Eldridge Cleaver called the Twist "a guided missile, launched from the ghetto into the very heart of suburbia." [62] Rock did have a profound impact, desegregating the radio waves and much of the music charts, bringing together different racial and ethnic groups at dances and concerts, and changing blacks' and whites' self-perceptions. In ways we don't yet know rock 'n' roll reconstructed the meanings of "whiteness" and "blackness," which as Tom Holt has argued are, of course, absolutely interdependent. [63] This is not to say that racial boundaries are not constantly rearticulated—they are, as in the gradual construction of rock itself as a "white" music. But if we want to get at the sixties, we will have to consider that Cleaver may be right that rock 'n' roll helped prepare the ground.

Still, what is missing from Cleaver's analysis (and what it shares with the sixties books under discussion here) is any acknowledgment of gender's role in the transformations of the sixties. This is especially striking since it was dissatisfaction with the dominant model of masculinity that in part fueled the birth of rock 'n' roll. Moreover, as rock 'n' roll destabilized the categories of whiteness and blackness so did it necessarily destabilize notions of masculinity and femininity. In fact, rock 'n' roll allows us to see the ways in which race, gender, class, and sexuality exist not as abstract and distinct categories, but are, rather, mutually constitutive identities. While it seems that rock 'n' roll did involve, at least initially, a greater challenge to domesticated masculinity than to domesticated femininity, further research may reveal that this is to some extent a function of the way in which histories of rock, like histories of the sixties, place women on the sidelines. Future studies may very well uncover ways in which young white women and girls also harnessed rock's subversive and rebellious possibilities. Then we may have a better understanding of the white women's side of the sixties generational revolt—the women's liberation movement—that is so vital a part of the sixties story.

NOTES

Acknowledgments: I presented different versions of this chapter at the October 1990 American Studies convention and the March 1991 conference on Contemporary Social Movements and Cultural Politics at the University of California, Santa Cruz. Many people helped me rethink and sharpen the arguments here, including the *Socialist Review* staff and Barbara Epstein in particular. Martha Vicinus encouraged me to think bigger. Connie Samaras, Paula Rabinowitz, Howard Brick, Becky Conekin, Laura Downs, Karen Merrill, and Peg Lourie provided thoughtful criticisms. In the end, of course, the essay's shortcomings should be laid at my doorstep. Finally, thanks to Jello Biafra, whose recent cover of the Animals' hit put the tune in my mind and in the title.

1. See, for example, the interview with Natalie Zemon Davis in Henry Abelove, et al., eds., *Visions of History* (New York: Pantheon, 1984), 114–115.

2. See Vincent Harding, "It's Not Enough to Honor King; We Have to Continue His Human Mission," *The Ann Arbor* (Michigan) *News,* January 18, 1988.

3. Citizenship, principled protest, and rock 'n' roll genius are formulated as male in *JFK, Born on the Fourth of July,* and *The Doors* respectively. In *JFK,* for instance, citizenship is constructed as masculine both in the closing courtroom scene where District Attorney Jim Garrison addresses his final remarks to his son, and in several scenes between Garrison and his son (played by Oliver Stone's son). Garrison's daughter is either absent or marginal to these scenes. The major female character, Garrison's wife, is depicted as aggressively antipolitical. Her interest is her family, certainly not her husband's apparently selfless and heroic struggle for truth and justice. In this film the public and private, formulated as masculine and feminine respectively, are opposed. One wonders if Stone's fascination with Kennedy and Garrison might stem in part from the antidomestic masculinity they seemed to embody.

4. For a discussion of Stone's engagement with the sixties, see Stephen Talbot, " '60's Something," *Mother Jones* 16, no. 2 (March–April 1991).

5. See, for example, James Miller, *Democracy Is in the Streets: From Port Huron to the Seige of Chicago* (New York: Simon & Schuster, 1987); Tom Hayden, *Re-*

union: A Memoir (New York: Random House, 1988); Todd Gitlin, *The Sixties: Years of Hope, Days of Rage* (New York: Bantam, 1987); David Caute, *The Year of the Barricades: A Journey Through 1968* (New York: Harper & Row, 1988); Nancy Zaroulis and Gerald Sullivan, *Who Spoke Up? American Protest against the War in Vietnam* (Garden City, N.Y.: Doubleday, 1984); Joan and Robert Morrison, *From Camelot to Kent State* (New York: Times Books, 1987); Abe Peck, *Uncovering the Sixties* (New York: Pantheon, 1985). The problem is not that most of these writers don't mention the women's liberation movement but that it is peripheral in their accounts. However, Zaroulis and Sullivan did manage to write a whole book on the antiwar movement without once mentioning women's liberation and its antiwar efforts. Worst of all is David Caute's five-hundred-page opus, which devotes less than five pages to women's liberation. Miller only alludes to the coming women's movement, but this exclusion is somewhat more excusable since his study ends with the Chicago Democratic Convention in August 1968. However, he, as well as the others listed above, could have explored the gendered politics of the New Left. *The Sixties Papers: Documents of a Rebellious Decade,* edited by Judith and Stewart Albert (New York: Praeger, 1984), include a section on the women's liberation movement. But the authors devote just five pages to it in their fifty-five page introductory essay. *The '60's without Apology,* edited by Sohnya Sayres, Anders Stephanson, Stanley Aronowitz, and Frederic Jameson (Minneapolis: University of Minnesota Press, 1984), is a collection of essays that, largely through the inclusion of Ellen Willis's important essay "Radical Feminism and Feminist Radicalism," makes some attempt to integrate women's liberation into its constructions of the sixties. The one book-length study of the sixties that does integrate the women's movement (both the liberal branch epitomized by NOW and the more radical women's liberation movement) is Stewart Burn's synthetic account, *Social Movements of the 1960's: Searching for Democracy* (Boston: Twayne, 1990).

6. Ellen DuBois, "Women Suffrage and the Left: An International Socialist Perspective," *New Left Review* no. 186 (March–April 1991).

7. Both the women's liberation movement and the New Left were overwhelmingly white. However, some have argued that by the late sixties feminist struggles were being waged within, for instance, the black freedom movement. According to this argument, historians who have defined the women's liberation movement as an autonomous movement primarily concerned with ending male dominance have erased the emergent black feminist struggle that was embedded within the black movement (Barbara Omolade, panel remarks at the roundtable discussion of my book *Daring to Be Bad* [Minneapolis: University of Minnesota Press, 1989], Berkshire conference on the history of women, June 1990). Tracye Matthews, a graduate student in the history department at the University of Michigan, is working on women in the Black Panther Party. Her research should tell us more about this.

8. Mary King, *Freedom Song: A Personal Story of the 1960's Civil Rights Movement*

(New York: Morrow, 1987); Angela Davis, *Angela Davis: An Autobiography* (New York: Random House, 1974); Jane Alpert, *Growing Up Underground* (New York: Morrow, 1981). One could add to this list Joan Baez, *And a Voice to Sing With* (New York: NAL, 1987). But Baez was a celebrity more outside than inside the Movement.

9. James Forman, *The Making of Black Revolutionaries* (New York: MacMillan, 1972); Cleveland Sellers with Robert Terrell, *The River of No Return: The Autobiography of a Black Militant and the Life and Death of SNCC* (New York: William Morrow, 1973); Anne Moody, *Coming of Age in Mississippi* (New York: Dell, 1971). However, this situation appears to be changing with the publication of two important Black Panther memoirs: Elaine Brown, *A Taste of Power: A Black Woman's Story* (New York: Pantheon, 1992) and David Hilliard and Lewis Cole, *The Side of Glory: The Autobiography of David Hilliard and the Story of the Black Panther Party* (Boston: Little Brown, 1993).

10. Carlos Muñoz, *Youth, Identity, Power: The Chicano Movement* (New York: Verso, 1989). Of course, Muñoz's book is problematic in the way it universalizes male experience. Vicki Ruiz discusses Muñoz's inattention to Chicanas in her review of his book in the *American Historical Review* (December 1991): 1638.

11. Solely in order to minimize confusion about which movement I am referring to, I will capitalize "Movement" when discussing the overlapping movements of the sixties (black freedom, student, antiwar, and New Left) and will use the lower-cased "movement" when discussing the women's liberation movement.

12. Despite their similar treatments of women's liberation, these are very different books. Hayden wrote his book as a memoir; Gitlin acknowledges the autobiographical basis of his book but presents his work as a more general history of the sixties. Gitlin's decision to write a history makes his book more useful than Hayden's, but more problematic as well because his experiences and feelings so inform his construction of the period.

13. Gitlin, *The Sixties*, 374, 375.

14. Hayden, *Reunion*, 419.

15. Hayden, like Gitlin, contrasts male and female experience in the movement at this time, noting that the women's consciousness-raising groups were "rather exhilarating, while the men went to morbid meetings" (*Reunion*, 421).

16. Gitlin, *The Sixties*, 427.

17. For a further elaboration of this idea see my book *Daring to Be Bad: Radical Feminism in America, 1967–1975* (Minneapolis: University of Minnesota Press, 1989), esp. 23–49 and 114–37.

18. Winifred Breines, "Whose New Left?" *Journal of American History* 75, no. 22 (September 1988).

19. Richard Flacks has critiqued the idea that the New Left "project" died in the late sixties. He points to the vitality of grassroots, collective experiments into the seventies. See his useful article "What Happened to the New Left?" *Socialist Review* 19, no. 1 (January–March 1989).

20. This is not to say that for either the New Left or the black freedom struggle the late sixties marked a time of unequivocal success. Indeed, many would argue that the organized black movement faltered when the struggle moved North. And SNCC fell apart long before SDS. But I would argue that any comprehensive history of the black freedom struggle would have to grapple with the significance of both black power and the Black Panther Party, which attempted to address both class and racial issues.

21. Quoted in Paula Rabinowitz, *Labor and Desire: Women's Revolutionary Fiction in Depression America* (Chapel Hill: University of North Carolina Press, 1991), 4.

22. In this groundbreaking article Epstein did problematize New Left men's masculinity. She maintained that both New Left men and women were ambivalent about commitment in their personal relationships. However, she suggested that women's ambivalence arose from their dissatisfaction with the quality of their relationships, while men were more apt to reject or at least feel ambivalent about the very idea of commitment. Epstein hypothesized that men's more global rejection of commitment might have stemmed from their memories of the "trapped quality of their fathers' lives." Epstein, "Family Politics and the New Left: Learning from Our Own Experience," *Socialist Review* nos. 63–64 (May–August 1982): 153–54. On the relative status of women in the Old and New Left, see Ellen Kay Trimberger, "Women in the Old and New Left: The Evolution of a Politics of Personal Life," *Feminist Studies* 5, no. 3 (Fall 1979); and Barbara Epstein (going by the name Easton then), "Women and the Left," *New American Movement* (Summer 1975).

23. See Wini Breines, "The 1950's: Gender and Some Social Science," *Sociological Inquiry* 56, no. 1 (Winter 1986).

24. See Rabinowitz, *Labor and Desire*, 37.

25. Mills's *White Collar: The American Middle Classes* (New York: Oxford University Press, 1953) opens with a quote from Charles Peguy: "No one could suspect that times were coming . . . when the man who did not gamble would lose all the time, even more surely than he who gambled."

26. Gitlin gets at this point, but without exploring gender, when he remarks, "Mills was a hero in student radical circles for his books, of course, but it was no small part of the persona for which he was cherished that he was a motorcycle-riding, cabin-building Texan, cultivating the image of a gunslinging homesteader of the old frontier" (*The Sixties*, 34).

27. Maurice Isserman, *If I Had a Hammer: The Death of the Old Left and the Birth of the New Left* (New York: Basic Books, 1987), 116–23.

28. Gitlin, *The Sixties*, 108.

29. Hayden, *Reunion*, 80.

30. Of course, they didn't identify with male homosexuals, who also occupied the margins of American society. Just as their attitudes toward women mirrored those of the dominant culture so did their attitudes toward homosexuality. Over the course of the period intolerance seems to have increased as many

white New Leftists equated militance with machismo and liberalism with wimpiness. See ex–SDS leader Gregory Calvert's review of Wini Breine's *Community and Organization in the New Left, 1962–68* in *Telos* (Winter 1982–1983).

31. Gitlin, *The Sixties*, 38.
32. Gitlin, quoted in Sara Evans, *Personal Politics: The Roots of Women's Liberation in the Civil Rights Movement and the New Left* (New York: Vintage, 1980), 128.
33. Davis quoted in Evans, *Personal Politics*, 151.
34. Max quoted in Evans, *Personal Politics*, 149.
35. Evans notes that by the second year of ERAP many New Left men were engaged in the business of sexual conquest (*Personal Politics*, 152).
36. Interestingly, feminist accounts tend to be much less critical of the black freedom movement. It could be, as Sara Evans suggests, that white women found the black freedom movement more hospitable than the New Left, which was such an intellectual proving ground. But even if this is true, and I am not yet convinced it is (there were, after all, female intellectuals in the New Left and intellectual discussions in SNCC), I think feminists' more charitable account of the black freedom movement stems from a feeling of affinity with the philosophy of black power and a desire to achieve legitimacy within the New Left through solidarity with that struggle. I have often thought that white women's liberationists' erroneous attribution of the first memo on sexism in the New Left to an African-American woman, Ruby Doris Smith Robinson, reflected in part their desire for an easy cross-racial sisterhood, as well as for political legitimacy, because black women were at least understood as oppressed, if not usually as women.
37. Morgan, "Rites of Passage," a 1975 article reprinted in her *Going Too Far* (New York: Vintage, 1978), 10.
38. Dworkin, "Why So-Called Radical Men Love and Need Pornography," in her *Letters from a War Zone* (New York: Dutton, 1989), 217. See Dworkin on the New Left in *Right-Wing Women* (New York: Perigree, 1983). She contends that before the revival of feminism, New Left men "fought for and argued for and even organized for and even provided political and economic resources for abortion rights for women" (95). They did so because "access to safe abortion made more women willing to be fucked more often by more men" (129). Dworkin claims these same men deserted abortion rights when feminists redefined the issue as one of women's control of their bodies. This is pure fiction: The New Left never mobilized in support of abortion rights in the days before feminism. See Suzanne Staggenborg, *The Pro-Choice Movement* (New York: Oxford University Press, 1991).
39. This was a slogan of the antidraft movement and it was, ironically, coined by folksinger and antiwar activist Joan Baez. See her memoir *And A Voice to Sing With*, 152.
40. Gitlin, *The Sixties*, 108. Hayden's wording differs a bit, but he too notes this remark (*Reunion, 107*).

41. Ellen Willis, "Radical Feminism and Feminist Radicalism," in Sohnya Sayres et al., eds., *The '60's without Apology*; Elinor Langer, "Notes for Next Time: A Memoir of the 1960's," *Working Papers for a New Society* 1, no. 3 (Fall 1973); Kathie Sarachild, "The Civil Rights Movement: Lessons for Women's Liberation" (unpublished 1983 speech delivered at the University of Massachusetts).

42. This genre of rancorous recollections was very much encouraged by the mid-seventies ascendance of cultural feminism. Briefly, cultural feminism is an antileft strain of feminism that reformulated the central task of feminism as the construction of a women's culture where female values would be nurtured and celebrated. The reasons for cultural feminism's ascendance within the movement are too complicated to discuss here, but it was related to the political circumstances of the mid-seventies—the political impasse feminists found themselves in, what Robin Morgan called the "futilitarian" politics of radical feminism, and, perhaps most crucially, the movement's fragmentation along lines of class, sexual preference, and race. Cultural feminism with its universalizing discourse of "sisterhood" and its concern with achieving tangible change in the form of a women's culture had extraordinary appeal. Those who tried to raise the issue of the differences between women were denounced as dupes of the male left, which, it was argued, was out to derail feminism. Cultural feminists had a certain stake in presenting the New Left as intrinsically and chronically sexist.

43. See Echols, *Daring to Be Bad*, especially chapter 2.

44. See Echols, *Daring to Be Bad*, chapters 1–3.

45. The idea that radicalism involved fighting one's own oppression had only recently found acceptance in the white left, largely as a result of the black movement's expulsion of whites and French theorists' invention of the "new working class"—an idea with complicated repercussions in the white left. The early New Left generally cast African Americans and the poor in the role of revolutionary agents of change. See Stanley Aronowitz's immensely instructive article "When the New Left Was New" in Sayres, et al., *The '60's without Apology*, 35.

46. Mary King, who with Casey Hayden was among the first to challenge Movement sexism, writes in *Freedom Song* that both she and Hayden were drawn to Beauvoir's writings in part because her female characters were not defined by men.

47. Rosenfelt and Stacey, "Second Thoughts on the Second Wave," *Feminist Studies* 13, no. 2 (Summer 1987): 351.

48. The Port Huron Statement is reprinted in its entirety in Miller's *Democracy Is in the Streets*. See p. 374 for this passage.

49. Ellen Kay Trimberger, "Women in the Old and New Left," in *Feminist Studies* 5, no. 3 (Fall 1979): 442.

50. Richard Flacks, "Some Problems, Issues, Proposals," in Paul Jacobs and Saul Landau, *The New Radicals: A Report with Documents* (New York: Vintage, 1966), 168.

51. I hesitate to use this term since it has been so successfully appropriated by the right to describe any and all things progressive and feminist, thus the quotation marks. See Barbara Epstein's timely and important "'Political Correctness' and Collective Powerlessness," *Socialist Review* 21, nos. 3–4 (July–December 1991).

52. Barbara Ehrenreich has used the term "self-proletarianization" to describe the mid-seventies Marxist-Leninist left. However, a version of this was certainly around a decade earlier. See her very useful critique of socialist feminism, "Life without Father: Reconsidering Socialist-Feminist Theory," *Social Review* 73 (January–February 1984): 49.

53. Ellen Willis, "Coming Down Again: Excess in the Age of Abstinence," *Village Voice*, January 24, 1989.

54. Frances Chapman, a talented writer for the Washington, D.C., women's liberation newspaper *off our backs*, invoked this line in her 1984 interview with me. Chapman characterized it as a good line from a bad book, the book being *Wild Women Don't Get the Blues*.

55. Elsa Barkley Brown, "Polyrhythms and Improvisation: Lessons for Women's History," *History Workshop Journal* 31 (Spring 1991).

56. According to Leila Rupp and Verta Taylor, resource mobilization theory, in contrast to earlier scholarship on social change movements, stresses the importance of resources—expertise, money, publicity, and the support of influential groups and individuals not involved in the movement—to a movement's success. Leila Rupp and Verta Taylor, *Survival in the Doldrums: The American Women's Rights Movement, 1945 to the 1960's* (New York: Oxford University Press, 1987). Aldon Morris, *The Origins of the Civil Rights Movement: Black Communities Organizing for Change* (New York: Free Press, 1984).

57. George Lipsitz, *A Life in the Struggle: Ivory Perry and the Culture of Opposition* (Philadelphia: Temple University Press, 1988; rev. ed. 1995), 47.

58. See, in particular, Barbara Ehrenreich, *The Hearts of Men: American Dreams and the Flight from Commitment* (Garden City, N.Y.: Anchor, 1983).

59. See Robert Draper, *Rolling Stone Magazine: The Uncensored History* (New York: Bantam, 1990), 61.

60. For the racial dimension of the attack on rock 'n' roll see Linda Martin and Kerry Segrave, *Anti-Rock: The Opposition to Rock 'n' Roll* (Hamden, Conn.: Archon Books, 1988).

61. The term "hillbilly cat" was slang for "white Negro." See Greil Marcus, *Mystery Train: Images of America in Rock 'n' Roll Music* (New York: Dutton, 1982), 181. Marcus's work was perhaps the first to grasp the full significance of Elvis's transgression of America's racial boundaries. See also George Lipsitz's inspired article "Land of a Thousand Dances: Youth, Minorities and the Rise of Rock and Roll," in Lary May, ed., *Recasting America: Culture and Politics in the Age of the Cold War* (Chicago: University of Chicago Press, 1985).

62. Eldridge Cleaver, *Soul On Ice* (New York: Dell, 1968), 197. Andrew Ross dis-

cusses Cleaver's observation in *No Respect: Intellectuals and Popular Culture* (New York: Routledge, 1989), 65–101.

63. Tom Holt, "Notes for a Paper: Reflections on Race-Making and Racist Practice: Toward a Working Hypothesis" (paper presented to the Committee for the Study of Social Transformation, University of Michigan, Spring 1991).

PART THREE

IDENTITY POLITICS
AND ACTIVIST PROJECTS

□

CHAPTER 8

Sisters and Queers:
The Decentering of Lesbian Feminism

Arlene Stein

□   □   □   □   □   □   □   □   □   □   □   □

Recently, a forty-four year-old mother of two boys told me that "in the old days," the 1970s, she could go to a particular place—a cafe or women's center, for example—to find the lesbian community in her medium-sized town. But by the late 1980s, when she broke up with a longtime lover, she went out searching again for that community and couldn't find it. Another woman I knew expressed fears about the number of lesbian friends she had lost to heterosexual conversions, having become convinced that more and more women were forsaking their lesbianism in exchange for what she saw as the greater public respectability afforded by living with men.

Lesbian feminism emerged out of the most radical sectors of the women's movement in the early 1970s. Young women who "came out through feminism," as the saying went, attempted to broaden the definition of lesbianism, to transform it from a medical condition, or at best, a sexual "preference," into a collective identity which transcended rampant individualism and its excesses as well as compulsory gender and sex roles. It was a movement which spawned the most vibrant and visible lesbian culture that had ever existed in this country.

But by the mid 1980s, the vision of a Lesbian Nation which would stand apart from the dominant culture, as a sort of haven in a heartless (male/heterosexual) world, began to appear ever more distant. In contrast to the previous decade, lesbian culture and community seemed placeless. This complaint was common, particularly among women who came of age in the 1970s, when becoming a lesbian meant coming into a community committed to some

This chapter is reprinted with revisions from an article of the same title in *Socialist Review* 22, no. 1 (1992): 33–55, by permission of *Socialist Review*. "No Dykes" is reprinted with permission from Alison Bechdel, *Dykes to Watch Out For: The Sequel* (Ithaca, N.Y.: Firebrand Books, 1992), strip 82, pp. 16–17. Copyright © 1992 by Alison Bechdel.

shared values. Philosopher Janice Raymond sounded the call of alarm in a women's studies journal in 1989: "We used to talk a lot about lesbianism as a political movement—back in the old days when lesbianism and feminism went together, and one heard the phrase lesbian feminism. Today we hear more about lesbian sadomasochism, lesbians having babies and everything lesbians need to know about sex."[1] As she and others explained it, the 1980s and 1990s brought a retrenchment from the radical visions of the previous decade. A triumphant conservatism had shattered previously cohesive lesbian communities.

While many of these assertions are unquestionably true, the death-of-community scenario cannot explain the apparent paradox that by 1990, in many urban centers, lesbian influence appeared to be nowhere *and* everywhere. In 1991 the *San Francisco Examiner* reported on the closing of the last lesbian bar in that city. How strange, the columnist noted, that "more lesbians than ever live in San Francisco but that the last lesbian bar was set to close." Bemoaning the loss of a "home base" for lesbians, the former owner of the bar said: "It's a victim of the lesbian community becoming more diverse. There is an absence of a lesbian community in the presence of a million lesbians."[2]

Reflecting this more decentered sense of community, today's lesbian "movement," if one can call it that, consists of a series of projects, often wildly disparate in approach, many of which incorporate radical and progressive elements. If the corner bar was once the only place in town, by the early 1990s in cities across the country there were lesbian parenting groups, support groups for women with cancer and other life-threatening diseases, new and often graphic sexual literature for lesbians, organizations for lesbian "career women" and lesbians of color, and mixed organizations where out lesbians played visible roles. What is new, I suggest, is the lack of any fundamental hegemonic logic or center to these projects.[3]

The once clear connection between lesbianism and feminism, in which the former was assumed to grow naturally out of the latter, is not all that clear today. Gone is the ideal of a culturally and ideologically unified Lesbian Nation. A series of challenges, largely from within lesbian communities themselves, have shaken many of the ordering principles of lesbian feminism. In the following, I want to explain this process of decentering. What does it mean? Why did it occur? And what might it tell us about the trajectory of identity-based movements?[4]

Identities and Movements

All movements engage identities, but in recent years "identity" has become a key term, signifying the sense in which the goal of movements is not only to mobilize identities toward some other end but also to act upon collective identities themselves. In the 1960s and 1970s, in response to the widespread perception of postwar social conformity, new social movements politicized the concern for autonomy and subjective identity, arguing for notions of political activity that challenged previously clear-cut distinctions between private and public, personal and political.[5]

Lesbian feminism, and the women's liberation movement in general, was committed to the goal of authenticity, to redefining and affirming the self. A movement such as this confounds the abstract universalism of theories such as Marxism or resource mobilization, which have typically conceptualized social movements as expressions of shared interests within a common structural location. In such theories, actors find their collective identities within a prevailing cultural model that is more or less fixed. The formation of collective identities is assumed to be relatively unproblematic, reflecting "essential" differences among persons that exist prior to mobilization. We refer, for example, to a supposedly unified subject such as the *women's* movement, searching for signs of collectivization and unity and downplaying evidence of discontinuities and ruptures.

Instead of assuming that collective identities simply reflect differences among persons that exist prior to mobilization, we need, I think, to look closely at the process by which movements remake identities. For it is through the process of mobilization that this sense of "group-ness" is constructed and individual identities are reshaped.[6] New social movement theories that emerged in the 1980s in Europe come closer to being able to answer some of the questions posed by movements such as lesbian feminism: for example, how do people develop politicized group identities? How do these identities change over time? Rather than conceiving of movements as narrowly concerned with achieving material benefits, theorists such as Alain Touraine have reconceptualized them as struggles for the "management of historicity," for the "social management" of culture. In this framework, movements emerge not simply as the expression of needs narrowly defined but as needs rooted in self-conceptions, in identities.[7]

With this in mind, I want to reread the history of lesbian feminism as a series of identity reconstructions that are partial and strategic. A social movement organized around sexuality may seem a peculiar site for such an examination, since sexual desires and behavior tend to be viewed as presocial and unchanging. Over the past two decades, however, a host of scholars have argued against such assumptions, claiming with respect to homosexuality that it is "socially constructed," that it is "situational, influenced and given meaning and character by its location in time and social space."[8]

Lesbian feminists took this constructionist critique very seriously. Indeed, they literally tried to remake lesbian life in this country by bringing together disaffected members of the homophile, gay liberation, and feminist movements, as well as unaffiliated women, to form autonomous lesbian organizations that would be part of the larger struggle for social and sexual freedom.[9] Yet in the end, I will argue, the movement failed to see the constructed, indeed fragile, nature of its own collective self-concepts.

Smashing the Categories

To my suggestion that lesbianism is becoming decentered, one could reply that the lesbian-feminist movement, consisting of hundreds of semi-autonomous small-scale efforts nationwide, was never centered. However, while it was never unified, it did have a hegemonic project. It was, firstly, an effort to reconstruct the category "lesbian," to wrest it from the definitions of

the medical experts and broaden its meaning. It was, secondly, an attempt to forge a stable collective identity around that category and to develop institutions which would nurture that identity. And thirdly, it sought to use those institutions as a base for the contestation of the dominant sex/gender system.

The medical model of homosexuality, dominant for most of the twentieth century, situated sexual object choice outside of society, declaring it fixed at birth or in early childhood, and deemed it an intractable property of the individual. The "old gay" pre-feminist world, a series of semi-secret subcultures located primarily in urban areas, formed in relation to the hegemonic belief that heterosexuality was natural and homosexuality an aberration. But for 1970s "new lesbians," the pre-feminist world and the conviction that lesbians were failed women were no longer tenable or tolerable. In place of the belief in a lesbian essence or fixed minority identity signified by an inversion of gender, long synonymous with the image of lesbianism in the popular imagination, they substituted the universal possibility of "woman-identified" behavior.[10] As a popular saying went, "feminism is the theory, lesbianism is the practice."

In critic Eve Sedgwick's terms, we see the "re-visioning, in female terms, of same-sex desire as being at the very definitional center of each gender, rather than occupying a cross-gender or liminal position between them. Thus women who loved women were seen as more female . . . than those whose desire crossed boundaries of gender. The axis of sexuality, in this view, was not only highly coextensive with the axis of gender but expressive of its most heightened essence."[11] Through its encounter with feminism, lesbianism straddled what Sedgwick has called "minoritizing" and "universalizing" strategies, between fixing lesbians as a stable minority group and seeking to liberate the "lesbian" in every woman. Feminism provided the ideological glue which wedded these two sometimes contradictory impulses.

The movement could not have emerged without the second-wave feminist insight that gender roles are socially constructed, or without the gay liberationist application of that insight to sexuality. If the "exchange of women"—compulsory heterosexuality—was the bedrock of the sex/gender system, as Gayle Rubin and others argued, then women who made lives with other women were subverting the dominant order.[12] Jill Johnston and others declared that a "conspiracy of silence" insured that for most women "identity was presumed to be heterosexual unless proven otherwise. . . . There was no lesbian identity. There was lesbian activity." Expressing the feelings of many middle-class women of her generation, Johnston wrote in 1973: "For most of us the chasm between social validation and private needs was so wide and deep that the society overwhelmed us for any number of significant individual reasons. . . . We were all heterosexually identified and that's the way we thought of ourselves, even of course when doing otherwise."[13]

If homophobia on the part of heterosexual feminists and in society at large deterred many women from claiming a lesbian identity, collapsing the distinction between identification and desire minimized stigma and broadened the definition of lesbianism, transforming it into "female bonding," a more inclusive category, with which a larger number of middle-class women could identify. Indeed, there was historical precedent for this vision in the "passionate friendships" common among women of the eighteenth and nineteenth centuries.[14]

Lesbianism represented a sense of connectedness based on mutuality and similarity rather than difference. Ultimately, it was more than simply a matter of sex, poet Judy Grahn declared: "Men who are obsessed with sex are convinced that lesbians are obsessed with sex. Actually, like other women, lesbians are obsessed with love and fidelity."[15] The new, broadened definition of lesbianism resonated with many women who had long experienced their sexuality in relational rather than simply erotic terms, and who considered sexuality a relatively nonsalient aspect of identity and an insufficient basis upon which to organize a mass movement.

Centering lesbianism upon female relationality and identification, these "new lesbians" challenged medicalized conceptions that focused upon gender inversion and masculinized sexual desire. They blurred the boundary between gay and straight women and transformed lesbianism into a normative identity which over time came to have as much—and sometimes more—to do with lifestyle preferences (such as choice of dress or leisure pursuits) and ideological proclivities (anticonsumerist, countercultural identifications) as with sexual desires or practices.

This shift in meaning enabled many women who had never considered the possibility of claiming a lesbian lifestyle to leave their husbands and boyfriends—some for political reasons, others in expression of deeply rooted desires, many for both. It allowed many of those who lived primarily closeted lives to come out and declare their lesbianism openly. Never before had so

much social space opened up so quickly to middle-class women who dared to defy deeply held social norms about their proper sexual place. As a result, the group of women who called themselves lesbians became increasingly heterogeneous, at least in terms of sexuality.

Remaking the Self

Historically, there have always been women who have had sexual/romantic relationships with other women but have not assumed the label "lesbian." There have also been women whose actual sexual desires and practices don't fit the common social definition of lesbian—women, for example, who identify as lesbian but who are bisexual in orientation and/or practice. There are many possible configurations of the relationship between desire, practice, and identity—many more such configurations than there are social categories to describe them.

Yet popular understandings of lesbianism assume a clear-cut relationship between sexual orientation/behavior and sexual identity. Lesbians are assumed to be women who are attracted exclusively to other women and who claim an identity on the basis of that attraction. But for many women, the relation between sexual orientation, sexual identity, and sexual practice is far from stable or uncomplicated.

Moreover, as I have suggested, such definitions change over time. Particularly before the advent of the lesbian-feminist movement, these definitions were situated primarily within the framework of medical expertise, which

fixed lesbianism as a "condition" and made it synonymous with cross-gender, or mannish, attributes. It meant that a woman who took on a lesbian identity needed to overcome extreme social disapproval and formulate a favorable sense of herself which included a "deviant" sexuality.[16] Those who took on this identity during the pre-Stonewall era were more apt to be women who never developed stable identities as heterosexuals.

Often these women either had never had significant sexual and emotional relationships with men, or they related to men only in an effort to hide or deny their lesbianism. One such woman described her coming out in the following terms: "I fell in love with a woman when I was about fifteen or sixteen. I don't know whether I used the term lesbian then; I knew that I loved women, and that was where I was and where I wanted to be. I didn't fall in love with men."[17] In sociologist Barbara Ponse's terminology, she would be considered a "primary" lesbian—someone who identified homosexual feelings in herself before she understood their social significance, who did so at a relatively early age, and who experienced homosexuality less as a choice than as a compulsion. If the "old gay" world largely comprised women for whom lesbianism was "primary," lesbian feminists claimed that the pool of potential lesbians was much larger. Young lesbians in the early 1970s universalized the critique of compulsory heterosexuality and emphasized the possibility of coming out or "electing" lesbianism, proclaiming that it was the "feminist solution." Not only was the institution of heterosexuality constructed, activists argued, but so too were heterosexual desires. Because they were constructed, they reasoned, such desires could just as easily be reconstructed.

This 52-year-old woman had been married for twenty-two years. Interviewed in the early 1970s, she described her coming out as follows:

> I began . . . to become involved with women's consciousness-raising groups, and I began to hear . . . of the idea of women being turned on to each other. It was the first time I heard about it in terms of people that I knew. . . . I was receptive but had no previous, immediate history. Like there was a part of me that had been thinking about it, and thinking, "Gee, that sounds like intellectually that's a good idea."[18]

The movement thus brought into the fold many "elective" lesbians like this woman, for whom relationships with men were often significant; some were married, some had long-term relationships with men with whom they felt they were in love and to whom they were sexually attracted. Nevertheless, they "discovered" women as sexual and emotional partners at some point, and came to identify as lesbians. Writing of this period several years later, a long-time activist recalled:

> Those of us who were active in 1971 and 72 witnessed the tremendous influx of formerly heterosexual women into the Lesbian Movement. They

came by the thousands. Lesbians of this background now compose the very backbone of the Lesbian Movement. . . . We put the world of men on notice that we were out to give their wives and lovers a CHOICE. We got a bad reputation as "chauvinistic." Lesbian feminism was called an "expansionist philosophy"—meaning that we were out to politically seduce (read: awaken) all women. In the years that have followed, it seems ironic to this old-gay-never-married dyke, that some of the most ardent, anti-straight women . . . were 1971's HOUSEWIVES![19]

The distinction Ponse and others have drawn between "primary" and "elective" lesbians—who differ as to their accounts of the origins of their lesbianism, the meaning of lesbian activity and lesbian feelings, and their age of entry into the lesbian community—thus suggests very different paths through which women have arrived at lesbian identity. Drawing upon object-relations psychoanalytic theory, Beverly Burch argues that the "early" or primary lesbian incorporates a greater sense of "differentness" within her sense of self than the "later-developing" or elective lesbian.

"Primary" lesbians generally have to struggle to establish a positive sense of themselves as lesbians during adolescence, when other issues of social identity are being negotiated. Women who come out later in life, on the other hand, may have already negotiated other issues of social identity before they assume a "deviant" sexual identity. They may have established a sense of self as relatively "normal," at least in terms of their sexuality. Taking on a lesbian identity at this stage, says Burch, means coping with somewhat different issues. "It may involve a sense of loss in terms of acceptability and social ease, but losing something one has had is an experience quite different from never having had it."[20]

Moreover, as I have suggested, historical evidence shows these sexual choices to be shaped by class position. Women who joined public lesbian subcultures before Stonewall were more likely to be of working-class origin, due at least in part to the fact that they tended to be less concerned with losing social status. Women encouraged to "elect" lesbianism through exposure to feminism, by contrast, were more likely to come from the middle classes. With time, these and other preexisting, largely unspoken, differences in identity would pose thorny problems for the process of collectivization. Smashing the categories, it turned out, was a much simpler task than remaking the self.

Border Skirmishes

Twelve hundred women attended the first West Coast Lesbian-Feminist Conference, held in Los Angeles in June 1973. The goal of the conference was to unify lesbian feminists under a common program, but almost immediately the gathering was wracked by internal disagreements over the definition of les-

bianism and, by extension, debates over who would be admitted. A male-to-female transsexual guitarist was shouted down by the crowd and prevented from performing. A prominent feminist writer and theorist was criticized for living with a man. Shortly after the conference, one woman's comment was telling: "If there was any point of unity it was that almost all lesbians are conscious of and hopeful for the development and existence of a lesbian-feminist culture/movement."[21] But a unified culture and movement implied a consensus on the meaning of lesbianism which did not exist.

During the early 1970s, such debates about who was a lesbian became commonplace throughout the country—at conferences, at women's music festivals, and within local communities. Border skirmishes around transsexualism, lesbians with boy children, bisexuality, and other issues deeply divided many lesbian events and communities. Symptomatic of the difficulty of defining the category "lesbian," they marked a growing preoccupation with fixing boundaries, making membership more exclusive, and hardening the notion of lesbian "difference."

The movement had earlier tried to broaden the base of lesbianism by loosening the boundaries around the group. But smashing some categories entailed the creation of others; identity politics requires defining an identity around which to mobilize. Boundary-setting became a preoccupation of the movement once it was faced with the challenge of insuring commitment and guarding against disaffection from the ranks, particularly in view of the pre-existing differences among women which I earlier identified.

If early lesbian feminism emphasized the fluidity of identity categories and the importance of self-description, with time the definition narrowed: Lesbians were biological women who do not sleep with men and who embrace

the lesbian label. If they shared certain values in common, foremost among then was their willingness to make lives apart from men. The growing symbolic importance of the notion of a "women's community" in the mid to late 1970s signified the importance of boundary definition.[22] It centered the movement upon a rejection of men and patriarchal society. It claimed that gender is the primary basis of lesbian identity (and that all other divisions are male-imposed), and argued that power was something imposed from without, by men. If power and hierarchy issues surfaced, members of the "women's community" saw this as the residue of patriarchy and male-identification, something that would fade away with time. If women within the community developed heterosexual desires, lesbians in the mid to late 1970s tended to see this as a sign that patriarchy had been insufficiently purged.

While the language of the movement was radically constructionist, at least in terms of sexuality, in practice it privileged the "primary" lesbian for whom desire, exclusively lesbian, was congruent with identity. Studying the lesbian community in a medium-sized southern city in the 1970s, Barbara Ponse described the "biographic norm" of lesbian communities as the "gay trajectory," popularly known as "coming out." Lesbians assumed that this process was unidirectional. In the highly politicized milieu of lesbian communities, one did not come out and then "go back in" without suffering the consequences of such a move. Ponse concluded that the fluidity and changeability of both identity and activity at the level of the individual "may elude classification within the frameworks of the paradigms of the lesbian world, which, like the dominant culture, assume a heterosexual-homosexual dichotomy."[23]

The movement also privileged white, middle-class women, for whom lesbianism represented both a sexual choice and an oppositional identity. But for many women of color, as well as white working-class women, the choices were never so clear and unambivalent. Women of color, in particular, often felt that they were forced to pick and choose among identities. Audre Lorde wrote in 1979: "As a Black lesbian feminist comfortable with the many different ingredients of my identity . . . I find I am constantly being encouraged to pluck out some one aspect of myself and present this as the meaningful whole, eclipsing or denying the other parts of self."[24] Many resisted pressures to make lesbianism their "dominant" or "master" identity.

What was problematic, I believe, was not so much that boundary-making took place—for it does in all identity-based movements—but that the discourse of the movement, rooted in notions of authenticity and inclusion, ran so completely counter to it. Lesbian feminism positioned itself as the expression of the aspirations of *all* women. Like other identity-based movements, it promised the realization of individual as well as collective identity, and saw the two as intimately linked. At its best, it provided women with the strength and support to proclaim their desires for one another. It allowed many to withdraw from difficult and often abusive situations and opened up social space never before possible in this country. But at its worst, it hardened the boundaries around lesbian communities, subsumed differences of race, class, and even sexual orientation, and set up rather rigid standards for living one's life.

Dilemmas of Identity

All identity-based movements have a tendency to fall into what Alberto Melucci has termed "integralism," the yearning for a totalizing identity, for a "master key which unlocks every door of reality." Integralism, says Melucci, rejects a pluralist and "disenchanted" attitude to life and encourages people to "turn their backs on complexity" and become incapable of recognizing difference.[25] Indeed, the contemporary sociological and historical literature on lesbian-feminist communities of the 1970s is rife with such observations.[26] Sociologist Susan Krieger looked at "the dilemmas of identity" posed by a women's community in the Midwest in the mid 1970s.

She found that individuals frequently experienced a loss of self, in which they felt either overwhelmed or abandoned by the community. While noting that "all social groups confront their members with this kind of conflict," Krieger admitted that "in some groups"—namely, those in which "the desire for personal affirmation from the group is great, and the complementary desire for assertion of individuality is also strong"—this experience is felt more intensely than in other groups and seems to occur more frequently.[27] Lesbian communities were often characterized by likeness, intimacy, and shared ideological orientation; they comprised women who were highly stigmatized. Krieger surmised that all these things contributed to the seeming difficulties their members had with maintaining their individuality amid pressures to merge and to become one with the community. Often this dynamic caused in-

dividuals to become more preoccupied with bolstering their own identities than with achieving political goals and led to internal struggles over who really belonged in the community.

While Krieger focused on gender as the primary locus of "likeness" within lesbian-feminist communities, one could also add race, class, and personal style to the mix. In many parts of the country, despite their efforts to free themselves from imposed social roles, subcultures often created new ones, prescribing sexual styles, political ideologies, and even standards of personal appearance which relatively few could successfully meet. This had the effect of excluding many women, particularly working-class women of all races, but also women who for any number of reasons may not have felt at home in the movement's countercultural milieu.

Particularly after the mid 1970s, many lesbian-feminist communities, scattered throughout the nation, became increasingly private enclaves. If earlier the movement tried to "smash the categories," substituting for the narrow, overly sexualized definitions of lesbianism a broad, normative definition which welcomed all women into the fold, over time these definitions themselves narrowed and became increasingly prescriptive. It is ironic, perhaps, that the very qualities that were once seen as a boon to the lesbian-feminist movement were coming to be viewed as seeds of its demise. Communities of intimacy, it turned out, were also communities of exclusion.

Individuals troubled by the inability of lesbian feminism to resolve the tension between identity and difference were faced with two basic options: They could reject identity as a basis for politics and strike out on their own, asserting their individual autonomy and personal difference. Or they could reshape identity politics and form new attachments which acknowledged "multiple" allegiances and the partial nature of lesbian identity. Indeed, as I will argue, both trends characterize the current phase of lesbian identity politics.

In the early 1980s, a series of structural and ideological shifts conspired to decenter the lesbian-feminist model of identity. First, the predominantly white and middle-class women who composed the base of the movement aged, underwent various life-cycle changes, and settled into careers and families of various stripes—often even heterosexual ones. Second, a growing revolt emerged from within: Women of color, working-class women, and sexual minorities, three separate but overlapping groups, asserted their claims on lesbian identity politics. The next section focuses on these shifts, particularly on how sexual difference posed a challenge to lesbian-feminist constructions of identity.

Sex, Race, and the Decline of the Male Threat?

From the mid 1970s to the early 1980s, the most visible political campaigns undertaken by the feminist movement were against pornography and sexual violence against women. For many women, straight and gay, pornography symbolized male sexuality and power and the fear that stalked women through the ordinary routines of daily life, representing all that was anathema to the vision of a female sexuality that emphasized relationality and reciprocity rather than power and coercion.

But new voices emerged, charging that the radical feminist vision glossed over the real, persistent differences among women and that it idealized women's sexuality and their relationships with one another. These women argued that all the attention upon sexual danger had minimized the possibility of women's pleasure. Highly polarized battles raged in the pages of feminist publications, as "sex radicals" branded their anti-porn, anti-s/m opponents as "good girls," and came to a head in the unlikely setting of a conference at Barnard College in 1982, when anti-s/m activists picketed a speak-out on "politically incorrect sex."[28]

These political clashes, which have come to be called the "sex debates" or "porn wars," rarely addressed the subject of lesbianism explicitly. But insofar as these debates called into question the normative basis of the lesbian-feminist model of identity, lesbianism was the salient subtext. Lesbian "sex radicals" charged that somewhere in the midst of defining sexuality as male, and lesbianism as a blow against the patriarchy, desire seemed to drop out of the picture. As the editor of *On Our Backs* magazine, a popularizer of the emergent "pro-sex" lesbian sensibility, brashly claimed: "The traditional notion of femininity as gentle and nurturing creates the stereotype that lesbianism is just a hand-holding society. 'Lesbians don't have sex,' the story goes. Or if they do, it is this really tiresome affair—five minutes of cunnilingus on each side, with a little timer nearby, and lots of talking about your feelings and career."[29] As "pro-sex" lesbians saw it, in all the talk about "woman identification," the specificity of lesbian existence as a sexual identity seemed to get lost.

In response, some tried to reengage with the tradition of pre-Stonewall lesbianism, which they saw as unencumbered by feminist ideological prescriptions and rooted in working-class bar culture and butch-femme roles.[30] A burgeoning sexual literature reasserted the centrality of desire and sexuality in lesbian identity and culture. Rather than making the distinction between male and female sexualities the primary political cleavage (as radical feminists had done), it acknowledged the sexual diversity implicit within the lesbian category and often invoked, symbolically at least, the sexual license of an earlier moment in gay male culture.

For many women, the onset of the AIDS crisis, which occurred nearly simultaneously, made coalition-building with gay men an even more immediate task. Centering post-Stonewall lesbian identity upon the shared rejection of men and patriarchy, lesbians had earlier disengaged from a gay liberation movement that was largely blind to their needs. But the tide of homophobia unleashed by the AIDS crisis affected lesbians as well as gay men and served at times to sharpen the differences between lesbians and heterosexual women. As the withered body of the person with AIDS replaced the once-pervasive image of the all-powerful male oppressor, the sense of male threat which underlay lesbian-feminist politics diminished further.

Lesbians in many urban centers joined the ranks of such predominantly gay male organizations as ACT UP and Queer Nation, which engaged in public actions across the nation to increase lesbian/gay visibility and puncture the "heterosexual assumption." Others attempted to construct sexualized subcultures which took their cue from an earlier era of gay male sexual experimentation. There were more co-ed gay bars, social events, and institutions. The new identifications between lesbians and gay men extended to personal style as well: clothing, music, and other forms of consumption.

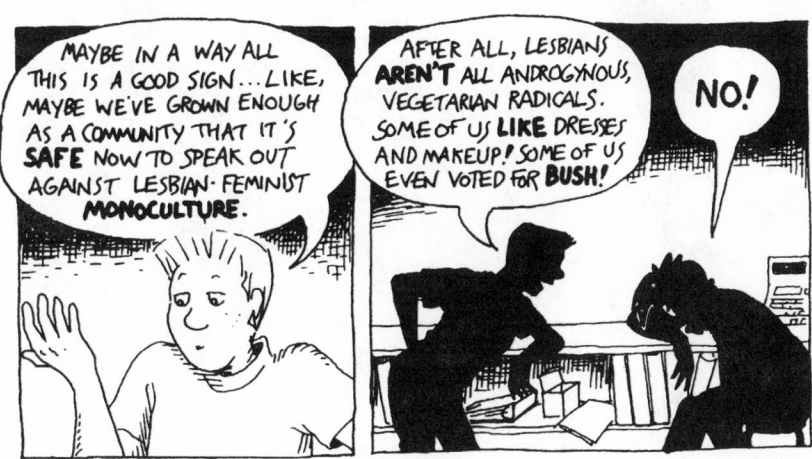

By the late 1980s, even if relatively few women were directly touched by these developments, their effects could be felt in many lesbian communities. The break was largely, though not entirely, generational. An emergent lesbian politics acknowledged the relative autonomy of gender and sexuality, sexism and heterosexism.[31] It suggested that lesbians shared with gay men a sense of "queerness," a non-normative sexuality which transcends the binary distinction homosexual/heterosexual to include all who feel disenfranchised by dominant sexual norms—lesbians and gay men, as well as bisexuals and transsexuals.[32]

As a partial replacement for "lesbian and gay," the term "queer" attempted to separate questions of sexuality from those of gender.[33] But in terms of practice, this separation was incomplete. The new coexistence of gay men and women was often uneasy: ACT UP and Queer Nation chapters in many cities were marred by gender (and racial) conflicts. The new "co-sexual" queer culture could not compensate for real, persistent structural differences in style, ideology, and access to resources among men and women. This recurring problem suggested that while the new queer politics represented the assertion of a sexual difference which could not be assimilated into feminism, neither could gender be completely subsumed under sexuality. Despite their apparent commonalities, lesbians and gay men were often divided along much the same lines as heterosexual women and men.[34]

A less noisy but no less significant challenge to lesbian feminism came through the assertion of racial and ethnic identifications. At conferences and national meetings, women of color argued for the importance of acknowledging the divisions of race and class, which had long been subsumed in the interest of building a unified culture and movement. A series of influential an-

thologies challenged the feminist belief in the primacy of the sex/gender system and led to the development of autonomous black, Asian, and Latina lesbian-feminist organizations.[35]

If lesbian feminism often presented itself as a totalizing identity which would subsume differences of race, class, and ethnicity and pose a united front against patriarchal society, these challenges pointed toward an understanding of lesbianism as situated in a web of multiple oppressions and identities. Lesbians of color and lesbian sex radicals questioned the belief that lesbian life could ever stand completely outside of or apart from the structures of the patriarchal culture. They problematized the once uncontested relationship between lesbianism and feminism. And they shifted lesbian politics away from its almost exclusive focus upon the "male threat," toward a more diffuse notion of power and resistance, acknowledging that lesbians necessarily operate in a society marked by inequalities of class and race as well as of gender and sexuality.

Seventies Questions for Nineties Women

Some might interpret the scenario I have painted, of the increasing spatial and ideological fragmentation of lesbian communities and the currently contested nature of the relationship between feminism and lesbianism, as indicative of a "post-feminist" era. Certainly, the series of cultural shifts I have described break with an earlier moment of lesbian-feminist politics. They result in large part from the difficulties lesbians have faced in mobilizing around a sense of group difference, even as these cultural shifts are made possible by the construction of that very sense of difference.

I have argued that the lesbian-feminist movement found itself torn between two projects: between fixing lesbians as a stable minority group, and seeking to liberate the "lesbian" in every woman. As I suggested earlier, feminism provided the ideological glue which wedded these two sometimes contradictory impulses. It redefined lesbianism in more expansive, universal terms, constructing a lesbian culture founded upon resistance to gender and sexual norms. While it opened up the possibility of lesbian identification to greater numbers of women than ever before, it could ultimately only achieve unity through exclusion, though a gender separatism which hardened the boundaries around it.

Younger women today are trying to carve out lesbian identities at a moment when many of the apparent certainties of the past have eroded—the meaning of lesbianism, the relationship between lesbianism and feminism, and the political potential of identity politics. They recognize that while marginalized groups construct symbolic fictions of their experience as a means of self-validation, and that compulsory heterosexuality necessitates the construction of a lesbian/gay identity, identities are always simultaneously enabling *and* constraining. As one 23-year-old New Yorker recently told me: "What I am is in many ways contradictory. I don't belong in the straight world, though I'm a white girl. . . . But I don't really belong in the feminist world because I read lesbian porn and refuse to go by a party line. On the other hand, I think I'm a feminist. It's a set of contradictions."[36] Even as they integrate feminism into their daily lives, she and others reject the view that lesbianism is *the* feminist act, that any sexual identity is more authentic or unmediated than any other. In this sense, they are in fact "post-feminist," if that term is descriptive of the consciousness of women and men who, while holding their distance from feminist identities or politics, have been profoundly influenced by them. They simultaneously locate themselves inside and outside the dominant culture, and feel a loyalty to a multiplicity of different projects, some of them feminist-oriented, others more queer-identified, many of them incorporating elements of both critiques. And they see themselves, and their lesbianism, as located in a complex world marked by racial, class, and sexual divisions.

Indeed, this indeterminacy is deeply troubling to many women, particularly those who once held out the hope of constructing a lesbian-feminist movement that was culturally and ideologically unified. But I want to suggest that today's more "decentered" movement may present new democratic potential. Many women who felt excluded by an earlier model of identity now feel that they can finally participate in politics on their own terms. As clashes over feminist issues such as abortion, sexual harassment, and pay equity heat up over the coming years, as they are likely to do, lesbians will be on the front lines, as they have always been—only this time they will be out as lesbians. Some will continue to organize primarily as lesbians.[37] Others will continue to participate in movements which are not necessarily feminist at all, but with greater visibility than ever before.

This suggests that any unified conception of lesbian identity is reductive and ahistorical; collective identity is a production, a process. Stuart Hall's comments on ethnic resistance are relevant here.[38] In any politicization of marginal groups, he says, there are two phases. The first comprises a rediscovery of roots, and implies a preoccupation with identity. Only when this "local" identity is in place can a consideration of more global questions and connections begin. For many lesbians in this country, the first phase of this movement has already occurred. We may now be seeing the arrival of the second.[39]

NOTES

Acknowledgments: For their comments on earlier drafts of this chapter, I am grateful to Elizabeth Armstrong, Deborah Gerson, Sabine Hark, Liz Kotz, Nancy Solomon, Pat Stevens, Carla Trujillo, and the *Socialist Review* Bay Area collective, especially Steve Epstein. Thanks also to the audience at the Conference on Contemporary Social Movements and Cultural Politics, University of California, Santa Cruz.

1. Janice Raymond, "Putting the Politics Back into Lesbianism," *Women's Studies International Forum* 12, no. 2 (1989).

2. *San Francisco Examiner*, November 12, 1991, p. 3.

3. Howard Winant makes a similar argument about the politics of race in "Post-modern Racial Politics: Difference and Inequality," in *Socialist Review* 20, no. 1 (January–March 1990).

4. These ideas are based on archival research and interviews conducted primarily in the San Francisco Bay Area. Parts of the analysis may not hold true for other parts of the country, particularly nonurban areas, where the pace of change may be slower.

5. Alain Touraine, *Return of the Actor* (Minneapolis: University of Minnesota Press, 1988); Alberto Melucci, *Nomads of the Present: Social Movements and Individual Needs in Contemporary Society* (London: Century Hutchinson, 1989); Ernesto Laclau and Chantal Mouffe, *Hegemony and Socialist Strategy: Towards a Radical Democratic Politics*, trans. Winston Moore and Paul Cammack (London: Verso, 1985).

6. Pierre Bourdieu, "What Makes a Social Class? On the Theoretical and Practical Existence of Groups," *Berkeley Journal of Sociology* 32 (1987): 13. Also see Scott Lash, *Sociology of Postmodernism* (New York, Routledge, 1990); Sandra Harding's discussion of epistemologies as "justificatory strategies," in "Feminism, Science and the Anti-Enlightenment Critiques," in *Feminism/Postmodernism*, Linda Nicholson, ed. (New York: Routledge, 1990), 87.

7. Looking at the construction of collective identity in social movements provides a link between the symbolic interactionist tradition and more recent theories of social movements. See Herbert Blumer, "Collective Behavior," in *New Outline of the Principles of Sociology*, A. M. Lee, ed. (New York: Barnes and Noble, 1946).

8. Jonathan Katz, *Gay American History* (New York: Harper and Row, 1976), 7. See also Jeffrey Weeks, "The Development of Sexual Theory and Sexual Politics," in Mike Brake, ed., *Human Sexual Relations* (New York: Pantheon, 1982).

9. See Rose Weitz, "From Accommodation to Rebellion: The Politicization of Lesbianism," in *Women-Identified Women*, Trudy Darty and Sandee Potter, eds. (Palo Alto: Mayfield, 1984); Barry Adam, *The Rise of a Gay and Lesbian Movement* (Boston: Twayne, 1987).

10. Radicalesbians, "The Woman-Identified Woman," reprinted in *For Lesbians Only*, Sarah Hoagland and Julia Penelope, eds. (London: Onlywoman Press, 1988); Adrienne Rich, "Compulsory Heterosexuality and Lesbian Existence," *Signs* (Summer 1980).

11. Eve Sedgwick, *Epistemology of the Closet* (Berkeley: University of California Press, 1990), 36.

12. Gayle Rubin, "The Traffic in Women," in *Toward an Anthropology of Women*, Rayna Reiter, ed. (New York: Monthly Review, 1975).

13. Jill Johnston, *Lesbian Nation: The Feminist Solution* (New York: Simon and Schuster, 1973), 58.

14. See Carole Smith-Rosenberg, *Disorderly Conduct* (New York: Knopf, 1985); "The Female World of Love and Ritual," in *Heritage of Her Own*, Nancy F. Cott and Elizabeth Pleck, eds. (New York: Simon and Schuster, 1979).

15. Judy Grahn, "Lesbians as Bogeywoman," in *Women: A Journal of Liberation* 1, no. 4 (Summer 1970): 36.

16. Vivienne C. Cass, "Homosexual Identity Formation: A Theoretical Model," in *Journal of Homosexuality* 4, no. 3 (1979).

17. Barbara Ponse, *Identities in the Lesbian World: The Social Construction of Self* (Westport, Conn.: Greenwood, 1978), 160.

18. Ibid., 162.

19. *Lesbian Tide* (May–June 1978), 19.

20. Beverly Burch, "Unconscious Bonding in Lesbian Relationships: The Road Not Taken" (unpublished dissertation, Institute for Clinical Social Work, Berkeley, Calif. 1989), 91.

21. Jeane Cordova, *Lesbian Tide* (May–June 1973).

22. Alice Echols, *Daring to Be Bad: Radical Feminism in America 1967–75* (Minneapolis: University of Minnesota Press, 1989); Bonnie Zimmerman, *The Safe Sea of Women: Lesbian Fiction 1969–1989* (Boston: Beacon Press, 1990).

23. Ponse, *Identities in the Lesbian World*, 139.

24. Audre Lorde, "Age, Race, Class and Sex: Women Redefining Difference," in *Sister Outsider* (Trumansburg, N.Y.: Crossing Press, 1984).

25. Alberto Melucci, *Nomads of the Present: Social Movements and Individual Needs in Contemporary Society* (London: Century Hutchinson, 1989), 209.

26. Iris Young, "The Ideal of Community and the Politics of Difference," in *Feminism/Postmodernism*, Linda J. Nicholson, ed. (New York: Routledge, 1990); Shane Phelan, *Identity Politics: Lesbian Feminism and the Limits of Community* (Philadelphia: Temple University Press, 1989); Cheryl Cole, "Ethnographic Sub/versions" (unpublished dissertation, University of Iowa, 1991).

27. Susan Krieger, *The Mirror Dance: Identity in a Woman's Community* (Philadelphia: Temple University Press, 1983), xv.

28. Carole Vance, ed., *Pleasure and Danger: Exploring Women's Sexuality* (Boston: Routledge, 1984); B. Ruby Rich, "Feminism and Sexuality in the 1980s," *Feminist Studies* 12, no. 3 (Fall 1986).

29. From an interview with Susie Bright, October 1989.

30. Joan Nestle, "Butch-Fem Relationships," *Heresies* 12 (Summer 1981).

31. Julia Creet, "Lesbian Sex/Gay Sex: What's the Difference?" *OUT/LOOK: National Lesbian and Gay Quarterly*, no. 11 (Winter 1991); Gayle Rubin, "Thinking Sex: Notes for a Radical Theory of the Politics of Sexuality," in Vance, *Pleasure and Danger*.

32. The autonomous bisexual movement suggested a politics along much the same lines, but tended to privilege self-identified bisexuals. See, for example,

Bi Any Other Name: Bisexual People Speak Out, Loraine Hutchins and Lani Kaahumanu, eds. (Boston: Alyson, 1990).

33. Michael Warner, "Fear of a Queer Planet," *Social Text* 29 (1991); Allan Bérubé and Jeffrey Escoffier, "Queer/Nation," *OUT/LOOK: National Lesbian and Gay Quarterly,* no. 11 (Winter 1991).

34. Dan Levy, "Queer Nation in S.F. Suspends Activities," *San Francisco Chronicle,* December 27, 1991; Michele DeRanleau, "How the Conscience of an Epidemic Unraveled," *San Francisco Examiner,* October 1, 1990.

35. These included *This Bridge Called My Back: Writings by Radical Women of Color,* Cherríe Moraga and Gloria Anzaldúa, eds. (Watertown, Mass.: Persephone Press, 1981); *All the Women are White, All the Blacks are Men, But Some of Us Are Brave,* Gloria Hull, Patricia Bell Scott, and Barbara Smith, eds. (New York: Feminist Press, 1982); *Home Girls: A Black Feminist Anthology,* Barbara Smith, ed. (New York: Kitchen Table/Women of Color Press, 1983).

36. From an interview with the author in 1989.

37. The appearance in 1992 of the organization Lesbian Avengers, a direct-action group whose principal goal was to increase lesbian visibility, marked the potential resurgence of lesbian identity politics.

38. Stuart Hall, "Cultural Identity and Cinematic Representation," *Framework,* no. 36 (1989).

39. See Arlene Stein, ed., *Sisters, Sexperts, Queers: Beyond the Lesbian Nation* (New York: Plume, 1993).

CHAPTER 9

Small Change:
Radical Politics since the 1960s

L. A. Kauffman

□　　□　　□　　□　　□　　□　　□　　□　　□　　□　　□　　□

One of the best places to take the erratic pulse of post-sixties culture is *Factsheet Five*, a thick, inexpensively produced bimonthly compendium of cultural and political marginalia. Boasting several thousand readers, *FF* primarily lists zines (with "zine" being short for "fanzine," which *FF*'s former editor once defined as "anything published on a non-commercial scale"). Not a publication to limit its boundaries, however, *Factsheet Five* has also reviewed music, comics, poetry, computer software, pamphlets, books, mail art, "artifacts," and videos.

In *FF*'s pages, one can find endless improbable juxtapositions: a review of *News and Notes from All Over* (the newsletter of the Society for the Eradication of Television) next to a listing for *No Other Way* ("a zine of punk Christianity"); side-by-side blurbs for *Left Green Notes*, an environmentalist newsletter, and *Lifestyles of the Bodily Dismembered*, a zine filled with movie reviews. *Gay Community News* is here and so is *Girlfriends* (a zine for transvestites, transsexuals, and cross-dressers with "straightforward advice on cross-dressing on a budget"). *Wage Slave World News* ("humor in a labor-activist vein") coexists with *Wrestling Then and Now*. *The Sacred Wilderness, Sherlockian Tidbits, Sneezing Jesus, Social Anarchism, The Subtle Journal of Raw Coinage*—just scanning the titles is a lesson in cultural eclecticism.

Most of these zines do not claim to be political, and most probably would not even call themselves radical. But they are all "alternative" in one way or another: out of the ordinary, to be sure; scruffily assembled, usually through photocopying; generally available only through the mail, or occasionally in the most specialized and offbeat of bookstores; and concerned with questions that mainstream America might deem trivial, bizarre, scandalous, or subversive. Beyond that, they have nothing substantive in common. Scale, not content, is the determining criterion. *Factsheet Five* will review just about anything, if it's small.

FF's fixation on (microscopic) scale—and, by extension, particularity—mirrors a crucial dimension of postwar economic and political restructuring in the United States, with major parallels in (and implications for) contemporary social movements: the growth of a culture and politics that valorizes the small. In recent years, as voter interest and turnout has steadily declined and "infotainment" has usurped the place of hard news, it has become commonplace to assert that American public life has weakened at the center. Political debate has become soulless and shallow in this account, and the so-called "public sphere" of rational and informed discussion on broad social and cultural matters has all but ceased to exist. Some blame television, some blame the retreat of intellectual life into the academy, some blame the American education system; all agree that the center no longer holds.

Jürgen Habermas's famous account of the decline of the public sphere, one of the most thoughtful of the genre, is a narrative of the progressive weakening of public life over the course of the nineteenth and twentieth centuries: the intertwining of public debate and private commerce through the rise of advertising and publishing for profit; the blurring of boundaries between public and private with the advent of the welfare state; the breakdown of the elite political realm with the spread of the franchise and mass democracy. But in the nearly thirty years since Habermas first published *The Structural Transformation of the Public Sphere,* another set of structural transformations have suggested a new plot twist in the familiar decline-and-fall storyline: the postwar proliferation of what might be called micro–public spheres, each with its own distinctive discourses, debates, and institutions.

There are, today, tiny-to-middling public spheres for hobbyists and enthusiasts of all kinds, for believers in this or that creed or this or that cause—small networks of public interaction marked by a level of vibrancy and engagement almost wholly lacking in the capital-p Public Sphere. It is not so much the *existence* of these microspheres that is new as their place within U.S. society, the fact that they have come to serve as the major contexts for public life, replacing rather than merely supplementing a larger, more unitary kind of public interaction.

Postmodern is the adjective that comes most quickly to mind as a way of describing this decentered and fragmented condition. But postmodernism is usually taken as a strictly cultural phenomenon, and this transformation of public life very significantly mirrors a large-scale social decentering, spurred on by the collapse of the traditional nuclear family and fostered by changes in the production and marketing strategies of multinational capital. Some of the most insightful analysts of these shifts have used a different terminology to describe the new economic and cultural configuration: "post-Fordism."

The relevant Ford is Henry Ford, who in the 1920s and 1930s laid the groundwork for mass consumer capitalism through a cluster of key innovations. The assembly line, and greater division of labor that accompanied its introduction, made it possible to produce large quantities of standardized goods at low cost. The relatively high wages Ford paid his top assembly-line employees—five dollars for an eight-hour day in 1914—encouraged mass consumption by giving the average worker disposable income with which to purchase the new goods. A more conciliatory approach to labor gave job stability to workers but also provided a more stable climate for business.

Fordism enabled the creation of a mass American culture both before and especially after World War II, in which consumer goods came to serve both as a mechanism for social homogenization and, by extension, as a kind of social glue. A sizable part of what made the postwar average American "average" were the things he or she bought and owned: a prefabricated suburban home, a Ford station wagon, Levi's jeans, Wonder Bread. Standardized production meant standardized consumption—sameness.

Fordist citizenship, too, was about homogeneity and consensus. The dominant postwar sense of being American was produced and reproduced with the same efficiency and predictability of Ford's automobile assembly lines. With a booming economy, a swaggering role in world politics, and the Communist enemy to define itself against, the United States—or at least its enfranchised white majority—had a strong, shared sense of identity. Indeed, as the General Motors–sponsored parades of the 1950s depicted in Michael Moore's film *Roger and Me* make clear, fostering such civic consciousness was a serious business, contributing to the very prosperity it celebrated.

In the wake of the economic downturn of the early 1970s, which convinced many businesspeople that the mass-production-and-consumption formula of Fordism no longer provided the conditions for steady economic growth, the major capitalist economies—U.S., English, French, and West German, frequently inspired by the Japanese—underwent a series of major restructurings. More specialized and smaller-scale batch production began to replace the mass production of identical goods. Where Ford had made its mark by producing large quantities of a handful of models, Toyota built its company strategy around consumer choice, producing fewer quantities of a larger number of cars and allowing buyers to customize their automobile by selecting from a long menu of optional add-ons. Where Levi's, until recently, produced huge quantities of only a handful of styles of jeans, Benetton developed an innovative "just-in-time" production process, using detailed sales information from its stores to determine production runs of different sizes, styles, and colors.

The emergence of post-Fordism led to the systematic targeting of more specialized groups of consumers (what industry consultants call market segmentation). Rather than simply producing and marketing products, companies increasingly invent and market specific "lifestyles"—one of several, depending on their size, ambitiousness, and strategy. Ralph Lauren, for example, branched out from clothes manufacturing to produce a vast range of paraphernalia for the actual and would-be leisured elite: linens, home accessories, and perfume. A new emphasis on "consumer choice" has led to a dizzying array of options: R. J. Reynolds now manufactures, for example, at least eight different kinds of Camel cigarettes—filterless, filtered, lights, ultralights, wides, light wides, 100s, and light 100s, all of course available in both soft pack and box.

Sometimes this new market segmentation—or "micromarketing," as it is sometimes also called—takes place on regional lines, for instance when General Motors produces more front-wheel-drive vehicles for shipment to northern states and more automobiles with car alarms for sale in New York City. It also takes place on lines of identity, as corporate planners with an eye on changing demography seek new markets: Revlon, Estée Lauder, and Maybelline have introduced lines of cosmetics for African-American consumers; Mattel recently began producing black Ken and Barbie dolls; Nordstrom and Target, among other big retailers, have been actively courting consumers with disabilities. The corporations behind this shift may themselves have dramatically expanded in size, but their continued profitability derives from simultaneously responding to and furthering the fracturing of American society on lines of affinity and identity.

Though it has not rescued U.S. capitalism from the twin problems of low growth rates and high trade imbalances, the shift to post-Fordism has successfully transformed many people's relationships to the goods that they buy: Product choices have come to be a major element in how people define their "individuality." Social identities in the postwar and especially post-sixties period have come to be formed in intimate relation to consumer goods, resulting in a mind-boggling array of communities and affinities defined in significant part by shared tastes in music, clothing, film, fiction, sports, and the like.

In the political realm, there is a remarkable parallel between this new importance of "taste cultures" and market segments in U.S. society and the move, since the 1960s, from a common counterculture to a plurality of radical subcultures. If the center no longer holds, neither does "the left" as a broad, shared context for political life.

The counterculture of thirties or sixties radicals was of course far from truly unified; but those generations had, at least (especially in the sixties) an aspiration toward building a broad, shared oppositional world. The counterculture of the 1960s had something of a messianic quality: It wanted not just to oppose but to include. Timothy Leary's famous incantation, "Tune In, Turn On, Drop Out," became an invitation not just to try LSD but to join those who were working to remake their lives in what seemed like revolutionary ways. Joining meant stepping over to the other side, leaving the culture of the "Establishment" to join a burgeoning nation of ragtags loosely united in opposition. Hippies, Yippies, anarchists, pacifists, and SDSers might sometimes seem like they were each other's worst enemies, but a common counterculture bound them together. A chain of association linked long hair, Bob Dylan's music, pot, communal living, and opposition to the war: Each seemed somehow inevitably to lead to the others.

For a while, anyway. The unity of the sixties counterculture began to break down in the last years of the decade. The separatist leanings of Black Power and women's liberation made for major fissures: black culture and the women's culture-in-the-making competed with the broad counterculture for oppositional allegiance. Proponents of the new identity politics actively rejected the counterculture, viewing radical counterhegemony as little more than a form of counter-homogeneity: "Goodbye, goodbye forever, counterfeit Left, counter-left, male-dominated cracked-glass-mirror reflection of the Amerikan nightmare. Women are the real Left," radical feminist Robin Morgan declared in a 1970 essay. They also saw themselves as creating new alternative cultures: "The Seven-fold path of Blackness is to Think Black, Talk Black, Act Black, Create Black, Buy Black, Vote Black, and Live Black," the cultural nationalist Maulana Ron Karenga wrote in 1967. In contrast to the welcoming posture of much of the counterculture, these new radicals set limits on who could belong in their oppositional worlds.

Each of the new identity-based movements of the late 1960s and early 1970s created its own oppositional world as an alternative to both the political mainstream and the counterculture. In the wake of the 1969 Stonewall rebellion, in which homosexuals physically fought back against a police raid on a Greenwich Village gay bar, gay liberationists founded newspapers, started activist organizations, began the annual Gay Pride Parade, and created gay community centers. Radical feminists, socialist feminists, lesbian feminists, black feminists, and Chicana feminists each took similar steps. Angered at the pretension of those who headed the institutions of the left—almost invariably white men—to speak for all, identity-based radicals usually opted for creating their own institutions rather than fighting for inclusion in the existing ones.

As a result, radical politics today consists of a congeries of subcultures: multiple environmentalist subcultures, multiple feminist subcultures, multiple Latino and African American subcultures, multiple gay and lesbian subcultures, and so forth. One can no longer speak of a common culture of "the left" or anything like an inclusive and all-encompassing oppositional world.

The language of contemporary radicalism reflects this shift. Though the linear metaphor of left and right for describing political positioning was always a clunky superimposition on complex political realities, in recent years the political categories of left and right have become even less apt as tags for the kinds of political movements and visions found both here and throughout the world. The notion of dividing political positions into "left" and "right" dates from the French Revolution, when delegates to the Estates-General of 1789 seated themselves according to their stances toward the monarchy. It is a simple and elegant model—Marat to the left of Danton, Robespierre to the left of Marat—a useful shorthand for categorizing political phenomena.

Instead of one or two dimensions of political positions, however, there now seem to be an unspecifiable number, or minimally, a sharpened awareness of the multitude of autonomous dimensions of political belief. Where one stands with respect to gender politics may have little to do, after all, with where one stands on racial politics; there are no necessary links between one's views on the economy and one's beliefs about sexual orientation. There are quite a few gay Republicans, for example, and plenty of Marxists who are thoroughly homophobic. Black nationalists can be sexist, and white feminists can be racist. Unexpected political configurations speak to the complexity of the political movement: radical feminist anti-pornography activists working in tandem with Christian fundamentalists; unionized workers in the logging industry facing off against environmentalists.

If the floor of the French Estates-General provided the basis for the spatial metaphor of left and right, the analogue for post-sixties politics would have to be some as yet unbuilt skyscraper, impossibly tall, with an infinity of twisting stairways and coiled elevator shafts potentially linking all spaces in the building with one another.

Radical activists of various sorts have tried to come up with new political metaphors more appropriate to the contemporary moment, most famously the image of the rainbow and the Green slogan, "Not left or right but out in front." But the most common form taken by new attempts at political synthesis is a rhetorical one that bespeaks the very fragmentation it attempts to counter: the list. Sometimes the list brings together forms of opposition, like antiracism, antisexism, anti-imperialism, and so on. Other times the list cites forms of oppression: racism, sexism, homophobia, classism, ableism, ageism, and so forth. The lists are often dizzying in their length, in an attempt to be inclusive: addition has replaced ideology.

The example of *Factsheet Five* also points to the other side of this fracturing, the side that is less about the divisions of identity and belief and more about a predilection for diminutive (activists usually say "manageable" or "human") scale. E. F. Schumacher declared in 1973 that small is beautiful, and radicals have for twenty years been taking that message more and more to heart as a prescription for how to go about political organizing. Most post-sixties activists opt for decentralized local campaigns rather than coordinated national ones; when groups do cooperate nationally, as the Green Committees of Correspondence have done, the networks are generally loose and relatively unstructured.

A big part of the vibrancy of contemporary radicalisms comes from their multiplicity and decentering. But it is striking and unsettling to contemplate how much the subcultural politics of particularity unwittingly echoes the structures of the post-Fordist economy. Multiplicity, choice, reshaping one's self, refining one's sense of identity—these days, these are the values of the marketplace as well as those of the opposition. Smallness has become a matter of both principle and profit in late-capitalist America: principle for the radical periphery, profit for the capitalist core. And the parallel makes it all the easier for the latter to capitalize on the former, often undermining opposition in the process. When the manufacturer of Agent Orange can cloak itself in a fuzzy green glow, and a company that purveys overpriced sweaters can position itself at the forefront of multiculturalism, a troubling symbiosis is at play.

"Think Globally, Act Locally" has become a mantra of sorts for post-sixties radical politics. Has this focus on the local and the small been a coy admission of the radical inability to *act* globally? As the scale of social problems—and of the institutions of power that resist attempts to address them—expands, the scale of radical politics has seemed to contract. The personal is political. An insistent localism. A retreat from questions of broad social and economic reform. Gestures instead of strategies. Short-lived campaigns rather than sustained institution-building.

It is too simple to label the post-sixties shift from counterculture to subculture, or from mass organizations to local campaigns, as a political retreat. The sixties counterculture, after all, was all too often racist, sexist, homophobic, and, well, *suffocating* in its cheery redemptiveness. And the big national organizations of former lefts—or international organizations, in the obvious case of the Communist Party—too often had thoroughly undemocratic and top-down organizing styles.

□ □ □

A politics of small change can function quite successfully as an end run around the depressingly obvious fact of radicals' marginalization. Can't beat capitalism? Carve out little alternative communities of principle within it. Can't credibly challenge the state? Set your sights lower and focus on remaking your daily life. Can't build long-term strategies? Opt for dramatic gestures instead. Can't come up with a compelling successor to the waning ideologies of liberalism and socialism? List your convictions, and leave it at that.

That's what we've got, and if we're to have something else, some politics with greater scope, exhortation isn't going to do the trick. It is not for lack of will that radical politics has become a politics of small change. The reasons are to be found by looking outside the micropublic spheres of radical political life, for every form of radicalism stands in closer relation to the conditions of its emergence than its adherents generally care to admit.

CHAPTER 10

Gay and Lesbian Experiences and Sensibilities in the Antiwar Movement

Mindy Spatt

□   □   □   □   □   □   □   □   □   □   □   □

I am a member of DAGGER, Dykes and Gay Guys Emergency Response. We first started meeting in San Francisco in September 1990 to plan a lesbian and gay response to the escalating U.S. intervention in the Persian Gulf.

We were very successful both organizing in our own community and working in coalition with other groups to plan a city-wide response when the United States invaded Iraq in January 1991. Our participation in antiwar efforts was rarely noted in the local media, except for the gay and lesbian press. Gay and lesbian publications across the nation reported that as individuals and as a community, lesbians and gay men were active and vocal in opposing the war. The failure of the mainstream media to cover us was a reflection both of the invisibility of lesbians and gay men in the media and of the extremely limited way the press covered the antiwar movement.

In the context of antiwar coverage that was cursory at best, San Francisco received both national and international media attention. Reporters focused on what they referred to as "violent" acts like police cars being burned or windows being broken. They didn't ask who the thousands of people in the streets of San Francisco were or what ideas, opinions, or feelings motivated a week of almost nonstop protests. There is more analysis of most situation comedies on TV than there was of the antiwar movement. It was as if the press bought the government line that only a few "radicals" opposed the war instead of a large and varied crowd desperately trying to make their voices heard.

Lesbian and gay participation in San Francisco political life is nothing new. One reason we were able to mobilize large numbers of people to demonstrate against the war is our long history of political involvement there. The size of our community and its financial clout have helped to create considerable political influence.

The gay community's electoral clout in San Francisco solidified in November 1990 when two lesbians joined gay supervisor Harry Britt on the city's

Board of Supervisors, making three out of eight supervisors openly gay. A gay man was also elected to the city's Board of Education, and domestic partnership legislation was passed. Candidates for city and state offices fight for the endorsements of San Francisco's powerful gay political clubs.

The community can be as vocal about its displeasure as about its choices. In 1979 several nights of rioting followed the lenient sentence given to Dan White after he was convicted of murdering San Francisco's first openly gay supervisor, Harvey Milk, and Mayor George Moscone; lesbians and gay men were prominent in the large protests against the U.S. military action in Honduras in 1988. Some of the Honduras response was organized by Lesbians and Gays Against Intervention (LAGAI), a group that formed out of a San Francisco–based campaign to resist U.S. military action in El Salvador in 1983. LAGAI has been an active anti-intervention presence in the community since that time, and it was responsible for calling together DAGGER shortly after U.S. troops were sent to the Middle East.

Other political actions coming out of the community range from the largest Gay Freedom Day parade in the world to special-interest groups such as SHOP, the Suburban Homosexual Outreach Project, which works to educate people in shopping malls about gay and lesbian life. Gays and lesbians are also active in the business community, unions, and other influential groups in the city.

The Castro area of San Francisco is sometimes referred to as the "gay ghetto," but in the context of political organizing, ghettoization has some advantages. One is that we have our own press. Two privately owned and fairly conservative weekly newspapers provided some means for the community to share information about the war's impact in our community and war-related events and protests. Having a distinct geographical neighborhood also facilitates the dissemination of information through tabling, postering, and leafleting. By leafleting Muni stops in the Castro at rush hour, we were able to reach hundreds of people, many of whom likely passed on the information to other people they spoke with throughout the day.

Those are some of the factors that contribute to the relatively high level of political organization in the gay community. The reasons why a large percentage of our community actively opposed the war can be traced to the origins of the gay liberation movement, a social activist campaign for gay rights that was part of the radical movements of the 1960s.

According to activist and author Kate Raphael, "Open lesbian/gay anti-war and anti-imperialist organizing goes back to the days immediately following Stonewall. The Gay Liberation Front, which linked itself very consciously with the Vietnamese National Liberation Front, was one of the largest organizations to spring up in the aftermath of Stonewall. There were other groups, such as the Gay Revolutionary Party, a group of mostly gay men of color, and WITCH (Women's International Terrorist Conspiracy from Hell). Most lesbian/gay liberation groups at that time had an anti-war focus."[1]

From those beginnings, though, lesbians and gay men went in divergent political directions. Gay men focused on building communities that were comfortable for them and on openly expressing their sexual identity. Gay bars and bathhouses proliferated, and political organizing focused on being "out" and unashamed about homosexuality. There was less focus on international politics than there had been in the early days of the Gay Liberation Front. Lesbians were increasingly active in anti-intervention politics in the seventies, although their participation was often unacknowledged.

During the late 1970s and early 1980s, I was involved in antiracist, anti-apartheid, Central America, and prisoner-support work in Portland, Oregon, and in San Francisco. Lesbians were in the majority in all the groups I worked in, none of which publicly presented itself as a lesbian group. The conflict between the commonality we felt with other liberation struggles and the homophobia we feared from people we considered our allies was very troubling to many women.

As lesbians developed sensitivity and respect for other cultures we were also developing our own culture and politics. "Women's music," often a euphemism for lesbian music, flourished nationally, along with newspapers, magazines, and art. Despite some conflicts with the straight feminist movement, the lesbian movement retained a feminist political perspective while creating somewhat independent communities in both rural and urban areas.

The 1980s saw lesbians trying to integrate their lesbianism with anti-intervention politics in a more open way. In San Francisco, that tendency gave rise to groups such as LISPP, Lesbians in Solidarity with the People of Palestine, which had originally been a group of lesbian women calling themselves Jewish Women for a Secular Middle East. Such organizations strengthened the theoretical, political, and personal ties between lesbians and other oppressed outsider groups.

At the same time, AIDS was bringing gay men back into radical activism all over the United States. During the eighties ACT UP and other AIDS activist groups began working to pressure the media, government, health establishment, and drug companies to respond to the growing epidemic. Initially the majority of people in these groups were young white gay men. They became very skillful at organizing high-profile demonstrations and civil disobedience actions. Combining media savvy and creativity, they succeeded in attracting a great deal of publicity and in forcing some changes. However, while their tactics were radical, they never developed a coherent political agenda and failed to form coalitions with other groups. As women and people of color became increasingly concerned about AIDS, many were drawn to groups like ACT UP, especially in large cities like Los Angeles and New York. But with their involvements concerns about racism, sexism, and classism came to be expressed with increased frequency. Conflict between those who wanted a narrow focus and those who felt AIDS or gay rights could not be addressed without drawing in other concerns caused several gay activist groups either to split or cease operations. But activist tactics and the ability to attract publicity have become part of the political culture in many cities among both gays and straights.

The San Francisco AIDS activist group SANOE (Stop Aids Now or Else) claims to have been the first group in the United States to blockade a bridge; they stopped traffic on the Golden Gate to dramatize the need for immediate action to stop AIDS. The group was widely criticized for the action and the resulting inconvenience to commuters. A couple of years later, antiwar groups in the Bay Area and throughout the United States blockaded bridges and stopped traffic to express their anger at the United States' military action in Iraq, but the roots of the action in gay and lesbian activism were never acknowledged.

One of the most positive things about lesbian and gay participation in the antiwar movement was the combination of all the resources, skills, and traditions I just described. The actions and other activities we planned reflected the broad range of concerns that are part of the gay community. For example, an antiwar demonstration organized by DAGGER marched through the Parc 55 Hotel in downtown San Francisco, which had been charged with over seventy unfair labor practices by the National Labor Relations Board in the year preceding our demonstration. As our leaflet pointed out, employees who were fighting for the right to unionize at the Parc included labor activists, people of color, and gay and lesbian people. Persons staying at the Parc did so despite a labor-organized boycott of the hotel. The theme of the demonstration, which was unfortunately cut short by the police, was "Bring the War to the Rich."

For me personally, as a Jewish woman who strongly supports Palestinian independence, it was very important to find a group within my own community that would share my view that the Gulf War and Palestinian self-determination were inseparable. The other members of DAGGER, several of whom are Jewish, shared my position, and we incorporated that position into our antiwar actions.

We joined with an Arab gay men's group to cosponsor a forum on the Middle East for the gay community. The event, which was extremely well attended, featured mostly Arab speakers who provided valuable historical and cultural background absent from mainstream media coverage of the Gulf War. We looked at the problems of the region as a whole and the role lesbians and gay men could play in making changes.

We also worked in coalition with other groups, most notably the San Francisco Pledge of Resistance, a group that organized civil disobedience in response to threats of U.S. intervention in El Salvador. Both ACT UP/San Francisco and DAGGER cosponsored blockades of the federal building with the pledge, and gay concerns were consistently visible. Queer Peace, a focus group of Queer Nation, organized a kiss-in, and ACT UP "built a huge gas pump showing the number of U.S. AIDS deaths (10,000 since the troops were sent to Kuwait in August) and the billions of dollars spent on the war."[2]

Despite our positive experiences with the pledge, many lesbians and gay men felt invisible during antiwar activities. Several marches organized by straight groups used the Castro as a rallying point but failed to include gay or lesbian speakers in their agendas. Many chants originated by ACT UP were modified to suit antiwar protests, but when gay people chanted gay chants we often did so alone. Straight people seemed to fear the implication of joining us in chants such as "Fags suck dick, Dykes lick labia, U.S. out of Saudi Arabia!"

Some of us have the feeling that the straight left picks and chooses which parts of queerness they can use and deal with and which parts they cannot. While we show up regularly to assist with organizing around primarily straight issues such as abortion, it is rare to see straight people at gay and lesbian protests and almost unheard of to see straight people forming contingents in gay and lesbian–organized demonstrations or marches.

As I said earlier, gay people, and especially lesbians, have had a long history of unacknowledged participation in other people's struggles. I think most of us believe that through this type of activity we can build cooperation and understanding between ourselves and other oppressed people who are our natural allies. The only chance that gay people, people of color, workers, and poor people have of seeing the federal government be more concerned with their needs for health care, jobs, and other services is to band together. In the face of the AIDS crisis, homelessness, unemployment, and cutbacks in education and health care, the federal government's ability to find billions of dollars to spend on killing innocent Iraqis was a sad measure of how far we have yet to go in building a society more responsive to our needs.

How can members of the university community become more involved in community-based political activism? It is, of course, for them to decide. I can only make suggestions based on my perspective from the outside. I think it is important to note that students in the Bay Area, especially from City College, were an organized and vocal force in the antiwar movement. We hope this signals a reawakening of campus activism. We also hope to see increased cooperation between students, faculty, and those of us outside of the academic community. Most of us in DAGGER, and probably most political activists, have full time jobs that do not leave us a lot of time for political activity. Writing leaflets and providing educational materials to our community can be a daunting task when only weekends and evenings are available for research and writing. People in the university have quick and easy access to a great deal of information. It would be wonderful to see that information made available to the public at large and to activist groups. For example, volunteers spending even an hour or two at the library could respond to specific requests for information. Information packets could be assembled by students and teachers in various disciplines. Media resources like film and video labs could be made available to community groups. Support for the war with Iraq was built up with an enormous propaganda campaign against Saddam Hussein. This kind of campaign is difficult to counter without access to equipment and materials.

In a more general sense, the racism and homophobia that pervade all the institutions in this country likewise pervade college campuses. As both individuals and as members of organized activist groups, we all have a role to play in breaking them down. I would hope that students and teachers alike would reject educational materials that are xenophobic or prejudiced. I would also hope they would demand diversity among faculty and staff. The war, the media's complicity in it, and the anti-Arab racism it spawned serve as sobering reminders of how much work remains to be done by progressives in this country.

NOTES

1. Kate Raphael, "Queers Come Out against the War," *San Francisco Sentinel* 19, no. 3 (January 17, 1991): 6.
2. Ibid.

CHAPTER 11

Reweaving the New World Order: An Ecofeminist Analysis

Ilene Rose Feinman

□   □   □   □   □   □   □   □   □   □   □   □

Of the 250,000 troops that the United States deployed during the Persian Gulf war, 33,000 were women.[1] The presence of these women in a military operation became a national obsession, sometimes extending to panic. Phyllis Schlafley of the Eagle Forum asked, "Have we lost our masculinity?"

Operation "Desert Shield" became "Desert Storm" with U.S. air attacks against Iraq on January 16, 1991, and congressional debate over the Defense Appropriation Bill for 1992 heated up. Proposals were introduced both to exempt from active duty the parents of young children and to permit women's increased participation in combat. The media quickly dubbed the Gulf conflict the "mom's war" and proliferated images of women soldiers on the nightly news, on the cover of *Time,* and in the daily press. Images of women marching, cleaning their guns, and loading missiles and supplies for the male fighters circulated widely. Male U.S. soldiers, appropriating this theme from an advertisement for Wranglers, popularized a most unusual pin-up. Jaqueline Phillips Guibord, a married Mormon who busts narcotics and prostitution rings in her work as an undercover cop, was posed, fully clothed, leaning against the hood of her police car in a Wrangler jean jacket, rifle by her side.

How are we to think about the jarring and largely unanticipated transgressions of gender boundaries in the images of women in this war? Women soldiers in and near battle zones are a direct challenge to essentialized images of women. How will this shift U.S. social perspectives and expectations? And how should feminist antimilitarism shift its focus in response?

A Socialist Ecofeminist Perspective

My concerns in this chapter revolve around the impact of women's changing roles in the military of the "new world order." I am particularly concerned about examining women's role in the military through the activist-based theories of feminist antimilitarism, including the evolving category of ecofeminism.

Feminist forms of antimilitarism have either fully or ironically endorsed the notion of women as peacekeepers. Clearly, the presence of women in the military sets this assumption on edge. As feminist antimilitarists we need to develop more nuanced accounts of women's roles in the world while maintaining the commitment against militarism. As struggles for equal rights interface with the Army's "be all that you can be" rhetoric directed at women recruits, we need to develop alternative visions. Moreover, feminist antimilitarism is now challenged to examine the roots of its privileged refusal of military service, thus raising the question of feminism in relation to race and class: Who does feminist antimilitarism speak for? And why are large numbers of women joining the military now?

There is, of course, nothing naturally female about loathing war. While public opinion polls conducted just before the Gulf War revealed that many more men than women supported war as a solution to Saddam Hussein's invasion of Kuwait, not surprisingly, the gap closed significantly once the war began, with over half of the women previously opposed now supporting the war effort. Nor should there be anything too surprising about women seeking economic success through military service, which has become one of the few avenues of equal opportunity in the United States.

A long history of feminist analyses inside the antinuclear, environmental, lesbian, gay, bisexual, and anti-intervention movements enabled an immediate reading of the Gulf War through gendered assessments of militarism. Opponents of the war stressed its unequal ramifications on people of different classes, races, and genders and pointed to the threats it posed to regional and planetary ecosystems. These analyses were often contradictory and invoked different systems of causality, although many of the slogans of the antiwar marches were explicit criticisms of the combined effects of patriarchy and capitalism. In fact, there have long been tensions among feminist antimilitarists about the extent to which women's role as peacemaker is biologically based and the extent to which it is a matter of socialization. From a socialist ecofeminist perspective, "woman" is a category that is socially constructed, yet at the same time pervasive and deliberately "naturalized"—and deeply reinscribed by the Gulf War.

I see potential in socialist ecofeminism as a social, political, spiritual, and personal practice of sustainability. With it, I am theorizing in terms of these practices on the basis of a feminist, nonviolent, nonracist, economically just, and ecologically sustainable set of criteria.[2] Socialist ecofeminism includes a critique of (and direct action against) capitalist, patriarchal, and hierarchical social relations. According to this model (or set of thinkers), nonhuman nature, children, women of all races and ethnicities, and men of color are "others" to the economically privileged white men who by and large hold world power. This perspective embodies some of the aforementioned tensions around women's prescribed roles yet consistently maintains the claim that patriarchal social relations and capitalist economic relations are central to the problems facing the planet.

Demonstrations of ecofeminism have included performance art, anthologies and articles, and direct action at military sites. Ecofeminists have woven webs across doorways and into fences; created animal images in the form of huge batik butterflies; built symbolic tunnels/birth canals under fences; carried out rituals of levitation, purification, and reclamation; and planted food and flower seeds on government property. Webs recur as a central metaphor in ecofeminist practice. The web of interconnected yet distinct life is simultaneously the web of resistance invoked against militarism and the capitalist exploitation and degradation of the planet. It also signifies a mirroring and mocking of the conditions of late capitalism and postmodernity, insisting on a widely differentiated yet necessarily interconnected ecology of social, political, and economic organization.

Socialist ecofeminism also puts a high value on collective work. This essay is an example. My motivation for writing it depended on a shared perception of the need to shift antimilitarist language to account for the rise in the numbers of women soldiers and the uses to which their images were being put. I have literally discussed, written, taught, and edited this essay through my organizing work against the war, much of which has been, pleasurably, collective work: co-teaching nonviolence preparations; helping to organize rallies and teach-ins; putting together workshops on women and war; transforming curricula into discussions on gender and war, gender and militarism, and the heretofore gendered imperatives of martial citizenship.

Martial Service and (Male) Citizenship

Martial duty in the United States has historically been a constitutive part of the bargain for male citizenship. Centerpiece of a host of rights and responsibilities, martial service has been seen as the ultimate form of patriotism and the key to male prestige and honor.[3] The object of martial duty has been the protection of the interests of the state and of its women and children during times of invasion. Women and children, traditionally the symbol of the homeland being protected by the warrior men, are seen as vulnerable and as critical to the literal reproduction of the nation state. Yet women have provided the critical social infrastructure for military bases and for the sustenance of soldiers in the military theater.[4]

The war in the Persian Gulf began to unravel these gendered notions: over 10 percent of the recruits there were women. Since the war, the number of women serving in the U.S. military has continued to increase.[5] The media and the polity have been at a loss to imagine how these women fit traditional notions of martial citizenship.

Women's roles are not fixed or stable and are particularly subject to change during wars and national emergencies. The unintended gender bending of these periods carries both short-term and long-term ramifications. During World War II, for example, "Rosie the Riveter" took on the country's industrial work and supplied weaponry to the troops. The brevity of the Persian Gulf War *(for the United States)* and the already enormous U.S. weapons stockpiles meant that women were not needed for "men's work" in the factories, although they did replace some temporary male workers in the service industries. Because U.S. casualties were so low, it was also unnecessary to encourage women to bear children in order to replenish the ranks, as has often been done in past wars. (In fact, women soldiers were fighting for access to abortion in base hospitals.) After World War II, the women who had been running the factories were coaxed back into the home to make dinners and babies. No such reorganization of women's roles in the U.S. economy was necessary after the brief Gulf War, yet women's visibility as soldiers sent shock waves through mainstream notions of women's place in the world order.

In the wars of the late twentieth century, the most noticeable changes in women's wartime roles have been close to the battlefront. Traditionally, women have played the all but invisible roles of support to the military as diplomatic wives, base wives, and prostitutes. Although women continue to be overrepresented in food service, nursing, and maintenance work, they have begun to work on the edges of battle. In the Gulf War, they flew the bombers but didn't sit in the gunner seats, drove the tanks but didn't shoot at targets, and so on. In numbers and position, the Gulf War moved U.S. women closer to the front lines, although not to the monetary "rewards" of combat duty.[6]

One of the most curious rhetorical moves by the press, and arguably by the White House, was to dub the Gulf War the "mom's war," constructing every woman soldier as a mother or potential mother. This slogan helped to domesticate the war as a way to cope both with women's presence and with domestic distaste for the conflict. It simultaneously distanced, "othered," and screened the situation, effects, and conditions of the war. It provoked previously unimaginable questions. How can women be fighting to protect our women and children? What horrors await the female POW?[7] How quaint and strange to see on the evening news women soldiers' husbands at home struggling with the double burden of wage and family work. How would the forces now incorporate the lesbians, gays, and bisexuals who, if they dared to be open or were forcibly outed, were swiftly discharged upon their return? As "victorious" U.S. soldiers returned to what press accounts called their "wives, children, and families," where were the women and men who didn't have them, or at least not the sort implied?

Although women soldiers have responded with enthusiasm to the Army's call to "be all that you can be," instead of meteoric ascents through the ranks, they came home to congressional battles over a new "mommy track" that would block women from combat service and allow special tracking for career women soldiers. Pending legislation was designed to "protect" women, as potentially occupied wombs, from actual battlefield deployment. Both women and men returned home to a domestic crisis that had been obscured by the war, one that has had enormous impact on the government's ability to fulfill its promise to help returning soldiers "be all that they can be." In contrast to the post–World War II prosperity that lasted roughly to the early 1970s, soldiers returning from the Gulf War faced cutbacks in social welfare, school funding, and employment opportunities. In short, the economic crises in the United States, which temporarily receded from view because of the war, reemerged very quickly with concurrent cutbacks and fights over social program funding. And as is always the case, these crises will be borne on the backs of the underprivileged men and women so notably overrepresented among the war's troops.

Wars and Wimps

From an ecofeminist perspective, the Gulf War was in part the result of a wimp crisis. Beginning with President George Bush's worried sense of self, its deeper manifestations were the decline of the American empire and the United States' economic crisis, which would be exacerbated by loss of control over Middle East oil. As corporations leave the United States for free trade zones and cheap labor, as we find our economy located in the web of international capital, we can no longer imagine the United States as a discrete political and economic entity.[8] Little remains that is "made in the USA" except for war technologies, and this affects the national identity. The inability to produce domestic goods for sustainability has generated the need for quick, reliable performance, for infallible success that can pull together a wavering public. We have been tied up in the yellow ribbon of military prowess.

While the end of the Cold War had signaled the waning of the "old world order," the Gulf War asserted the ongoing right and ability of the United States to lead the world in military action. The new world order was thus apparently birthed by the Gulf War, gleefully courted and conceived with George Bush as the father. The mother-of-all-battles metaphor originated in Saddam Hussein's proclamation at the start of the war and became a sound bite that was used to characterize everything from sporting events to Senate races. The Gulf War, accepted as the mother of the new world order, was also seen as the mother of a reborn Star Wars: At the end of the first week of the war, the Pentagon announced its first successful test of the Strategic Defense Initiative program, and President Bush pressed for increased SDI funding.

These rebirths cured the United States' warriors of the Vietnam syndrome and inscribed new feelings of success and power.

Who was this mother, and why was she being invoked? The metaphor domesticated the associated notions of mother and nature, transforming both from things dark and wild into something techno-strategically manageable. What was birthed here was an American-made monster capable of regenerating itself through techno-military replication, through cloning. The once-fallible war hero became at once the patriot (a deeply gendered role in the tradition of martial citizenry) and the mother, reproducing his own technologies. This copulatory merging enabled the mother to be divested of "she-ness" and of a "natural" care-taking role and to be transformed into a catalyst for massive violence staged as the (re)production of the new world order. Simultaneously, we were busy in the United States revisioning our images of soldiers, with men home as mothers and mothers cleaning guns and loading weapons in Saudi Arabia.

The actual visual and visceral impact of the Gulf War was kept off-screen for American viewers. The desert theater and the women and men of the countries we were fighting for and against remained mysterious. To our TV-trained eyes, it was a barren landscape noted for its hostility to the Bradley Fighting Vehicles, its massive oil fires attributed only to Saddam Hussein, and for its one trespassing inhabitant, an Iraqi soldier characterized in a U.S. soldier's account as a desert ground squirrel who came popping out of the ground to surrender after Desert Storm. The new world order, orchestrated from above by its father, George Bush, disconnected the Iraqi soldier from his national identity, turning him into a pitiful bastard child to whom U.S. soldiers demonstrated kindness by rescuing him from his foxhole.

□ □ □

Reweaving a new world order in socialist ecofeminist terms requires a vision. We need to understand the ways that the national and international fabrics are unraveling, to grasp the shifting discourses, and to rewrite them in ways that appeal to the interconnectedness of lives without subsuming them to one core identity or causality. We need to develop careful analyses that touch real lives. Our strategies need to be locally situated in our own bodies of knowledge and our own communities, with an eye to their international ramifications. We have to practice our theories and theorize our practice so that we know what we mean, and develop ourselves in terms of our communities and our coalitions in ways that practice sustainability. Identity politics are not something to do while waiting for the real movement to start. They are part of a total refiguring of our relationships to each other and to the planet. They are an integral strand in the web of resistance to domination.

NOTES

Acknowledgments: This chapter represents the beginning of what has evolved into an in-depth analysis of the relationship of U.S. women to soldiering in the new world order and of appropriate strategies for feminist antimilitarist response. I owe much to conversations in the Santa Cruz Nonviolence Preparers Collective, in the short-lived affinity group Post Mod Squad, and in Graduate Students against the War; and with Marcy Darnovsky, Giovanna Di Chiro, Barbara Epstein, Deena Hurwitz, Nöel Sturgeon, Marita Sturken, Kenny Welcher; and to the inevitable and insistent reshaping of my thinking that comes through the work of translating this odd world for my eight-year-old son, Ben.

1. Carolyn Becraft, *Women in the Armed Services: The War in the Persian Gulf* (Washington, D.C.: Women's Research and Education Institute, 1991).
2. For key examples of this tendency in ecofeminism, see Adrienne Harris and Ynestra King, eds., *Rocking the Ship of State* (Boulder, Colo.: Westview Press, 1989). This anthology offers articles examining the relationships between women of all colors and the militarist state.
3. For a careful history of the causal links between soldiering and citizenship, see Linda Kerber, "May All Our Citizens Be Soldiers and All Our Soldiers Citizens: The Ambiguities of Female Citizenship in the New Nation: in *Arms at Rest,* ed. Joan R. Challinor and Robert L. Beisner (New York: Greenwood Press, 1987).
4. For documentation of women's wartime support work see Micaela di Leonardo, "Morals, Mothers and Militarism," *Feminist Studies* 13 (Fall 1985); Cynthia Enloe, *Bananas, Beaches and Bases* (Berkeley: University of California Press, 1989); and Jean Bethke Elshtain, *Women and War* (New York: Basic Books, 1987).
5. As of November 1992 the Department of Defense reported 35,000 enlisted women in the U.S. armed forces.
6. As of August 1992, a number of bills dealing with women's work roles in the military were moving through Congress. One, which has passed the House Armed Services Committee, allows women to fly in combat; another, which President Bush vetoed, would have made abortion on demand available to military personnel and their dependents on bases.
7. During the summer of 1992, stories emerged about women soldiers being raped both as prisoners of war and by fellow male soldiers, providing fuel for the argument that women need to be protected from the battlefield. A story about a male soldier who claimed to have been raped was given very short shrift in the press and by Congress.
8. See Aihwa Ong, *Spirits of Resistance and Capitalist Discipline* (Albany: State University of New York Press, 1987); Karen Stallard, Barbara Ehrenreich, and Holly Sklar, *Poverty in the American Dream: Women and Children First* (Boston: South End Press, 1983); Maria Fernández-Kelly, *For We Are Sold, I and My People: Women and Industry in Mexico's Frontier* (Albany: State University of New York Press, 1983); Enloe, *Bananas, Beaches and Bases.*

CHAPTER 12

Race: Theory, Culture, and Politics in the United States Today

Howard Winant

□   □   □   □   □   □   □   □   □   □   □   □

The theme of race continues to occupy a central place in U.S. cultural, political, and economic life. But what does race *mean* in the United States today? How can a concept with no scientific significance, a concept that is understood in such varied and often irrational ways, retain such force in our societal life? Why is race such an important source of meaning, identity, (dis)advantage, power, and powerlessness? What are the consequences of racial identity for its bearers, and how does the racial culture—the system of racial meanings and identities—shape the U.S. political order?

The persistence of these questions has defied the predictions of most government officials, social critics, and movement leaders. Until quite recently, mainstream economists and Marxists, liberals and conservatives, ethnicity theorists and nationalists, all expected the dissolution of race in some greater entity: free market or class struggle, cultural pluralism or nation-state.

To examine such matters is to enter the thickets of racial theory. No task is more urgent today. The mere fact that these questions are at once so obvious and so obviously unanswered suggests the enormity and urgency of theoretical work on race. One must approach the effort modestly, for the problematic of race is in some ways as large as social theory itself.

My strategy here is to examine contemporary U.S. racial dynamics from the standpoint of racial formation theory, an approach developed specifically to address the shifting meanings and power relationships inherent in race today. I begin with some basic propositions about racial formation. Then I look at recent U.S. racial history, which, I suggest, is in transition from a pattern of dom-

This chapter reprinted in a similar form as that in "Where Culture Meets Structure: Race in the 1990s," chap. 3 of *Racial Conditions: Politics, Theory, Comparisons,* by Howard Winant (University of Minnesota Press, 1994), 22–36, by permission of the publisher. Copyright © 1994 by Howard Winant.

ination to one of hegemony. Next I discuss the range of contemporary racial projects, focusing on the contest for racial hegemony. Finally I assess the system of racial hegemony in the 1990s.

Racial Formation Theory

Racial formation theory was developed as a response to postwar understandings of race, both mainstream and radical, that practiced "reductionism." By this I mean the explanation of racial phenomena as manifestations of some other, supposedly more significant, social relationship. Examples of racial reductionism include treatments of racial dynamics as epiphenomena of class relationships, or as the result of "national oppression," or as variations on the ethnicity paradigm established in the early twentieth century, after successive waves of European immigration.

In contrast to these approaches, racial formation theory looks at race as a phenomenon whose meaning is contested throughout social life.[1] In this account race is a constituent of the individual psyche and of relationships among individuals as well as an irreducible component of collective identities and social structures.

Because race is not a "natural" attribute but a socially and historically constructed one, it becomes possible to analyze the processes by which racial meanings are attributed, and racial identities assigned, in a given society. These processes of "racial signification" are inherently discursive. They are variable, conflictual, and contested at every level of society from the intrapsychic to the supranational. Inevitably, many interpretations of race, many racial discourses, exist at any given time. The political character of the racial formation process stems from this: elites, popular movements, state agencies, cultural and religious organizations, and intellectuals of all types develop racial projects that interpret and reinterpret the meaning of race.

The theoretical concept of racial projects is a key element of racial formation theory. A racial project is simultaneously an interpretation, representation, or explanation of racial dynamics, and an effort to reorganize and redistribute resources along particular racial lines. Every project is therefore both a discursive and cultural initiative, an attempt at racial signification and identity formation, on the one hand, and a political initiative, an attempt at political mobilization and resource redistribution, on the other.

Interpreting the meaning of race is thus a multidimensional process in which competing projects intersect and clash. These projects are often explicitly, but always at least implicitly, political. Racial projects potentially draw on phenomena that are both "objective" or institutional and those that are "subjective" or experiential. That such social structural phenomena as movements and parties, state institutions and policies, or market processes should be the source of political initiatives regarding race is hardly controversial.

Racial formation theory, however, also finds the source of racial projects in less familiar social practices: in the manipulation and rearticulation of racial identities by their bearers, in the enunciation and transformation of racial "common sense," and in the various subversive, evasive, or parodic forms of racial opposition that closely resemble other forms of subordinated and postcolonial resistance.[2] In a later section of this chapter I offer a "map," in table form, of contemporary U.S. racial projects.

Recent U.S. Racial History: From Domination to Hegemony

From this theoretical vantage point, I propose now to examine, in what must necessarily be a fairly schematic account, the evolution of U.S. racial politics in the postwar period. To frame this account properly, let me present my key argument at the outset. The black movement upsurge of the 1950s and 1960s ended the epoch of racial domination and initiated the epoch of racial hegemony. It transformed the dynamics of racial politics away from outright coercion and toward democratic inclusion. Of course, the movement did not fully attain that goal. But it did initiate sweeping political and cultural changes: it created new organizations, new political norms, new collective identities, new modalities of expression and representation; it challenged past racial practices and stereotypes; and it ushered in a wave of democratizing social reform that ultimately extended well beyond the issue of race.

The Pre–Civil Rights Era

In the pre–civil rights era the U.S. racial order was maintained largely, though of course not exclusively, through domination. The most visible manifestations of this regime were all enforced by coercive means: segregation, racial exclusion, and physical violence culminating in extralegal terror. Periodic mob assaults on urban ghettos and barrios, deportations to Mexico in the Southwest, plunder and outright extermination of native peoples, anti-Asian pogroms, physical intimidation and murder by police, and of course the practice of lynching were all fairly characteristic of this epoch.[3] It was not until well into the twentieth century, and even then only in certain areas where racially defined minorities had been able to establish themselves in large numbers and to initiate negotiations between the white establishment and minority elites, that a measure of "protection," and even patronage and political influence, were sometimes available. But even these gains were highly limited and fragile.

The Political Effects of the Black Movement

The black movement upsurge changed all that. It permitted the entry of millions of racial minority group members into the political process—first among blacks, and later among Latinos, Asian Americans, and Native Americans. It initiated a trajectory of reform that exposed the limits of all previously existing political orientations—conservative, liberal, and radical. With very few exceptions, all these currents had colluded with the denial of fundamental political rights to members of racially defined minorities.

The aftermath of this prodigious movement upsurge was a racial order in which domination had been replaced by hegemony. Political mobilization along racial lines resulted in the enactment of reforms that dramatically restructured the racial order, reorganized state institutions, and initiated whole new realms of state activity. The achievement of the franchise, the establishment of limited but real avenues of economic and social mobility, the destruction of de jure segregation, the reform of immigration law, and the institution of a measure of state enforcement of civil rights were but a few of the movement's more dramatic accomplishments.

The Cultural Effects of the Black Movement

Furthermore, by transforming the meaning of race and the contours of racial politics, the racially based movements also transformed the meaning and contours of American culture. Indeed, they made identity, difference, the "personal," and language itself political issues in very new ways. They made mainstream society—that is, white people—take notice of "difference"; they created awareness not only of different racial identities but ultimately of the multiple differences inherent in U.S. culture and society. In short, the new movements "politicized the social," vastly expanding the terrain of politics and transfiguring U.S. culture.

Thus, where previously U.S. culture had been monolithic and stratified, and indeed racially segregated ("race records" on which such singers as Bessie Smith and Bukka White performed, and other segregated media), it now became far more polyvalent, far more complexly articulated. Without being able to argue the point fully, I think it fair to assert that since the mid-1950s—I am taking as a fairly arbitrary demarcating point the advent of rock 'n' roll—U.S. culture has adopted a far more pluralistic cast. With respect to race, this means that genres of music, art, and language retain their bases in particular communities while at the same time "crossing over" into the national culture with far greater regularity than was previously the case. Cultural differences coexist without requiring any overarching synthesis, yet partial syntheses take place continually.[4]

This does not mean that a "cultural revolution," along the lines proposed by Harold Cruse in the 1960s, has been or even could be achieved.[5] As in the political sphere, much of the increased presence of "darker" visions and "other" voices in the cultural sphere is the result of tokenism and co-optation, of pragmatic liberal practices advocating tolerance and diversity, rather than radical democratic practices celebrating difference. Even granting all this, the present-day proliferation of artistic and popular cultural forms with roots in racially defined minority communities is quite astonishing when seen from a historical and comparative vantage point; much has changed in a few short decades. And this too must be judged an accomplishment of the movement.

The Racial Reaction

The achievements and legacy of the black movement were hardly greeted with universal acclaim. Various currents on the right strongly objected to the politicization of the social and to the new-found assertiveness and proliferation of cultural difference.

The very successes of the movement, however, set limits on the reaction that followed it. Because such movement themes as equality, group identity, and difference could not simply be rolled back, it became necessary, from the late 1960s onward, to rearticulate these ideas in a conservative ideological framework of competition, individualism, and homogeneity. In other words, since the movement's introduction of new political themes could not be undone, opponents had to learn how to manage these political themes as well.

This is why today's political debates about racial inequality are dominated by charges of "reverse discrimination" and repudiation of "quotas," why demands for "community control" have reappeared in opposition to school desegregation, and why high government officials claim that we are moving toward a "color-blind society." Cultural debates are dominated by the right's rejection of difference and otherness (whether racial, gender-based, sexual, or any other kind). The right's strong defense of "traditional values," of individualism, and of mainstream culture, its discourse about family, nation, and our "proud heritage of freedom," betoken intense resistance to the very idea of a polyvalent racial culture. Many of the notes struck by the right in contemporary cultural debates over race are, shall we say, white notes. They reflect a deep-seated fear, perhaps unconscious and only occasionally expressed, of the racialized other who has plagued the European for so long.[6]

The "Decentering" of Racial Conflict

By the end of the 1960s the emancipatory effects of the black movement upsurge (and of its sequelae in other communities and constituencies) had been blunted by the racial reaction. Indeed the dominant racial theory since World War II—ethnicity theory—which had once allied itself with the minority movements, reappeared as one of their chief theoretical antagonists: neoconservatism. Along with a reconstituted far right, the new right and neoconservative currents would emerge by the 1980s as related but distinct right-wing racial projects.

Neoconservatism was largely a movement of intellectuals who sought to intervene in policy debates over race. Its chief concern was the threat to political and cultural traditions it discerned in racial minority demands for group rights or "equality of result." The new right, heir apparent of backlash politics and the Wallace campaigns, was a far more grassroots movement, linked to the religious conservatism fostered by some sectors of Catholicism and Protestant televangelism; it has been a key component of every Republican presidential victory from 1968 to 1988. The far right was a more motley crew consisting of the traditional assortment of bigots and race baiters but also newly possessed of a modernized wing. The latter emerged in the mid-1980s when Klan leader and Nazi David Duke decided to swap his robe for a sport coat, get a blow-dried haircut, and undergo extensive plastic surgery, both on his face and in his rhetoric.

On the left, the movement upsurge fell victim to its own success. In the effort to adapt to the new racial politics they themselves had created, racial movements lost their unity and raison d'être. Working within the newly reformed racial state was more possible, and confronting it more difficult, than during the preceding period. Opposition to the backward and coercive racial order of the South had permitted a tenuous alliance between moderate and radical currents of the movement, an alliance that the winning of civil rights reforms ruptured. The "triumph" of liberal democracy failed to placate radicals who sought not only rights but power and resources as well. The conferring of rights did not appreciably change the circumstances of a black youth in North Philly or a *vato loco* (roughly translatable as a Chicano homeboy) in East Los Angeles. What was heralded as a great victory by liberals appeared to radicals as merely a more streamlined version of racial oppression.

By the late 1960s, then, the U.S. racial order had largely absorbed the challenge posed by the civil rights movement, responding effectively (from the standpoint of rule) with a series of reforms. At the same time it had largely insulated itself from the more radical of its racial challengers—for example, revolutionary Marxist and nationalist currents—by drawing upon traditional coercive means, but also by exploiting the ideological weaknesses inherent in these viewpoints.

Over the following two decades what remained of the movement evolved into two loosely knit racial projects: the pragmatic liberals and the radical democrats. In the former group I include the surviving civil rights organizations, the liberal religious establishment, and the Democratic Party. In the latter group I include grassroots organizations that continue to function at the local level, cultural radicals and nationalist groups that have avoided mystical and demagogic pitfalls, and survivors of the debacle of the socialist left who have retained their antiracist commitments.

This spectrum of racial projects, running from right to left, characterizes the United States today. In contrast to the earlier postwar period, the political logic of race in the United States is now "decentered" because the racial formation process operates in the absence of a coherent conflict. Only a comprehensive challenge to the racial order as a whole could generate such coherence. This decenteredness reflects not only the incomplete and fragmented character of the available racial projects but also the complexity of contemporary racial politics and culture. None of the extant racial projects seems capable of presenting a durable and comprehensive vision of race. None can realistically address in even a minimally adequate way both the volatility of racial expression, meaning, and identities, on the one hand, and the in-depth racialization of the social structure and political system in the United States. Indeed, such a totalizing vision of race may no longer be possible.

This decentered racial situation reflects an unprecedented level of societal uncertainty about race. The various racial projects listed here are merely efforts to advance one or another current, one or another political agenda, in a society wracked by racial anxiety and conflict. They may compete in the effort to construct a new racial hegemony, but they do not offer any real prospect of clarifying or resolving ambivalent racial meanings or identities. Despite occasional appearances to the contrary, the right-wing racial projects have no more gained racial hegemony than have those of the left. Rather, the state, business, media, and religious and educational institutions appear permanently divided, riven, inconsistent, and uncertain about racial conflicts and issues, much as we as individuals are confused and ambivalent.

The System of Racial Hegemony:
Contemporary U.S. Racial Projects

Hegemony is a system in which politics operates largely through the incorporation of oppositional currents in the prevailing system of rule, and culture operates largely through the reinterpretation of oppositional discourse in the prevailing framework of social expression, representation, and debate.[7] Of course, not everything in a hegemonic system works this way. For example, there is certainly plenty of room in contemporary U.S. racial politics and culture for exclusion, segregation, discrimination, malevolence, ignorance, and outright violence. Highlighting the hegemonic dimensions of present-day U.S. racial dynamics emphasizes the effects of several decades of racial formation processes and the qualitative shifts that have occurred in the meaning and structure of race since the movement upsurge of the 1960s.

Under hegemonic conditions opposition and difference are not repressed, excluded, or silenced (at least not primarily). Rather they are inserted, often after suitable modification, within a modern (or perhaps postmodern) social order. Hegemony therefore involves a splitting or doubling of opposition, which simultaneously wins and loses, gains entrance into the halls of power and is co-opted, crosses over into mainstream culture and is deprived of its critical content.

What is the logic of racial hegemony in the present-day United States? Today there can no longer be any single axis of racial domination and subordination. There can no longer be any explicitly segregationist politics, nor can there be expressive forms of culture reserved exclusively for whites.[8] Just as these once-powerful forms of racial domination have been eroded or even destroyed, so too has their opposition. Racial hegemony has gradually evolved from this situation, which is a crisis of the movement legacy of the 1960s.

Racial Hegemony and Racial Projects

The evolution of racial hegemony means that the outmoded antinomy of racial domination and racial subordination has been replaced by a range of racial projects whose "formation and superseding" (in Gramsci's words) constituted the process of racial formation in the United States.

In the contemporary United States, racial formation proceeds, and racial hegemony is organized, through the interplay of these projects. Hegemony operates through the adoption by the state, the media, large corporations, and other key societal institutions of political initiatives and cultural narratives drawn from competing racial projects. Through the state and the major parties, for example, racial policies are worked out across the entire national political agenda. Thomas Byrne Edsall and Mary D. Edsall describe some of the items on the agenda:

> Considerations of race are now deeply imbedded in the strategy and tactics of politics, in competing concepts of the functions and responsibilities of government, and in each voter's conceptual structure of moral and partisan identity. Race helps define liberal and conservative ideologies, shapes the presidential coalitions of the Democratic and Republican parties, provides a harsh new dimension to concern over taxes and crime, drives a wedge through alliances of the working classes and the poor, and gives both momentum and vitality to the drive to establish a national majority inclined by income and demography to support policies benefiting the affluent and the upper middle class.[9]

Race provides a key cultural marker, a central signifier, in the reproduction and expression of identity, collectivity, language, and agency itself. Race generates an "inside" and an "outside" of society and mediates the unclear border between these zones; all social space, from the territory of the intrapsychic to that of the U.S. "national character," is fair game for racial dilemmas, doubts, fears, and desires. The conceptualization and representation of these sentiments, whether articulated in a track by Public Enemy or a TV commercial for Jesse Helms, is framed in one or more racial projects.

By the 1980s, then, the racial order consisted of a range of conflicting racial projects, each descended from the days of racial domination and movement opposition, each seeking to advance its own conception of the significance of race in contemporary U.S. society. At the core of each project was a particular

TABLE 12.1
Racial Hegemony in the United States (c. 1990)

	CULTURE ← ARTICULATION → STRUCTURE	
Project	Racial Discourse: Concept of Identity, "Difference," and the Meaning of Race	Political/Programmatic Agenda: Orientation to the State, (In)Equality
Far Right	Represents race in terms of inherent, natural characteristics; rights and privileges assigned accordingly; traditional far right operates through terror; renovated far right organizes whites politically.	Open racial conflict; equality seen as a subversion of the "natural order"; the state is in the hands of the "race-mixers." Whites need to form their own organizations, pressure the state for "white rights."
New Right	Understands racial mobilization as a threat to "traditional values"; perceives racial meanings and identities as operating "subtextually"; engages in racial "coding"; articulates class and gender interests as racial.	Racial conflict focuses on the state; racial (in)equality determined by access to state institutions and relative political power.

articulation of the culture and structure of race, of racial discourse and racial politics. This range of projects, which together constitute racial hegemony, can be "mapped," somewhat schematically (see Table 12.1).

The linkage between culture and structure, which is at the core of the racial formation process, gives each project its coherence and unity. Indeed, once it is argued that the United States is inherently a "white man's country" (as in certain far right racial discourses), or that race is a spurious anachronism beneath the notice of the state (as in neoconservative positions), or that racial difference is a matter of "self-determination" (as in radical democratic racial discourse), the appropriate political orientation and economic and social programs follow quite naturally.

Racial Hegemony in the 1990s

Racial formation theory tells us that the racial order is in constant flux. Contested meanings and identities, conflict over political and economic resources, rivalries over territory and systems of cultural expression: these are the

TABLE 12.1 *(Cont.)*

Racial Hegemony in the United States (c. 1990)

	CULTURE ← ARTICULATION → STRUCTURE	
Project	Racial Discourse: Concept of Identity, "Difference," and the Meaning of Race	Political/Programmatic Agenda: Orientation to the State, (In)Equality
Neoconservatism	Denies the salience of racial "difference" or argues it is a vestige of the past, when invidious distinctions and practices had not yet been reformed; after the passage of civil rights laws, any collective articulation of racial "difference" amounts to "racism in reverse."	Conservative egalitarianism; individualism, meritocracy, universalism; rejection of any form of group rights; "color-blind" state.
Pragmatic Liberalism	Racial identities serve to organize interests and channel political and cultural activities; as long as principles of pluralism and tolerance are upheld, a certain degree of group identity and racial mobilization can be accepted as the price of social peace.	Cultural and political pluralism; affirmative action as "goals, not quotas"; state racial policy as moderating and eroding the legacy of discrimination.
Radical Democracy	Racial difference accepted and celebrated; flexibility of racial identities; multiplicity and "decenteredness" of various forms of "difference," including race.	State racial policy as redistribution; racial politics as part of "decentered" but interconnected pattern of "new social movements"; extension of democratic rights and of societal control over the state.

processes that continue to frame the complex problem of race in the United States. Thus there is nothing eternal about the five racial projects outlined here. Indeed they are framed somewhat schematically, in an effort to clarify divisions and antagonisms. In many respects the overlaps between these five projects are as significant as the distinctions between them.

This last point is quite important, since ultimately, as Gramsci argued, hegemony is constructed out of differing social forces welded together in what he called a "historical bloc." There are clear grounds for potential polarization in the five-part typology developed here: if racial hegemony today is in flux and divided among many initiatives, tomorrow it may be bifurcated by left and right currents.

Furthermore, the racial dimensions of political conflict and cultural representation are becoming ever more central as we approach the end of the twentieth century. Racial hegemony is converging in important respects with overall societal hegemony. In this situation the political and cultural currents that most effectively establish the link between racial difference and social inequality will win the contest for hegemony in the United States.

The right enjoys considerable privileges in this situation. Besides the institutional advantages realized during the Reagan years, right-wing racial projects have been able to portray minority racial identities, and minority insistence on the continuing significance of race and racism, as anachronistic, pernicious, and unfair. Left racial projects have only intermittently and partially succeeded in countering these views (as in the Jackson campaigns) and often appear mired in outmoded conceptions and proposals.

Indeed at present throughout U.S. society, including in racially defined minority communities and on the left, there is an unwillingness to enter into discussions about race. This reluctance is not illogical: it is born of fear and bitter experience. But it is also politically dangerous. As the projects of the right advance a view of race that links difference and diversity to national weakness, economic decline, and widespread racist fears,[10] those on the left cannot refuse to debate the contemporary meaning of race and the programmatic alternatives before us. Such issues as the relationship among minority middle classes and "underclasses," the relevance of nationalist and integrationist traditions today, and, perhaps most centrally, the relationship between race and class must be extensively discussed in an atmosphere where dogma and orthodoxy are effectively resisted.

Race and Class

In the contemporary United States, hegemony is determined by the articulation of race and class. The ability of the right to represent class issues in racial terms is central to the current pattern of conservative racial hegemony. All three rightist projects—those of the far right, the new right, and the neoconservatives—partake of this logic. Conservative/reactionary politics today disguise class issues in racial terms. In so doing they build on a thematic current that is as deep and wide as U.S. history itself. This theme can be called "divide and conquer," dual labor markets, white skin privilege, Eurocentrism, immigrant exclusion, or internal colonialism: its clearest name is racism.

Conversely, any challenge to this current, any counterhegemonic initiative, must be explicitly race-conscious in its approach to issues of class or fall victim to the same hegemonic strategies that have doomed so many other progressive political initiatives. Traditional left politics have consistently failed to do this; they have steadily refused to afford race the centrality it receives on the right. Rather, left politics—both moderate and radical—have been steeped in class reductionism. In the particular conditions of U.S. politics, the subordination of race to class has never been viable; it is less logical in the contemporary period than ever before.

Making race consciousness explicit and central to class politics means recognizing the irreducibility of race in U.S. political and cultural life and thinking about class, inequality, and redistribution in ways that take racial divisions and conflicts into primary account. How might the racial projects of the left articulate the relationship of race and class? A full answer to this question must await large-scale political and cultural experimentation, but a more limited and schematic response is already possible.

First, such approaches cannot be mere inversions (whether innocent or cynical) of the new-right uses of racial coding, nor of the neoconservative strategic denial of the significance of race. Left racial projects must affirm the ongoing reality of racial difference in U.S. cultural and political life. Indeed, in their radical democratic aspects at least, they must go further and create (or recreate) a joyful recognition of racial difference that goes well beyond mere tolerance. One of the striking features of the contemporary racial situation is that many examples of such an appreciation exist in cultural life and in everyday experience—in music and art, sexual relationships, educational and religious settings, the media—without finding any political articulation at all.

Additionally, a radical democratic articulation of race and class must acknowledge that racial minority status still serves as a negative marker, a stigma, in the class formation process. Although somewhat attenuated since the 1960s with the rise of significant minority middle classes, dark skin still correlates with poverty.[11] Class position is in many respects racially assigned in the U.S.

It follows from this that radical democratic challengers should reopen the question of discrimination as a racial process with class consequences. The reactionary redefinition of the nature of racial discrimination (in the "reverse discrimination" arguments of the 1970s and 1980s) as something that only happens to individuals and thus is disconnected from history, and from any preponderant collective logic in the present, conveniently suppresses the fact that discrimination drives all wages down.

Linking race and class in a manner that does not reduce race to class involves a democratic challenge to the fundamental authoritarianism of the right. It involves rethinking populism and the economic and cultural logics of equality and fairness. As a mass politics with strong themes of social injustice, exclusion, and resentment, U.S. populism has traditionally been directed at one of two main targets: on the one hand, at big business, the conglomerates, the trusts; on the other hand, at racial minorities—the blacks, the "yellow peril."

Efforts to reconstruct the far-right racial project along populist lines are indicative of the latter tendency. David Duke ran for president in 1988 on the ticket of the "Populist Party," which was exhumed in the mid-1980s almost a century after its heyday of free silver, agrarian revolt, and southern lynching. This time around the scapegoating of blacks was particularly central.

To counter this approach a left populism will be needed. One such set of proposals, whose advocates have included William J. Wilson and Orlando Patterson, involves the resuscitation of class-based New Deal policies (extensive public investment and job creation, expansion of the welfare state in a social democratic direction) combined with race-specific measures where discrimination per se is the issue.[12] At present this sort of proposal appears rather utopian, given the lethargy of the Democratic Party, the perpetual fiscal crisis of the state, the political profits still available through playing the "racist card" (quotas, Willie Horton), and the absence of a strong and independent minority movement. Some circumstances, however, do seem to favor a swing back toward left populist initiatives. These might potentially include the end of the Cold War and the decline of the arms-demanding Moloch of the Pentagon, the widespread perception of government neglect of domestic social problems, and the rise of class resentment toward the beneficiaries of the regressive policies of the 1980s.

If there is to be any counterhegemonic initiative, such left populist currents will have to be combined with an ethical thrust, as Cornel West has recently argued.[13] In this view, social justice in all its forms—class-based, race-based, and gender-based—is achieved only through a combined political and moral vision. This suggests that the pragmatic liberal and radical democratic projects can learn from the right, just as the racial reaction learned from the minority movements of the 1960s.

In order to overcome right-wing populism's racist politics of resentment, notions of equality and fairness must be rethought in the combined light of race and class and gender. Thinking of discrimination in terms of the restriction of the individual's rights and opportunities—in a "color-blind" way, as the right-wing projects would have us do—becomes a lot more logical in a state committed to social and class justice. In a situation of tight labor markets, such as the one Wilson proposes, the problem of "reverse discrimination" would be far less conflictual than it is in a situation where the gap between rich and poor is widening and middle-income people's life chances are eroding. Thus linking race and class justice concerns would facilitate efforts to overcome historic patterns of racial discrimination without unduly threatening whites.[14]

Similarly the right-wing appeal to racial fears requires careful scrutiny. The right must employ the "politics of resentment" in this process; at a minimum, it must articulate these resentments and fears in coded racial terms such as "quotas." David Duke, Lee Atwater, and Jesse Helms offer an authoritarian and exclusive program: to protect whites against nonwhites, against people they do not trust or understand. This authoritarian politics is open to a democratic challenge: it can be rearticulated as inclusion, not exclusion. Jesse Jackson demonstrated this with his rhetoric of "common ground" and his talk of "adding another patch to the quilt." By accepting and celebrating racial, gender, and sexual difference within a plural community, by offering and accepting a place under the "quilt," such a program reaffirms the themes mentioned above: equality, fairness, social justice, and an ethical society.

Racial hegemony is being reconstituted as overall hegemony; unfortunately it is the right that is largely responsible for this trend and that stands to benefit the most from it. The task now is to provide an alternative, emancipatory account of the virtues of racial difference and racial diversity, and to reconstruct the links between the fate of racially defined minorities and the fate of U.S. society as a whole.

NOTES

1. Michael Omi and Howard Winant, *Racial Formation in the United States: From the 1960s to the 1990s*, 2nd ed. (London and New York: Routledge, 1994).

2. James Scott, *Weapons of the Weak: Everyday Forms of Peasant Resistance* (New Haven: Yale University Press, 1985); Homi K. Bhabha, "DissemiNation: Time, Narrative, and the Margins of the Modern Nation," in idem, ed., *Nation and Narration* (London: Routledge, 1990).

3. Neil R. McMillen, *Dark Journey: Black Mississippians in the Age of Jim Crow* (Urbana and Chicago: University of Illinois Press, 1989); David Montejano, *Anglos and Mexicans in the Making of Texas, 1836–1986* (Austin: University of Texas Press, 1987); Ronald T. Takaki, *Stranger from a Different Shore: A History of Asian Americans* (Boston: Little Brown, 1989); Omi and Winant, *Racial Formation*, 73–74.

4. For developments in rock, rap, and race see the excellent magazine edited by Dave Marsh, *Rock and Rap Confidential*. On rap the best source is the magazine *The Source*.

5. Harold Cruse, *Rebellion or Revolution?* (New York: William Morrow, 1968), 111–12.

6. Studies on the general subject of postcoloniality are replete with examples and analyses of this complex. For some representative analyses see Henry Louis Gates, Jr., ed., *"Race," Writing, and Difference* (Chicago: University of Chicago Press, 1986).

7. This approach obviously involves an interpretation of Gramsci that cannot be spelled out within the limits of the present essay. The Gramsci literature is vast and rewarding for students of race. I rely here upon Antonio Gramsci, *Selections from the Prison Notebooks*, Geoffrey Nowell-Smith and Quentin Hoare, eds. (New York: International Publishers, 1971); Stuart Hall, "Gramsci's Relevance for the Study of Race and Ethnicity," *Journal of Communication Inquiry* 10, no. 2 (1986); and Chantal Mouffe and Ernesto Laclau, *Hegemony and Socialist Strategy: Towards a Radical Democratic Politics* (London: Verso, 1985). I have also found useful material in Ranajit Guha and Gayatri Chakravorty Spivak, eds., *Selected Subaltern Studies* (New York: Oxford University Press, 1988).

8. Nor for nonwhites. As I have argued above, even cultural forms deriving from the experiences of particular racially defined minorities (such as rap, hip-hop, or for that matter norteña) have "crossed over." A related issue is whether any group may legitimately retain its exclusive racial character. Various minority organizations on university campuses—the African American student unions, the Asian and Pacific Islanders associations, the Chicano student groups such as MECHA—have been attacked as exclusionary. Here I think the resemblance is more superficial than real between past segregation and white exclusivism, on the one hand, and present racial minority efforts to construct associations solely for members of their own group, on the other. Exclusivism acquires force when it is directed by a dominant majority against a subordinated minority. Hence neoconservative criticisms leveled at such groups (or at events scheduled "for women only," or gay dances, for that matter) seem either misconceived or disingenuous.

9. Thomas Byrne Edsall and Mary D. Edsall, "Race," *Atlantic Monthly*, May 1991, 53.

10. Ronald Walters, "White Racial Nationalism in the United States," *Without Prejudice* 1, no. 1 (Fall 1987).

11. In 1986, blacks were three times as likely to be poor as whites; 44 percent of black children lived in poverty in 1985, as compared to 16 percent of white children. Latinos were roughly twice as likely to be poor as whites, though this group is far more stratified than are blacks. Similar variations exist for Asians. For Native Americans, poverty rates approach or exceed those of blacks.

12. William Julius Wilson, *The Truly Disadvantaged: The Inner City, the Underclass, and Public Policy* (Chicago: University of Chicago Press, 1987); Orlando Patterson, "The Black Community: Is There a Future?" in *The Third Century: America as a Post-Industrial Society*, Seymour Martin Lipset, ed. (Stanford, Calif.: Hoover Institution Press, 1979).

13. Cornel West, "Nihilism in Black America," *Dissent* (Spring 1991).

14. For a sustained argument on some of these points, see Gertrude Ezorsky, *Racism and Justice: The Case for Affirmative Action* (Ithaca: Cornell University Press, 1991).

CHAPTER 13

Industrial Racism, the Environmental Crisis, and the Denial of Social Justice

Cynthia Hamilton

□   □   □   □   □   □   □   □   □   □   □   □

The future of capitalism depends on its capacity to expand, and today we are witnessing both its desperation and its extraordinary ability to appropriate everything in its own interest. Environmentalism is not escaping its grasp. As James O'Connor writes, "a certain amount of green capitalism is possible to the degree that such a system does not challenge or threaten the structures of privilege and power which capitalism depends on."[1]

Green capitalism's free-market rhetoric is fostering a great deal of confusion among those concerned about environmental degradation, and it will continue to do so unless and until we develop an independent analysis of the economy and the environmental crisis—one that identifies alternative development strategies, technologies, and values, beginning with renewable resources and nonpolluting processes. We are embarking on no less than a search for alternatives to the two hundred years of technological development known as the industrial revolution, an era that has crescendoed with the most toxic conditions in the history of humanity.

Both Western liberalism and conservatism believe in individualism, private property, and the free market, notions that provide the philosophical structure for the model of industrial democracy that dominates modern thought and society. Communist systems, too, accepted the tenets of the industrial revolution: The domination of nature by humanity has been an imperative for capitalism and communism alike.

Now, however, the model of industrial development embellished by notions of infinite supply, progress, and growth is bankrupt. Industrial society is no longer able to sustain or manage itself. Structural inflation, structural un-

A version of this chapter appears in Robert D. Bullard, ed., *Confronting Environmental Racism: Voices from the Grassroots* (Boston: South End Press, 1993), 63–76. The excerpt originally titled "Avoiding Western Chauvinism" (pp. 70–72) is reprinted by permission of South End Press. (See chapter endnotes 7 and 8 for poetry acknowledgments.)

employment, depleted resources, and destruction of the environment are now constants. In the words of Herbert Marcuse, "intensified progress seems to be bound up with intensified unfreedom. . . . Concentration camps, mass exterminations, world wars, and atom bombs are no 'relapse into barbarism,' but the unrepressed implementation of the achievements of modern science, technology and domination."[2]

In the East and the West, cultural values have been predicated on cultural chauvinism; difference has always been dismissed. New paradigms must begin by relinquishing both cultural chauvinism and what Hazel Henderson describes as the "belief system of industrialism—continual economic expansion, technological determinism and Cartesian rationalism."[3] Traditional approaches to growth and expansion, which embrace the notion that more is better, must be replaced by a more balanced approach that challenges the existing structures of privilege and power.

If a new paradigm is to emerge, a theoretical reconceptualization is necessary. We must go beyond questions of the ownership of production and address the means of production directly. Green capitalism—taking the form of pollution credits, debt for nature swaps, adding "greens" to the boards of directors of major polluting companies—represents an effort to obscure and reappropriate meaning without challenging structures of privilege and power.

America's uneven domestic economic development is responsible for the environmental problems we confront. Real alternatives must begin with the rejection of economic expansion in favor of the idea of a steady-state economy based on renewable energy. Acceptable levels of production must replace the current insatiable appetite for more. Existing technology should be reassessed and appropriate technology, all of it energy efficient, substituted wherever necessary. In housing, manufactured solar construction should replace traditional structures. In agriculture, economies of scale should replace the conglomerates that now dominate; organic agricultural methods and appropriate technology will prove to be ecologically sound and economically viable.

A social overhaul as well as a technological one is necessary. New ownership structures (for example, cooperatives) must be introduced to guarantee consumer services. The principles of the new environmentalism must reflect real democratic options and mechanisms for inclusion in substantive decision making. Without a decentralization of power, we are doomed to totalitarian measures imposed to control crises of resource scarcity.

Movements that challenge environmental abuse must be rooted in cultural as well as political critique. This necessitates that the old cultural chauvinism of Europeans, in both the West and the East, be replaced by an acknowledgment of the cultural traditions of people of color who have respected other life forms and sought balance rather than the domination of nature. The independent critique of development expressed by people of color domestically and internationally represents the best alternative to capitalism's blind commitment to expansion and growth. It also represents an expanded definition of environmentalism, one that demands that we think of the problem in terms of its causes. Ironically, those considered new arrivals to the environmental movement—blacks, Chicanos, and Native Americans—come to it with the most useful tools. Their efforts are focused on saving their communities, the embodiment of culture. That is precisely what continued growth and ecological destruction threaten.

The traditional environmental movement has tended toward conservatism because of its ties to the political and economic establishment and its uncritical acceptance of industrial growth. The new urban environmental movements of people of color and working-class women are now on the cutting edge of environmental politics. In their efforts to save their communities from development and industrial policies that threaten them, the black community and other communities of color (especially Chicanos and Native Americans, because they too have been victims of de facto segregation) are formulating a new kind of politics that emphasizes direct democracy, popular control, and decentralization. Sometimes these new social movements demand the dismantling of productive forces, but more often they offer an alternative conception of power that is based in community.

The emphasis on community is far from an abstraction: It is the source of an important contribution to alternative models, values, and lifestyles. It is also a direct response to new development and environmental hazards that literally threaten homes and neighborhoods, a response that fosters the transformation of individual fears and concerns into group efforts. In these situations, the cry to "save community" is synonymous with the cry to "save the earth."

The manner in which routine development policies have affected communities of color in the United States has made most grassroots organizations wary of capital-intensive projects such as highways, office towers, shopping malls, and condominiums. Unsurprisingly, the social and environmental crises caused by this sort of development have manifested themselves most visibly in communities of color. These communities have experienced both the most severe deindustrialization and the greatest contamination from industrialization. According to the United Church of Christ, three out of five black and Hispanic Americans live in communities with uncontrolled toxic waste sites.

The health consequences of these realities have had and will have catastrophic consequences for minority communities. Most of these will not manifest themselves for many years, but already we know that Navajo teenagers have organ cancer seventeen times the national average, that 50 percent of the children suffering from lead paint poisoning (resulting in short attention spans, limited vocabulary, and behavior problems) are black. These are the implications of America's institutional racism and development strategies, which ignore human and social costs and which have significantly eroded the quality of life in America's urban areas.

These problems are the consequences of decades of land-use decisions that insure that those with the most consistent residential proximity to industry in America's cities are poor people of color. In the early twentieth century, central business districts were always at the center of the industrial circumference, with people of lower socioeconomic status living closer to the center. As whites moved away from the inner cores of industrial cities to escape their noise and foul air, water, and land, blacks were allowed to move into the houses left behind. In many instances, this housing had been built on landfills or garbage dumps. In the inner cities of the Northeast and the Midwest, elevated trains emerged from subway tunnels to traverse the length of the black community, with business continuing as usual below.

Blacks completely replaced the European ethnic working class in these areas by the end of World War II. Today, noise, dirt, railroad tracks, and pollution from factories, warehouses, and stockyards have become the trademark of black communities and a guarantor of de facto segregation. The boundaries of black communities are distinct: highways or freeways, or natural divisions such as rivers or lakes, form the boundaries of industrial districts. The concentration of industry and its proximity to housing increases the likelihood that routine emissions and waste will be transformed into dangerous pollution.

The environmental organizing being done around the country by communities of color is not based on a narrow populism that demands participation in the decision to move debris from one neighborhood to someone else's. Communities of color are unlikely to be attracted to a NIMBY (Not in My Back Yard) approach, which doesn't move us any closer to environmental solutions or alternatives. Precisely because they have been so abused, communities of color begin their organizing with a recognition of limited options and allies, a clear view of community development, and a recognition of the inequities of industrialization. And they are unlikely to be confused when environmental problems are linked to economic development and underdevelopment.

A Culture of Alienation

Conceptions of economic development not only produce cultural attitudes and behavior, they are also shaped by them. Native Americans, for example, have always insisted that their culture, which emphasizes harmony between humans and nature, was the source of their economic system. In Western culture the emphasis has always been on humanity's control of nature. Ironically, those in the West who have been closest to the products of industrial development have been least likely to explore its consequences. Quite possibly the reason for this is alienation from the land and nature, lack of contact with the mythic beginnings of the land.

Many of the cultural symbols and mythical heroes of Western societies, such as Prometheus, are embodiments of domination and production. It is the antiheroes of the West such as Orpheus, Narcissus, and Dionysus who are antagonists of domination, and they are considered weak and disruptive. In these antiheroic mythical images, the opposition between humans and nature, subject and object, is overcome.[4] They represent a different reality. According to Herbert Marcuse, "theirs is the image of joy and fulfillment; the voice which does not command but sings; the gesture which offers and receives; the deed which is peace and ends the labor of conquest; the liberation from time which unites man with god, man with nature."[5]

Given the prevalence of Western chauvinism, it is not surprising that many Western scholars have attributed the characteristics of these antiheroes to "Africa, . . . the land of childhood, lying beyond the day of self-conscious history"[6] or have dismissed them as effeminate. But Western scholars were always quick to allege that Africa's proximity to nature was a source of weakness. Feelings, emotions, and sensations—never reason—were said to characterize the "sons of Ham."

This idea was stood on its head by African and West Indian writers and activists from French colonies in the 1930s. The negritude movement that they launched portrayed the technological achievements of the West as symbols of colonialism and oppression and the West itself as a civilization of "cannons and machines." Renaissance Africa, in contrast, offered "humanism" and pointed to the importance of taming technology and subjugating it to human needs. The negritude writers celebrated precisely those qualities denigrated by the West. Léopold Senghor wrote in "Prayer to the Masks,"

For who would teach rhythm to a dead world of cannons and machines?
Who would give the shout of joy at dawn to wake the dead and orphaned?
Tell me, who would restore the memory of life to men whose hopes are
   disemboweled?[7]

These are not voices of the rejection of technology as such. Rather, they seek to point out the errors of technology and the need to infuse it with the spirit of people. This poetic critique of industrialization and technology therefore points a way to alternatives:

Eia for those who never invented anything.
Who never explored anything.
Who never conquered anything,
But who abandon themselves to the essence of all things,
Ignorant of surfaces, caught by the motion of all things.
Indifferent to conquering but playing the game of the world. . . .

Listen to the white world
Horribly weary from its enormous effort,

Its rebellious joints crack beneath the hard stars.
Its rigid, blue steel penetrates the mystic flesh;
Hear its traitorous victories trumpet its defeats;
Hear the grandiose alibis for its sorry stumbling,
Pity for our conquerors, omniscient and naive![8]

Contemporary Sources of Alternatives

The persistent criticisms of environmental destruction and domination by non-Western societies articulate the direction that new paradigms must explore. Alienated from the processes and the fruits of modern development, feminism and the black movement (as well as Native Americans and Chicanos) have taken up themes of environmental destruction as a consequence of alienation and domination.

Carolyn Merchant has called our attention to the congruence of the principles of feminism and those of an emergent ecological theory: (a) the idea of earth as a home; (b) the acceptance of all parts of a system as possessing equal value; (c) the acknowledgment of process; and (d) the recognition that capitalist growth has social costs.[9] Ironically, the feminist contribution at the level of theory may reflect the socialization experiences of women. The separation of the so-called public and the domestic spheres has made women likely to be aware of and sensitive to hierarchy, leadership styles and function, and relations between individuals.

Women, both white and black, tend to be comfortable in decentralized, nonhierarchical, nonbureaucratized structures; men often find them inefficient and incomprehensible. Women's innovative contributions to organization are the antithesis of bureaucracy: Women have rejected the division of labor, specialization, depersonalization, mechanization, and routine as oppressive and adverse to personal freedom. Their principles encourage individual initiative while emphasizing respect for interdependence and cooperation; ironically, they also maximize the use and expression of women's qualities as nurturers. (Examples include the Greenham Common experience, the Student Nonviolent Coordinating Committee under the direction of Ella Baker, and the settlement house movement at the turn of the century.)

Black women have developed these alternatives in their political work in the civil rights movement and in organizing efforts where they have been the majority, as is often the case in urban environmental movements. Where the issues are close to the domestic sphere—home, health, family, community—women have been comfortable taking the lead and doing so in a participatory and democratic manner.

When politics becomes personal, and when groups previously left out of formal parliamentary and electoral processes of participation begin to demand access or develop new modes of development, the philosophy of individualism is challenged. The legitimate structures and framework of modern industrial societies make it difficult to address social or community consider- ations, and the benefits of modern society accrue to individuals. Those who put group or collective needs above individual ones are forced to confront ex- isting institutional arrangements. The movement for civil rights, for example, was conceptually bound to the collective good.

The black struggle has also made major contributions to an emergent the- ory and praxis of economic democracy. Black communities are on the front lines of the crises of growth and development—unemployment, displace- ment, and pollution. In 1960s struggles for self-help and community control over development, blacks connected their work toward local alternatives with the needs of national and even international communities of color. These struggles added the dimensions of morality and values to American politics, eloquently voiced by Dr. Martin Luther King, and bequeathed a language of participation and challenge to contemporary political movements:

> The 1960s revolt of central-city minority neighborhoods invented a political vocabulary which has been embraced not only by service professionals choosing to reside in the central city, but by suburban dwellers as well. This has induced government agencies and local political leaders to become much more neighborhood-oriented and participation-oriented at least in their rhetorical style.[10]

The struggles of blacks and women thus provide images of alternatives. Both groups have incorporated political and moral choices into their lived ex- perience and made politics the basis of everyday life. For blacks in a legally segregated society, demanding broad social change was a prerequisite for ex- panded personal rights and freedom. For women challenging the separation of the domestic and public spheres, action in the form of personal expression is aimed at a more comprehensive social transformation.

Blacks have historically been relegated to concerns of an urban and do- mestic nature; the arena of international politics was defined as off-limits. Similarly, "women's issues" have been portrayed as separate from politics; women's concerns have been seen as limited to domestic issues such as child care, education, and health. Both groups have responded with demands to de- fine their own concerns; both have moved beyond notions of individualism in doing so. And both have used the limits imposed by their socialization to ad- vantage, taking up leadership roles in urban environmental organizing in part because the environmental crisis has manifested itself as a threat to health, family, and community.

Human progress in the Western world has been synonymous with alien- ation, a concept that is becoming important to ecological concerns. Only the struggle against alienation and its perversion of values, against artificial divi- sions among humans and within ourselves, can bring us closer to an alternative political system predicated on a healthy physical environment. The transcendence of alienation must be our primary task as we undertake the construction of a new economic democracy, seeking to replace our lost social justice. In the words of the negritude poet Aimé Césaire:

[For] it is not true that the work of man is finished,
That there is nothing for us to do in this world,
That we are parasites on this earth,
That it is enough for us to keep in step with the world,
But the work of man has only just begun,
And it is up to man to vanquish all deprivations immobilized in the
  corners of his fervor,
And no race has the monopoly on beauty, intelligence, or strength,
And there is a place for all at the rendezvous of conquest.[11]

NOTES

1. James O'Connor, "Is Sustainable Capitalism Possible?" *Conference Papers on Capitalism and Nature,* Capitalism Nature Socialism / Center for Ecological Socialism Pamphlet 1 (Santa Cruz: Center for Political Ecology, 1991), 14–15.
2. Herbert Marcuse, *Eros and Civilization: A Philosophical Inquiry into Freud* (New York: Vintage, 1961), 4.
3. Hazel Henderson, *The Politics of the Solar Age: Alternatives to Economics* (New York: Anchor Press/Doubleday, 1981), 355.
4. Marcuse, *Eros and Civilization,* 15.
5. Ibid., 147.
6. Georg W. F. Hegel, *Philosophy of History* (New York: Dover, 1956), 91.
7. Léopold Senghor, "Prayer to Masks," in Ellen Conroy Kennedy, ed. and trans., *The Negritude Poets* (New York: Thunder's Mouth Press, 1989), 132–33. Copyright © 1975 by Ellen Conroy Kennedy. Foreword copyright © by Maya Angelou. All rights reserved. Reprinted by permission of Thunder's Mouth Press.
8. Aimé Césaire, "Return to My Native Land," in Ellen Conroy Kennedy, ed. and trans., *The Negritude Poets* (New York: Thunder's Mouth Press, 1989), 76. Copyright © 1975 by Ellen Conroy Kennedy. Foreword copyright © by Maya Angelou. All rights reserved. Reprinted by permission of Thunder's Mouth Press.
9. Carolyn Merchant, *The Death of Nature* (San Francisco: Harper and Row, 1981), 26.
10. Michael Dear and Alan Scott, eds., *Urbanization and Urban Planning in Capitalist Society* (New York: Routledge, Chapman, and Hall, 1981), 331.
11. Césaire, "Return to My Native Land," *The Negritude Poets,* 79.

CHAPTER 14

The Iconography of Hazardous Waste

Andrew Szasz

□   □   □   □   □   □   □   □   □   □   □   □

The issue of hazardous industrial wastes has been arguably the most dynamic environmental issue of the past two decades. Even as other movements struggled just to stay alive during the conservative 1980s, concern about toxic industrial waste sparked a widespread, vigorous social movement. Thousands of local, community-based groups formed. A rich infrastructure of more permanent social movement organizations was built. The movement's understanding of the toxics problem deepened, becoming more systematic and more radical. The movement's combination of radical critique and direct, grassroots tactics is perhaps best described as "radical environmental populism."

The movement brought a new mass base of working people and people of color to environmentalism. It forged practical and conceptual links between environmentalism and the struggles against racism and sexism. Most recently, some of the more thoughtful voices in the movement have begun to suggest that environmental populism is not only the vehicle for achieving a better environment but is also the most promising candidate for leading the next phase of the larger movement for social change. Reflecting these advances in self-understanding, the movement has begun to call itself a movement for environmental justice.[1]

This remarkable decade of organizational and ideological development was preceded by, and in part made possible by, a vast change in public attitude toward toxic waste.

"The Nation's Most Important Environmental Problem"

A 1989 poll taken by the Environmental Protection Agency (EPA) found that the American public thought of hazardous industrial waste sites as the most

A longer version of this chapter appears as chapter 3 of Andrew Szasz, *EcoPopulism: Toxic Waste and the Movement for Environmental Justice* (Minneapolis, 1994), 38–68, by permission of the publisher. Copyright 1994 by the Regents of the University of Minnesota. Published by the University of Minnesota Press.

serious environmental risks facing the nation.[2] That was not always the case. Before 1978, "toxic waste" did not yet exist as a distinct entity in the popular imagination; by 1980, it had become one of the most dreaded of environmental risks. Perhaps the best way to highlight this change is to contrast two surveys of public attitudes toward the classic risk issue of "How close is close enough?"

In 1973, the EPA sought to determine people's attitudes toward the prospect of having a federally owned hazardous waste disposal facility in their community.[3] Almost 60 percent of the sample were willing to live within five miles of a hazardous waste disposal facility (see Table 14.1). With the hindsight conferred by knowing popular sentiment today, citizens in 1973 appear to have been remarkably unruffled by the prospect of having a hazardous waste disposal facility for a neighbor. Clearly, the phrase "hazardous waste" had not yet entered popular discourse; nor had it yet come clearly to signify something to be dreaded and avoided at all cost.

In sharp contrast, a survey done in 1980 for the Council on Environmental Quality[4] showed that the percentage of people willing to accept a disposal site within five miles of their home had dropped below 20 percent. The 60 percent acceptance mark by 1980 was passed only at the distance of one hundred miles (see Figure 14.1). By 1980, then, attitudes toward hazardous waste disposal sites closely resembled post–Three Mile Island attitudes toward living near nuclear power plants, the technology that risk-perception researchers always single out as *the* exemplar of technology that inspires extraordinary levels of popular dread.[5]

The toxics (now environmental justice) movement would have been much less likely to have developed as vigorously as it did had this sea change in mass perception not happened. Yes, certainly, there would still have been instances of communities protesting local contamination or resisting the proposed siting a new toxic waste facility. But it is likely that such protests would have been like those of the early 1970s, sporadic and isolated.[6] Mass dread of toxic waste was the perceptual basis, the fertile ground, upon which local protests proliferated, linked up with each other, and began that dramatic

TABLE 14.1

Acceptable Proximity of a National Disposal Site (in percent)

	Willing	Unsure	Unwilling	Don't Know
Within 1 mile	36.8	27.9	35.0	0.3
Within 5 miles	59.9	21.4	20.4	0.3
Within 10 miles	67.4	18.8	13.5	0.3
Within 25 miles	70.1	17.4	12.2	0.3

Source: L. L. Lackey, T. O. Jacobs, and S. R. Steward, "Public Attitudes toward Hazardous Waste Disposal Facilities," EPA 670/2-73-086, prepared for the National Environmental Research Center, U.S. Environmental Protection Agency, Alexandria, Va.: Human Resources Research Organization, 1973.

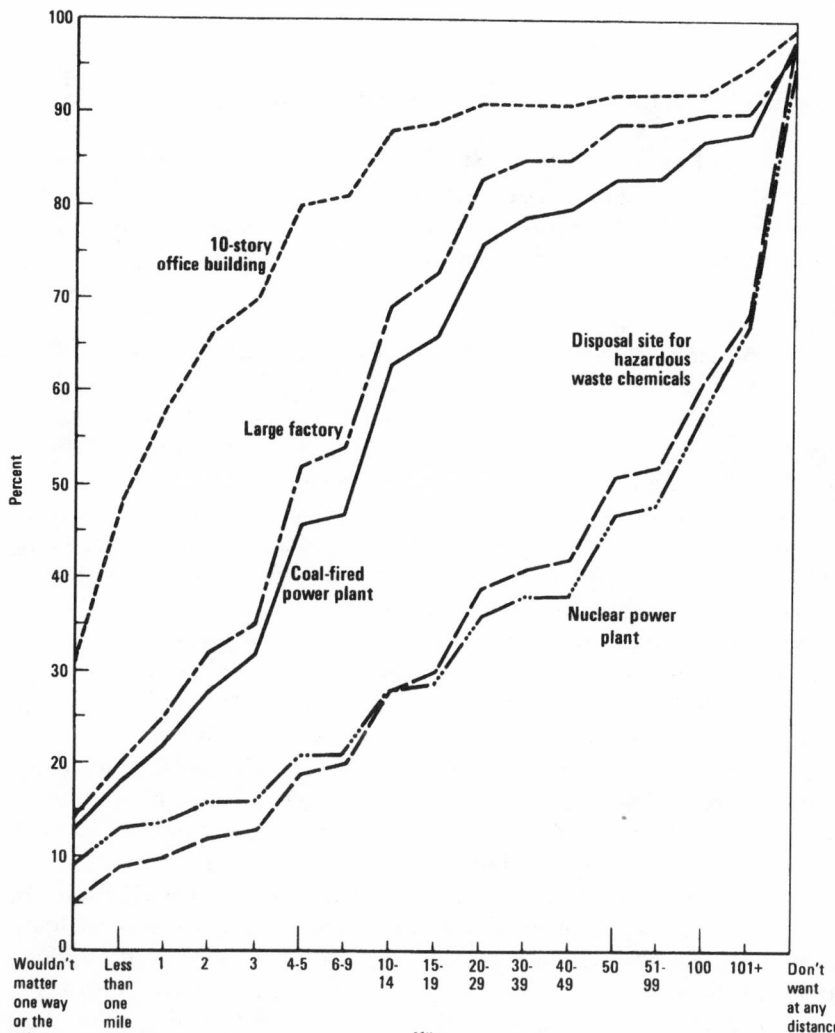

Figure 14.1. Cumulative Percentage of People Willing to Accept New Industrial Installations at Various Distances from Their Homes

Source: U.S. Council on Environmental Quality, "Public Opinion on Environmental Issues: Results of a National Public Opinion Survey" (Washington, D.C.: Government Printing Office, 1980), 31.

process of organizational and ideological evolution that, in a mere decade, generated a new, vibrant, innovative phase of American environmentalism. I describe here how this change in popular perception happened. I then explore how we might best understand the process of mass attitude formation more generally. I end with a brief discussion of the problematic connection between popular perception and political action.

Toxic Waste on Television and in the Popular Press

People's perception of hazardous waste changed when intense media coverage made "Love Canal" and "toxic waste" into household words that conjured up frightening images with terrifying meanings.

Local environmental conflict had become widespread during the 1970s.[7] Dozens of these local conflicts were about toxic waste, some opposed to the siting of a new waste disposal facility, others demanding the cleanup of wastes that had contaminated their community.[8]

Sociological studies have shown that television news loves "disorder" stories that feature disasters, victims, protesters; stories with action and color; stories in which abstract social issues are personalized and thus made accessible.[9] Contamination protests fit television's story selection and stylistic preferences perfectly. All the right elements were there: industrial chemicals, cancer and birth defects, innocent victims, and great "visuals" in the form of sinister piles of drums, discolored pools of water, sick children, distraught parents, angry community gatherings.

It would take only one case among the many to break out and become the symbolic kernel of a national opinion-formation process, only one case to become the grain of sand around which the perceptual pearl would begin to form. The breakthrough came, as we know, with the case of Love Canal.

Here, I am not so much interested in the actual events in that unfortunate community.[10] If one wishes to study perceptual change on a mass, national level, one has to bracket the local news story and look only at how Love Canal was seen on TV and represented in the popular press.[11]

Hazardous Waste on the Television

The nation first heard about hazardous waste when CBS and ABC carried stories about events at Love Canal on August 2, 1978. Over the next two years, the networks' nightly news programs alone carried about 190 minutes of news about hazardous waste.[12] Whether people watched television in the morning (*CBS Morning News; Today Show; Good Morning, America*), during the day (*Donahue*), the dinner hour (McNeil-Lehrer; the networks' nightly news shows; *60 Minutes*), or late at night (*Nightline*), they saw stories about Love Canal.[13] I acquired copies of fifty-one stories that, together, accounted for about two thirds of the time (120 minutes) devoted to this topic by the networks' nightly newscasts and carefully examined them in order to identify their most characteristic qualities and their most repetitive verbal and visual messages. Below, as I cite images and words from these stories, I refer to them by letter—A for ABC; C for CBS; N for NBC—and story number; a key matching story number with the date on which the story is aired is provided in note 14.[14]

Love Canal's First Appearance on Television: During the first month of coverage, reports provided the basic background information: Decades earlier, Hooker Chemical Company in Niagara Falls, New York, dumped toxic chemical waste, "thousands of drums" (C1) of it, into Love Canal, a partially completed and abandoned navigation channel. In 1952, the canal was covered up. A year later, Hooker sold the land to the Niagara Falls Board of Education, and a school was built. Then developers built homes and "unsuspecting families" (C1) moved in. In the 1970s, after heavy rains, chemical wastes began to seep to the surface, both on the school grounds and into people's yards and basements. Federal and state officials confirmed the presence of eighty-eight chemicals, some in concentrations 250 to 5000 times higher than acceptable safety levels. Eleven of these chemicals were suspected or known carcinogens; others were said to cause liver and kidney ailments (C1, A1, A6).

The sense that this was a disaster was conveyed explicitly: a "calamity that has been steadily and silently building up for a long time" (A1) was now "seeping . . . coming out of the ground" (C1) into people's lives. More subtly, the reports conveyed the ominousness of the events at Love Canal by showing visuals that seemed to signify normalcy, but then undermining or reversing the impression, signifying the opposite, through voice-over narration. Some examples: A boy bicycles along a quiet suburban street while the narrator says, "There have been instances of birth defects and miscarriages among families" (C1). Kids play on a community playground while the narrator reports the New York Health Department's recommendation that pregnant women and small children evacuate (C1). Aerial views sweep across beautiful Niagara Falls and a boatful of admiring sightseers while the narrator quotes officials' fear that wastes are contaminating the Niagara River and Lake Ontario (N1). Shots of people's backyards, lawns, and swimming pools are followed by pictures of holes in the ground filled with ominously colorful soups of liquid chemical. "More than eighty chemical mixtures had worked their way up through the earth . . . into nearly backyards and basements," (N2) ruining swimming pools, "destroying much of the vegetation" (C1). This advice, often found in horror movies, conveyed a sense of insidiousness, of the benign and everyday suddenly becoming nightmarish.

Known or suspected health impacts were by far the most important aspect of the story. High rates of miscarriage and birth defects were reported (C1, C2, A1–A4, A6, N2). "Fear and concern [are] gripping this community" (A1). Lois Heisner, a housewife and former Hooker employee, describes two miscarriages and two children born prematurely, one who "has a defect" (A1). Karen

Schroeder, interviewed with her daughter Sherry, a little girl with large, sad eyes, sitting at her side, says her daughter was born with a cleft palate, and two rows of bottom teeth and has congenital hearing problems (A6; also shown and described in C1).

"You could see the fear on faces," says the reporter (C2) as the camera shows residents lined up to have their blood tested for "abnormalities." A state health official tells the reporter that they are looking for evidence of abnormalities associated with leukemia, anemia, and toxic liver conditions. He says, "I would expect to find more than the normal level of these kinds of illnesses" (C2). Indeed, CBS reports that "of those who have been told [the results] of their blood tests], abnormalities have shown up in 40 percent of the cases" (C5). A housewife worries about leukemia. There is a report of abnormalities in some residents' liver function, and another mother, Jean Guagliano, tells the reporter that both her children have kidney disease (C5). The reporter from ABC sums up: an "environmental disaster . . . people who lived here . . . [are] damaged for life" (A6).

Families are shown grappling with financial tragedy as well. Visuals of working-class or lower-middle-class homes convey the message that most are barely making ends meet; how will they ever pay for medical treatment? Their one major source of savings, their home, suddenly has no market value. A reporter asks a young woman, Mary Heeney, "Have you thought about trying to sell [your home]?" She laughs bitterly: "They won't put for-sale signs on any of these homes and who'd be crazy enough to buy one? I can't imagine why anybody would" (C2). They want to get away, to flee the hazard, but how can they afford to go? Lois Heisner, holding her child: "We have decided we are going to get out one way or another, but right now, you know, you can't just jump; where are we going to go?" (C1).

Stories indicate that community life is totally disrupted. The grade school is closed; the schoolyard, located on top of the canal, "where children have played for 24 years," (N2) is fenced off and signs warn, "No Trespassing Dangerous Area." Officials recommend that the people most affected should evacuate the area, first 37 families with pregnant women and children under two, then 97 families, eventually 239. There are shots of homes, now boarded up. At least those folks *are* getting away; families who have not persuaded officials to relocate them are frightened and angry. *Their* houses have protest signs: "We want out now" and "Evacuate us *now*!" (C2). Children are demonstrating, holding signs: "Children of *all* ages should be evacuated"; "Love Canal stinks and kills" (C2).

The most frequent, most persistent images throughout these news stories depict community land (schoolyard, suburban field, backyards) that ought to be green and vibrant with suburban vegetation but instead has only sparse, half-dead plant cover punctuated with holes containing an unnatural-looking chemical soup. Viewers see yards and basements invaded by chemical ooze, disrupted neighborhood life, a closed school, boarded-up homes, mass blood testing. Families packing and moving. Protest signs on houses. Worried housewives and mothers. (The stories contain nine interviews with residents, all women, all working class or lower-middle class, all articulate, competent, smart, some angry, all worried about the health of their families.)

Stories then began to suggest that what happened to the people at Love Canal could well happen in many other communities, that the horror movie of chemicals coming out of the ground into homes and children's bodies could soon be playing at a theater near you. U.S. industry was said to be annually generating 30–40 million tons of hazardous waste that "could have a severe adverse effect on human and animal life" (C4). Said the reporter, "Proper disposal of chemicals is the exception, not the rule," repeating the EPA's estimate that 80 percent of waste was being disposed of "improperly, inadequately or illegally" (C4).

The EPA was said to have found at least 400 other cases (C4); or 638 instances in which improperly disposed wastes might be threatening public health (A6); there might, in fact, be thousands (A6). Dumps sites were said to be "like ticking time bombs" (C4). Indeed, in the two years following initial coverage of Love Canal, television news featured a steady stream of stories that, taken together, communicated that toxic chemical contamination was widespread: PCBs, pesticide residues, dioxin, mercury fluorine, asbestos, chlorine, phosphorous, thousands of drums stacked haphazardly in various out-of-the-way rural spots, sick farm animals, contaminated water supplies, reports of illnesses ranging from rashes to cancer. No wonder that Walter Cronkite, one of the most trusted men in America, introduced one story with these words: "The problem of hazardous chemical waste drifts across the nation these days like a bad dream" (C6).

Love Canal Back in the News: In May 1980, Love Canal once again became the focus of the networks' attention, with eight stories over five days. The EPA released a study that found that eleven of thirty-six residents tested had chromosomal damage (C26, N4). A doctor from the EPA, the scientist who had conducted the study, and a cancer researcher working with the community all stated to reporters that the kind of chromosome damage found could cause cancer, miscarriage, and birth defects (C26, N4, A7). Interviews with distraught citizens were the emotional core of the coverage.

Reporter: "What do you think about when you think about tomorrow, next month, next year?"

Pat Sandonato, one of the eleven found to have chromosome damage: "My kids dying, coming down with something they can't cure" (C26).

Phyllis Whitenight, another of the eleven, says she has had cancer and "will probably get it again" (N4). Still another, Barbara Quimby, says she is not surprised to hear the findings since her eight-year-old has birth defects and is retarded (N4). Marie Pozniak, who has had cancer and whose daughter has central nervous system problems and asthma, says, "Every child I look at in this area, I wonder, 'Do you have hidden dangers in you?' How many cancers are growing in their body?" (N6).

Residents who were not part of the original relocation are "furious" and "desperate to move" (N4). They demand that the government "evacuate them immediately" (N5). Leonard Whitenight rages that the government has money for Cuban refugees or to get bodies out of Guyana but "won't help its own people" (C26).

Everyday life has come to a halt. People are in an uproar, standing in nervous groups, milling about in the streets. Barbara Quimby: "The people are just at their wits' end. They just can't handle any more mentally. Not when it comes down to your children. That's the worst" (A7).

The following day, citizens hold two EPA officials hostage for five hours. Barbara Quimby, holding a small child: "The people even scared me. They're my friends, my neighbors. They're calm, law abiding citizens, but they just can't handle it anymore. It's not only the risk to you. When you hear that this could affect your children. I mean, anybody who's a parent has to sympathize with us" (C27).

The following day, Love Canal is on all three networks, the lead story on two of them (C28, A8, N6). President Carter has declared an emergency; temporary relocation of seven hundred additional families is announced. Some declare they will stay until the government provides a permanent solution, but most go and go quickly. One mother, her family already in the car, tells the reporter that her nephew has cancer and she "can't put my children through that; I can't take the chance" (N6). Pat Sandonato, the one who thinks about her kids dying, says, "I just want my kids out of here" (C28). Another family is shown leaving just two and a half hours after the announcement. The kids say goodby to their pet, a Saint Bernard, left behind as they drive off to a motel (A8).

Scope Stories: Meanwhile, reported estimates of the national scope of the problem kept growing. The EPA reported at various points that there were "more than eight hundred" sites that were a serious threat to public health (C19); that there might be "as many as two thousand" that would need Superfund cleanups (C14); that there might be as many as thirty thousand sites with some waste (C7, C19, A10). In 1978, it was said that industry was generating 35 million tons of hazardous waste a year (C8); by 1980, that estimate had nearly doubled, to "125 billion pounds" (A10). The EPA's estimate that 80–90 percent of this material was being disposed of in unsafe ways was reported over and over (C4, C17).

Industry and government officials: These amounts might have been less frightening if the news had shown corporate generators and the disposal industry acting in a responsible manner and if government regulators had been shown to be competent to protect public health. Viewers, however, got just the opposite impression.

EPA officials repeatedly condemned past industry practices, saying that industry had left the nation a legacy of vast levels of contamination. The chemical industry was shown resisting stronger regulation. Ralph Nader charged that congressman opposed to the Superfund were getting big campaign contributions from the chemical industry (C31). Tennessee Congressman Albert Gore, Jr., charged that "the chemical industry is engaged in a very cynical effort to try to kill this legislation" (A9). A Union Carbide spokesman complained that "there's too many regulations, with standards that simply spend money" (C35), and a DuPont vice president called the proposed Resource Conservation and Recovery Act (RCRA) waste disposal standards "silly" (A10). As RCRA was about to go into effect, Walter Cronkite said that anticipation of new, stricter, more costly disposal rules had "triggered a vast, illegal dumping." There were picture of tanker trucks clogging the roads as the voice-over reported, "As the midnight deadline approached, there were reports of massive amounts of toxic chemicals on the move around the country, all in an effort, according to EPA officials, to dump the wastes before the new reporting requirements take effect" (C35). This was hardly the kind of news that would reassure worried citizens.

Could government provide the needed protection? Not likely, according to the network news. If safe disposal methods existed (C4, N1) and strong regulations had been on the books since 1976, why were 80 to 90 percent of wastes still improperly disposed of? The networks explained that delays in rule making had undermined implementation. EPA's enforcement efforts were weak, "infinitesimal in comparison to the size of the problem . . . grossly inadequate," according to a spokesman for the Environmental Defense Fund (C19). EPA was said to have only eighty inspectors to monitor compliance at twenty thousand disposal sites and thirty thousand factories (C35). "Without a larger enforcement staff," said the reporter, "few expect that the new law will quickly clean up the toxic waste problem" (C35).

TV Iconography of Hazardous Waste in a Forty-Second Précis: By November 1980, television's visual and rhetorical vocabulary of hazardous waste had become so highly conventionalized that Rebecca Chase could show it all and tell it all in forty seconds of snapshots and sound bites (A10):

Visuals	Voice-over
Boarded up homes	[no narration. Clicking of a slide
Chemical plant	projector carousel advancing
Polluted, dead ground	to the next slide.]
Boarded-up homes	*Love Canal was just the beginning.*
Chemicals leaking from container	*Deadly chemicals seeping into*
Backyards of boarded-up homes	*basements and backyards from*
Sign: "Hazardous Chemicals—	*an abandoned dump.*
Unauthorized Entry	*A national disaster declared.*
Prohibited"	

Boarded-up homes	*Residents evacuated.*
Drums of waste	*Once officials started looking,*
Truck discharging liquid waste	*They found toxic chemicals*
	throughout the nation,
Drums	*improperly stored . . .*
Drums	*abandoned . . .*
Polluted water	*contaminating drinking water . . .*
Caterpillar tractor putting dead	*killing cattle . . .*
cattle in a mass grave	
Person in a wheelchair	*making people sick . . .*
Child from Woburn, Mass.	*cancer . . .*
Woman	*miscarriages . . .*
Child from Love Canal	*birth defects.*
Aerial view of a dump site	*The EPA has discovered*
	30,000 dumps . . .
Workers sampling from drums	*4,000 are considered hazardous.*
Houses	*From New York . . .*
Drums	*to Kentucky . . .*
Drums	*to Illinois . . .*
Polluted water	*to Louisiana . . .*
Drums	*to California, toxic time bombs.*
Explosions at Elizabeth, N.J.	*Some have already blown up.*

Hazardous Waste in the Popular Press

Although television is the critical medium today for issue formation, the process is amplified if a message is conveyed in other media as well. Love Canal stories appeared in almost every type of popular magazine, the newsweeklies (*Time, Newsweek, U.S. News and World Report*), the business press (*Business Week, Fortune*), the left/movement press (*The Nation, The Progressive*), science journals (*Science*), highbrow literary magazines (*Atlantic Monthly, Saturday Review*), women's magazines (*Redbook, McCall's, Glamour*), *Mechanix Illustrated, People, Reader's Digest*.

The sheer level of news saturation is, itself, an important datum. By 1980, one would have had to be militantly uninterested in the world, uninterested in reading *anything*, in order to avoid reading something about Love Canal and hazardous waste.

I examined stories that appeared in *Time, Newsweek, Redbook, McCall's, Glamour,* and *Mechanix Illustrated.*[15] How was hazardous waste represented in the popular press? What impression did people get when they looked at these stories? It all depended on how deeply or how carefully the reader confronted these articles.

Carefully read, the articles conveyed a frightening story, certainly, but they also attempted to be balanced and fair. The reader who went beyond the over-

heated rhetoric—"witches' brew" "nightmare" "environmental disaster"—
would have learned that there were substantial doubts about the health impacts of toxic waste. The famous chromosome-damage study at Love Canal
may have been flawed; more generally, the connection between hazardous-
waste dumping and health problems had not been firmly established.

One would, however, have to read these stories with undivided attention
for these reservations to have equal weight. We know, instead, that many
"readers" glance rather than read. They look at the pictures, read the captions
and headlines, perhaps the first paragraph, and then turn the page. Such superficial readings produce a much more extreme, one-sided message, highly
stereotyped, top-heavy with charged, inflammatory rhetoric and imagery.
Some headlines:

"A Nightmare in Niagara" (*Time*, August 14, 1978)

"The Poisoning of America: Those Toxic Chemical Wastes" (*Time* cover
story, September 22, 1980)

"The Tragedy of Love Canal" (*Redbook*, April 1979)

"Underground Time Bombs: Chemical Waste Dumps" (*Mechanix Illustrated*,
September 1980)

"Our Fear Never Ends" (*McCall's*, June 1980)

Some picture captions:

"Environmental disaster area: a witches' brew of long-buried chemicals
turns the Love Canal district into ghost town" (*Newsweek*, August 21, 1978)

"Ending a nightmare: Jo Ann Kott's family packs up and heads for a motel"
(*Newsweek*, June 2, 1980)

". . . eruption at the Three Mile Island of waste dumps" (*Time*, May 5, 1980)

" 'You don't want them near you—nor do I' " (*Time*, September 22, 1980)

" 'We didn't understand that every barrel stuck into the ground was a ticking time bomb' " (*Time*, September 22, 1980)

"Incessant medical tests are part of the tragedy of the Love Canal disaster"
(*Mechanix Illustrated*, September 1980)

"A high incidence of cancer, birth defects and respiratory and neurological
problems" (*Time*, September 22, 1980)

"Today it is a ghost town of empty houses and abandoned dreams, but the
people of Love Canal have an important story to tell, for every day it becomes clearer that what happened to them could happen again—to any of
us" (*Redbook*, April 1979)

"A vivid illustration of the problems facing many communities throughout the U.S.: thousands of drums containing toxic wastes" (*Time*, September 22, 1980)

Finally, and perhaps most importantly, the photographs accompanying these stories repeated, and thus reinforced, the highly stylized vocabulary of hazardous-waste images shown by television news: contaminated patches of earth, haphazard piles of rusted and broken industrial drums, workers encased in protective safety gear, disrupted homes and community, common folk victimized and angry.

Polling Confirms that a New Issue is Formed

Opinion polls soon confirmed that all this media attention had had a big impact on people's perceptions of the toxic waste problem. An ABC News/Harris poll found that 93 percent of the public favored making federal disposal standards "much more strict;" 86 percent favored making "toxic chemical dumps and spills a very high priority for federal action;" 88 percent favored "providing funds to allow people who live in such areas and whose health may have been impaired to move out as soon as possible".[16] A poll conducted by Robert Cameron Mitchell for the U.S. Council on Environmental Quality found that 64 percent of the public was concerned "a great deal" about chemical waste disposal.[17] (It was this poll that yielded the "how close is close enough" curve reproduced in Figure 14.1.) A third poll, commissioned by the Chemical Manufacturers Association, found that 93 percent of politically active individuals felt either "very" or "extremely" concerned about chemical industry waste disposal practices.[18] *Glamour* magazine devoted its regular reader poll, "Tell Us What You Think About," to Love Canal in August 1980. Ninety-two percent of the respondents said news reports of Love Canal had made them "more alert to the dangers of living near a waste site;" 86 percent said the government was not doing enough to protect the public; 98 percent favored new legislation "to prevent dumping problems in the future."[19]

Understanding Perceptual Change in Contemporary Society

The development of widespread popular dread was a key moment in the creation of contemporary toxic waste politics. Certainly, there is nothing original in saying that the process of mass attitude formation is a centrally important condition for social movement growth. Still, the specific case of toxic waste suggests that the quality of opinion formation in the contemporary period is changing. As the account above shows, attitude change seems today to be based less on one's own experience than on media spectatorship, on a media-led witnessing of others' experience. This, in turn, causes other changes. The pace of attitude change, its "rate of spread" among people, seems to have sped up. At the same time, its *depth* or meaningfulness has become more suspect: Are attitudes borne of television watching as likely as direct experience to lead to actual political behavior?

Can we find a way of thinking about the contemporary attitude-formation process that sheds light on the implications of such changes?

Leading Theories of Risk Perception and Issue Creation

The phenomenon of widespread fear or dread of technological developments is referred to, in both academic and policy discourse, as the problem of lay "risk perception." The best-known approach to risk perception comes out of a rather specialized subfield of psychological research known as "decision theory." Decision theory has shown that people use a small number of simplifying "heuristics" when making judgments under uncertainty. Turning their attention to the question of lay perception of technological risks, decision theorists argued that two of these heuristics, "availability" and "overconfidence," are especially important. "Availability" means that people judge events to be "likely or frequent if instances of it are easy to imagine or recall"; "overconfidence" leads people to have unwarranted confidence in their judgments.[20]

Decision theorists have also studied lay risk perception empirically. They found that people judged something to be risky to the degree that it was "unknown to those exposed and unknown to science, and to a lesser extent by newness, involuntariness, and delay of effect . . . [and by the] severity of consequences (certainty of being fatal), dread, and catastrophic potential."[21]

The decision-theory approach certainly tells us something, but it also has serious flaws. The methodology used, questionnaires administered to artificially assembled samples of populations in experimental settings in no way connected to actual social events, is itself a denial of process. The findings are necessarily static and ahistorical. The findings are then explained in terms of fixed characteristics of human perception, "heuristics," or in terms of supposedly inherent and unchanging characteristics of certain technologies—their disaster potential, for example, or their uncontrollability.

The approach has difficulty capturing perhaps the central fact of lay perception, the fact that jumps out at the most casual observer, namely, that people's perception of risk *changes over time*. A process or technology may be accepted by the public, perceived as benign; later, it comes to be perceived as threatening, possibly catastrophic. This happened in the important case of nuclear power as well as in regard to hazardous waste.[22] Decision theory describes the end result of this process; it does not focus much on the dynamics of the process itself.

Long before the recent interest in "risk," sociologists and political scientists had sought to understand and describe the issue-creation process more generally. In sociology, advocates of the "constructivist" approach questioned the purported objectivity of "social problems," thereby focusing attention on the process through which claims that a problem exists are successfully made.[23] In political science, Cobb and Elder offered an essentially similar description of the process of "issue creation" in American politics.[24]

These approaches are attractive because they are explicitly concerned with describing process. They are, nonetheless, problematic because they continue to emphasize the word-centered production of meaning (with central terms like "claims," "rhetoric," "discourse") at a time when, many now argue, political communication and the production of meaning is increasingly accomplished through images, not words, through visual rather than verbal representation.

Words, claims, rhetoric certainly played a role in making "hazardous waste" an issue, but exclusive reliance on word-oriented notions of issue creation misses the distinctive qualities of an issue that was largely made on and by television. We need to find a way of thinking about issue-creation that relies more on the image than the word, a process that is more figural than discursive, a process that creates "meanings" in which the cognitive content is underarticulated and is dominated by highly charged value and emotional components. Some in the constructivist tradition have begun to examine this shift from word to image,[25] but this development has been explored most thoroughly in the literature on postmodernity.

Postmodern Perspectives on Mass Attitude Formation

The term "postmodern" suggests that society has decisively entered a qualitatively new and distinct historical phase.[26] Although I do not embrace this view fully or uncritically,[27] I believe this literature has trenchant, illuminating things to say about contemporary society. More specifically, I believe that its description of changes in the production and reception of political messages captures important aspects of the process of contemporary issue creation.

Theorists broadly agree that "postmodern" means, first, a new and original style of cultural production, a new fusion of high and low, elite and mass culture. This new amalgam of elite and mass culture is said to be inseparably bound up with the process of commodification: self-consciously postmodern art derives much of its raw material from the mass-produced output of the culture industry and from advertising.

We must hasten to note that "culture" means much more than the self-conscious practice of the visual and performing arts or of literature. Culture must be conceived of much more broadly, as that ensemble of languages, codes, or systems of representation that constitute a "particular way of experiencing, interpreting, and being in the world."[28] Culture, in this sense, is woven into the very fabric of social life; it is coextensive with and constitutive of social life. Theorists' depictions of "what is postmodern about contemporary society" thus move from a narrow focus on cultural objects to more encompassing descriptions of a social life that embraces "ephemerality, fragmentation, discontinuity, and the chaotic."[29]

The literature depicts postmodernity as a fundamental alteration of the texture of everyday life. The economy no longer produces only commodities but "commodity-texts" that are some combination of commodity, representation, image, and discourse. People no longer consume just things but thing-images.

Clearly, the very existence of such developments is unthinkable without the creation of a vast infrastructure of mass communications, television, and other increasingly sophisticated mass technologies of media and entertainment. Representation- and image-consumption has increasingly become the substance of everyday activity. The distinction between reality and representation threatens to become meaningless. Jameson says the "world [is] transformed into sheer images of itself . . . pseudo-events and 'spectacles,'"[30] and Lash talks of a society "whose very empirical reality is largely made up of images or representations."[31]

This confounding of daily living and representation-consumption transforms people's relationship to history, to community, to family. At the level of individual experience, theorists of postmodernity are relatively united in describing a subjectivity that is increasingly fragmented, distracted, attuned more to surface sensation and stimulation than to deeper feelings and meanings.[32]

Theorists of postmodernity also agree that politics, too, has been fundamentally altered, but they have diametrically opposed views as to *how*. Here, David Harvey's concern about "a mine-field of conflicting notions" is indeed apt. Some theorists claim that postmodernity is liberatory. To break with modernity means, fundamentally, to break with the domination of white, male, bourgeois, Eurocentric discourses, to open up cultural space for discourses by heretofore voiceless others and make possible the celebration of multiplicity and difference. Other observers are considerably more pessimistic. To them, postmodernity means that people are radically apolitical, ignorant of political facts, indifferent to public matters, unwilling to participate. Postmodern people are not able or willing to be citizens; participatory democracy, in the full sense of that term, is no longer possible. What politics remains is transformed into theater, into spectacle, into the production and consumption of superficial political imagery. Taking place in and through the media, particularly television, political discourse becomes ever more shallow, superficial, trivial.[33]

The first, or "utopian," interpretation of postmodernity's political implications is certainly appealing. The second, or "co-optative" interpretation is, I believe, more relevant to the task at hand. It allows us to think about the conditions that make meaningful political communication and, therefore, the process of issue creation, so problematic.

Production of Political Messages: In contemporary society, political discourse takes place increasingly in and through the same media circuits that provide commodified ways to fill leisure time and satisfy desires. The mass media are not neutral vehicles for communication, for discursive circulation. Stories must meet quite exacting requirements for both form and content. On television, specifically, the colorful image works better than the crafted word, and talk is best kept brief and simple. Striving for action and color, working within severe time constraints, news reports shy away from complex explanation; social issues are, instead, dramatized and personalized.

Consumption of Political Messages: Here, critiques of postmodernity point to two kinds of problems: first, the general qualities of postmodern subjectivity; second, people's indifference to public matters.

We have alluded to the first of these above. The postmodern subject is depicted as distracted, as addicted to fleeting and fragmentary sensation, as resistant to meanings. Baudrillard says the masses refuse "the sublime imperative of meaning";[34] they are a sink for all attempts to energize them.

> "[T]he masses scandalously resist this imperative of rational communication. They are given meaning: they want spectacle. . . . they idolize the play of signs and stereotypes, they idolize any content so long as it resolves itself into a spectacular sequence. . . . the political has long been the agent of nothing but spectacle on the screen of private life. Digested as a form of entertainment, half-sports, half-games . . . at once both fascinating and ludicrous."[35]

Further, theories of postmodernity share with many other perspectives the view that the people experience a radical split between public and private realms. To the average person, the realm of the "public," of national political events, seems distant, insignificant in comparison to the obvious importance and salience of the mundane, proximal concerns of everyday life.[36] People are not interested in the "larger issues;" their knowledge of that world is, at best, hazy.

Both casual observation and social scientific studies confirm that these depictions are to a great degree justified. Signs of ignorance and disinterest are everywhere. Study after study shows that Americans know little about most public matters.[37] Millions say they follow the news, but research finds that they do so in a superficial and evanescent manner.[38] The steady decline in the percentage of people who vote shows that many people refuse to participate even superficially in the political process. In 1990 the Markle Commission on the Media and the Electorate reported an "astonishing" level of ignorance about, and a "widespread, glacial indifference" toward even presidential campaigns.[39]

How can political communications proceed if these descriptions of mass political subjectivity are true, even if they are true only in tendency? What can politicians and issue makers do to overcome the public's indifference? How can they capture people's attention and influence their attitudes?

A *Solution: Production of Political Icons:* Politicians and issue makers are sharp students of practical communications who know full well that electronic media are the dominant vehicle for political communication. They have learned to reduce the message to the dramatic visual and the sound bite. They also act as if postmodern theorists' most pessimistic interpretations of the state of the masses is, in fact, correct. Their solution, their antidote to indifferent, distracted attention is, in fact, identical to the solution of the requirements-of-the-medium problem: make political messages ever more simple, vivid, colorful, repetitive.

I would like to suggest at this point that the semiological concept of the "icon" can be appropriated to capture and summarize the quality of this changes in political communication. We are most familiar with "icon" as religious representation. The American semiologist C. S. Peirce appropriated the term in order to capture the uniqueness of the one type of sign, "a sign which refers to the object that it denotes merely by virtue of characters of its own, . . . Anything whatever . . . is an icon of anything in so far as it is like that thing and used as a sign of it."[40] Sturrock's clarifying commentary is that "There is thus a picture-element in an *icon*, . . . The relation of expression to content is one of physical similarity."[41]

Recently, as cultural criticism has come under the influence of semiological and poststructuralist theories, we have seen the term "icon" applied to pop-culture figures (Elvis, Marilyn Monroe, and the like) who are no longer just people but have metamorphosed into fixed, highly stylized, mythical figures in the popular imagination. In fact, by 1992 cultural critics had seized upon the term with such enthusiasm that it had begun to be used too often and too loosely.

Still, the term has yet to be consistently applied to political phenomena or political communication. The preferred term is still "political symbol." However, to the degree that political messages are carried by images rather than words, so that meaning or signification takes place more through nonverbal spectacle than through narrative, the term "political icon" is a more appropriate expression for what is occurring than is the more traditional term "political symbol."[42]

Lash argues that there has been a general shift in society's regime of signification from words to images, from the discursive to the figural, from narrative to spectacle. The notion of the icon suggests that political communication has been transformed (or, if you like, degraded) exactly as Lash says. Political communication increasingly relies on the production and display of political icons rather than symbols, iconography rather than rhetoric, both because the means of communication require it stylistically and because it is assumed that displays of spectacular images are the only way to break through the indifference of the intended audience.[43]

Strengths and Weaknesses
of the Postmodern Interpretation

Notions of icon production and display seem a fruitful way to think about the events that made hazardous waste an issue and, more generally, about how one can meaningfully update theories of social-problem construction and issue creation. Conceiving of political communications as taking the form of icons, as opposed to rhetoric or even symbols, emphasizes the image-oriented style of such communications. It conveys the central role of mass media and, hence, the way that attitude formation is based more on being a passive consumer of media messages than on direct, personal experience. That, in turn, accounts for the rapid pace of attitude diffusion. Those are all observations that ring true and that suggest that a postmodern reading of attitude formation has considerable merit.

A final implication of the postmodern interpretation is, however, more questionable. Were we to accept the most extreme postmodernist readings of contemporary social process, we would believe that attitude changes generated by icon production and consumption are never really meaningful ones. How do people receive, assimilate, and retain iconic political messages? If people's experience, and hence the texture of mass attention, is indeed fragmented, superficial, evanescent, do the attitude changes induced by iconography have any real depth or staying power? Do such attitudes ever produce actual, overt political behavior?

In a society in which episodic attention is the norm, the argument goes, issue importance can evaporate as quickly as it forms, and nothing guarantees that even widespread political discourses will have staying power. One tunes in and consumes some imagery about environmental destruction—say, Bhopal or the Exxon Valdez. One cares, one can even care a great deal, during those brief bursts of attention given over to monitoring national and world events. However, if such stories do not connect with something in the viewer's immediate life sphere, if there is no material, experiential basis for the opinion formed, that person will believe that a problem, an issue, exists without being more than momentarily upset about it. Absent a real connection to their immediate interests, concern will fade and the story will be forgotten when the kaleidoscopic flux of news moves on to other things.

Some evidence supports this view that the attitudinal changes produced by iconic communications are shallow and evanescent. Researchers have repeatedly found that increased media coverage produces an immediate leap in expressions of concern about an issue, but the same research also shows that expressions of concern tend to fade rapidly as soon as coverage wanes.[44]

But if this kind of attitude formation is always essentially hollow and politically meaningless, why do technologists and their politically conservative allies worry? People such as Chauncey Starr, the author of a seminal article on risk who is affiliated with the utility industry's pro-nuclear Electric Power Research Institute, or Aaron Wildavsky, the well-known conservative political scientist, fret when public opinion crystallizes around highly charged images and names.[45] And why do environmentalists believe it is worthwhile to change popular attitudes by means of inventing and displaying icons? They have, after all, mastered the art of icon-making and have used it to excellent effect, creating and successfully throwing into discursive circulation both *images* (the baby harp seal, the whale, the cooling tower, the haphazard pile of rusting fifty-five-gallon drums) and *names* (acid rain, greenhouse effect, ozone hole, Love Canal, and toxic waste).

The answer is that icon-fostered attitudes do *not* always and inevitably fade without trace. That would be the sole outcome only if postmodern conditions had totally erased all other, earlier practices, only if all other forms of politics had ceased to exist. But, as I suggested above, depictions of postmodernity tend to totalize too much, tend to overstate the degree of transformation. Other, more traditional forms of political practice do persist.

If so, we might imagine that things can go one of two ways: The iconogenic moment occurs, producing in mass perception the kind of extreme feelings of dread described by Slovic and other decision theorists. If nothing else happens, people's sense of foreboding, of being at risk, passes. If, however, the attitudes and beliefs formed in the iconogenic moment *do* connect with immediate experience and interests—if, for example, people see toxic waste stories on TV and think that *their* community may be contaminated or that the waste facility to be built in their neighborhood might ruin their health and well-being—then the attitudes fostered by the icon, far from being shallow or hollow or evanescent, can instead lead to rapid, even explosive social movement growth.

NOTES

1. For details about the development of this movement, see Andrew Szasz, *EcoPopulism: Toxic Waste and the Movement for Environmental Justice* (Minneapolis: University of Minnesota Press, 1994), 69–99, 150–161.

2. Adam Clymer, "Polls Contrast U.S.'s and Public's Views," *New York Times*, May 22, 1989.

3. U.S. Environmental Protection Agency, "Public Attitudes toward Hazardous Waste Disposal Facilities" (Washington, D.C.: Government Printing Office, 1973).

4. U.S. Council on Environmental Quality, "Public Opinion on Environmental Issues: Results of a National Public Opinion Survey" (Washington, D.C.: Government Printing Office, 1980).

5. Paul Slovic, Baruch Fischhoff, and Sarah Lichtenstein, "Characterizing Perceived Risk," in Robert W. Kates, Christoph Hohenemser, and Jeanne X. Kasperson, eds., *Perilous Progress: Managing the Hazards of Technology* (Boulder and London: Westview Press, 1985), 91–125.

6. Szasz, *EcoPopulism*, 69–70.

7. Thomas N. Gladwin, "Patterns of Environmental Conflict over Industrial Facilities in the United States, 1970–78," in Robert W. Lake, ed., *Resolving Locational Conflict* (New Brunswick, N.J.: Center for Urban Policy Research, 1987), 14–44.

8. U.S. Environmental Protection Agency, "Siting of Hazardous Waste Management Facilities and Public Opposition," SW 809 (Washington, D.C.: Government Printing Office, 1979).

9. W. Lance Bennett, *News: The Politics of Illusion,* 2d ed. (New York: Longman, 1988); Herbert J. Gans, *Deciding What's News: A Study of CBS Evening News, NBC Nightly News, Newsweek and* Time (New York: Pantheon, 1979).

10. The story of Love Canal has been told often and well by participants, journalists, environmental activists, government officials, sociologists, and other social scientists: Lois Marie Gibbs, *Love Canal: My Story* (Albany: State University of New York Press, 1982); Michael Brown, *Laying Waste: The Poisoning of America by Toxic Chemicals* (New York: Pantheon, 1979); Samuel S. Epstein, Lester O. Brown, and Carl Pope, *Hazardous Waste in America* (San Francisco: Sierra Club Books, 1982); Nicholas Freudenberg, *Not in Our Backyards! Community Action for Health and the Environment* (New York: Monthly Review Press, 1984); Mark E. Anthony Reische, "A Legislative History of the Comprehensive Environmental Response, Compensation, and Liability Act of 1980 (Superfund), Public Law 96-510," prepared by the Environment and Natural Resources Policy Division of the Congressional Research Service of the Library of Congress for the Committee on Environment and Public Works, U.S. Senate, 3 vols. (Washington, D.C.: U.S. Government Printing Office, 1983), 1:700–704; Martha R. Fowlkes and Patricia Y. Miller, *Love Canal: The Social Construction of Disaster* (Washington D.C.: Federal Emergency Management Agency, 1982); Adeline G. Levine, *Love Canal: Science, Politics, and People* (Lexington, Mass.: Lexington Books, 1982).

11. Harvey Moloch and Marilyn Lester in their important article on the Santa Barbara oil spill, "Accidental News: The Great Oil Spill as Local Occurrence and National Event," *American Journal of Sociology* 81, no. 2 (1975), make the important distinction between asking how an event is experienced locally and how it is represented nationally.

12. Based on an inspection of *Television News Index and Abstracts* (Nashville, Tenn.: Vanderbilt University Television News Archive).

13. Levine, *Love Canal,* 100, 156, 171, 192, 207.

14. The coverage was uneven, with CBS providing the most coverage, about 83 minutes, ABC about 63 minutes, and NBC about 47. Regardless of any variations in content, the sheer difference in time devoted to the story would have meant that viewers loyal to NBC's David Brinkley and Jessica Savitch would have gotten a somewhat different impression of the importance of the story than, say, devotees of Walter Cronkite and Roger Mudd.

I selected the full set of CBS stories and a smaller number from the other networks. Below is a key for identifying the stories referred to in the text:

CBS: C1—August 2, 1978; C2–August 7, 1978; C3—August 8, 1978; C4–August 9, 1978; C5—September 1, 1978; C6—September 6, 1978; C7—November 21, 1978; C8—December 14, 1978; C9—January 5, 1979; C10—January 10, 1979; C11—February 6, 1979; C12—February 9, 1979; C13—February 16, 1979; C14—March 2, 1979; C15—April 10, 1979; C16—April 17, 1979; C17—April 30, 1979; C18—April 30, 1979; C19—May 8, 1979; C20—June 13, 1979; C21—December 20, 1979; C22—February 26, 1980; C23—March 22, 1980; C24—April 28, 1980; C25—May 5, 1980; C26—May 17, 1980; C27—May 20, 1980; C28—May 21, 1980; C29—May 29, 1980; C30—June 6, 1980; C31—August 24, 1980; C32—September 19, 1980; C33—September 29, 1980; C34—October 1, 1980; C35—November 18, 1980.

ABC: A1—August 2, 1978; A2—August 4, 1978; A3—August 7, 1978; A4—August 11, 1978; A5—September 8, 1978; A6—November 21, 1978; A7—May 17, 1980; A8—May 21, 1980; A9—September 11, 1980; A10—November 20, 1980.

NBC: N1—August 9, 1978; N2—September 24, 1978; N3—April 22, 1980; N4—May 17, 1980; N5—May 18, 1980; N6—May 21, 1980.

15. In addition to the obvious choice of *Time* and *Newsweek,* I chose the women's magazines because women have played such a central role in the hazardous-waste movement. The articles are: "Tell Us What You Think about . . . Love Canal," *Glamour,* August 1980; "What You Thought about . . . Love Canal," *Glamour,* November 1980; "A Nightmare in Niagara," *Time,* August 14, 1978; "Explosion of a Toxic Time Bomb: New Jersey blaze spotlights growing problem of chemical waste," *Time,* May 5, 1980; "The Neighborhood of Fear: Carter orders a further evacuation from polluted Love Canal," *Time,* June 2, 1980; "Skeptical View: Another Look at Love Canal," *Time,* November 3, 1980; Melinda Beck, Mary Lord, and Jerry Buckley, "More Love Canals?" *Newsweek,* May 14, 1979; Melinda Beck and Mary Lord, "A Caustic Report on Chemical Dumps," *Newsweek,* October 22, 1979; Sharon Begley, "Toxic Waste Still Pollutes Roadways," *Newsweek,* October 27, 1980; Matt Clark, Mary Hager, Dan Shapiro, William Marbach, "Fleeing the Love Canal," *Newsweek,* June 2, 1980; Fern Marja Eckman, "Our Fear Never Ends," *McCall's,* June 1980; Dorothy Gallagher, "The Tragedy of Love Canal," *Redbook,* April 1979; Peter Gwynne, et al., "The Chemicals around Us," *Newsweek,* August 21, 1978; Ed Magnuson, Peter Stoler, and J. Madeleine Nash, "The Poisoning of America: Belatedly, the campaign begins to control hazardous chemical wastes," *Time,* September 22, 1980; Tom Morganthau and Mary Hager, "Coping with Toxic Waste," *Newsweek,* May 19, 1980; Merrill Sheilds, et al., "Fiery Cloud over Earth Day," *Newsweek,* May 5, 1980; Michael J. Weiss, "Underground Time Bombs: Chemical Waste Dumps," *Mechanix Illustrated,* September 1980.

16. Steven Cohen and Marc Tipermas, "Superfund: Preimplementation Planning and Bureaucratic Politics," in James P. Lester and Ann O. Bowman, eds., *The Politics of Hazardous Waste Management* (Durham, N.C.: Duke University Press, 1983), 43–59; Allan Mazur, "The Journalists and Technology: Reporting about

Love Canal and Three Mile Island," *Minerva,* 22, no. 1 (1984); Andrew Szasz, "The Dynamics of Social Regulation: A Study of the Formation and Evolution of the Occupational Safety and Health Administration" (Ph.D. diss., University of Wisconsin, 1982), 350.

17. U.S. Council on Environmental Quality, "Public Opinion on Environmental Issues;" Robert Cameron Mitchell, "Public Opinion and Environmental Politics in the 1970s and 1980s," in Norman J. Vig and Michael E. Kraft, eds., *Environmental Policy in the 1980s: Reagan's New Agenda* (Washington, D.C.: Congressional Quarterly Press, 1984), 51–74; Robert Cameron Mitchell, "Rationality and Irrationality in the Public's Perception of Nuclear Power," in William R. Freudenburg and Eugene A. Rosa, eds., *Public Reactions in Nuclear Power: Are There Critical Masses?* (Boulder, Colo.: Westview, 1984), 137–79.

18. Paul D. Bush, "Citizen Response to Industrial Waste," in C. P. Huang, ed., *Industrial Waste: Proceedings of the Thirteenth Mid-Atlantic Conference* (Ann Arbor, Mich.: Ann Arbor Science Publishers, 1981), 533–36; Reisch, "A Legislative History of (Superfund)," 1:708–9.

19. "What You Thought about . . . Love Canal," *Glamour,* November 1980.

20. Paul Slovic, Baruch Fischhoff, and Sarah Lichtenstein, "Facts versus Fears: Understanding Perceived Risk," in Richard C. Schwing and Walter A. Alberts, Jr., eds., *Societal Risk Assessment: How Safe Is Safe Enough?* (New York: Plenum, 1980), 181–214; Amos Tversky and Daniel Kahneman, "Judgment under Uncertainty: Heuristics and Biases," in Daniel Kahneman, Paul Slovic, and Amos Tversky, eds., *Judgment under Uncertainty: Heuristics and Biases* (New York: Cambridge University Press, 1982), 3–20.

21. Slovic, Fischhoff, and Lichtenstein, "Characterizing Perceived Risk," 100.

22. William R. Freudenburg and Rodney K. Baxter, "Public Attitudes toward Local Nuclear Power Plants: A Reassessment" (paper presented at the American Sociological Association, Detroit, 1983); Allan Mazur, *The Dynamics of Technical Controversy* (Washington, D.C.: Communications Press, 1981); Allan Mazur, "The Journalists and Technology: Reporting about Love Canal and Three Mile Island," *Minerva* 22 (1984): 45–66; Allan Mazur, "Media Influences on Public Attitudes toward Nuclear Power," in Freudenburg and Rosa, *Public Reactions to Nuclear Power,* pp. 97–114; William L. Rankin, Stanley M. Nealey, and Barbara Desow Melber, "Overview of National Attitudes toward Nuclear Energy: A Longitudinal Analysis," in Freudenburg and Rosa, *Public Reactions to Nuclear Power,* pp. 41–68.

23. Malcolm Spector and John I. Kitsuse, *Constructing Social Problems* (New York: Aldine deGruyter, 1987).

24. Roger W. Cobb and Charles D. Elder, *Participation in American Politics: The Dynamics of Agenda-Building,* 2d ed. (Baltimore: Johns Hopkins University Press, 1983).

25. William A. Gamsow, and Andre Modigliani, "Media Discourse and Public Opinion on Nuclear Power: A Constructionist Approach," *American Journal of Sociology* 95, no. 1 (1989): 1–37.

26. This discussion is based on Frederic Jameson, "Postmodernism, or The Cultural Logic of Late Capitalism," *New Left Review*, no. 146, (1984); Jameson, *Postmodernism, or The Cultural Logic of Late Capitalism* (Durham: Duke University Press, 1991); Scott Lash, *Sociology of Postmodernity* (London: Routledge, 1990); David Harvey, *The Condition of Postmodernity* (Cambridge, Mass.: Basil Blackwell, 1989); Jean Baudrillard, "In the Shadow of the Silent Majorities," in *In the Shadow of the Silent Majorities, Or the End of the Social, and Other Essays* (New York: Semiotext(e), 1983), 1–61; Murray Edelman, *Constructing the Political Spectacle* (Chicago: University of Chicago Press, 1988).

27. The claim that society has entered an absolutely new moment seems too extreme, overstated. Some of the developments that are cited as quintessentially "postmodern" have existed for many decades; conversely, these developments have not completely displaced older, more traditional or modernist ones.

   Anyone familiar with critical theory (Max Horkheimer and Theodor Adorno, *The Dialectics of Enlightenment* [New York: Continuum, 1987]; Herbert Marcuse, *One-Dimensional Man: Studies in the Ideology of Advanced Industrial Society* [Boston: Beacon Press, 1964]), the Situationists (Guy Debord, *Society of the Spectacle* [Detroit: Black & Red, 1977]), or earlier studies of the connection between economic growth and advertising-driven production of demand (Paul A. Baran, *The Political Economy of Growth* [New York: Monthly Review Press, 1957]; Paul A. Baran and Paul M. Sweezy, *Monopoly Capital: An Essay on the American Economic and Social Order* [New York: Monthly Review Press, 1966]; Stuart Ewen, *Captains of Consciousness: Advertising and the Social Roots of the Consumer Culture* [New York: McGraw-Hill Book Company, 1976]) knows that some of what is now labeled "postmodern" has been with us for quite some time. Similarly, political scientist Murray Edelman has argued, in a series of works dating from 1964 (*The Symbolic Uses of Politics* [Urbana: University of Illinois Press, 1964]; *Politics as Symbolic Action: Mass Arousal and Quiescence* [New York: Academic Press, 1971]; *Political Language: Words That Succeed and Policies That Fail* [New York: Academic Press, 1977]), that American politics has long been dominated by symbolic gestures rather than substance. Marcy Darnovsky ("Social Movements in the Media Environment," University of California at Santa Cruz, 1990) shows that image management, public relations methods derived from advertising, found their way into American politics as far back as the Wilson administration. What are said to be defining features of "postmodern" politics, then, do not seem unprecedented, dramatically new, or original; they appear as American as apple pie. If there is truth in these descriptions, as I think there is, their power and importance are not diminished if we forbear from characterizing them as radical and unprecedented developments. We should see them, instead, as a fuller expression of tendencies already present.

   The second point is that postmodern forms and practices have not taken over as totally as is depicted in some works on postmodernity. Cogent as these descriptions are, the most cursory examination of contemporary events suggests that they describe only part of what is happening politically in American society. Indifference to public matters may be endemic, but it is far from total and uniform. Citizens vary widely in their levels of attention and concern about issues. Earlier forms of political practices, traditional social movement forms and strategies, for examples, persist. Contemporary society is complex and heterogeneous with a culture that has traditional, modern, and postmodern elements.

Thus, postmodernity seems, simultaneously, to have been with us for a long time and not yet fully to have arrived. Though much of the literature on postmodernity suffers from the tendency to totalize what it describes, some authors are careful to state that postmodernity is only one facet of a complex and multilayered social formation and are groping toward a careful and detailed theorization of uneven and combined cultural development. For example, see Lash, *Sociology of Postmodernity*, 13; Jameson, *Postmodernism*, 3–4. Still, as with other academic developments that catch fire and become fashionable, the term has now been used so promiscuously that it has become increasingly hard to pin down what it does and does not signify. David Harvey comments, quite correctly, that the literature on postmodernity is "a mine-field of conflicting notions" (*Condition of Postmodernity*, ix).

28. Harvey, *Condition of Postmodernity*, 53.

29. Ibid., 44.

30. *Postmodernism*, 18.

31. *Sociology of Postmodernity*, 14.

32. Jameson, "Postmodernism," has an especially thorough discussion of postmodernity and subjectivity.

33. Kaplan labels these "utopian" versus "coopted" postmodernisms in E. Ann Kaplan, ed., *Postmodernism and its Discontents: Theories, Practices* (London: Verso, 1988), 4. Lash makes a similar distinction with his notion of "oppositional" versus "mainstream" postmodernisms (*Sociology of Postmodernity*, 37).

34. Baudrillard, "In the Shadow of the Silent Majorities," 7.

35. Ibid., 10, 37–38.

36. "To hear or read the news is to live intermittently in a world one does not touch in daily life. . . . Most experiences that make life joyful, poignant, boring, or worrisome are not part of the news: the grounds for personal concern, frustration, . . . the conditions that matter at work, at home . . . the events people touch, as distinct from those that are 'reported' " (Edelman, *Constructing the Political Spectacle*, 35). As a result, "Nonvoters constitute a larger political grouping in America than the adherents of any political party. Only a small proportion of the population contributes money for political purposes, engages in any other kind of political activity, or pays more than passing attention to political news" (ibid., 7).

37. See, for example, Robert S. Erikson, Norman R. Luttbeg, and Kent L. Tedin, *American Public Opinion*, 2d ed. (New York: Wiley, 1980); W. Russell Neu-

mann, *The Paradox of Mass Politics: Knowledge and Opinion in the American Electorate* (Cambridge, Mass.: Harvard University Press, 1986).

38. Alex S. Jones, "Survey Finds That Americans Want News but Are Not Very Well Informed," *New York Times*, July 15, 1990.

39. Michael Oreskes, "Study Finds 'Astonishing' Indifference to Elections," *New York Times*, May 6, 1990.

40. Quoted in John Sturrock, *Structuralism* (London: Paladin Grafton Books, 1986), 84.

41. Ibid., 85.

42. See Sturrock's useful review of different types of signs, *Structuralism*, 84–85.

43. Certainly, politics has always relied heavily on slogans to carry emotionally loaded, condensed meanings in the longer signifying chains of political discourse. We are talking here about a *tendency*, not an absolute, a tendency in which the discursive rhetoric fades out, is no longer performed, leaving the visual image and the sound bite to carry all the freight of the political message by themselves. Postmodern theorists' depictions here converge with the laments of the political pundits. Editorialists, observers of the co-ed variety, agree that the influence of the media has altered every aspect of the political process, mutating it in form and degrading it quality. Electoral campaigns are run along the lines of commercial product advertising. Candidates' positions on the issues are trivialized, "communicated" with a few carefully chosen images and sound bites. Lawmakers are now continuously preoccupied with the politics of image management. They are reluctant to push an issue unless they are sure that it will play well on the news. Concern that a particular vote could be "made into an effective 30-second spot" by opponents creates a "politics of avoidance," politics that is "timid and irrelevant." See Michael Oreskes, "America's Politics Loses Way As Its Vision Changes World," *New York Times*, March 18, 1990; and Oreskes, " 'Wars' Wound Candidates and the Process," *New York Times*, March 19, 1990.

44. Anthony Downs, "Up and Down with Ecology—the 'Issue-Attention Cycle,' " *The Public Interest* 28 (Summer 1972); Riley E. Dunlap, "Two Decades of Public Concern for Environmental Quality: Up, Down and Up Again" (paper presented at the annual meeting of the American Sociological Association, New York, 1986); Shanto Iyengar and Donald R. Kinder, *News That Matters: Television and American Opinion* (Chicago: University of Chicago Press, 1987); A. Clay Schoenfeld, Robert F. Meier, and Robert J. Griffin, "Constructing a Social Problem: The Press and the Environment," *Social Problems* 27 (1979). We should not have been surprised, then, when a recent media study found that even the most avid news consumer "retained . . . little more than a hazy familiarity" with what they read, heard, or saw in the news (Jones, "Survey Finds That Americans Want News").

45. Starr's original paper on risk was "Social Benefit versus Technological Risk," *Science* 165 (September 1969). Keynoting a General Motors Research Laboratory symposium on societal risk assessment, Starr told the audience that "the

perceptions [of the 'great population of this country'] may be so far from reality that you and I know that they're absurd, but that's how they feel about it . . ." (reported in "The Risks We Run and the Risks We 'Accept,' " in Schwing and Albers, *Societal Risk Assessment,* 4). In a recent article, Starr cautioned that, "Public fears can always be aroused by the concept of man's tampering with nature, creating global catastrophes. Such fears can easily be used to stop new scientific developments. . . . anticipatory arousal of public anxiety can inhibit the creation of new technology" ("Risk Management, Assessment and Acceptability," *Risk Analysis* 5, no. 2 [1985]: 98–99). Aaron Wildavsky accuses Americans of suffering from unfounded fears, mass paranoia: "How extraordinary! The richest, longest-lived, best-protected, most resourceful civilization, with the highest degree of insight into its own technology, is on its way to becoming the most frightened. . . . It isn't much, really, in dispute—only the land we live on, the water we drink, the air we breathe, the food we eat, the energy that supports us. Chicken Little is alive and well in America" (in "No Risk Is the Highest Risk of All," *American Scientist* 67, no. 1 (January–February 1979):32.

CHAPTER 15

The Media Environment
after Desert Storm

Marcy Darnovsky

□   □   □   □   □   □   □   □   □   □   □

One of the major themes of media coverage during the 1991 Gulf War was itself media coverage of the Gulf War. Denunciations and defenses of the media's performance abounded in every genre of television and radio show and in every sort of newspaper and magazine. Stories about Pentagon press censorship and public approval of it,[1] about fan clubs for a CNN reporter and the slickness of the networks' graphics, about Saddam Hussein's television strategy—all of these "angles" provided grist for the saturation coverage of the war.[2]

This pattern of media self-absorption was more than institutional conceit: The media in fact constituted a crucial battlefield in the Gulf War. The Bush administration and the Pentagon saw control of media coverage as crucial to their success. They derived the political logic of their media strategy from the revisionist history of the Vietnam War that became popular during the Reagan regime. Television and press news, that story goes, had coddled antiwar critics or caved in to their pressure tactics, helping to turn Americans against pursuit of a military victory in Southeast Asia and acting as a primary vector of the highly infectious "Vietnam syndrome."

Twenty years later, media considerations were thus central in both the selling of the Gulf War and the fighting of it. Planning for Desert Storm as a media event, in fact, rivaled preparations for Desert Storm as military action. Writing a few weeks after the cease-fire, Michael Klare, defense correspondent for *The Nation*, argued that the conflict in the Gulf

> was the first war in history whose overarching strategic design was dictated more by concern about the resurgence of antiwar protests than in response to actual battlefield conditions. . . . [Bush's] every move was dictated by his fear of the Vietnam syndrome. This can be seen in his decision to act quickly

and with overwhelming force, and in the muzzling and manipulation of the mass media.[3]

From the point of view of the administration and the Pentagon, then, the carpet bombing and massive death in Iraq were preventive measures and not only in a strictly military sense. If U.S. troops were to get "bogged down" or killed in unacceptably large numbers, the U.S. media might report these developments, and they would then become risk factors for a recurrence of the Vietnam syndrome. The war makers understood public approval and a popular culture of enthusiasm as crucial to their success and deployed a media strategy that skillfully combined censorship and state-of-the-art spectacle, brute control of information with a carefully orchestrated ensemble of emotion-charged images, stories, and mythic themes.

For the U.S. movement that mobilized to protest the Gulf War, media coverage was also a central concern. From the very beginning of the crisis, antiwar activists stressed the media's influence on public opinion and, therefore, its effects on the outcome of the war.[4] More quickly and more fully than in any previous political mobilization, antiwar activists sharpened their media analysis and critique and experimented with new tactics for resisting and pressuring news organizations.

Among the hundreds of hand-made signs at the major antiwar demonstrations, dozens addressed media themes. In a number of cities including New York, San Francisco, Chicago, and Los Angeles, critics of the war mounted demonstrations as large as twelve hundred people at the offices of newspapers, radios, and television stations. In the San Francisco Bay area, a newly formed group called Artists and Writers Out Loud rallied each week for five weeks at a different local television station. A group of New York City ACT UP (AIDS Coalition to Unleash Power) protesters invaded the network news studios during their evening news broadcasts. The New York–based media-watch group FAIR (Fairness and Accuracy in Reporting) distributed over a hundred thousand copies of a media-response flyer that listed the addresses and phone numbers of national news outlets. Alternative media such as the Pacifica radio network, the video production group Paper Tiger TV, and the computer bulletin board Peacenet leapt into high gear. Forums, discussions, and panels on the war and the media proliferated and continued to draw overflow audiences for the duration of the conflict; many articles about the media and the war were written during and after the conflict.[5]

This chapter examines the assumptions that drove most left media activism during the Gulf War and that continue to underlie many activist media strategies. Without rejecting the importance of traditional left media strategies, it argues for augmenting them with insights from theoretical work done under the umbrella of "cultural studies," which John O'Kane has described (very aptly for the purposes of understanding what might be called the popular culture of the Gulf War) as "the academic label for examining connections between seemingly rational and autonomous structures of political expression and the circulation of popular pleasures, social identities, and regressive fantasies."[6]

The Information Model of Media

Most antiwar media efforts were predicated on the assumption that many Americans would oppose the Gulf War if they knew more about it. The problem of the media, according to this approach, is that of access to information: If Americans were aware of such circumstances as the political situation in the Middle East, the U.S. government's involvement with Saddam Hussein, and the huge numbers of Iraqi civilian deaths, they would turn against the war.

From this point of view, the Pentagon's press restrictions and the news media's omissions and distortions were nearly complete explanations for the overwhelming popularity in the United States of the troop deployments and bombing raids in the Gulf region. The major thrust of antiwar media strategy, therefore, was to encourage a rift in the collaboration between the Pentagon and the media: to pressure news organizations to defy military censorship and to rise above their own biases—in other words, to "tell the truth" about the Gulf War.

Many of the media-related signs at the massive antiwar demonstrations in San Francisco on January 19 and 26, 1991, expressed these assumptions. Some of them focused on Pentagon censorship: "This sign has *not* been cleared by the U.S. military," "Free the Press," "The Pentagon is making (up) history," "Question Pentagon-censored news." Others blamed the media, implying that they were responsible for public support of the war or, sometimes, for the war itself: "Corporate media's Operation Ignorance," "Mainstream media are propaganda pimps," "U.S. media: The blood is on your hands," "Break the media blockade." Still other signs were direct appeals to the media: "Media: Give us the truth," "We have a first amendment right to truth," "See us! Count us! Report the truth!"

Ironically, these demands for access to the media and truth from them share the standard assumptions about objectivity and neutrality that the media often use as self-justification. They also echo the conservative academic tradition of studying "media effects" defined in a narrow, quantifiable, behaviorist sense. Of course, left and antiwar media analyses are far more critical in their intent and application, even when they adhere to the information model. According to the critical formulation of the information model, the media cannot and will not deliver a fair or accurate picture of the world because they are owned by corporate giants and underwritten by advertisers and because the practices and expectations of journalists correspond to an elite view of the world.[7]

This critical formulation of the information model is an important contribution to a theory of the media and to strategies of media resistance. We cannot do without information; it matters very much that most Americans were unaware of the Bush administration's long-standing support for Saddam Hussein, that most of the tens of thousands of bombs dropped on Iraq were *not* the so-called "smart missiles" shown over and over in video game–style newscasts, that as many as two hundred thousand Iraqis died as a result of the war.[8] It makes a difference that only twenty-nine out of almost twenty-nine hundred minutes (about 1 percent) of network-news war coverage during the first five months of the Gulf crisis were devoted to grassroots dissent against Bush's military buildup.[9] Exposing the ways in which the major media failed to live up to their self-proclaimed standards of objectivity, fairness, accuracy, and balance can be an effective tactic.

But the information model of media is insufficient if only because it doesn't explain the depth or breadth of popular support for the war in the United States. The patriotic bumper stickers and yellow ribbons that festooned the country were not, after all, issued by the Pentagon but adopted in a surge of grassroots fervor, and they were affixed on pickup trucks as well as on BMWs. Many commentators attributed these displays of patriotism to the "rally 'round the flag" effect, but that is a way of labeling the problem rather than explaining it. Information, access, censorship, truth, and disinformation touch only the surface of the media-related dilemmas of national identity and emotional identification in which the wild enthusiasm for the Gulf War was tangled.

The Manipulation Model of Media

Another set of inadequate assumptions about media that is widespread among leftwing critics and activists can be termed the manipulation model of media. This model coexists, usually in unacknowledged and unlikely combination, with the information model. According to the manipulation model, the media audience is not only information deprived but also stupefied, duped, even brainwashed. It credits the media with persuasive powers of almost magical proportion, sometimes describing the media's operating procedures as conspiracy. Some antiwar activists, following this model, posited a simple and direct causal relationship between "media manipulation" and the outpouring of support for the Gulf War.

As with the information model, there is more than a grain of truth here. Techniques that are by definition manipulative—public relations, advertising, marketing—are routinely accepted in the contemporary United States as tools of both commerce and governance. The Reagan and Bush administrations developed an impressive arsenal for managing media relations and public perceptions. Beginning in 1980 they staged a series of "national identity spectacles"[10]—the patriotic orgies that surrounded the 1984 Olympics and the 1986 birthday celebration for the Statue of Liberty; the Libyan terrorist scare followed by Reagan's 1986 bombing attack, which Noam Chomsky called "the first bombing in history staged for prime time television"; and, of course, the Grenada and Panama invasions, which served to work out the details of media control and to test-market public response to military adventures.

The Pentagon began its own intensive study of public relations more than a decade ago, just as the revisionist history of the Vietnam War gained popularity. In planning sessions and classes at war colleges, through military exercises and models of recent military actions, and by adapting the principles of commercial advertising and marketing, the Pentagon honed its media and perception management skills.[11]

According to retired U.S. Army Col. Darryl Henderson, the Army has been sending top officers to civilian marketing seminars since the early 1980s. The basic lesson they learned: advertise the good news, bury the bad. Bad news from the Persian Gulf that couldn't be suppressed was therefore leaked out slowly, after an initial favorable, though false, impression had been created. The military briefers' enthusiasm about the precision accuracy of "smart missiles" is an example: Several days after the first triumphant reports, the Pentagon began to dribble out contradictory stories about the Iraqi's successful use of plywood decoys and about attacks on Israel by Scud missiles from launchers that had reportedly been destroyed. Henderson credited the strength of public support for the Gulf War to these sorts of "Army and Pentagon good-news marketing efforts."[12]

Although the information and the manipulation models are often invoked as though they were compatible, they actually make very different assumptions about the media's audiences. The ideal audience in the information model is the rational, autonomous liberal individual, the citizen with the time, ability, and impulse to synthesize facts and to make calculations based on information combined with abstract concepts of justice, truth, and freedom. The manipulation model, on the other hand, posits a nation of passive, suggestible people easily roused to frenzy.

The manipulation model is often invoked when the information model is obviously inadequate. A comment by Noam Chomsky during a speech in Berkeley, California—one of a series of addresses he made to overflow audiences during the Gulf War—provides an example. Probably the most influential media critic on the U.S. left, Chomsky followed his usual practice, marshaling an impressive array of facts (citing sources from memory when asked) and putting this information together into a coherent picture of U.S. militarism and foreign policy. He was completely uncompromising in telling the truth as he saw it. His talk was brilliant, a masterpiece of the critical information model of media. At the end of the talk, an audience member asked why so many Americans had supported the war. Suddenly dropping the information model, Chomsky answered that they had been "terrorized by media propaganda about Saddam Hussein."

Most Americans are probably both less ignorant and less terrorized than critics such as Chomsky assume. But to whatever extent they *are* ignorant and terrorized, these conditions are the starting points for understanding rather than an adequate explanation. The media's role in producing them is a process to be analyzed and understood rather than simply invoked.

The Media Environment

The information model is particularly unhelpful in understanding that the media in the late twentieth century operate not as a series of discrete effects, channels, or programs but as an environment—a constantly evolving, self-referential surrounding whose pervasiveness makes it difficult both to escape and to bring into focus. Within this media environment, meanings are produced not only by facts and information but also by style, form, and the televisual experience of blurred programs, commercials, previews, and station breaks that Raymond Williams called "flow."[13] Meanings are produced not only by analysis but also by images and stories.

The manipulation model, on the other hand, tends to misidentify the powers of media. As much recent work on media has demonstrated, media audiences aren't the blank slates or shapeless lumps of clay that charges of manipulation and intimations of brainwashing imply. The media derive their powers not from the ability to conjure chauvinism, mindless enthusiasm, and blind support out of thin air, but from their capacity to rework existing identities, histories, and understandings.

The logic that prevails in the media environment is not straightforwardly ideological but what Jochen Schulte-Sasse has called "sentimentological" and "televisualogical." These are hybrid logics that rely heavily on emotionally charged appeals, that are most effectively mobilized by television images, and that borrow liberally from the conventions of fiction entertainment.[14] Critics who rely on the information model of media tend to consider these sorts of logics politically or intellectually suspect. Yet insights into the media environment, and effective strategies of resistance to it, depend on acknowledging and understanding them. Thus it is crucial to notice and investigate why television coverage of the Gulf War was part video game, part sportscast, part mini-series; why the networks quickly incorporated images of bombers and tanks into their logos and promotions, aestheticizing war beyond recognition; why George Bush chose to deliver several rousing speeches about the war during the 1991 playoff and Super Bowl halftimes.

Neither the information model nor the manipulation model make visible the complex web of emotions and identifications that raveled and unraveled during the Gulf War. Defiant disingenousness, willful ignorance, and selective attention to information[15] overwhelmed feelings of guilt, responsibility, and sympathy for the enormous suffering of Iraqis. Deep unease about America's economic downturn and its standing in the world system could be temporarily shelved as far too many Americans reveled in the pleasures of triumph and of a solidarity based on demonizing the enemy. The thrills of omnipotence traditionally obtained by identifying with a strong leader were exacerbated by the new titillation of identifying with the high-tech precision weapons themselves as television viewers were treated again and again to a bomb's-eye view of the world. The administration worked with this range of reactions, trying to mobilize them in the service of Reagan-Bush era efforts to forge a new American identity: a post-Vietnam syndrome, post–Cold War Americanism that draws deeply on unapologetic militarism.

The information model and the manipulation model also fail to capture the importance of the metaphors and stories told about the Gulf War. George Bush never really offered a rational or coherent explanation for why he was taking the country to war, but he spun a spellbinding tale. He told a simple but incredibly powerful story of Saddam Hussein as the dark and devious villain and the U.S. military as a white knight rushing to rescue Kuwait, that innocent sheikdom as damsel in distress.[16] This fairy tale about Saddam-the-bad and America-the-good drew on deep reservoirs of racism and sexism and fit them into simplistic but satisfying structures of good and evil. Ella Shohat has pointed out that villain-hero-rescue stories are typical of colonial narratives, especially when the villain is a dark-skinned rapist. "The civilizing mission involved precisely teaching a lesson to the dark man who dared to disobey," Shohat writes. The imperial rescue fantasy was reinforced by the media's frequent use of the phrase "the rape of Kuwait," by reports about Iraqis raping Kuwaitis, and by intimations that captured American women soldiers were likely to suffer sexual abuse.[17]

If the media and the administration insinuated that Saddam Hussein was a rapist, they explicitly portrayed him as Hitler born again. *The New Republic* went as far as touching up a photo of Hussein for its cover, clipping his moustache into the Führer's style. The Hussein-Hitler analogy, of course, was an effort to rewrite history and reshape collective memory, to bury the Vietnam syndrome by constructing the Gulf War as another World War II—the good war in which the United States rescued Hitler's victims and saved the home front from a horrible fate. In the Gulf War, the administration belatedly suggested that the United States was not just the rescuer of innocent Kuwait but that it was itself likely to come under nuclear attack by Iraq. When the images of high-tech weapons that dominated television coverage during the air bombardment and the short ground attack gave way to images of American soldiers returning home to their families, one of the subtexts was the suggestion that the home front had been saved from destruction.

The movement against the Gulf War did begin to offer stories and metaphors to challenge those deployed by the administration, the Pentagon, and the media. Frequently used slogans—"No Oil War" and "Support the Troops, Bring Them Home Alive"—were important efforts to disrupt the dominant narratives about moral crusades and patriotism. A few of the signs at rallies referred to the aestheticization of war in the media environment: "War is not a video game," "Sellavision presents The Gulf War: The Mini-series," "Death, lies & video war!" In the aftermath of the war, a number of media critics questioned the notions of information and manipulation, either implicitly or explicitly.[18] Acknowledging the limits (as well as the strengths) of the information and manipulation models of media may help clear the way for appreciating the insights of these activists and theorists and for beginning the work of formulating new strategies of media resistance and a more complex understanding of late-twentieth-century "media wars."

NOTES

Acknowledgments: Thanks to the members of the Bay Area editorial collective of *Socialist Review* (of which I am a member) and to the friends who met with us for several insightful discussions that deeply informed my understanding of the Gulf War and the media's role in it. A collaboratively written essay, "Warring Stories: Reading and Contesting the New World Order," also draws heavily on these discussions; see *Socialist Review* 91/1 (vol. 21, no. 1, January–March 1991).

1. A Times Mirror poll found that 79 percent of Americans approved the Pentagon's press restrictions and 57 percent favored even stricter controls: "The People, the Press and the War in the Gulf: A Special Times Mirror News Interest Index" (Washington, D.C.: Times Mirror Center for the People and the Press, January 31, 1991).

2. A striking exception to the media's voraciousness for news about the media was its treatment of a federal lawsuit challenging the Pentagon's press restrictions on constitutional grounds. The suit was filed by five writers and eleven mostly small, left news organizations. The major broadcast and print media not only refused to join the lawsuit but ignored or barely mentioned it (Sydney H. Schanberg, "Censoring for Military Political Security," *Washington Journalism Review*, March 1991).

3. Michael Klare, "The Peace Movement's Next Steps," *The Nation*, March 25, 1991.

4. In this sense, many critics of the Gulf War shared the Bush administration's belief in the Vietnam syndrome, arguing that the American people would turn against the Gulf War "when the body bags started coming home."

5. Many left and progressive analyses of media coverage were written during the war, most of them in alternative weekly newspapers. Exceptions were several op-ed pieces by Jeff Cohen, executive director of FAIR, which appeared in major newspapers. Articles about media written after the Gulf War include Tom Engelhardt, "The Gulf War as Total Television," *The Nation*, May 11, 1992; Ernest Larsen, "Gulf War TV," *Jump Cut* no. 36 (1991); Ella Shohat, "The Media's War," *Social Text* 28 (vol. 9, no. 3, 1991); Danny Schechter, "Gulf War Coverage," *Z*, December 1991; Robert Stam, "Mobilizing Fictions: The Gulf War, the Media, and the Recruitment of the Spectator," *Public Culture* 4, no. 2

(Spring 1992); McKenzie Wark, "News Bites: War TV in the Gulf," *Meanjin* 50, no. 1 (Autumn 1991).

6. John O'Kane, "At the Edge of Bohemian Populism," *Socialist Review* 92/2 (vol. 22, no. 2, April–June 1992): 143.

7. See, for example, Edward S. Herman and Noam Chomsky, *Manufacturing Consent: The Political Economy of the U.S. Media* (New York: Pantheon, 1988), especially chapter 1, "A Propaganda Model."

8. The Pentagon refused to give estimates of Iraqi casualties, either civilian or military, instead emphasizing losses of Iraqi military equipment. Generals Norman Schwarzkopf and Colin Powell, in fact, both made comments about finding Iraqi casualties "not of interest." For months after the war, nongovernmental organizations such as Greenpeace were the only source of estimates of Iraqi civilian deaths.

9. Documented by FAIR and reported in the special Gulf War issue of its publication: *Extra!* 4, no. 3 (May 1991).

10. The term is suggested by Sut Jhally and Ian H. Angus in their introduction to the anthology *Cultural Politics in Contemporary America* (New York: Routledge, 1989), which they edited.

11. Thomas B. Rosenstiel, "The Media Take a Pounding," *Los Angeles Times*, February 20, 1991.

12. Col. Darryl Henderson (ret.), "How Army is Marketing the Gulf War to 'Soft' Public," *San Francisco Examiner*, February 10, 1991.

13. Raymond Williams, *Television: Technology and Cultural Form* (New York: Schocken Books, 1974).

14. Jochen Schulte-Sasse, "Electronic Media and Cultural Politics in the Reagan Era: The Attack on Libya and *Hands Across America* as Postmodern Events," *Cultural Critique* no. 8 (Winter 1987–88).

15. Michael Morgan, Justin Lewis, and Sut Jhally designed a survey to investigate the knowledge that underlay public support for the Gulf War and found that the more television people watched during the war, the less they knew about "information that might have reflected badly upon the Administration's policy." For example, only 13 percent of the sample responded correctly when asked how the U.S. State Department reacted in July 1990, when Saddam Hussein indicated before the fact that he might invade Kuwait. (The U.S. ambassador in Baghdad, April Glaspie, indicated to Hussein that the U.S. would take no action. A transcript of Glaspie's discussion with Hussein was later made public by Iraq and was widely reported in the U.S. media.) On the other hand, most respondents (80 percent) knew such facts as the name of the missile used to shoot down the Iraqis' Scud missiles (the Patriot) (Michael Morgan, Justin Lewis, and Sut Jhally, "More Viewing, Less Knowledge," in *Triumph of the Image: The Media's War in the Persian Gulf—A Global Perspective,* ed. Hamid Mowlana, George Gerbner, and Herbert I. Schiller [Boulder, Colo.: Westview Press, 1992]). These findings can be interpreted either as support for the information model (as signs of insufficient knowledge) or in the context of the

construction of meaning on the basis of the basic narrative and metaphoric structures deployed in the media environment.

16. This argument is elaborated by George Lakoff, "Metaphor and War," *Journal of Urban and Cultural Studies* 2, no. 1 (1991), first published in *East Bay Express* 13, no. 20 (February 22, 1991).
17. Ella Shohat, "The Media's War."
18. See especially Engelhardt, "The Gulf War;" Shohat, "The Media's War;" and Stam, "Mobilizing Fictions."

PART FOUR

SEARCHING FOR STRATEGY:
DILEMMAS OF ACTIVISM

□

CHAPTER 16

Movements and Dissensus Politics

Frances Fox Piven and Richard A. Cloward

□   □   □   □   □   □   □   □   □   □   □   □

Social movements unfold within a larger political context dominated by electoral politics. Recently, a number of analysts have puzzled over the question of how this context influences the rise and evolution of movements.[1] In this chapter we reverse the inquiry and examine the impact of social movements on electoral politics. We think the evidence suggests that movements play a large role, perhaps a determining role, in the periodic electoral dealignments and realignments that bring new regimes to power and usher in new public policy eras in American history.

Social movements thrive on conflict. By contrast, electoral politics demands strategies of consensus and coalition. We will argue that movements have the impact they do on electoral politics mainly because the issues they raise and the strife they generate widens cleavages among voter groups. We call this "dissensus politics" to differentiate it from the usual process of building electoral influence by recruiting adherents and assembling coalitions, or what might be called "consensus" politics.

Of course, other conditions must also be present before movements can cause destabilizing cleavages. Movements are not likely to have much impact unless economic and social conditions are already eroding established electoral allegiances and coalitions. But then it is also the case that significant change-oriented movements are not likely to emerge except during periods of economic and social instability.

To understand the significance of dissensus politics, we need to go back to the common and taken-for-granted model of popular influence through electoral politics because we think there is a gap in this model that points to the critical role of movements. Ordinary people are said to have influence in democratic systems because their assent at the voting booth is a condition for gaining or retaining state power. Numerous analysts have pointed out, however, that even apart from the perennial problems of corruption and manipulation, the wide distribution of the franchise cannot guarantee that majorities will prevail so long as voters remain disorganized. If voters are atomized, casting their ballots as disconnected individuals, politicians need muster only small minorities to prevail.[2] For democratic majorities to prevail, voters must be organized, a task that falls to political parties. Parties make voters effective by delineating and publicizing a limited number of alternative policies and candidates, on the one hand, and by mobilizing and aggregating voters for one or another of these alternatives on the other hand.

Once the role of parties in electoral democracy is acknowledged, so is the likelihood of a host of systematic distortions of voter preferences, owing to the influence of wealth, the capacity for symbol manipulation and the control of public information, and the organized and often legal corruption of the election process. However, these problems are widely discussed, and in any case are not our subject here. To understand the importance of movements in electoral politics, we must appreciate not only the influences that distort the essentially democratic mission of organizing voter majorities, but the deeply conservative tendencies of electoral politics even apart from such distortions, especially in a two-party system. To win state office, party leaders and their candidates must build broad majorities. They strive to do this by holding the allegiance of those who voted for them in the past while also attracting marginal voters from the contending party. To do this, they try to avoid conflict and search instead for the consensual appeals and promises that preserve and if possible enlarge existing voter coalitions.[3] (Campaign ads that try to recruit voters with shots of beaming families and beautiful sunrises are only the ludicrous ultimate expression of this tendency.) The operatives in a two-party system where majorities must be constructed in the face of diversity are necessarily the conservators of coalitions.

There are, however, eras in which established electoral coalitions break apart and new coalitions form, producing "realignments." These realigning periods are usually treated as the key turning points in American electoral history, both because of the large electoral shifts that occur and because these shifts in turn bring new governing regimes to power and inaugurate new policy eras.[4] Thus the stasis and immobility bred by a two-party system has in the past been at least partly overcome by the periodic convulsions called realignments. This view of the role of realignments in overcoming the conservative tendencies of the American party system is consistent with Walter Dean Burnham's account of electoral realignments as an expression of the accumulated political tensions that result from the failure of the party system to respond to the problems generated by a dynamic capitalist economy. So far, so good.

Still, something is missing. There is a marked tendency in the literature on realignments toward reification or even mystification, as if realignments were an inherent and natural feature of American politics, occurring with an inevitable regularity at thirty-year intervals or so. But why? Unless we revert to a sort of mystical naturalism connoted by the idea of cycles, we need to understand what or who makes realignments happen. The discontinuities between social experience and electoral politics that result from a static party system may well set the stage for realignment. And signs of electoral discontent may even prompt some rhetorical shifts in campaign appeals by major party operatives. Still, overall, political leaders remain timid and conservative, trying to suppress the potential for realignment by bridging potential cleavages with general symbols and vague promises. Under these confusing conditions, discontented voters may be as atomized and ineffective as all voters are said to be in the absence of parties.

Just as people have to be mobilized to support parties and the issues and candidates they put forward, so do they have to be mobilized to desert them. Social movements are often the mobilizers of disaffection. In particular, we think social movements are politically effective precisely when they mobilize electoral disaffection. (We hasten to add that while movements win what they win as a result of their divisive impact on electoral coalitions, electoral dissensus does not necessarily guarantee victories, and such victories as are won may not last, as we will explain.)

If parties worked as they are supposed to, they would play the role we claim for social movements. Periodic elections would spur the party out of power to mobilize the potentially disaffected. Or third parties would emerge in response to the limited options offered by the major parties. Obviously, some of this does happen. However, the role of parties in generating conflict and mobilizing the disaffected is less than the principles of party competition would suggest. A fragmented governmental system in the United States means that the opposition party usually continues to control some part of the government apparatus, and so it is itself constrained by the need to hold together a majority by promoting consensus. As for third-party efforts, it has often been pointed out that they are made difficult in the American system by majority-take-all electoral arrangements, which require that a fledgling party produce instant majorities in a district to win the representation and patronage that sustains the party for another effort. Other procedural barriers to third-party efforts include obstructive registration laws that narrow participation, particularly among the lower classes, rigged ballot access laws, and the enormous cost of campaigning, particularly in this century. These obstacles to third-party organizing as popular undertakings help explain why the task of mobilizing electoral disaffection has often fallen to social movements and why such third-party efforts as do emerge are themselves often dependent on energizing social movements. From the abolitionists to the populists to the civil rights movement to the pro-lifers, social movements and third-party efforts have been intertwined, so that a firm distinction between the electoral impact of movements and third parties is difficult to draw.[5]

To appreciate the role of social movements in helping to precipitate electoral convulsion and realignment, we have to pay attention to the distinctive dynamics of social movements that enable them to do what party politicians do not do. Elsewhere, in connection with our studies of "poor peoples' movements," we emphasized the defiant and disruptive strategies of protest movements that arise among lower strata groups that have few regular political resources. We think the argument we are making here helps account for why disruptive protests, such as strikes or riots, sometimes force reform responses from the state. But we think our argument about the interplay of movements and electoral politics applies to social movements generally, including movements that enlist the middle strata and those that eschew the tactics of institutional disruption.

Social movements, even movements that are not particularly disruptive, can do what party leaders and contenders for office in a two-party system will not do: They can raise deeply divisive issues. In fact, social movements thrive on the drama and urgency and solidarity that result from raising divisive issues. If conflict is deadly to the strategy of a party trying to build a majority coalition, it is the very stuff that makes social movements grow.

Moreover, social movements tend to emerge at moments when the electoral system itself signals the emergence of new potential conflicts. Signs of increased volatility appear in electoral politics, usually traceable to changes in the economy or social life that generate new discontents or encourage new aspirations. The evidence of voter volatility in turn may prompt party leaders to do what they characteristically do, to attempt to hold together their coalition. Only now they will employ a more expansive rhetoric, acknowledging grievances among their constituents that are ordinarily ignored or naming and thus perhaps fueling aspirations that are only beginning to emerge. Even the threat of defections that jeopardize a majority can prompt electoral leaders to make the pronouncements that contribute to the climate of change and possibility that nourishes movements.

But politicians are not the only communicators. The conflicts that movements generate often lend them considerable communicative force. This is no small thing. Ordinarily, political communication is dominated by political leaders and the mass media, who together define the parameters of the political universe, including understandings of which sorts of problems should properly be considered political problems and which sorts of remedies are available. Just how deeply this communication penetrates popular understandings is disputed.[6] But whatever the hidden beliefs of people, it is hard to dispute the monopoly by the powerful on public and political communication, at least in the absence of movements.

Movements can break that monopoly, at least for a brief moment. Movements mount marches and rallies, strikes and sit-ins, theatrical and sometimes violent confrontations.[7] The inflammatory rhetoric and dramatic representations of collective indignation associated with these tactics project new definitions of social reality, or definitions of the social reality of new groups, into public discourse. They change understandings not only of what is real but of what is possible and of what is just. As a result, grievances that are otherwise naturalized or submerged become political issues.

Movements do what Schattschneider long ago said had to be done to change the outcome of political contests. Movements raise new issues, and when new issues take center stage of politics, the balance of political forces changes, in two ways. First, by raising new issues or articulating latent issues, movements activate groups that might otherwise remain inactive.[8] Second, new issues are likely to create new cleavages, with far-reaching consequences for the balance between contending forces. Cleavages are what electoral politicians seek to avoid, but they are the key to understanding the impact of movements on electoral politics, and in particular, to understanding why movements sometimes win victories.

Ordinarily, movement strategists explain their activities in terms similar to electoral organizers, as efforts to mobilize adherents and even to mobilize voters and voter majorities. The dramatic projection of movement issues can activate followers, to be sure; and in rare instances, as in the case of the nuclear freeze movement, the consensual causes advanced by the movement are of a kind that arouse little overt opposition. But most often movements polarize while they activate. Typically, the processes that mobilize hitherto inactive groups to the movement's cause also mobilize an opposition. Moreover, because movements raise new issues, they frequently polarize groups along different axes than those that organize and divide the major parties. The new cleavages create problems for electoral leaders trying to hold together voter majorities, forcing reluctant politicians to make choices on issues they would otherwise avoid. Movements wrest concessions from reluctant political leaders when concessions are seen as a way to avert threatened defections, or to staunch the flow of defections already occurring, or sometimes when concessions are viewed as a way to rebuild an already fragmented coalition by enlarging or solidifying support from one side of the cleavage line.

Of course, the choices between constituent groups that are forced on electoral leaders by movement-generated conflict may well continue to fuel conflict and therefore threaten a new wave of electoral defections. Under these conditions, movement victories may be shortlived. The opposition provoked by the movement, and goaded and perhaps strengthened by its victories, may thus eventually prevail in intraparty contests. Or the electoral fragmentation that nourished the movement in the first place, and that the movement in turn worsened, can lead to the defeat of the party that is both the target and the social base of the polarizing movement.

In sum, movements grow when electoral leaders, prodded by signs of instability in their coalitions, communicate new possibilities to hold together their majorities. But as movements grow, nourished by the mood of hope generated by efforts at conciliation, they become the agents of widening cleavages, even dividing or shattering electoral coalitions. In this sense, movements mobilize electoral dealignments. The conflicts movements generate may also set in motion the voter shifts that eventually result in new electoral alignments.

□ □ □

We think the dissensual politics provoked by the interaction of movements and the coalition builders of the two-party system is illustrated by a number of twentieth century movements, including the labor movement of the 1930s, the civil rights movement of the 1960s, and the "new social movements" of the 1970s, particularly the dual movements focused on gender roles: the feminist movement, on the one hand, and the allied pro-life and Christian right movements on the other.

The emergence of the New Deal realignment is typically traced to the election of 1932, when Franklin Delano Roosevelt won office after a long period of Republican domination of the national government.[9] In this version of the story, dealignment and realignment in the 1930s were a simple voter response to economic catastrophe. It is no doubt true that economic collapse prompted many voters to turn against the majority Republican Party, setting dealignment in motion. And Roosevelt tried to take advantage of the discontent generated by economic hardship in his campaign rhetoric denouncing economic royalists and celebrating the common man. However, when the 1932 returns were in, there was little pattern to the Roosevelt sweep. He had carried all but a few states in the Northeast and had won among all income groups. In other words, economic collapse had shattered the old Republican majority, but the electoral coalition of the New Deal era had not yet emerged.

In fact, Roosevelt came to office oriented toward measures that would revive business and bring order to the financial markets. It was escalating protests among the unemployed and workers, protests fueled by hardship and the sense of political possibility that Roosevelt's rhetoric communicated, that changed FDR's course, forcing him to inaugurate extensive emergency relief and public works measures. Later, Roosevelt tried to conciliate growing demands among workers for government protection of the right to organize, demands that had been encouraged if not precipitated by New Deal promises encoded in the National Industrial Recovery Act. Throughout 1934 and 1935, the administration tried to pick a path between growing worker anger at the failure of the administration to enforce the right to organize and growing business indignation at the disruptive strikes staged by workers encouraged by federal appeasement. As the strike movement escalated, a series of administration halfway measures only backfired, encouraging worker demands precisely because appeasement revealed the political vulnerability of the regime. Meanwhile, federal conciliation and the strike wars it seemed to encourage drove a substantial segment of the business leadership virtually to declare war on the administration and in the 1934 election to go so far as to launch a short-lived third-party effort. Finally and reluctantly, Roosevelt was forced to choose between escalating worker demands and an enraged business community. With the 1936 election approaching, Roosevelt threw his support behind the National Labor Relations act, despite "bitter and sustained opposition to the act by employers before and after its passage."[10]

The polarizing impact of the labor movement had forced Roosevelt's hand. It also helped to shape the New Deal coalition that emerged from the interplay of movements and electoral politics, to which movements among the aged and farmers contributed. The shapeless—and classless—Democratic majority of 1932 was steadily reconstituted, and by the late 1930s the pattern was clear. Workers, especially less skilled workers, were identified with the Democrats, and business and professional strata tilted sharply to the Republicans.[11] The New Deal realignment had taken form, and the conflicts generated by the movements of the era had helped to form it.

□ □ □

While the electoral realignment that emerged from the 1930s was defined in part by class, it was just as importantly defined by section. Working-class voters in the urban North were linked in an electoral alliance with the Democratic white South. This regional coalition was not entirely new, since the Democrats had been the party of both big-city machines and the one-party South since the nineteenth century. And the coalition had not always held together, as was evident in the elections of the 1920s, and particularly in the election of 1928, when the Democratic alliance had temporarily shattered on the shoals of sectional religious and cultural conflict. But in the 1930s New Deal conciliation of the South, together with the temptations and rewards of national power, brought the southern political stratum home to the national Democratic Party and, for a time, kept it loyal.

These rewards, however, contributed to the ultimate fragmentation of the coalition. New Deal policies promoted the industrialization of the South and also subsidized a more capital-intensive agriculture. Economic development, in turn, had political repercussions that first weakened and then destroyed the coalition. In that process, movements that were themselves a reflection of economic change and the ensuing electoral repercussions played a critical □ role.

The economic modernization of the South had two main effects that bear on the role of movements in the ultimate fragmentation of the New Deal coalition. First, modernization changed the class structure of the South, spurring the growth of a new middle class, including a professional middle class, who in the 1950s became natural recruits for a resurgent southern Republicanism.[12] Second, a more capital-intensive agriculture led to the displacement of millions of black and white sharecroppers and tenants, as well as small farmers whose land was gobbled up by large owners who were mechanizing with federal subsidies and who were better able to make use of federal subsidies for idle land. Most of the displaced whites gravitated to nearby towns and small cities, where they were not unwelcome. But displaced blacks tended to migrate to the big cities of the South and North, where ghetto neighborhoods established earlier provided a kind of protective haven. In the cities, they became voters and increasingly important constituents of the urban and northern wing of the Democratic Party. And because segregation had thus concentrated their numbers, blacks became a potentially critical voter bloc in the industrial states with the largest number of electoral votes.

The events that followed reveal first the role of third parties as agents of electoral dissensus, and then the similar and in this case more definitive role of social movements. As the 1948 election approached, Harry Truman, the Democratic incumbent, confronted Henry Wallace's third-party challenge from the left, which threatened to attract black (and labor) voters. This explains Truman's attempt to conciliate blacks before the 1948 election by appointing a U.S. Commission on Civil Rights and then by incorporating some of the commission's recommendations into the Democratic platform.

With that, the blow was struck that revealed an emerging fissure in the New Deal coalition. Four deep South delegates bolted the nominating convention, and angry southern politicians formed a States Rights Party with Strom Thurmond as their candidate. Truman won the election, but the Democratic percentage of the southern white vote plummeted, to 53 percent from FDR's 85 percent in 1936.

Once the Henry Wallace threat evaporated, the Democrats tried to conciliate the South. But the forces unleashed by southern modernization now had a momentum of their own. Each gesture of recognition of civil rights from northern liberals fueled the anger of southern whites even as it sparked the hopes of urban blacks in both the South and the North. Many observers treat the 1954 Supreme Court *Brown* decision striking down the "separate but equal" doctrine in public education as the instigator of this conflict. Certainly it was an important trigger, perhaps comparable to the "right to organize" announced in the National Industrial Recovery Act of 1933.[13] In the wake of the decision, southern whites mobilized in a movement of "massive resistance" led by the political leaders of the southern states. And with this new legitimation from the highest court in the land, the southern black movement for civil rights began in earnest with the Tallahassee and Montgomery boycotts.

In the campaigns of 1952 and again in 1956, Democratic nominee Adlai Stevenson tried earnestly to soothe an alarmed white South with talk of "states' rights." The deep South did in fact return to Democratic columns, but in the more industrial states of the outer South, the Republican trend among middle class voters accelerated, encouraged of course by the popularity of Eisenhower.[14]

Moreover, to worsen Democratic troubles, heretofore loyal black voters began to defect from the Democratic Party in the 1956 election. The extraordinary excitement that must have been generated by early civil rights protests, combined with Stevenson's less-than-heroic efforts to placate the white South, spurred marked defections among urban blacks, among whom Democratic voting fell from 80 percent in 1952 to 60 percent in 1956. And black turnout fell as well, especially in northern cities.[15] This last development was also a warning of growing racial conflict within the party's ranks in the big cities, which was immobilizing Democratic mayors who might otherwise have worked to recruit black voters.

In the 1960 campaign, Kennedy confronted these troubles in the party and, influenced one suspects by Stevenson's sorry record in the South, decided to try to win back defecting black voters by reviving the civil rights promises of Harry Truman in his platform (and by the widely publicized telephone call from Robert Kennedy to Coretta King when Martin Luther King was jailed in Atlanta during the campaign.) The strategy scored a modest success. Despite losing much of the South—Florida, Tennessee, and Virginia, as well as Alabama and Mississippi, whose electors were unpledged—Kennedy won a narrow victory. A modest upturn in the black Democratic vote, from 60 to 68 percent, was part of the reason.

But necessarily, party leaders trying to hold majorities together are not brinksmen. After he took office, Kennedy tried to heal the growing fissure in the party by avoiding civil rights initiatives and conciliating the white South. The escalating civil rights movement and the tide of support it generated in the North, especially among black voters, and escalating white southern anger and resistance, forced his hand. By the summer of 1963, in the wake of the turbulent Birmingham civil rights demonstrations and Governor George Wallace's flamboyant personal confrontation with federal officials to bar two black students from entering the University of Alabama, Kennedy finally moved on his promises of 1960, sending major civil rights legislation to the Congress, which Lyndon Johnson pushed through after Kennedy's assassination.[16] A year later, as the civil rights demonstrators were again locked in combat with Governor Wallace at Selma, Johnson called on Congress for a voting rights act, which was signed into law in August 1964, even as civil rights demonstrations escalated.

As everyone now agrees, the party that finally and reluctantly conceded these historic civil rights victories was badly damaged by them, and its chances to win the presidency were especially damaged. The solid South, which had kept the Democratic Party alive as a national party during the lean years of Republican domination before 1932, and had been its most reliable base after 1932, was gone. As early as 1964, George Wallace made a primary bid in the presidential contest and did alarmingly well in the early primaries in Indiana and Wisconsin, although his candidacy in the South was blocked by southern leaders who were now ready to support Republican nominee Barry Goldwater. Wallace ran again in 1968, this time as a third-party candidate. In the aftermath of the debacle of patched battles between police and demonstrators at the 1968 Democratic convention, he drew support not only from the white South but from previously Democratic working-class whites in the North who felt themselves besieged by mounting black demands over jobs, housing, welfare, schools, and for a share of local political power, on the one hand, and by the student antiwar movement and its class and cultural provocations on the other hand.

Republican strategists had taken note of the fracturing impact of race conflict on the Democratic Party, and they maneuvered to take advantage of it, beginning in the early 1960s with the creation by the Republican National Committee of its own "Operation Dixie" campaign to build a Republican Party in the South.[17] Later, as race conflict spread to the North, turning black and white Democratic constituencies against one another, the Nixon administration added fuel to the flames with the "Philadelphia Plan," which called for affirmative action in the construction trades,[18] and it used the Justice Department to secure the court orders for school busing that precipitated virtual race war in many cities. When the black movement subsided and the dust settled, the South had become the most solidly Republican section in the nation, and a majority of the white working class had joined the ranks of "Reagan Republicans."

So, if there is a final reckoning, it must be that the civil rights movement won, but in the process badly damaged the electoral base of the party that yielded it victories, helping to bring a Republican administration to power for most of the past quarter century. Still, it is hard to see how the movement had much of a choice. The southern wing of the Democratic Party had been the implacable foe of black political and economic aspirations for a century. Only as the southern political establishment was being driven out of the party were national Democratic leaders willing to act on black demands. Democratic leaders resisted this hemorrhaging, trying by delay and evasion to hold their coalition together. But the combined impact of movements and third parties in galvanizing voters doomed their efforts, so the divisions widened, civil rights victories became possible, and except in the aftermath of Watergate, the party that ceded them did not regain the presidency for a quarter of a century.

□ □ □

The black movement had not yet subsided before a series of other movements emerged focusing on peace, environmental, and gender issues, which have come to be called the "new social movements." Certainly these movements took heart, strategy, and in some cases activists from the civil rights movement and also from the student antiwar movement of the 1960s. And they were similar to the black movement in contributing to the conflicts that continued to beset the Democrats in 1972 when, after a chaotic Democratic convention, George McGovern was defeated by Richard Nixon in a landslide, an outcome foreshadowed in the 1968 election when the Wallace and Nixon candidacies together had claimed an "emerging Republican majority" of 57 percent.[19]

But the strand in the complicated interplay of movements and electoral politics that we want to try to disentangle here has to do with gender and with the movements focusing specifically on gender issues that emerged in the tumultuous late 1960s and early 1970s. We think a good case can be made that as much of the movement activity of this era subsided, the gender-focused movements actually escalated and were especially important in the dissensus politics of the past two decades. The gender politics advanced by social movements of the right and the left first added to the fracturing of the Democratic Party that race conflict had begun, helping to keep a new Republican majority in power. But gender conflicts continued, and even escalated, particularly as the pro-life movement gained courage and momentum from the conciliatory stance of Republican leaders. By the end of the 1980s, the stage was set again for a new period of electoral dissensus and dealignment, this time working its way through the Republican majority coalition.

The movements that forced gender issues to the fore of national politics in the 1970s were expressions of profound and long-term changes in American society, including the loosening of family forms, the entry of women into the labor market, and the rise in the 1960s of an era of cultural permissiveness. These developments in turn helped give rise to a liberatory movement among women, especially among better-educated and better-placed women positioned to take advantage of the relaxation of old restrictions in the family and the labor market. The "women's liberation" movement that emerged fought on a number of fronts for enlarged economic and political opportunities for women, and movement activists naturally fought for these liberal causes within the Democratic Party. But these particular battles were framed by a larger one: the movement both directly and by implication challenged the most ancient of subordinations, the subordination of women to men that had always been understood as rooted in biology and therefore as inevitable and fated.

A social movement that strikes at such primordial understandings inevitably provokes strong reactions, especially among people still rooted in traditional relationships and traditional communities who feel that their very identities are at risk.[20] In fact, there is a strong parallel between the civil rights and women's movements that is not often recognized, since both dared to challenge deeply imprinted identities rooted in ideas about biological destiny. No wonder both movements provoked counter movements of intractable fury. And no wonder that the pro-life movement and the Christian right to which it was allied, by reasserting the sanctity of traditional gender roles, of childbearing, and of "family values," emerged as the most significant protest movements of the 1980s.

Both civil rights and gender issues also contributed to the fracturing of the Democratic Party, which had formerly housed the constituencies who were now aroused and at war. True, the conventional wisdom attributes little significance to gender conflict, ascribing the fracturing of the Democratic Party mainly to race conflict and to a lesser extent to the "new class" activists in the new social movements. But conflict over gender roles was also cleaving the party, probably along the same or similar fault lines. The white southerners and white working-class northerners who were initially incensed by racial challenges were only a few years later reacting against the threat to traditional gender roles posed by the modernizing women's movement.

Or so Republican strategists clearly thought. How else explain the centrality given to symbolic gender issues by the Republican leadership, beginning in 1980? The elimination from the Republican platform that year of the traditional Republican endorsement of the ERA is one example. Then there is the use of *Roe v. Wade* as a virtual litmus test for Supreme Court nominations. The hard-line positions against abortion publicized by Republican presidents and presidential contenders is another example. Consider the international furor created when the administration refused to fund family-planning programs that included abortion in the third world. Or the notoriety generated here by the "gag rule" prohibiting the provision of abortion information in U.S. family-planning agencies that received federal funds.

These highly publicized moves by Republican national leaders begin to make sense when we view them as a strategy to worsen the cleavages that had been created within the Democratic Party by the deeply conflictual issues of the feminist and pro-life movements. It was within the Democratic Party that the women's movement's demands for an emancipatory understanding of gender were played out, and it was primarily among traditional Democratic constituencies that these issues had provoked anguish, fear, and partisan defection. For more than a decade, the Republican leadership worked both to exacerbate and assuage these anxieties, creating the odd spectacle of the powerful leaders of the richest and most technologically advanced country in the world in the grip of an anachronistic fundamentalism.

The election of 1992 and the campaign that preceded it suggests, however, that the majority coalition forged in part by conflict over gender politics is itself vulnerable to the continuing conflict and fragmentation caused by the dualistic movements advancing gender politics. The Republicans continued to stress their appeals to the traditionalist movements. Their 1992 convention was virtually given over to a theatrical celebration of a gender traditionalism and the celebrities associated with it, a kind of mirror image of the Democratic convention of 1972 where social movement activists also seemed to have a commanding role. But as the pro-life and Christian right movements escalate, forcing more strident affirmation of traditional gender roles, they may well be generating new cleavages, this time within the Republican coalition. This is what the Democrats seemed to hope for, styling a convention and campaign that was modern and socially liberal, pro-choice, and in which women politicians figured prominently. The election returns suggest the outcome of the issues raised by the dual gender movements and the fissures they generated. It is not so much that the Republican candidate lost, for that outcome has many causes. Rather, what bears on our argument about the role of social movements in generating dissensus politics is the shift of women voters away from Republican columns, especially the single mothers and working women who, whether through circumstances or choice, are not traditionalists.

□ □ □

In sum, we think a good deal of light can be cast on both movements and electoral politics by examining their interaction, and particularly by examining the contribution of movements to catalytic moments of electoral convulsion. The conflicts that give rise to movements, and that movements in turn escalate, sometimes overcome the stasis inherent in two-party electoral politics. Movements raise issues and generate conflicts that spur dealignment and realignment. In the process they may win victories from party leaders straining to hold majorities together. We think that the great domestic reforms of the twentieth century—from labor rights to civil rights to reproductive rights— were forced on party leaders who used reform to avert or stem voter defections.

But whether victorious or defeated, social movements are short-lived. The usual explanations point to the co-optation of movement leaders or to the exhaustion of movement participants, who grow weary of the taxing forms of political action that movements demand, both of which surely happen. More to the point of our argument here, however, social movements subside precisely because they transform the electoral context that brings them into being and nourishes them for a time. The conflicts promoted by social movements and the electoral shifts they set in motion tend to fragment and defeat the dominant party whose latent cleavages both made social movement politics possible and became the arena of movement action. That process unfolded in the Republican electoral coalition as the 1980s came to a close and helped to account for the defeat of the Republican contender in the presidential election of 1992.

What can movement leaders do then? During each of the historical episodes we have described, there was a moment when hope flourished that the mutual limits of movement and electoral politics could be overcome. Growing movements and the electoral instabilities they created combined to nourish the idea that something more enduring was possible than the perennial convulsive encounters between transient movement politics and intransigent electoral politics. The movements should turn to electoral politics, enter the party, and reform it, as when Bayard Rustin, standing at the cusp of the civil rights movement in 1965, called for a turn from "protest to politics."[21] As the civil rights movement lost momentum, its leaders did indeed move into electoral politics. SNCC leaders ran for local offices or for Congress, just as women are now doing and as they did in the 1920s, in the wake of winning the franchise.[22] So too, at least in a general way, did union leaders turn to electoral politics when they entered the inner councils of the Democratic Party some fifty years ago. But the record of these efforts in the past argues that the hope for a synthesis of party and movement is likely to be disappointed. When movement leaders become electoral politicians, they necessarily leave behind the distinctive movement power born of contention. The imperatives of coalition building that shape electoral politics in a two-party system demand that leaders shun conflictual issues in order to build majorities. And, as former movement agitators bend to the dictates of electoral politics, the hope of reform necessarily awaits the next social movement.

NOTES

1. See for example Frances Fox Piven and Richard A. Cloward, *Poor People's Movements: Why they Succeed, How they Fail* (New York: Pantheon Books, 1977); Doug McAdam, *Political Process and the Development of Black Insurgency, 1930–1970* (Chicago: University of Chicago Press, 1982); Sidney Tarrow, *Power in Movement: Social Movements, Collective Action, and Politics* (New York: Cambridge University Press, 1994); Anne Costain, *Inviting Women's Rebellion* (Baltimore: Johns Hopkins University Press, 1992).
2. See for example E. E. Schattschneider, *Party Government* (New York: Rinehart and Co., 1942).
3. Theodore Lowi even suggests that the major parties collaborate with each other in a "tacit contract to avoid taking important issues to the voters." See his "The Party Crasher," *New York Times Magazine,* August 23, 1992.
4. See V. O. Key, "A Theory of Critical Elections," *Journal of Politics* 17 (February 1955); James Sundquist, *Politics and Policy* (Washington D.C.: Brookings Institution, 1973); Walter Dean Burnham, *Critical Elections and the Mainsprings of American Politics* (New York: W. W. Norton, 1970); Benjamin Ginsberg, "Critical Elections and the Substance of Party Conflict, 1844–1968," *Midwest Journal of Political Science* no. 16 (1972); Richard L. McCormick, *The Party Period and Public Policy* (New York: Oxford University Press, 1986).
5. For historical accounts of third-party efforts in the United States see Richard Hofstadter, *The Age of Reform: From Bryan to F.D.R.* (New York: Alfred A. Knopf, 1955); Keith J. Polakoff, *Political Parties in American History* (New York: Alfred A. Knopf, 1981); Lawrence Goodwyn, *Democratic Promise: The Populist Movement in America* (New York: Oxford University Press, 1976); Steven J. Rosenstone, Roy L. Behr, and Edward H. Lazarus, *Third Parties in America: Citizen Response to Major Party Failures* (Princeton, N.J.: Princeton University Press, 1984).
6. See James C. Scott, *Weapons of the Weak* (New Haven, Conn.: Yale University Press, 1985).
7. On the dramaturgical strategies of movements, see Robert Benford and Scott A. Hunt, "Dramaturgy and Social Movements: The Social Construction and Communication of Power," *Sociological Inquiry* 62 (February 1962).

8. On the relationship of issues to cleavages, see E. E. Schattschneider, *The Semi-sovereign People* (New York: Holt, Rinehart and Winston, 1960).

9. Some analysts, however, date the beginnings of realignments in the election of 1928, when the candidacy of Catholic Al Smith made religion the pivotal—and polarizing—issue of the campaign, attracting new voters from among Catholics and driving Southern voters out of Democratic columns.

10. The quote is from William G. Domhoff, *The Power Elite and the State: How Policy Is Made in America* (New York: Aldine de Gruyter, 1990), 65. On the political forces responsible for the NLRA, see also Piven and Cloward, *Poor People's Movements*, chapter 3, and *Why Americans Don't Vote* (New York: Pantheon Books, 1988), chapter 5; Irving Bernstein, *The Lean Years: A History of the American Worker, 1930–33* (Baltimore: Penguin Books, 1970); Michael Goldfield, "Labor's Subordination to the New Deal. Part One: The Influence of Labor on New Deal Labor Legislation" (paper delivered at the annual meeting of the American Political Science Association, New Orleans, 1985); Thomas Ferguson, "From Normalcy to New Deal: Industrial Structure, Party Competition and American Public Policy in the Great Depression," *International Organization* 38 (Winter 1984).

11. By 1936, "businessmen switched to Landon while workers went the other way." See Richard Jensen, *The Winning of the Midwest: Social and Political Conflict, 1888–1896* (Chicago: University of Chicago Press, 1981), 212. Among high-income voters, Roosevelt ran 29 percentage points behind the Republican candidate. For responses to a Gallup poll on party identification in 1940, see James Sundquist, *Dynamics of the Party System: Alignment and Realignment of Political Parties in the United States* (Washington, D.C.: Brookings Institution, 1973), 202.

12. On this development, see Thomas Sugrue, "The Origins of White Backlash in the Urban North" (prepared for delivery at the annual meeting of the American Political Science Association, Chicago, September 3–6, 1992).

13. The decision itself however was the culmination of a long series of efforts by the NAACP, aided by civil rights lawyers in the Department of Justice. See Richard M. Valelly, "National Parties and Racial Disenfranchisement," ed. Paul E. Peterson, *Classifying by Race* (Princeton: Princeton University Press, 1985).

14. In 1948, the Democrats lost Alabama, Louisiana, Mississippi, and South Carolina. In 1952 and 1956 they recaptured these states, only to lose Florida, Virginia, Tennessee, and Texas, and Louisiana as well in 1956.

15. This discussion draws from Piven and Cloward, *Poor People's Movements*, chapter 4. On black voting patterns in 1956, see Henry Lee Moon, *Balance of Power: The Negro Vote* (Garden City: Doubleday, 1948), 221; Samuel Lubell, *White and Black*, 2d ed. rev. (New York: Harper Colophon Books, 1966); and Oscar Glantz, "The Negro Voter in Northern Industrial Cities," *Western Political Quarterly*, no. 13 (December 1960).

16. On the impact of the civil rights movement on presidential decision making in

this period, see Mark Stern, "Calculating Visions: Civil Rights Legislation in the Kennedy and Johnson Years," *Journal of Policy History* 5 (1993); Arthur Schlesinger, Jr., *A Thousand Days* (Boston: Houghton Mifflin, 1965); Theodore Sorenson, *Kennedy* (New York: Harper & Row, 1965); and Sundquist, *Politics and Policy*.

17. See Philip A. Klinkner, "Race and the Republican Party: The Rise of the Southern Strategy in the Republican National Committee, 1960–1964" (paper delivered at the annual meeting of the American Political Science Association, Chicago, September 3–6, 1992).

18. See Jill Quadagno, *Unfinished Democracy: Rights, Race and American Social Policy* (New York: Oxford University Press, 1994).

19. This is of course the title of Kevin Phillips's 1969 book.

20. For interpretations of these "existential" screams, see Jane Sherron De Hart, "Gender on the Right: Meanings behind the Existential Scream," *Gender and History* 3 (Autumn 1991): 261; Kristen Luker, *Abortion and the Politics of Motherhood* (Berkeley: University of California Press, 1984); and Jane Mansbridge, *Why We Lost the ERA* (Chicago: University of Chicago Press, 1986).

21. Bayard Rustin, "From Protest to Politics," *Commentary*, no. 39 (February 1965).

22. For a discussion of the failed electoral strategy of the suffrage movement, see Anna L. Harvey, "Uncertain Victory: The Electoral Incorporation of Women into the Republican Party, 1920–1928" (paper delivered at the annual meeting of the American Political Science Association, Chicago, September 3–6, 1992).

CHAPTER 17

Think Globally, Act Politically: Some Notes toward New Movement Strategy

Richard Flacks

□   □   □   □   □   □   □   □   □   □   □   □

Social movements arise when normal politics fail. The great American movements of labor, women, and blacks expressed the exclusion of their constituencies from the central political processes. Workers had no rights in their workplace to defend their life interests; at the same time, they could not find adequate political representation. Women and blacks could not vote at all, nor did they have institutional power to protect themselves.

The primary victories of these movements were political: the right to vote, the right to organize and strike, the development of electoral constituencies with leverage, the achievement of legislative and judicial acknowledgement of and protection for rights, the establishment of organizational infrastructures that formulate public policies and lobby for them, the achievement of some veto power in the political arena, the capacity to elect representatives in localities were the movement has been strong. In the course of decades of struggle by these movements, the American definition of citizenship rights became more inclusive. Groups previously denied full citizenship achieved legal recognition. Areas of life previously excluded from government intervention became subject to it.

Movements and Electoral Politics after the Sixties

By the end of the 1960s, movement activists came to see that the achievement of political inclusion and citizenship as defined by the Constitution and mainstream political culture had been accomplished. This achievement, however, was insufficient: Millions of workers—black and white—remained poor and insecure, women remained subordinated, major social needs remained unfulfilled, the quality of urban life was deteriorating, militarism and war remained the first priority of the state.

In short, despite movement gains, normal politics were still not a framework in which the pressing needs and interests of movement constituencies could be fulfilled. Indeed, some groups who had previously felt represented (especially members of the growing intellectual/professional strata) were experiencing the established political framework as irrational and closed. Elite domination of the state and of the political parties frequently thwarted the popular will; at the same time, racial, ethnic, and other organized minorities were necessarily disadvantaged within the electoral process.

A number of movement projects were initiated in that period whose purpose was to restructure electoral and governmental processes:

The Reform of the Democratic Party

Labor activists had sought representation in the Democratic Party since the New Deal days and during the 1940s and 1950s had taken considerable control of particular state and local Democratic Party organizations. Similar representation was one of the main goals of the southern civil rights movement; by the late sixties, black voting blocs in the South became the basis for considerable party realignment. By the early 1970s, a wide range of movement-based activists pressed for party reform that would undermine the power of traditional machine politicians and compel the recognition of women and minorities. The McGovern candidacy in 1972 offered hope that a new national Democratic Party could be created that would be rooted in the mass constituencies mobilized for change in the sixties, combined with the working-class base that formed during the New Deal. It turned out, of course, to be impossible to forge such a coalition, given the racial and cultural barriers among the constituencies and, indeed, among the activist leaderships as well.

Twenty years later, many activists still hope for a progressive national political party as the key to an effective political strategy for change. Each movement has some capacity to advance a particular agenda to protect certain interests and to veto certain threats. But no movement on its own has the potential to achieve the redistribution of wealth, power, and social priorities that would significantly improve the life chances of their constituents or sustain their deepest aspirations. A political party representing the common ground of progressive movements would seem to be the obvious framework for mobilizing the political resources and formulating the programmatic agenda for change. And yet, no leadership has emerged in the last twenty years to work systematically to create such a party. Movements continue to act as pressure groups within the Democratic Party. The Jesse Jackson campaigns created moments in which a "common ground" politics seemed to promise results. Experiments in the creation of third parties have had some local success. But in the climate of the last fifteen years, as mainstream politics moved rightward and movement gains came under attack, prospects for a progressive national force seemed always receding.

Single-Issue Coalitions

Although systematic efforts to create a national electoral coalition did not eventuate, single-issue, ad hoc coalition projects became increasingly evident and effective in the 1980s and 1990s. Some examples: the campaign against Robert Bork's Supreme Court nomination; the campaigns against aid to the contras in Nicaragua; the anti-apartheid disinvestment efforts; the anti-NAFTA campaign; the campaign for national health care reform. In all of these, national and local organizations and activists from diverse movements were able to collaborate on common projects focused on a particular well-defined and short-term objective. Seemingly insurmountable barriers—for example, those between labor unions and the peace movement—were in some cases overcome. New institutional sources for activist energy came into being—for example, liberal religious communities. The ad hoc nature of these efforts meant that they did not seem to build on one another; still, they offered evidence that, despite the fragmentation of the left and the rise of a politics of identity, coalescence, at least under immediate conditions of practical necessity and opportunity, was possible.

Localism

Since the sixties, movement activists have had substantial success in influencing electoral politics and governmental policy at city and state levels. Considerable numbers of New Left activists came to see that the student movement as such was a limited vehicle for advancing far-reaching social change. The university campus, despite its significance in postindustrial society, remained too isolated from the political and cultural mainstream; students, despite their capacity for dramatic and effective disruption, could not achieve their goals without substantial links to potential majorities. And, from a biographical perspective, students had to graduate into a wider world and find new arenas in which to fulfill their political commitments.

Many student activists, accordingly, sought to overcome their political and cultural isolation and searched for activist vocations by settling into particular local communities. What we mean by "new social movements" has much to do with these post-sixties organizing efforts, for it is out of these that feminism, environmentalism, gay liberation, and the antinuclear movements emerged.

The localist emphasis of post-sixties activism resulted in part from the limited resources available to the left; most particularly the absence of any central organizational authority that could have directed a national strategy. But localism derived also from the ideological perspectives that dominated the New Left—the emphasis on participatory democracy, on decentralization, on human scale. The feminist critique of patriarchal leadership reinforced these perspectives by encouraging both male and female activists to work in non-hierarchical, face-to-face ways—rather than in the self-promoting, top-down manner that seems required by efforts to assert national leadership.

The new movements developed, accordingly, in highly decentralized ways. Although each of them contained national organizational structures, these had relatively little to do with directing the manifold movement activities that emerged out of issues arising in particular regions, communities, neighborhoods, and workplaces.

The environmental movement is a prototypical case. Environmentalism did not become a mass movement because of the initiatives of national organizations; rather, the movement was constructed out of a host of seemingly disparate local protests and projects: struggles over land use, urban development, population growth, toxic waste disposal, nuclear power, neighborhood preservation, defense of traditional culture, occupational hazards, and so forth. Typically, members of a local community came together and acted in response to a locally experienced threat—at times, using the resources (language, know-how, material support) made available by the formal organizations of the national movement. In the midst of such local struggles there were often some veteran activists—people whose identities were shaped in the Old or New Left. Over the course of time, the influence of experienced activists was no longer a necessary ingredient for enabling local protest to take off. After twenty-five years, many who don't consider themselves to be activists have acquired the consciousness and skills to act effectively in local protest.[1]

The local creativity of the new social movements was an important, if largely hidden, feature of American social history during the last quarter century. Local protests often succeeded in deflecting the particular threats that initially sparked them, or won certain concessions and accommodations from the corporate and state bureaucracies that encroached on community life. Moreover, locally based movement activity rather quickly developed a certain strategic thrust that went beyond the merely reactive. The political aim of grassroots activism was to win a degree of direct voice in the decisions and policies that determine the community's future. This implicit strategy was implemented in a variety of political projects.

Beginning in the early seventies, new social movement activists, especially in towns with sizable university populations, began competing directly for local office. In the eighties this effort widened with the development of local "rainbow" coalition politics in a number of cities, whereby black community activists made electoral alliance with feminist, environmentalist, gay, and peace constituencies. Eventually progressive coalitions came to local power in a variety of places rather different from the progressive university town. Indeed, there is probably no major city in the country whose politics has not been affected by the separate and combined efforts of movement activists to win at least a piece of local power.[2]

In addition to seeking electoral office, locally based movements have pressed for structural reform at the local and state level—reform that would provide movement constituencies with legal bases for intervening in the decision-making process and holding government directly accountable. Decisions previously reserved for specialized or elite arenas were now subject to public scrutiny and voice.

A major example of movement initiatives in this regard with the Environmental Quality Act in California (CEQA), which requires that all local development be subject to environmental impact review. The EIR process compels a public weighing of social costs and provides an arena for public testimony and an opportunity for public negotiation of "mitigations" with respect to all changes of land use. Governmental procedures such as mandatory public hearings provide community movements with significant opportunities for mobilization, public education, the development of expertise, and the exercise of community leadership. From the perspective of public authority, the process was agreed to in an effort to get community residents "off the streets" and into the bureaucratic structure; in practice, however, it has provided a degree of information and opportunity for public participation not previously available.

In general, in the last twenty-five years, a variety of mechanisms embodying principles of public review and participatory planning have emerged in American community and institutional life. Public mechanisms similar to those provided by the EIR exist in some locales with respect to job hiring and promotion policies, police practices, health service provision, provision of services for the aged, and public education (where local control has, of course, a long tradition in the United States). The development of these mechanisms has meant considerable change in the structure of power at the local level.

But the local democracy achieved during this past quarter century is a limited one: American communities are now places where social movements have some ability to veto or modify unwanted decisions. Largely missing at the community level are institutional mechanisms for promoting economic redistribution, for effectively controlling the flow of capital, or for effectively determining the planning processes that shape their futures. These processes are determined beyond the locality.

Having learned to "act locally while thinking globally," movement activists discovered that the innovative post-sixties political strategies had effective limits: They could not provide a significant way to protect local communities from the incursions of globalized megacorporations nor from the globalizing cultural frameworks provided by the megamedia.

The Failure of Normal Politics

In general, movement activists hope that the outcome of mass protest will be the democratizing of normal politics. Normalcy is necessary in the aftermath of protest. Grassroots movement participants need eventually to go home to raise their families and live in the freer space that their protests have helped open. Meanwhile, committed activists hope to find long-term careers within stable political institutions, representing the grassroots, serving the people as professionals, administrators, politicians.

The sixties generation's hopes for the establishment of a liveable normal politics were exercised through the strategies I have enumerated above. These were, I have suggested, not unsuccessful. The most egregious denials of human rights characteristic of American society prior to the sixties have been removed. Avenues for democratic participation for a variety of previously excluded groups have been opened; arenas of life previously subject to authoritarian control are now less so; daily life and human relations are in many ways more free and cultural expression far less repressed and homogenized.

We do not, however, now have a normal politics in which the relatively disadvantaged groups in society believe that their interests and needs and aspirations can be effectively expressed and addressed. Indeed, the evidence is that millions of Americans who formerly thought themselves to be represented politically are increasingly alienated. Few constituencies feel adequately represented by political leadership; populist mistrust of politicians is pervasive; government is perceived largely as a burden rather than a resource.

Normal politics worked in the aftermath of the thirties. The labor movement and radical ferment of the Depression years helped solidify the Keynesian–welfare state model for sustaining political stability and steady economic growth. After World War II, mass parties, claiming to represent workers and other mobilized constituencies, effectively determined national policies in many countries.

These mass parties established their dominance not only by being a voice for disadvantaged mass constituencies but by maintaining the *silence* of some of these (women, ethnic minorities, the least skilled, for example). The upsurges of the sixties were in large part due to the prior underrepresentation or exclusion of such groups from the normal politics that the labor movement of thirties had helped create.

Sixties activists in Europe and the United States assumed initially that the established mass parties could be made more inclusive. As we have seen, one of the key strategic projects of activists in the United States in the early seventies was the reform of the Democratic Party so that it could effectively represent the claims of previously marginalized constituencies and thereby establish a new majority coalition. Hopes for a revitalization of the European social democratic parties were also prevalent in the seventies.

Efforts to broaden the mass parties as effective vehicles of economic redistribution and democratization were largely frustrated. Much discussion in Europe and the United States in the seventies envisioned a new social democratic program "beyond the welfare state"—that is, reasserting efforts to promote popular democratic control of planning and investment, workplace democracy, environmentalism, and women's liberation. Programmatic change in these directions did occur in some of the European parties. Once in power, however, European social democratic parties (for example, in France and Spain) reverted to versions of neoliberalism, abandoning even their prior commitment to preserving the welfare state. A similar shift to the right has been evident during the brief periods when the Democratic Party has controlled the White House.

Why did this eminently rational hope for the revitalization of social democracy remain unfulfilled? Part of the problem the mass parties faced was the splintering of their traditional base. The very success of the post–World War II social contract in raising living standards of industrial workers and promoting economic growth meant that large numbers of workers sought to protect their relative advantage, resented taxation that supported the welfare state, and hoped for more opportunity to own things. Against this, traditional party rhetoric about solidarity and equality and the common good seemed stultifying. Just when parts of the working class "bourgeoisified," these parties were, at the same time, compelled to respond to the rising demands of ethnic minorities, women, and the less skilled for recognition, justice, and voice. Class identity, which had undergirded the political strength of these parties, broke into many fragments. No single leadership could claim to speak for these diverse and conflicting parts. Indeed, white male working- and middle-class voters resonated far more to Reaganite and Thatcherite political appeals than to the increasingly hollow rhetoric of their putative party leaderships.

The heart of the problem is that the mass parties no longer can muster the resources within the scope of their domestic political economies to sustain the programs and policies required by Keynesian and welfare-state logics. The globalization of the world economy weakens the capacity of mass parties to use the state as an instrument for allocating resources to benefit their constituencies. Welfare states face intensifying fiscal crisis, capital flow is beyond state control, and Keynesian policies supporting high wages seem to conflict with the need to revitalize national competitiveness. The social-democratic/welfare-state program no longer seems sustainable, and promises made in its name lose credibility.

As a result, the parties find themselves paralyzed, no longer able to offer a credible majoritarian program that meets the needs of both the relatively advantaged and the newly emergent groups that constitute their base. Limited on the one hand by the conservatism of their more advantaged constituents and on the other hand by the fiscal constraints resulting from dependency on global capital flows, these once-dominant parties appear mired in compromise and contradiction. Because state-based strategies of social reform—whether called socialist, capitalist, corporatist, or something else—appear to be politically and economically unviable, the parties whose programs were based on such strategies seem to have had their day as embodiments of popular hope.

The United States has, of course, always lacked a European-style social-democratic party. But after the 1960s the Democratic Party's dilemmas were quite similar to those experienced by mass parties elsewhere. Many movement activists, either explicitly or implicitly, imagined that a movement coalition on the national level would revitalize the Democratic Party and usher in a scenario of the following sort: a progressive Democrat would enter the White House with the promise of completing the welfare state agenda of the New Deal and the Great Society. The bloated military budget would be redistributed to domestic investment that would create full employment by rebuilding the inner cities, constructing affordable housing, expanding education and other human services, and so on. The social wage would be expanded by providing universal health care, reforming welfare, and establishing entitlements for child care, lifelong education, and the like. In such a climate, the social movements would be institutionalized as frameworks for the advancement of constituencies' rights and interests within the electoral and judicial process. Movement activists would find fruitful vocations as advocates, representatives, and professionals in service to their constituencies.

There was, of course, no such new New Deal in the postwar America of the 1970s and the 1980s. Public policy was moved sharply rightward, and so the hope of a normal politics into which the pursuit of equality and social justice could be incorporated never materialized. The movements did become institutionalized: in the seventies a host of lobbying organizations emerged out of the civil rights, women's, peace, and environmental movements; a vast industry of direct-mail solicitation for such causes largely replaced street-level protest; large numbers of activists entered electoral politics, public service, and academic and professional roles with some continuing commitment to their movement identities guiding their work.

In the eighties, the movements lost much of their will and capacity to mobilize direct-action and anti-institutional protest. But it would be quite wrong to describe the seventies and eighties as a period of popular demobilization. As we have seen, at the level of town and neighborhood and local institution, within workplaces and families, the "abnormal" politics of new social movements continued. It was in this period that environmentalism and feminism became integral to the practices of daily life of millions and was incorporated into the political and social life of communities and institutions. This was the era of gay liberation, of collective action by the disabled, and of the cultural politics of racial identity.

Indeed, in the last few years, there has been a tendency among movement-oriented intellectuals and academics to want to redefine the historical meaning of social movements. Rather than measure movements' impacts in terms of political reform, we increasingly stress their impact on culture, consciousness, and identity. (The conference at Santa Cruz from which this volume derived was a kind of symptom of this reassessment.) A number of recent efforts to theorize movements are very much in this vein.[3]

This interpretation of social movements is paralleled by the apparently interminable debate within academia about "multiculturalism" and "political correctness." The so-called "culture wars" in higher education derive from the effort by academically rooted movement activists, begun in the 1960s, to make higher education more demographically and intellectually inclusive and from counter-efforts to block or dilute this thrust.

The cultural turn, from one angle, represents an important advance in the theory and practice of democratic social action. A new complex of understandings about social power and about the institutional sources of social change is embedded in efforts consciously to reconstruct identity, redefine the boundaries of social knowledge, and reform education. But certainly there is a dark side to this emphasis: the turn to culture is a turn away from efforts to analyze and strategize economic and state power on the part of movement activists and intellectuals. And the emphasis on "new" social movements focused on racial, ethnic, sexual, and other status-based identities has seemed to invalidate class as a basis for collective action.

The political vacuum left by the decline of socialist organizations and social-democratic parties cannot adequately be filled by the politics of culture and identity. Cultural projects are inherently nonstrategic; they don't redistribute wealth or address state power; they don't require the mobilization of grassroots collective action to challenge institutionalized power structures. Societal reconstruction requires that people organize in their shared interest while also defending and fulfilling their collective identities. Movements must embody material goals and debate strategies for achieving them, even as members engage in re-envisionings of the terms and meanings of their lives.

Elements of a New Movement Strategy

The parties and organizations of the left, for a century, provided the primary space within which questions of strategy, program, and class interest were thrashed out. Such space is now largely gone. Where does such discussion now take place? Primarily in the periodicals and journals of leftward orientation and in the forums provided by the university. Accordingly, public discourse about movement strategy and program is largely the province of intellectuals, whose life situation is likely to be at least somewhat removed from that experienced by movement constituencies. Political discussion under university auspices, moreover, is constrained in a number of ways by canons of academic discourse. Until some organizational format is created to permit university-based intellectuals to connect with movement-based activists and intellectuals, efforts to reconstitute a political strategy and program will be hampered.

Despite the absence of such an organizational format, I think those who are concerned about sustaining democratic action—whether we are housed in universities or in movements—need to carry on strategic discussion where we can and perhaps by so doing begin to open the social space a new politics requires. So, for the sake of discussion, I would like to suggest some possible lines along which movement strategy might develop in the coming period. Such strategy must begin with the fact that the capacities of states to do economic steering, allocate capital, and redistribute income have been largely superseded by global capital flow, transnational corporate organization, and the dynamic of the world market.

The globalization dynamic has ravaging effects on the daily lives of many who once believed themselves to be secure, provoking widening ripples of anxiety in the great majority of people in the apparently affluent regions of the world. The most evident expressions of popular insecurity and grievance take the form of protectionism, expressed in varying degrees of virulence. Alongside resistance to "free trade" policies are demands to exclude immigrants, violent "ethnic cleansing" projects, tax revolts, popular support for xenophobic and demagogic politicians, a general disgust with the political mainstream (a disgust endlessly reinforced by the discovery and mongering of political and personal scandal). The one remaining power clearly controlled by national states—the power to police—becomes, increasingly, the defining political issue.

In this situation, it seems to me, there are several strategic imperatives shared by democratic movements—lines of action required for their common defense that, at the same time, have the potential of advancing the possibilities for democratic alternatives to protectionism. The following strategic directions are applicable, at least, to the American movements:

A New Internationalism

Protectionism resists economic changes that threaten the wages and well-being of relatively well-off sectors of the working class. The alternative is to support improved living standards for workers in the poor countries. How? The most obvious way would be for American unions and labor organizers to provide direct assistance to labor struggles in those countries to which industrial jobs and capital have been and are being exported. Concerted action by Americans in support of such struggles—sympathetic demonstrations, political action, and job action—is necessary. Environmental internationalism (already evident in growing international networks of environmental activists and global environmental conferences) provides a second, equally important, track for strategic internationalism.

Americans have not been averse to mass action that either directly or indirectly expresses cross-national solidarity. Such action was integral to the antiwar and anti-interventionist activity during the Vietnam War, and of course manifested by strong grassroots opposition to U.S. policy in Central America.

The most effective and relevant solidarity movement was the antiapartheid struggle, which made extensive use of economic leverage. The campaign against NAFTA, although labeled as protectionist, undoubtedly raised popular awareness about the plight of Mexican workers and peasants and may well have stimulated movement networks that could be activated for longer-term internationalist projects.

Such projects are made more likely by a fundamentally new social reality: Americans increasingly are in the same boat as the rest of the world. If, historically, American living standards were enhanced by imperialism, today the American population is increasingly being colonized by the same supranational forces that are at work in the rest of the planet. American elites can no longer credibly promise Americans that they will be advantaged in the global economy. The increasing congruence of interests between the peoples of the northern and southern hemispheres provides a material basis for a new internationalist consciousness. The growing popularity of "world music" is a cultural manifestation of this potential.

Community Empowerment

As the nation state declines, the local community becomes the focus of hope for collective power to maintain everyday life. Whenever corporate decisions threaten economic loss and social dislocation, community-based mobilization has been an increasingly frequent—and often surprisingly effective—response. Struggles to prevent or mitigate plant closings and relocations, to oppose corporate pollution or destructive development—or force the mitigation of these—are integral to local scenes everywhere. Increasingly, communities seem to have developed considerable expertise about means of resistance; the need for "outside" organizers seems less than in the past as indigenous leadership grows in sophistication and creativity.

In the United States, as we have seen, a growing body of law has provided some legal foundation for community empowerment. State and national environmental legislation adopted over the last twenty-five years provides rights previously unavailable for local movements to challenge proposed developments because of their environmental impacts. Efforts to win similar legal protection for communities that are threatened with *economic* disruption— as, for example, the effort to pass plant-closing legislation—have been less successful.

In addition to legal support for community voices in corporate decisions, communities need access to capital for local investment, capital not now available from conventional private sources of finance. Community economic development grounded in democratic planning may be a fundamental strategy for protecting living standards against the ravages of the global market. I refer here not to the commonplace and often disastrous efforts by communities to invite their own rape by corporations and developers, but to efforts to develop community investment and ownership of enterprises that might be job creating and locally beneficial. Moreover, the provision of life necessities—including food, housing, recreation, child care—through community-directed, nonmarket mechanisms can provide social wage substitutions for declining or insecure private wages.

A promising strategic direction for community-based movement activists, therefore, would be to formulate an agenda for national legislation to empower localities. Such an agenda would include establishing national rules requiring the inclusion of community voices in corporate decisions that affect localities, and providing major national resources to support community planning, development, ownership, and control aimed at sustainable local and regional economies.

Participatory Democracy

The global market and the decline of the state compel the restructuring of private and public institutions. Corporate and bureaucratic downsizing, when carried out from above, is designed to protect the incomes and perquisites of those at the top while imposing the costs of economic realism on those with the least leverage. Within each institution, fear, demoralization, and resentment are the result. In the larger society, increasing economic insecurity and dislocation for previously comfortable middle layers accompany the further degradation of the poorest. In the name of efficiency, environmental protections are threatened, previously taken-for-granted fringe benefits are liquidated, all of the institutional "frills" that make up a reasonably varied daily life are abolished. Rearguard resistance to such changes often proves frustratingly ineffective.

The alternative is to enable—and indeed compel—all of the constituencies of a given institution (workplace, school, government bureaucracy) to participate in the planning of institutional change. This means, of course, open books, the diffusion of expert knowledge, the development of institutional mechanisms of representation, voice, and accountability.

There is considerable evidence that demands for participation are a typical response to the threat of retrenchment and downsizing. Cuts are often administered so quickly that the opportunity to mobilize a response from below is short-circuited. But in instances, such as in universities, where retrenchment warnings have happened in advance of implementation, the mobilization of energy and the capacity of affected groups to grasp technical issues and to bargain about these is evident.

Instead of simple resistance to such threats (which often does not materialize because people see cuts as necessary or inevitable, or otherwise become hopeless) movement strategy might focus on demands for the democratic restructuring of institutional life. Such demands are not for self-interested or privileged protection of particular groups. They are in fact quite the opposite:

The aspiration to exercise institutional voice is integrally connected with the need to take institutional responsibility.

□ □ □

To conclude: Social movements arise and are revitalized when normal politics fail. We seem to have entered an epoch in which normal politics not only are failing but cannot be restored in the traditional ways. Government based on representation through political parties and capable of steering national economies is now obsolete. Social polarization, tribalistic fragmentation, and cultural despair are looming dangers. Social movements—the semi-spontaneous upsurges of grassroots initiative—have until now been understood as spasmodic moments in which popular intervention revitalized and reformed institutions. Now that the parties are over, the fate of democracy and the chances for social justice will depend on the movements' capacity to take ongoing responsibility for the social future.

NOTES

1. For illustrative descriptions of local activism, see the chapters in this volume by Andrew Szasz and Mindy Spatt.
2. The rise of progressive electoral coalitions has been described in Pierre Clavel, *The Progressive City* (New Brunswick, N.J.: Rutgers University Press, 1986). Studies of two key cases include Mark Kann, *Middle Class Radicalism in Santa Monica* (Philadelphia: Temple University Press, 1986); W. J. Conroy, *Challenging the Boundaries of Reform: Socialism in Burlington* (Philadelphia: Temple University Press, 1990); J. M. Berry et al., *The Rebirth of Urban Democracy* (Washington: Brookings Institution, 1993); R. E. DeLeon, *Left Coast City* (Lawrence: University of Kansas Press, 1992). See also J. M. Kling and P. S. Posner, *Dilemmas of Activism* (Philadelphia: Temple University Press, 1990).
3. See, for example, the chapter by Alberto Melucci in this volume. Important discussion of the impact of movements on culture and consciousness may be found in Alberto Melucci, *Nomads of the Present* (Philadelphia: Temple University Press, 1989); Ron Eyerman and Andrew Jamison, *Social Movements* (University Park: Pennsylvania State University Press, 1991), and Barbara Epstein, *Political Protest and Cultural Revolution* (Berkeley: University of California Press, 1991).

CHAPTER 18

The Uses of Freedom: Postcommunist Transformation in Eastern Europe

Bronislaw Misztal

□   □   □   □   □   □   □   □   □   □   □   □

"Caminante, no hay camino. Se hace camino al andar."
(Traveler, there is no road. One makes the road by walking.)
Latin American proverb

From the Uses of Adversity to the Uses of Freedom

There is no doubt that a profound change occurred somewhere between the time when, in Poland in June 1989, the deal negotiated by the Communists and the opposition had spontaneously fallen through (leaving both forces in a new parliamentary arrangement that was neither Communist controlled nor dominated by the non-Communists) and the moment when the Berlin Wall was dismantled in November of the very same year; between the death of Nicolae Ceauşescu in the winter of 1989, the relinquishing of Soviet presidential power by Gorbachev in winter of 1991, and the trial of Honnecker in the winter of 1992. The end, one would like to say: the end of communism as we knew it, the end of the totalitarianism and state violence we lived in, the end to the political and economic backwardness we suffered, the end to social inequalities that frustrated us. Hopes flew high between the fall of 1989, when the "autumn of the people" captivated human minds as an overture to democracy and freedom, and the fall of 1993, when the governmental use of violence on the streets of Moscow and the electoral fiasco of the post-Solidarity elites in Poland produced a real "winter of the politicians." It was the end of the "old" and the beginning of the "new".

All this excitement was produced by previously powerless and otherwise frequently politically marginal actors (intellectuals like Mazowiecki, Havel, Antall, and workers like Walesa) who brought the communist polity first to the negotiating table, and next to an apparent end, by the wise "uses of adversity."[1] In circumstances where all dissent from the monolithic ideological line of state socialism had been made extremely costly, and hence unlikely to mobilize broad constituencies, and where the communist apparatus of the state kept political opportunities shut, this sudden "end" was both unpredicted and truly against the odds. It did happen, however, and immediately produced "end of history" musings among members of the Western intellectual community, who should have recalled that when something sounds too good to be true, it probably is.[2]

The "end of history" hypothesis had multiple dimensions. First, it referred to the actual "death of communism," which had two meanings.[3] In the simpler version, it suggested that communism as a system of oppression had come to a historical end. If this were true, oppression (state violence) would be eliminated along with the prospect of totalitarianism in the postcommunist world. Earlier, the end of totalitarian communism had been anticipated as coming about either through the emergence of an alternative to "disorganized capitalism" or through the end of the "garrison state," which would no longer be legitimated by external political crusades and therefore would be defeated by the powerless classes.[4] A more sophisticated hypothesis alleged that the end of communism signified the end of a project of modernization (of previously backward societies); it would be replaced by another project, possibly the Enlightment one. While both theories were optimistic, the latter implied the overall superiority of capitalism, whereas the former still believed that, having experienced the intolerant hand of communist dictators, and having also seen the indiscriminate marketization of social life by the capitalists, the newly emerging civil societies would attempt to form new state organisms capable of resisting both extremes.

Secondly, the "end of history" hypothesis, especially as developed by Fukuyama, offered an assessment of the character of social, political, and economic change in East-Central Europe. It was based on a presumption of the linearity and unavoidability of progress, with the trajectory of social change being determined by Western cultural and political standards. In this sense, the "end of history" is a proposition that divides political or economic transformations from their cultural roots. It becomes an interesting theory of innovation through "social transplant" or by decree. It supposes that the import of ideas from without would not be met with cultural obstacles and that such ideas could be transplanted by political, economic, or social experts. "Better" solutions would win over the "worse" ones in an overall triumph of rationality, necessity, and progress. The "end of history" means nothing less than the end of the past cultural restraints that had halted, slowed down, or otherwise deflected the trajectory of progress. In particular, it suggests the end of structural processes that historically have propelled conflicts and separatisms: nationalisms, ethnocentrisms, racism, antisemitism, and other cultural phenomena. This premise is essentially deterministic in nature. It, too, is optimistic.[5]

The two hypotheses have one thing in common: they presume the linearity of agency: from the uses of adversity (that is, from the uses of the structural conditions that made the system appear to be unchangeable) to the uses of freedom (that is, to the uses of conditions that are conducive to social change). Agency remains vested in certain main actors—presumably intellectuals, the architects of the original transformations, or in workers, since at least in Poland they gave the initial impulse to struggles against the adverse conditions.

From "Making the World" to "Thinking the World"

That state socialism was not a real alternative to Western capitalism has been obvious for some time.[6] Leading socialist intellectuals have either accepted the questionable future of the socialist idea, ruminated about its limited political application in Eastern Europe, or imagined a completely new global conception of socialism divorced from its historical mistakes.[7] But for Western intellectuals concerned about progress and social change, the variegated image of the events of 1989—unequivocally labeled a revolution by so many scholars and fine-minded observers—is far from being comprehensive.[8]

Linz is right to indicate that scholars had overestimated the "penetration, control, and bureaucratic power" of the ruling communist elites. Such overestimation has more profound roots in the certitude with which the students of social change and social movements have assumed the unlikelihood, even in theoretical terms, of the success of a movement over the polity. Who could have better offered this prediction than Alberto Melucci, a longtime researcher and observer of new movements, who remarked in 1984: "the idea of a movement transforming itself into power while maintaining the transparency of its own expressed demand was revealed as an illusion the day after the October Revolution." Was Melucci right in arguing this limitation of the historical role of social movements? Or is it just a question of how broad a historical generalization one attempts to make?[9]

One might believe that Melucci's sweeping generalization was rendered invalid when communism was wiped off the face of Eastern Europe in what apparently was a wave of democratic social movements. The unexpected social change in the Soviet-controlled part of the world, was, therefore, the most perplexing event of the late twentieth century—equal in its impact, perhaps, to the astonishment that the original communist revolution must have caused some seventy-one years earlier.

What social and political factors were at work during this transformation? What is the meaning of such change, and what direction is it going in? Such were the most general intellectual queries arising from these unexpected events. If social change gave birth to a rudimentary social and political freedom, then the question was as much "what are the recent *uses of freedom*," in the newly emerging societies as "what were the *uses of adversity*" that had freed those societies from totalitarian domination?

Lawrence Goodwyn, in an attempt to answer the latter question, links together various pieces of the sociohistorical puzzle, whereby the state, the
economy, the morale of the people, and several other elements require some
sort of analytical order: "A reciprocal relationship exists between the collapse
of Leninist economies, the creation of Solidarnosc, the emergence of Gorbachev, and sweeping opportunities (and dangers) now visible throughout
what so recently had been the exclusive sphere of the Soviets."[10]

While it is possible to ascertain the magnitude of social change, assessment
of its character and direction presents considerable problems. To win freedom
is one thing, and to know how to use it is quite another.

If Western intellectuals were caught by surprise that communism had finally collapsed, East European intellectuals have been more astonished by
how the dismantling of state socialism is being done and with what is it being
replaced. This is most clearly acknowledged by Ivan Szelenyi, who admits
that many observers believed that East European socialism would most likely
evolve into a more complex system with pluralized ownership and class relations. Other projections, cast from within Eastern Europe, foresaw either the
imposition of martial law from above (a selective repression enabling the authorities to increase food prices, stimulate domestic consumption, and force
changes in property rights) followed by further centralization of the state or,
conversely, a populist-introduced state of emergency (with a cultural revolution look-alike that would paralyze the communist system itself). Therefore,
the initial gasp of excitement one heard at the time the Berlin Wall was crumbling meant two different things: Western intellectuals were surprised that
something they thought of as immutable was finally moving on; East European intellectuals, on the other hand, were surprised that something they
thought of as capable of being reformed was falling apart and that a truly new
social and political formation was emerging.[11]

These processes of social change have affected our way of thinking and our
use of symbols; even the semiotics of politics has changed. As Charles Lemert
sees it: "Many suppose that the world has changed. This supposition, so al-
luring today, is not without its troubles. If the world is changed, then in what
does the change consist? If there is change in world magnitude, it is more
likely an upheaval, deep and wide, in how people think the world."[12] Although the way we "make the world" has changed, it is still possible that the
way we "think the world" has not changed that much and that we are still per-
petuating old patterns. There are, after all, structural constraints on the use of
freedom that limit the effective consequences of what has just been won. In
this chapter I maintain that:

1. the "uses of adversity" have not been transformed into proper "uses of
   freedom." While social forces that brought about the deconstruction of
   state socialism certainly won the struggle, by removing something that
   was obsolete and apparently not working well, the postcommunist trans-

formation has not become a successful reconstruction; instead it remains a process of undoing the previous system;

2. the replacement of state socialism with postcommunist arrangements did not occur as a planned or otherwise controlled process of social reconstruction; instead it was a spontaneous and frequently chaotic removal of everything that was reminiscent of the past, subsequently adversely affecting the continuity of societal history;

3. the establishment of democracy and freedoms did not produce, or coincide with, broader frames of citizenship *rights* for society's members; instead it produced the redefinition, or restructuring, of *privileges;*

4. the role of former agents of change—the intellectuals and the workers—in the political and economic processes of postcommunism was shrinking, frequently leading to paradoxical denials of previously held values and programs; what this implied, therefore, was that notions about the linearity of historical agency could not be upheld;

5. the project of transition from state socialism to postcommunism lost its national autonomy relatively early. Foreign interests not only focused on the region of East-Central Europe but also influenced the fate of this project by producing external necessities that the new countries had to cope with—for example, World Bank loans with conditions attached;

6. autonomy and democracy did not bring to an end previous structural problems and strains that characterized the region; to the contrary, such problems have suddenly been magnified; and finally,

7. the "end of history" hypothesis cannot be upheld and should be refuted.

Constraints on the Uses of Freedom

The actual uses of freedom are determined by two factors: by the constraints resulting from the circumstances surrounding its attainment, and by the preexisting cleavages within the state socialist society.

The uses of freedoms by those who won them are constrained by circumstances that cause considerable unpredictability of the outcomes of the intended democratization processes. Such processes "always contain a significant risk of failure," regardless of the skills, prudence, and mere luck of their advocates.[13]

General theories that attempt the correlation of democracy with some level of economic development (frequently referred to as "modernization") abstract from such unpredictability, thus assuming a linear causality: freedoms produce democracy, which in turn magnifies the scope of freedoms. Recent academic debates among students of East-Central Europe indicate that it is easier to describe the system's collapse than to evaluate transformations that follow in terms of the freedoms or democracy they bring about. Few observers have so far had any serious doubts as to the nature or direction of change.[14]

Favored outcomes scarcely prompt inquisitiveness, hence careful inquiry into the character of postcommunist transformation has yet to be made. Although existing analyses are of little help in explaining "the timing, the longevity, or the geographical incidence of the recent experiences of democratization,"[15] they can illuminate various constraints on the uses of freedoms. Elsewhere, I discuss these hypotheses in greater detail; what follows is a brief summary of the existing explanations of ongoing structural changes, with an indication of constraints they present.[16]

1. *Arguments about the withering away of the state:* The collapse of state socialism resulted from the state's diminishing capacity to create conditions conducive to its own reproduction.[17] In other words, at some point the system of state socialism lost its capacity for reconstitution of society and, what is even more important, was widely perceived as being incapable of providing social, historical, economic, or even biological continuity according to its promises. The erosion of legal-rational authority has adversely affected the ability of the state to protect the constitutional rights of its citizens, and, insofar as postcommunism is indeed starting from scratch, weaker or more disorganized political actors have benefited from few measures that enable their interests and needs to be satisfied. The system undergoing reorganization instead grants more freedoms to more powerful political actors by allowing the receding of established legal institutions.
2. *Arguments about the decline of welfare policies:* Similar in nature to the argument about the declining capacity of the state, these arguments point to the abandonment of social welfare policies as being "too expensive" for the state to implement. This particular situation renders certain categories of society's members (for example, women, adolescents, retirees) especially vulnerable to the worsening of their economic, and subsequently, political positions.[18]
3. *Arguments about the contagious nature of social change:* Social change diffuses the very same way that cultural innovations do, frequently in the form of "free ideas made public," and therefore it becomes freely available to the society at large. This is intrinsically an activist explanation of social change, since it accords similar roles and significance to all segments of society, who are expected to have equal chances of stepping in and using their freedoms. By the simple inversion of this argument, however, it becomes obvious that only a part of society is active in this process and ends up represented in a political system.[19]
4. *Arguments about differential openings and closures of political opportunity structures:* The political system is capable of encouraging or discouraging political actors to use their internal resources to form social movements. This argument implies that achieving certain goals depends on certain configurations of institutionalized circumstances combined with substantial investments of time, energy, initiative, activity, freedom, and security by

those actors who can forego certain other assets (status, earnings, privacy, professional improvement). The uses of freedom are therefore dependent on the actual "terms of trade" between goals that political actors want to accomplish and the assets that they are willing to forego. But under no circumstances are those "terms of trade" universal equations for all collective actors. Accordingly, some will engage in the process of change, while others stand back when this activity becomes "too expensive."[20]

These constraints have manifested themselves in the following areas: erosion of the legal institutions and in particular a declining role of the state; erosion of welfare policies and the subsequent production of economically and politically feeble actors; sectarian politics that make possible differential "uses of freedoms" for those actors who have more political "seniority" within the new system; and the emerging denominational state that arranges for special opportunities for religious or fundamentalist actors.

The Instrumental Uses of Freedom

Freedom, apart from its abstract meaning, is an ability to access and employ legal and political options on the part of groups of citizens whose interests can be articulated and translated into action. More broadly, freedom is also an ability to articulate and to pursue one's personal life options in terms of one's own cultural preferences in combination with one's intellectual, religious, and ethnic identities. In this sense it is obvious that the communist-governed societies of Eastern Europe never produced freedoms, first because interest articulation was limited to internal political elites of the party and, secondly, access to legal and political options was nonexistent, even for relatively high-ranking administrative structures of the communist establishment. Postcommunism has brought about formal legal and political options, and in this sense it constitutes a considerable improvement. Yet *access* to such options has been structured by a complex set of factors, with the result that the way freedom is used is considerably different in postcommunist countries from the way it is known in the Western democracies.

Sectarian Politics

Some constraints on freedoms in the postcommunist era are the result of preexisting, overtly undemocratic political opportunity structures. These were reproduced by apparently nonviolent procedures through which the succession of power took place.

I surmise that two aspects of the transition to postcommunism have influenced the sectarian or elitist character of politics in these initial years of "uses of freedom." First, the revolution in East-Central Europe was negotiated.

Nowhere did the disgruntled masses eliminate the old political order by violent and repressive actions. Instead, roundtables were created and become frameworks for discussing how power would be transferred.[21] This *reforma pactada*, or "negotiated agreement between democratic forces and interests from the old regime," was not an open or spontaneous process.[22] Such agreements never are. In general, the participants came from two groups: on the one side, there were the communist power wielders, who were facing the prospect of being held accountable for everything that had happened under their rule and therefore were motivated to keep the spectrum of other participants as narrow as possible; on the other side were various representatives of the political opposition together with recent recruits: experts and intellectual supporters, who were co-opted hastily.

Andras Bozoki puts it this way:

[W]ith the collapse of the post-Stalinist system, not only did the third stage of socialism fail to appear, but socialism as a system collapsed. The intelligentsia had not been victorious as an organized class, but as the "vanguard of the building of capitalism." Wishing to modernize and westernize, it accomplished victory as an ad hoc, heterogenous coalition of intellectual strata, estates and "tribes."[23]

The second factor that has constrained the uses of freedom results from the very paradox of the succession of power: the former opposition, and now ascending power elite, was destined to execute shock therapy to the economy (a therapy of which it had no experience), at the same time protecting labor from the costs of such a therapy.[24] In other words, those who were elected to use the freedoms were also historically charged with the task of curtailing them.

Although historical analyses of the overall immediate transfer of power are yet to appear, one may already outline certain characteristics of this process:

1. Everywhere (except Poland, where it was foreshadowed by earlier policies of the communists) this process caught society unprepared, and therefore no network of civic institutions was in place to monitor such negotiations;
2. Most social classes, not only intellectuals, were disorganized, confused, and misinformed, since fragmentation was an intended product of communist policies;
3. The attention of various societal groups was, to an extent, concentrated on economic (and not on political) issues, since the decade of the 1980s saw a dramatic lowering of living standards and dwindling economies;
4. Neither the top-ranking Communists nor the opposition groups consulted their respective constituents. Most Communist Party members in Poland, the Soviet Union, Czechoslovakia, and Bulgaria were caught by surprise when these parties announced their dissolution or were declared illegal. Likewise, the repressive apparatus of the communist states was ill pre-

pared and did not expect its immediate demise. The facts that the Communists decided to run for offices in the June 1989 elections in Poland, or that they tried to withstand the popular protest with harsh repressions in Prague in November 1989, indicate that the political apparatuses of the communist states were unprepared for this transition, the idea of which had been conceived in the narrow circles of leadership. Many political groups were absent at the roundtables because they did not realize they were taking place. It is also possible that they were deliberately excluded from the process;

5. Selection of participants to the negotiation tables was frequently accidental and involved members of intellectual "estates" or "tribes" within narrow opposition circles;

6. Democratization was taking place in "a conflict-ridden context" whereby pacts were "shortcuts to habituation."[25] Because of the structure of political forces, such pacts accommodated the members of the state apparatus, the intellectual circles, and occasionally the anticipated interests of the post-nomenklatural economic bourgeoisie.

Such political determinants have affected the range of precipitously legalized social forces. As Wlodzimierz Wesolowski observed, in Poland for two years,

> there existed a different type of a parliament—a contractual one. Its political composition was meticulously planned before the voters ever reached the polls. Its real role, according to the communist strategists, was to co-opt the opposition into the state apparatus without giving it a decisive voice or influence. History changed this plan. . . . The new parliament was accomplishing objectives of an anticommunist, democratic, and capitalist breakthrough despite its composition. It did not initiate the breakthrough, since the causative forces were located elsewhere.[26]

Wesolowski's statement subscribes to a theory of elite consensus, one that accords autonomy to the elites and frees them from accountability of responsibility to society at large.[27] But *reformas pactadas* do not always produce an effect in the form of a *garantismo;* instead, they frequently lead to what is called a *democradura.*[28]

Recent analysis by one of the foremost leaders of the anticommunist political opposition between 1945 and 1989 sheds more light on how access to legal-political options in postcommunist Poland was structured. The thrust of his argument is that the postcommunist political setup is not only a legacy but also a product of the deal that was struck with the Communist powers in 1989. In this sense, although gone from the political scene, the Communists remain the architects of the existing political order. Major political parties of postcommunism are "the children of one mother, namely, the agreement between the communist authorities and the Solidarity."[29] This constitutes the first significant limitation of freedom, since the existing options have not been produced freely.

That this freedom, in its limited provision, did not bring a universal and general sense of happiness, or simply satisfaction, is apparent from opinion polls that were conducted three months after the presidential election in Poland. Those polls indicate considerable erosion of moral and political authority and a growing disenchantment of the masses, whose detachment from political values undermines their ability to use new options of freedom. Wladyslaw Sila-Nowicki argues that despite winning freedom, Poland has remained basically an unjust society, whereby social inequalities of the communist era have only been magnified by those produced by the postcommunist transformation:

> It has remained the country of privileges for the few and inequalities for many, where a lack of moral scruples and shrewdness are worth more than honest work, and where the arrogance of people in power prompts them to disregard the individual man. . . . Too frequently the heroes who claim major contributions to dismantling the communist system. . . . fight fiercely for privileges. . . . and for positions in state administration regardless of whether they possess adequate skills. . . . The downfall of the ethos of Solidarity results from the fact that the heirs of Solidarity too frequently follow the path of the dignitaries of the communist party.[30]

The uses of freedom are restricted to the original participants of the deal with the outgoing communist powers. Many nonparliamentary political groupings complain that they have no access to interest articulation—that, for instance, the remnants of the formerly communist-monopolized mass media have now been partitioned among the original participants of the deal and as such are unavailable to the newcomers to the political scene.

Receding Role of Legal Institutions

Along with restricted access to parliamentary representation that excluded groups either too small to be present during the partition of power with the Communists, or that only emerged after this historical fact, another process shapes the postcommunist reality. Of the two orientations toward state organization—one that proposes the reinstatement of the rule of law, and another that argues for strong executive powers in the office of president—the former has considerably receded while the latter has been relatively strengthened in almost all postcommunist countries. This is most evident in Russia, where the power of the president is probably far greater (and less democratic) than the power enjoyed by his Soviet predecessor.

Immediately after the political takeover of power from the Communists, the prolegal orientation dominated, and an effort to build a system in which the laws passed by parliaments would be the major instrument of social transformation characterized the first postcommunist governments in the region. But the parliamentary initiatives in postcommunist countries were doubly handicapped: by the past histories of the new lawmakers (they were frequently political converts—former Communists turned democrats) and by the inhibiting effects of existing legal regulations, frequently inherited from the nondemocratic era. The new lawmakers were unable to garner political support for substantial reforms since the parliament itself was lacking legitimacy. The compromised pasts of many opposition deputies, who perhaps were former police collaborators if not *agents provocateurs*, certainly did not help in the legitimization process, but the crucial issue was that the postcommunist reconstruction was particularly slow in legislating new institutional structures of power. The intended uses of freedom of the lawmakers were directed at restricting the individual political authority of the new presidents (in Czechoslovakia, Poland, Russia, and Romania most notably), while the intended uses of freedom by the elected presidents were directed against all those who wished to shed more light on the clandestine deals between the communists and their former secret collaborators that were made during opposition roundtable talks.

The conflict over the uses of freedom was therefore a permanent element of the political landscapes of the postcommunists. In Russia, the clash between the speaker of the parliament, Ruslan Khasbulatov, and President Boris Yeltsin exemplified the first situation. In Poland, the battle between the intellectuals-turned-politicians who sought the identities of the collaborators of the communist secret services, and the president who successfully blocked their efforts, was an illustration of the second type of conflict. Certainly, as a result of *reformas pactadas*, the new states are not states of law, and "crafting democracy" by necessity includes also "grafting democracy."

Interestingly, the prolegal orientation has a strong and clear class correlation, since it characterizes those political groups with primarily intellectual constituencies (like the former OKP (Citizens' Parliamentary Club) in Poland or OF (Citizens' Forum) in Czechoslovakia, or Sajudis in Lithuania). The parliaments, because they were compromise assemblages of the communist and opposition groupings, turned out to be ineffective instruments to implement legal processes of reform. The right-centrist orientations of the impatient political elites inclined them not to wait for the end of protracted democratic processes of rewriting the laws. The centrist forces (in Poland and in Russia most notably) proposed "acceleration" policies that would use extra-parliamentary and extralegal measures to speed up decommunization and privatization, leaving the processes of legal and social modernization to await their day in the lawmaking institutions. As a result, the role of parliaments has eroded, both in actual fact and in public expectation.

Several major political decisions have been precipitated by the extra-parliamentary forces and through the use of extralegal and frequently populist measures that were certainly undemocratic. The most typical examples in Poland included the presidential elections in 1990. The major contender (and the subsequent winner of the presidential race, Mr. Walesa) had precipitated presidential elections before the legal work on the bill of the office of president has been completed. He also set the date for the new general elections in 1991, before the new constitution has been written (that is, new free elections took place when the bill of rights was still that of a communist country) and even prior to the completion of work on electoral law. The continuing rule of the compromised cabinet for six months after it had lost a nonconfidence vote in 1993 is another illustration of the dominant influence of nonparliamentarian and undemocratic politics. Likewise, in Russia, in the fall of 1993, the parliament was disbanded and the new elections were called before election laws were reformed and before a new constitution was worked out. There is no doubt that postcommunist governments are resorting to undemocratic politics as a prosthetic device where there is no institutional mechanism for political change and innovation. It remains to be seen whether such undemocratic methods can lead to democratic outcomes.

The instrumental and frequently precipitous use of freedom in the conditions of postcommunism erodes the prestige of law, curtails the role of the institution of parliament, and creates a system of dual power whereby two centers compete to be able to issue laws or decrees to replace the outmoded communist laws. The result is that neither one can act effectively and a certain political vacuum is created. The vacuum is subsequently filled by nonsecular and frequently fundamentalist forces.

The Emerging Denominational State

The denominational state is the opposite of the state of law. The latter concept refers to situations in which the institutions of the polity render the public space effectively controlled by the legislature and the judiciary, with the executive branch being constitutionally unable to introduce extralegal (ideological/totalitarian or exclusive/religious) values into state policies. The denominational state emerges when institutional arrangements allow religious and thus extralegal considerations to determine "the course of state policies, to penetrate into the contents of the legislative activity and affect the overall operation of the state, including personnel recruitment."[31] In such a state the legitimation of political decisions is sought in or created by constituencies other than those of citizens enjoying their liberties, and backed up by value systems other than universal citizenship rights of democracy, freedom, or equal opportunities. In particular, such legitimation is obtained by appealing to specific, nonuniversal values held by part (even if this is a majority) of the constituency.

My overall premise (the premise that underlies my analysis of the denominational state) is that the state's institutional weakness and its inability to coalesce the forces of secular power into a viable coalition has allowed religious elements to play a pivotal role in politics. It is as much a matter of a weak state as of strong religious organizations. A denominational state emerges where there is a conflict between crucial political actors over whether some general, yet controversial, policies should be implemented in order to gain consent from the constituencies. Such policies may involve modernization (or substantial social change), reorganization of social structures (or social revolution), changes in gender relations and politics, emphasizing or de-emphasizing national cultural values, shifting priorities in economic relations of production (for example, from agricultural to industrial or vice versa), patterns of redistribution of the national product (from egalitarian to elitist or vice versa), patterns of elite recruitment, and so on.

Whenever such conflicts cannot be negotiated and settled by the secular actors, there is a likelihood that some political forces will be willing to broaden the spectrum of power by either inviting or yielding to the aspirations of the military or the clergy. In either case, at the expense of a compromise among the secular forces, such new forces are politicized and import their repertory of particularistic value into the national politics.

The communist states were also denominational states, since the ideology of the leading party was nothing less than a system of quasi-religious regulations. Communism required faith in its ideology; and when it relaxed this requirement sometime in the 1970s, it still did not allow schism. The curtailment of freedoms under communism eliminated the Christian/Catholic moral orientation from political representation in Poland and Hungary and other nations in the Eastern bloc.

In Poland, at least, the postcommunist social order has been, to a considerable degree, established with the support and resources of the Catholic Church, which is not only a moral power but also an efficient bureaucracy. The prototype of free political representation, the advisory committee created by Lech Walesa in 1988, was housed in the offices of the diocese of Warsaw.

Although the clergy do not hold political offices, they are present in most political bodies in Poland. Three issues dominated political life in Poland in the years 1991–93. One was the issue of the abortion law, the second was the teaching of religion in schools, and the third was the role of the church in organizing political campaigning. In all three cases the Catholic Church managed to advance its interests. The abortion law is one of the most restrictive in the contemporary world, effectively eliminating choice by women. The education system has been saturated with religious content, and pressure is effected upon students to pursue religious education at state schools. Finally, despite parliamentary opposition, the president apparently has managed to work out an agreement to use religious institutions for political campaigning, and indeed his first campaign appearance for the 1991 election took place in church.

The increased presence of religious interest articulation in state social and political life has not, however, broadened the scope of religious freedom in Poland. In a fascinating study Mucha documents that the "democratization process of the late 1980s and early 1990s meant in Poland not the granting to everybody the citizenship rights, but instead changing the scope of privileges. The minority that was privileged before, lost their privileges, the majority of society gained them. Citizens who do not belong to the majority are actually deprived of many rights."[32] Political domination by the Catholic moral orientation has limited the scope of freedoms enjoyed by agnostic, lay citizens (who constitute Poland's largest minority) and has also led to the erosion of social space enjoyed by some ethnic/religious communities, like the Muslim Tartars. While the future shape of the state still remains undefined, it is obvious that in Poland the Catholic Church bureaucracy has been incorporated in the power system. Likewise, the erosion of secular values has allowed sacred ones to penetrate previously nonreligious institutions. In this sense, the freedoms brought about by dismantling state socialism have been used more astutely by the existing bureaucratic infrastructure of the Catholic Church than, say, by the citizen groups at large.

Elsewhere, the penetration of religious content into the politics of the state plays no less a role. In Russia, the Orthodox reawakening has become a significant element in the power struggle of the executive faction against the constitutional one, and in fact the former has managed to gain considerable support from the clergy, while the latter failed to realize that religious elements of political ideology may play a pivotal role in gaining popular support. It is just a matter of time before the Russian state becomes saturated with religious, and possibly fundamentalist, content and social life there becomes defined by nonsecular political actors who may determine elite recruitment patterns and the policy objectives of the state.

In the countries of the former Yugoslavia, the impact of religious differences has been even more significant. Yugoslavia has been the meeting point for three distinct cultural forces: that of the West (otherwise frequently perceived as European), including both Catholic and Protestant religious denominations; that of the East (East European), including Byzantine and Orthodox denominations; and that of the South-East (Asian, Middle-Eastern), which include Ottoman and Islamic influences. After the fall of communism many nonreligious and nonpracticing people have become religious again as a way of manifesting their national identities. Mestrovic et al. demonstrate that the mother-centeredness of the Catholic faith, through its veneration of St. Mary, is the force that allows religious values to merge with nationalist identities.[33] Thus, nationalist aspirations can be relegitimized and strengthened if they are sufficiently vested with religious denotations. A denominational state becomes an answer to new claims for political autonomy, secession from the imperial polity, and reorganization of political and moral allegiance. Its results are devastating to the very foundations of society's existence, giving rise to genocide, nationalisms, and war.

Fukuyama is therefore wrong in his assertion that the roles of religion and nationalism can be "modernized".[34] Instead, it appears that both can penetrate the political institutions, turn them into denominational ones, and overshadow the *reformas pactadas*. The postcommunist state is an institution of a current majority and as such is denominational, since it does not extend citizenship rights to the minorities and frequently, indeed, allows saturation of the legal processes with nationalistic, religious, or intolerant contents. As I put it elsewhere, the

> post-Communist state is especially vulnerable to the penetration of fundamentalist meanings, symbols and contents. With massive mobilization and popular discontent, with lack of democratic legal traditions, any extensive claims to the public space by the state can either precipitate some type of fundamentalist assault on democracy or prompt authoritarian defenses of the etatistic apparatus. Restricting its own claims to the public space [the state makes it possible] that religion will become fused with its own ideology. Allowing protracted conflict over access to public space may produce a situation of ungovernability, weak executive branch and disillusioned masses. A cautious approach to interest intermediation, frequently referred to as corporatist arrangement, will debase social movements of their class origin, replacing it with a denominational-religious identity, thus allowing liberal, non-reformist persuasion to dominate. . . . the fast moves by the etatistic structure to claim and appropriate public space prior to the organization of interests by the Church can lead to the absolutist regime that would slowly yet in a limited way control the reform process.[35]

Erosion of the Institutions of the Welfare State

Imperfect as it was, the system of state socialism had worked out certain elements of the welfare state whereby decommodification of the national economy allowed some goods to be included in the sphere of state-subsidized social consumption. Full employment, higher education, health care, maternity support, vacation time, housing, youth camps, public transportation, sick leave, and cultural production (movies, theater, opera, books) were just a few spheres where the state attempted equalization of consumption. Despite communist claims, such consumption was always class structured, yet to various degrees it was available to most segments of society.

With the dismantling of state socialism most of those social-consumption provisions were immediately commodified in part or entirely. Unemployment rose in Poland from zero to 1988 to 17 percent in 1993. Housing, education, social services, and cultural production lost their state subsidies and subsequently became regular commodities. With the impoverishment rate of the populations reaching 25 percent in Poland (measuring real income in 1991 against real income in 1989) and perhaps 50 percent in Russia, access to certain commodities became more class structured than it had ever been (such as vacation, sick leave, youth camps, and housing or health care). Privatization of national industries and of several spheres of social life was meant to bring about social and economic pluralism. It is important to notice that this process commenced with the forceful lowering of living standards of the most vulnerable segments of society: of workers in nonprimary industries (like textile or food processing) located in small and middle-sized towns; and of the so-called intelligentsia or nonmanual workers (mostly university-trained employees of the former state administration, colleges, and social-service agencies) whose peripheral position with respect to the postcommunist governments did not allow them to negotiate betterment of their labor contracts. At the same time the new class of private entrepreneurs and the employees of foreign companies have enjoyed conspicuous living standards in Hungary, Russia, and Poland.

This paradox is best encapsulated in Michael Burawoy's remark that while state socialism prompted the appearance of movements for workers' direction of society, "in order to be effective struggles for workers' control require the trappings of bourgeois society." But, as one currently sees, during the first stages of the postcommunist social order, "those trappings may also demobilize and atomize the working class."[36] Unemployment, homelessness, underinsurance, living below the poverty line, inability to send children to college—all those social evils have affected those segments of society that put high stakes in abolishing state socialism and in winning rudimentary freedoms. As Adam Michnik aptly put it:

> Under state socialism I was frequently in prison. As such I was not free. Yet I knew where am I sleeping tonight, what I am going to eat and what shall I do the next day. Abolishing state socialism brought me freedom. Today,. however, being free, I do not know where am I going to sleep tonight, whether or not I shall have my job tomorrow and what am I going to eat.[37]

In this way freedom brought about the insecurity and social malaise characteristic of capitalist society.

Cleavages in the System and the Uses of Freedom

The reconstruction of society (civil society), economy (free market), and polity (the state of law) can neither be reduced to component practices (citizenship rights; production and distribution based on market prices; equal opportunities) nor separated from the interplay of cultural and structural factors that determine change. By the same token, the interaction of these three processes constitutes the social context of the life-world.[38] State socialism left a considerable heritage of conflicts, tensions, and cleavages that took the form of structural and cultural inconsistencies. The uses of freedom have to be adequate to the magnitude of those inconsistencies (the needs to reconstruct) and to the scope of cultural possibilities in the East European societies. But, as Lukacs and Burawoy aptly remark, if state socialism "was so hard to reform in the direction of socialist ideals, how easy is it to move in the direction of capitalism?"[39]

Therefore, the key issue is whether the extent of social reconstruction is adequate to the magnitude of the structural inconsistencies of state socialism and whether such transformative effort can remedy any of the recurring problems that the state socialist system was unable to settle. Such inconsistencies had manifested themselves in the domains of labor (material production, organization of work, property and power) and in the domains of ideas (generation of ideologies, consisting of appealing symbols; ability to unite around common goals and to stand by them). It is, therefore, within those areas that the remedial effort should be concentrated.

Below, I argue that the reconstruction of society through the uses of freedoms misses this very important point: it ignores the particularities of these societies, affects the superstructural level, and leaves the cultural and economic foundations unaffected.

Although the rapid defeat of state socialism was unanticipated, the structural cleavages and contradictions within the system of state socialism have been studied and analyzed for quite some time.[40] In the labor sector state socialism was the system in which the working majority of society had "no control over the conditions, process or results of its own labor," nor was it able to influence "what to produce and how to employ the gross product." The labor sector was overwhelmingly dependent upon "a distinct and separate social group (the bureaucracy) whose corpus [was] continuously replenished through mechanisms of a selective cooptation."[41]

In reality there was an overlap between the domain of production and two other areas. Staniszkis demonstrated that the state had functioned as the force of production, since the state bureaucratic apparatus (in the absence of other mechanisms) provided an artificial link between production and distribution. As a result, the unclearly defined property rights did not transmit the interests of any social group. In brief, the diminishing capacity of the socialist state resulted from a yawning gap between requirements of material production and structured actual group interests. What people expected, wanted, and needed was not delivered, and instead they were provided with what the state bureaucratic apparatus determined they needed to have.[42]

The example of public transportation versus the development of an auto industry may shed some light on this problem. For several decades the countries of East Central Europe either did not manufacture their own automobiles or they produced them in small quantities. Instead, citizens were provided with inexpensive public transportation networks, both intra- and inter-urban ones. While the practical issue of getting people where they wanted to go was resolved, the social need, which was for convenient individual transport, was not satisfied.

Another observation indicates that a social order that eliminated property as the basic driving force of social behavior had a triply devastating effect: it made citizens passive, it rendered consumers helpless, and it made producers irresponsible.[43] The basic contradiction of state socialism resulted from the fact that a social order based on plan and control was expected to become the remedy for insecurity and injustice, yet it had denied everybody's natural responsibilities and duties. Citizens did not select representative bodies, so local government was not accountable; consumers had no instrument to communicate their interests, hence production plans did not have to correspond with consumers' needs; producers were not bound by actual cost efficiency, availability of labor, wages, and so on.

In the aggregate, one could say that the cleavages and contradictions of state socialism, which had manifested themselves as early as the mid-1960s, resulted in the necessity of a total overhaul of the entire system. However, as Staniszkis put it: "the challenge of current transformative efforts lies in the fact that they are undertaken by the parties that have been formed by the very intellectual tradition that they attempt to change if social change is to be sufficiently durable and profound. . . . This is far more than a theoretical question."[44]

Even in Poland, where dissent had the broadest social base, the bulk of society rather passively accepted the transition. In the course of the revolutionary transformations, common people, and even some successful politicians, have discovered that freedom and democracy are sorts of levers that can help advance the political objectives of some forces and individuals while bypassing, ignoring, or otherwise reducing other political interests to the secondary level. The uses of freedom can, therefore, be instrumental.

Moreover, as Mestrovic et al. demonstrate, the uses of freedom may be limited by historical traditions and the inability of particular societies to overcome their historically produced national characters. As we have seen in the countries of the former Yugoslavia, it was not possible to overcome their social character and conflicts, which have been reborn, or reemerged from latency, virtually overnight. Mestrovic's argument is that while in the Western countries the socially shaped elements of personality were gradually controlled by the emerging modern Western order, in the formerly communist countries the unconscious and the collective id were forced underground and were never really transformed, but only hidden from the damaging influence of the totalitarian state. Newly gained freedoms are therefore used to regain identity by "return of the repressed.":

Communists as well as Western capitalists have been suppressing national aspirations for well over a century, on both sides of the Iron Curtain. Now that these two ideologies begin to slide into one another, actually mutating into their opposites as they undergo a fatal reversal of meaning, their repressive functions have been weakened, and nationalism, the equivalent of the id, is emerging again. In much of Eastern Europe and the former USSR, the modernist nation-state has been splintered into the nation as the "will of the people" versus the State as an arbitrary, conceptual category.

The uses of freedom are not free, and, moreover, they can turn against the rational project of the uses of freedom that has been associated with the concept of modernity. Long forgotten, repressed by the totalitarian powers of the now-defunct communist states, the "habits of the heart" of the East European people make a comeback, and in the last instance they can alter if not completely reverse the nature of the project of transformation.[45]

Conclusions

Replacing state socialism with a somewhat more democratic social order is an endeavor whose magnitude cannot be appreciated in full at the present time. The first stage of this process consists in dismantling the political and economic infrastructure that was already in place as a result of previous reconstructions. In the past this infrastructure shielded the most vulnerable elements of society, which in the absence of civil society turned to the state for protection. This shield is immediately removed with the instauration of the new social order. Consequently, those who led the overthrow of the old order because they were the most affected by the inequalities of state socialism are likewise most affected by the new inequalities brought by new freedoms. In this sense, the immediate use of new freedoms turns frequently against those who needed them most. The political and economic priorities of the newly emerging states contribute to this situation greatly. In most postcommunist states the new governments declare that their foremost intention is to produce a new middle class of private entrepreneurs, since those are seen as a source of the initiative and ingenuity that state socialism muffled so effectively. In the process one can expect an intensified stratification, with new poor, growing crime rates, substantial unemployment, extremely differentiated living standards, and so on.

Replacement of state socialism is also a process that exhibits some symptoms of elitism, so that having the status of a veteran of the struggle against communism (but not necessarily the accompanying political objectives) legitimizes individuals to take part in it. Those who at any point have been "stained" by collaboration with the communist regime are automatically eliminated from politically active life, while those who were formerly stigmatized by being oppositionists are automatically considered qualified to occupy political positions. In Poland such an exclusion, planned by the post-Solidarity elites as a "decommunization" bill, could have affected approximately three million people. Likewise, in the aftermath of the political failure of the post-

Solidarity forces comparable "de-Solidarization" practices, if implemented, could decimate the political class. This 1990s version of McCarthyism cannot by any means be considered to be a democratic measure, yet settling historical accounts frequently involves attacking intellectuals. In countries where a considerable part of the educated strata of society were forced to be dependent to some degree on and hence to collaborate with the state socialist regime, the extralegal or legalized, yet undemocratic, settlement of past accounts can result in a new version of the Chinese cultural revolution, or Peronism, at the very best.

While in legal terms democracy and freedom have been achieved and are properly used in postcommunist countries, it is obvious that, in the absence of dominant classes (that yet would have to be produced), the power vacuum is filled by a compromise, with strong dominance by religious and populist components who call for measures of vindication and exclusion that are essentially undemocratic.

Furthermore, it is widely accepted by the politicians of postcommunist Europe that the most undemocratic element of state socialism was that it eliminated the market. In an effort to reinstate market mechanisms as the guarantee of structural freedoms and democracy, the postcommunist regimes have to pay the price of the immediate social inequality that accompanies the marketization of social life. In this sense, the uses of freedom in postcommunist conditions amount to a restricted version of democracy.

In brief, the change of political and economic formation, whether peaceful or violent on the surface, unleashes processes that are intrinsically conflictual, aspirations that are exclusionist, and economic programs that are frequently unfair and unjust (at least to those classes that cannot convert their capital rapidly enough) and initiates mechanisms for replacement of personnel and institutions that redefine and limit the uses of freedom. Profound, universal democratization is therefore an unlikely result of the uses of freedom that follow the uses of adversity. This particular sequence of historical events is therefore an overture toward the future and not the end of anything.

NOTES

1. Timothy Garton Ash, *The Uses of Adversity* (New York: Vintage Books, 1990).
2. Martin Malia, "The August Revolution," *New York Review of Books,* September 26, 1991, 22–28; "To the Stalin Mausoleum," in *Eastern Europe . . . Central Europe . . . Europe,* ed. Stephen R. Graubard (Boulder, Colo.: Westview Press, 1991).
3. Zbigniew Brzezinski, *The Grand Failure: The Birth and Death of Communism* (New York: Scribners, 1989).
4. Claus Offe, *Disorganized Capitalism* (Oxford: Oxford University Press, 1985); Andrew C. Janos, "Post Communist Eastern Europe: A Survey of Opinion," *East European Politics and Society* 4 (1990): 153–207.

5. Francis Fukuyama, *The End of History and the Last Man* (New York: Free Press, 1992).

6. Howard Davis and Richard Scase, *Western Capitalism and State Socialism* (Oxford and New York: Basil Blackwell, 1985).

7. Ferenc Feher and Agnes Heller, *Dictatorship over Needs: An Analysis of Soviet Societies* (New York: Basil Blackwell, 1983); Stanley Aronowitz, *The Crisis of Historical Materialism* (New York: Praeger, 1981); Michael Harrington, *Socialism: Past and Future* (New York: Arcade Publishing, 1989).

8. Ash, *The Uses of Adversity,* and *The Magic Lantern: The Revolution of 1989 Witnessed in Warsaw, Budapest, Berlin, and Prague* (New York: Random House, 1990); Charles C. Lemert, "Introduction," in *Intellectuals and Politics: Social Theory in a Changing World* (Newbury Park, Calif.: Sage, 1991); Ivan Szelenyi, "Post Communist Eastern Europe: A Survey of Opinion," *East European Politics and Society* 4 (1990):153–207.

9. Juan Linz, "Post Communist Eastern Europe: A Survey of Opinion," *East European Politics and Society* 4 (1990): 157; Alberto Melucci, "An End to Social Movements?" *Social Science Information* 23 (1984): 254.

10. Lawrence Goodwyn, *Breaking the Barrier: The Rise of Solidarity in Poland* (New York and Oxford: Oxford University Press, 1991), xxx.

11. Szelenyi, "A Survey of Opinion," 165–167; Jadwiga Staniszkis, *Ontologia Socjalizmu* (Warsaw: Krytyka, 1989), 94–95.

12. Lemert, *Intellectuals and Politics,* vii.

13. Lawrence Whitehead, Guillermo O'Donnell, and Philippe Schmitter, eds., *Transitions from Authoritarian Rule: Prospects for Democracy* (Baltimore: Johns Hopkins University Press, 1986), 38.

14. Exceptions include Michael Burawoy and Janos Lukacs, *The Radiant Past: Ideology and Reality in Hungary's Road to Capitalism* (Chicago: University of Chicago Press, 1992); and Stjepan Mestrovic, Miroslav Goreta, and Slaven Letica, *The Road from Paradise: Prospects for Democracy in Eastern Europe* (Lexington: University Press of Kentucky, 1993).

15. Whitehead, O'Donnell, and Schmitter, *Transitions from Authoritarian Rule,* 38.

16. Bronislaw Misztal and Craig J. Jenkins, "Starting from Scratch Is Not Always the Same: The Politics of Protest and the Post-Communist Transitions in Poland and Hungary," in *The Politics of Social Movements: Comparative Perspectives on States and Social Movements,* ed. Craig J. Jenkins and Bert Klandermans (Minneapolis: University of Minnesota Press, 1993).

17. Michael Burawoy and Pavel Krotov, "The Soviet Transition from Socialism to Capitalism: Worker Control and Economic Bargaining in the Wood Industry," *American Sociological Review* 57 (February 1992): 16–38; Elmer Hankiss, "In Search of a Paradigm," *Daedalus* 119, no. 1 (Winter 1990): 183–89; Bronislaw Misztal and Barbara A. Misztal, "The State's Capacity to Change: The Case of Poland and the Philippines," *International Journal of Comparative Sociology* 27 (July–October 1987): 141–61; David Stark, "Privatization in Hungary—From

Plan to Market or from Plan to Clan," *East European Politics and Societies* 4, no. 3 (Fall 1990): 351–92.

18. Bronislaw Misztal, "Social Movements against the State: Theoretical Legacy of the Welfare State," in *Poland after Solidarity: Social Movements versus the State,* ed. Bronislaw Misztal (New Brunswick, N.J.: Transaction Books, 1985), 143–65; Miroslawa Marody, "Miec aby byc" [To have in order to be], in *Spoleczenstwo polskie u progu przemian* [Polish society on the verge of a change], ed. Janusz Mucha et al. (Wroclaw: Ossolineum, 1991); Miroslawa Marody, ed., *Co nam z tych lat . . . Spoleczenstwo polskie u progu zmiany systemowej* [What's left from those years . . . Polish society facing systematic changes] (London: Aneks, 1991).

19. Andrew Arato, "Revolution in East-Central Europe: Interpretations," in *Demokratikus atmenetek* [Democratic transitions], ed. G. Szoboszlai (Budapest: MPT, 1991); Andras Bozoki, "Intellectuals and Democratization in Hungary" (Budapest University, 1993), 11.

20. Herbert Kitschelt, "Political Opportunity Structures and Political Protest," *British Journal of Political Science* 16 (1986): 57–85; Hanspeter Kriesi, "The Political Opportunity Structure of New Social Movements: Its Impact on Their Development" (paper presented at the workshop on "Social Movements, Counterforces and Public Bystanders," Berlin, July 5–7, 1990, WZB, 1–3); Bronislaw Misztal, "Political Opportunity Structures and the Dismantling of State Socialism in Poland and Hungary," *Hungarian Journal of Political Science* 3 (1993); Sidney G. Tarrow, *Power in Movement: Social Movements, Collective Action, and Politics* (Cambridge: Cambridge University Press, 1994).

21. Bozoki, "Intellectuals and Democratization in Hungary"; Laszlo Bruszt, "The Negotiated Revolution of Hungary," *Social Research* 57 (Winter 1990): 365–87; Ferenc Feher and Agnes Heller, *Kelet-Europa dicsoseges forradalmai* [Glorious revolutions of Eastern Europe] (Budapest: T-Twins, 1992).

22. Giuseppe DiPalma, *To Craft Democracies: An Essay on Democratic Transitions* (Berkeley: University of California Press, 1990), 8.

23. Bozoki, "Intellectuals and Democratization in Hungary," 11.

24. Jacek Wasilewski, "Dilemmas and Controversies Concerning Leadership Recruitment in Eastern Europe," *Praxis International* 11, no. 2 (July 1991): 240–48.

25. DiPalma, *To Craft Democracies,* 87.

26. Wlodzimierz Wesolowski, "Parliamentarzysci jako czesc elity politycznej" [Parliamentarians as part of a political elite], in *Poczatki Parlamentarnej Elity: Poslowie kontraktowego Sejmu* [The beginnings of parliamentary elite: The deputies to the contractual parliament], ed. Jacek Wasilewski and Wlodzimierz Wesolewski (Warsaw; IFiS PAN, 1992), 47. Author's translation.

27. Paul Cammack, "A Critical Assessment of the New Elite Paradigm," *American Sociological Review* 55, no. 3 (1990): 415–20. John Higley et al., "In Defense of Elite Theory: A Reply to Cammack," *American Sociological Review* 55 (1990): 421–26.

28. DiPalma (*To Craft Democracies*) distinguishes between three different situa-

tions. A *reforma pactada* is the agreement between elites concerning the negotiable nature of politics. A *garantismo* is the subsequent legal/political framework that is supposed to back up the reforms through agreements. A *democradura* is a situation whereby, under the guise of democracy, undemocratic and dictatorial arrangements are implemented by the current political elites. The first situation existed in Hungary, Poland, and the Czech Republic in 1989–92. A *garantismo* has never been fully implemented in any of the postcommunist countries. A *democradura*-like situation has existed in Russia since 1993.

29. Wladyslaw Sila-Nowicki, "Dokad idziesz Polsko ojczyzno moja?" [Poland, where are you heading?] *Polityka,* April 30, 1991. Author's translation.

30. Sila-Nowicki, "Dokad idziesz Polsko ojczyzno moja?"

31. Bronislaw Misztal, "The Conflict between the Denominational State and the State of Law," in *Religion and Politics in Comparative Perspective: Revival of Religious Fundamentalism East and West,* ed. Bronislaw Misztal and Anson Shupe (Westport, Conn.: Praeger, 1992), 166.

32. Janusz Mucha, "Democratization and Cultural Minorities. The Polish Case of the 1980s/90s," *East European Quarterly* 25 (1992): 479.

33. Mestrovic et al., *The Road from Paradise,* 139.

34. Fukuyama, *The End of History,* 271.

35. Misztal and Shupe, *Religion and Politics in Comparative Perspective,* 479.

36. Michael Burawoy, *The Politics of Production* (London and New York: Verso, 1990), 202.

37. Adam Michnik, "Dismantling of the State Socialism as Seen by an East European Intellectual" (paper presented at the Conference on Cultural Politics and New Social Movements, Santa Cruz, California, 1991).

38. Gert Mueller, *Sociology and Ontology: The Analytical Foundations of Sociological Theory* (Lanham, Md., and London: University Press of America, 1989), 33.

39. Burawoy and Lukacs, *The Radiant Past,* 148.

40. Andrzej M. Zawislak, "Panstwo kontra gospodarka: Prawidlowosc czy patologia" [The state versus the economy: A rule or a pathology?], in *Zalamanie Porzadku Etatystycznego* [The breakdown of the etatistic order], ed. Witold Morawski and Wieslawa Kozek (Warsaw: University of Warsaw Press, 1988); Ivan Szelenyi, *Socialist Entreprenuers: Embourgeoisement in Rural Hungary* (Madison: University of Wisconsin Press, 1988); Feher and Heller, *Dictatorship over Needs;* Davis and Scase, *Western Capitalism and State Socialism.*

41. Feher and Heller, *Dictatorship over Needs,* 45.

42. Staniszkis, *Ontologia Socjalizmu,* 15.

43. Zawislak, "Panstwo kontra gospodarka: Prawidlowosc czy patologia," 32.

44. Staniszkis, *Ontologia Socjalizmu,* 140.

45. Mestrovic et al., *The Road from Paradise,* 168, 24–45, 44.

CHAPTER 19

The Global Planet and the Internal Planet: New Frontiers for Collective Action and Individual Transformation

Alberto Melucci

□   □   □   □   □   □   □   □   □   □   □

> Nan-in, a Japanese master of the Meiji period, received a visit from a university professor, who had come to learn something about Zen. Nan-in served tea. He filled his guest's cup to the brim, and kept right on pouring. The professor watched as the cup overflowed, until he was no longer able to restrain himself. "It's full up," he exclaimed. "It won't hold another drop!" "Like this cup," said Nan-in, "you too are full up, of your opinions and theories. How can I explain Zen to you until you have first emptied your cup?"

Social Movements are Messages

I believe that contemporary social movements act as signals to remind us that both the external planet, the Earth as our homeland, and the internal planet, our "nature" as human beings, are undergoing radical transformations.

The so-called "new social movements" have made inroads into scientific and political debate as well as into the collective consciousness. Such movements as feminism, youth mobilizations, environmentalism, and pacifism have helped to write new political agendas; they have provided economic, political, and cultural institutions with new leadership resources and with personnel selected through mobilizing activities; they have become stable components of the market as their symbols, discourses, and practices are rapidly transformed into new goods and commodities; they have, finally, changed many of our daily habits, forms of relationship, and moral values.[1]

But in spite of this multifaceted "success" (whose ambiguous nature must be recognized), academic and political attention has restricted itself, for the most part, to the role that new social movements play in the political arena and, in the case of environmental issues, to concern for the fate of the planet, understood as the socio-physiological habitat of the human species. It is this "external planet" that commands public attention, expressed in the fears, appeals, or projects fed by the wave of new social movements. I have criticized elsewhere both the notion of new social movements defined by a simplistic and unidimensional view of phenomena that are analytically multidimensional and composed of very differentiated collective actors; and the notion of "success" that is measured only in terms of political effectiveness and institutional modernization.[2]

In this Chapter I would like to point out that there is another "planet" involved in the transformational processes that contemporary movements are part of and contribute to: the internal planet. I refer to the biological, emotional, and cognitive structures on which we base the construction of our experience and relationships. It is the relation of contemporary collective action to this internal planet that I would like to examine. Attention to this dimension seems to have been relegated to a marginal role, being entrusted either to what has become a kind of ritual reference to the "feminine difference" or to purely intellectual debate. Even appeals to an ecology of mind have rapidly transformed into fashion or a hurried maquillage of obsolete kinds of language and have not brought about any real assimilation of an alternative point of view.[3] Thus, to speak of the internal planet is not to add another theme to the agenda of theoretical and political issues concerning contemporary forms of collective action, already overflowing with urgent problems, as much as it is to point out the need to modify our perspective.

Just as with a physical symptom (a message from the body), when we are faced with contemporary movements we can assume one of two attitudes— that of "resolving" or that of "listening." Modern medical technology with its practice of intervention claims victory for the "resolutionary" approach and makes it impossible to listen. In response to contemporary social movements, a similar approach may prevail: an approach where the nature of the phenomenon is ignored in favor of immediate remedial action. Thus, in the case of social movements, a perspective comparable to the medical takes them seriously solely because of their capacity (or lack of capacity) to modernize institutions or to produce political reform. But this ignores that the reduction of contemporary social movements to their political dimension is like the suppression of a symptom: it is not the cure for a disease but merely a way to move it about.

Social movements bring to the fore *cultural dimension* of human action, its self-reflexive and symbolic qualities. Industrial society organized its experience around the inevitability of the laws of economics and the power of technology. Social movements reveal that the heart of survival can no longer be based on the system of means on which instrumental rationality (cost-benefit calculations) is founded but must be shifted to the problem of goals, that is, of the cultural models that shape action. It is not possible to imagine a livable future without some kind of conscious intervention and reappropriation of social relationships, symbolic systems, the dissemination of information. These must be viewed as equally, if not more, important than the technical apparatuses. Those who try to govern complexity by simply addressing its technological and political elements run the risk of a faulty perspective, a kind of substantial myopia. Dealing with the "real things" of the world today means paying ever-greater attention to the symbolic codes that organize everyday life, political systems, and the forms of production and consumption.

The reality in which we live is a cultural construct, and our representations of it serve as filters for our relationship with the world. For the first time in the history of the human species, this assertion is also true in a literal sense. That is, the world we inhabit today is a global, planetary-scale world, and this is only made possible by information, or the cultural processes with which we represent our world to ourselves.

The consequences of this change are enormous. The first is the growing inadequacy of the international system, of relations among sovereign nation states, to deal with global problems. But the emerging of a transnational dimension to issues and social agents, more than a political question, is a sign of the fact that human action is now capable of culturally creating its own space. The planet is no longer just a physical location: it is also a unified social space that is culturally and symbolically perceived.

The nature of contemporary social movements as signals is confirmed by the fact that they address individuals *as individuals,* and not as members of a group, a class, or a ·state. These aggregating factors, which in the modern world have been the basis for the formation of interests and solidarity, will not disappear. But it is increasingly evident that the destiny of the species and of the ecosystem is today a problem that affects the life of each and every individual. Change cannot be divorced from individual responsibility, and a direct personal investment becomes the condition and principal resource for intervention in the system.

Finally, social movements reveal that *conflict* is an inherent dimension of complex systems. The differentiation of interests and of cultures, and the uncertainty that has become a permanent condition of human action, create an unavoidable quantity of conflicts. Industrial culture used to consider conflict to be a necessary consequence of exploitation, or a kind of social pathology. Recognizing that conflict cannot be eliminated but merely managed, negotiated, resolved, means redefining the criteria of coexistence. Only an effort to make differences, possibilities, and the constraints of coexistence transparent and negotiable can bring about a new solidarity, both in micro-relations and in macro-systems.

Dilemmas

If social movements are symptoms that signal the presence of something else, what do they have to say to the conscience of the inhabitants of the global village? There are problems that have no solutions and that define the cultural and social boundaries of complexity; they are polarities that present impossible choices, inasmuch as their tension is the source of existence and renewed equilibrium of a highly differentiated system. These are problems we cannot help trying to solve but whose solutions only transfer the uncertainty elsewhere. We try to deal with them by making decisions; but decisions can be the avoidance of tension that has become unbearable, a means of neither seeing nor speaking of these dilemmas.

The first such dilemma is that between *autonomy and control*, between the opportunity to realize the potential of individual capacities and choices versus the tendency to create capillary systems of behavior manipulation, which today impact both the brain and the genetic structure itself. Contemporary societies have extended their power to control beyond the boundaries of any similar phenomena in the past. The use of nuclear power and genetic engineering bear witness in different ways to the extreme capacity of contemporary societies to "produce" themselves until they are at the point of self-destruction. This gives birth to a new dilemma, that between *responsibility and omnipotence*, between the tendency to expand the capacity of human systems to intervene in their own development versus the need to take account of and respond (response-ability) to the limits of "nature," both within ourselves and externally.

The power of the human species to act upon itself and upon its environment is based on irreversible scientific knowledge, which can no longer be canceled out (except in the case of a regressive catastrophe that takes evolutionary progress back to zero). At the same time the way this knowledge is utilized is based upon choices that can be reversed, tied to energy, scientific, and military policies and to the behavior of the political apparatus that administers these choices. The dilemma of *irreversible information and reversible choices* opens up new dramatic but also exciting possibilities for public ethics in the postnuclear era.

Finally, the planetary dimension of the world system means that there is no longer an "outside world": territories, cultures, languages exist only as the internal elements of a planetary system. But this "internalization" of differences opens up another dilemma, that between *inclusion and exclusion*. Inclusion processes tend toward a leveling of cultural differences and transform peripheral or marginal cultures into insignificant folk and ethnic appendages to the few major centers that govern the elaboration of cultural codes and their dissemination through the great market of the media. Forms of resistance to this homogenizing effect are almost inevitably destined to produce phenomena of exclusion, which means being reduced to silence and cultural death. How to preserve differences without marginalization and separatedness?

These great dilemmas lie, nearly always unmentioned, in the background of the decisions that aim at the management of complexity. The neutrality of technical procedures removes from debate and control by the "civil society" many of the questions that affect the life of each individual and the destiny of the species.[4] In order to bring these background dilemmas to light, we have today to make an additional effort of consciousness and action. It will be by confronting these dilemmas that we will be able to redefine the notion of freedom inherited from the modern era and to design a new framework for human rights.

In postmaterialist societies, where primary needs are generally satisfied, demands for freedom *from* needs are replaced by the freedom *to* need. The cultural construction of needs takes first place, opening up for a potentially large number of people the unpredictable space of the project, the creation, the gratuitous desire. The freedom to *have* that characterized *homo oeconomicus* of industrial capitalism is replaced by the freedom to *be*. From the right to *equality*, the flag of modern revolutions still far from being achieved, what we seek today is the right to be *different*. Recognition of, and respect for, diversity among individuals, languages, and cultures can open the way for a completely new definition of solidarity and coexistence.

The world in which we live is still far from incorporating these rights, especially in the light of the well-nigh hopeless gaps between geopolitical blocs, nearly unbridgeable North-South differences, and the mounting anger of those who feel themselves to be excluded. But it is also true that these rights are already present and are making themselves felt in people's everyday lives and in civic culture. Whether the challenges of these great contemporary dilemmas will be met depends upon our capacity to bring these rights into existence.

Around these rights a moral, cultural, and political climate has grown up that calls for a new culture for the human species. Its premise is that living as human beings brings with it the responsibility to live on the earth in acceptance of the insurmountable boundaries imposed on the destructive production of our species, and with silence and respect for all that exists for the simple reason that it does exist. This awareness brings to the fore the necessity to define human action as *a construction of possibilities within limits. Limits* have a double meaning here. Limits indicate a finite reality, imply the recognition of the body and death as part of the human condition. The body that lives, suffers, and dies continues to remind human beings of the transient quality of their existence despite faith in technology, a faith that is unlikely to help individuals come to terms with their physical fragility and the certainty that they will die.

In a second sense, however, limits also mean boundaries, frontiers, separations. They imply the acceptance of that which is "other," different, irreducible. Confrontation with that which is alien to us is always a challenge, a test of our "otherness" to others: we often try to reduce the difference by force, by denying or suppressing differences; but when we accept out limits, we become able to meet the challenge of communication across borders.

Within limits, however, an accent on possibility acknowledges, in the first place, the unarrestable tendency of human action to seek to overcome the limits of pain and death, to move the boundaries of time and space that frame our experience. Secondly, it bears witness to the human tendency to neocortical development and its plasticity, which raise the body to the level of the higher cognitive and spiritual faculties. We are nature, but we continue to look for and to produce meaning from nature. Finally, it makes visible the dimension of solidarity and communication, as an effort to make diversity less opaque and insurmountable.

The increasing awareness that this tension between possibilities and limits always shapes human action challenges the concept of rationality as it was defined in the modern Western world. By revealing the precarious nature of a rationality based entirely upon the instrumental relation between means and ends, the recognition of such a tension opens the way for new kinds of knowledge. Emotions, intuition, creativity, "feminine" perceptions of the world are equally part of our experience and vital elements in the process of constructing our individual and social reality.[5]

In this perspective the ethical capacity also loses the certainty of absolute ends and is entrusted to the responsibility and risk involved in the coexistence of differences. As the gravity of cleavages and unbalances between areas and peoples on our planet grows, such responsibility becomes all the more a matter that concerns every single individual as well as a collective challenge for mankind. Equally, the survival of the ecosystem depends on our ability to make conscious choices.

Individualization and Choice

From the beginning, the modern world has presented itself as an open field of possibilities and chances offered to the individual. The myths of progress and freedom have fed the Promethean dream of victory over the limits of nature through the power of technology; the promise of victory also affected the life of the individual, for whom an irresistible progress toward autonomy and personal realization was envisioned.

These orientations describe the historical horizon of modernity in all its variations, rationalistic or utopian; in spite of everything that has happened, our hopes and fears are still expressed within the frame of reference of this inheritance.[6] To be sure, the scenario of a system that is by now irreversibly planetary and whose future teeters on the edge of catastrophe has deeply undermined the optimism of the salvation myths based on technological faith.

But, in spite of disenchantment, we are still not free of the most exciting and dramatic inheritance of modernism: the need and the responsibility to be *fulfilled as individuals*. This legacy of modernity is still an unaccomplished task and a leading cultural impulse. The challenge is that of becoming the individuals that we are and at the same time of being connected with others. Every woman and man on this planet is invited to become what they are: true *social actors*, self-reflexive and responsible beings, perpetrators of actions that have direction and meaning—and also to be nodes in a network of coexistence and communication.

The dilemmas I have described above lay daily siege to the children of the disenchantment. Individuals find themselves caught up in a plurality of social systems that result from the multiplication of social positions, membership networks, reference groups. We move in and out of these relationships with much greater ease and speed than in the past, like migrant animals in the labyrinths of the metropolis, planetary travelers, nomads of the present.

We transform ourselves into sensitive terminals, transmitting and receiving unparalleled quantities of information without historical precedent. The media, the workplace, interpersonal relations, even leisure time, all produce data aimed at the individual, who must receive, analyze, memorize, and nearly always respond to this informational flow.

The accelerated number of possible affiliations and memberships, the glut of possibilities and of messages that widen our cognitive and emotional experience, all combine to weaken the traditional points of reference upon which individuals based the consistency and continuity of their existence (family, church, party, race, class).

The capacity of each of us to be able to declare with confidence over time "I am X or Y" has become unreliable and uncertain. Yet, we have constantly to respond to the query "Who am I?" We search for anchors to make permanence more possible, and we are forced to doubt our own biographies.

The time frame of everyday life becomes multiple and discontinuous because it involves passing from one universe of experience to another: from one network of affiliation to another, from the language and codes of one particular territory to social spaces very distant from the semantic and affective points of reference of the former. Time loses its uniformity and takes on a variable rhythm that is created by the flow and quality of the data we receive and transmit. Our perception widens and narrows, slows down and accelerates with the variations in the migrations in which we participate or by which we are swept away.

In the process of asserting itself, modernity had erased the cyclical time frame of myth and had appropriated the linear, teleological time frame of Christianity. In the secular version of an appeal to progress or to revolution, the modern world had insisted on the idea that human history was directed toward salvation and that the present had meaning because the end, the goal of the linear time, was already known to all.

Today, as often perplexed witnesses to the obsolescence of the great narratives of salvation, our destiny is that of choice. In the face of the possible, which seduces and threatens us, there is no avoiding the risk of making decisions (for which catastrophe is the extreme metaphorical figure). Choice means possibility and limitation, chances and constraints, option and self-restraint.

It is precisely this paradox of a process of opening without limits but also without egress (since it is impossible not to choose between the possibilities) that reveals for the first time, and so evidently, the uniqueness of each individual's experience, the irresistible call to individuation. If we have lost the sense of time's end and goal, then every moment in time acquires a dimension of infinity. Time carries with it no sense apart from that created by each individual for his or her life and environment. In other words, meaning derives from that which every individual is able to produce and to share with others.

This does not mean that unity of individual experience is any less important, or that permanence will be less sought after in the midst of change. But the continuity of individual experience can no longer be entrusted to a stable identification with a model, a group, a culture, or perhaps even a biography. It might appear that the quality most needed by the inhabitants of the disenchanted world would be cynical detachment. However, no one is more immobile than a cynic, and there is no greater rigidity than that which we adopt in the cool defense of our undeclared fragility. It is not this type of coldness that is required by the inhabitants of the world of complexity but rather a passionate ability to *transform* ourselves, to redefine ourselves in the present, to render choices and decisions reversible.

Metamorphosis is the answer to a world that asks us to multiply faces, languages, relationships. We must try for a "warm" response, never free from fear and trembling, but unstinting with love. Without compassion for ourselves and for other beings, without hope and humility, it is not possible to change one's form. It is only possible to change masks, trusting (and for how long?) in the empty game of self-representation.

As the point of intersection of numerous circuits of information, at the crossroads of complex networks of relationships, the individual risks drowning in all the noise, lacerated by too many exchanges and too many desires. We can maintain the integrity of our experience only if we learn both to *open and close*, to participate and to isolate ourselves from the message flow, from the call of the possible, from the demands for affection and communication. Being involved in so many relationships, each individual must discover an entering and leaving rhythm that enables him or her to give and receive information without losing the sense of communication, but also without causing the subject who communicates to disappear or to disintegrate.

Existence and Coexistence

Since relationships between humans are no longer determined by biological necessity or by the inevitability of historical laws, they become a field of choice, of uncertainty and risk. The gratuitous nature of the encounter as gift and reciprocity goes beyond personal relations and expands to embrace the encounter between human beings and the cosmos.

When relations between humans are entrusted almost entirely to choice, the foundation of solidarity becomes fragile and the social contract leans toward the precarious. The social fabric threatens to unravel, and a catastrophic individualism could take its place.

The very acceptance of the fact that everything in our relations cannot be calculated, that our exchanges will not necessarily be all-satisfying, that an indomitable uniqueness characterizes the experience of every individual—this acceptance can become the foundation for a new autonomy, one able to strengthen solidarity with a lucid passion. This awareness of fragility can be the beginning of a reformulation of the ethical choices necessary for coexistence.

We need new ethics that do not exempt us from the risk of choice and that will enable us to meta-communicate about the goals and criterion behind the choices themselves. We need a situational ethic capable of lending dignity to the individual decision and of repairing the ties between the individual and the species, living beings, the cosmos. An ethic that preserves our ability to marvel in the face of what exists without ceasing to change form.

The discovery that our salvation is no longer guaranteed by historical destiny is the rocky coastline upon which the ship of Western rationalism has been wrecked, along with its claims to absolute truth and its will to supremacy. What floats to the surface is a hope for meaningful human existence, grounded in coexistence and in the experience of our limits.

If values no longer bear the seal of the absolute, their only foundation lies in our capacity for agreement. *Homo sapiens,* the erect species with the gift of thought, is faced with the task of recognizing his position "between heaven and earth," as the ancient wisdom of the East would put it: accepting his roots in the earth under his feet and reaffirming his heavenly aspirations, symbolized by his head's skyward orientation.

We are, then, detached from nature by our capacity for language but tied to it by our bodies. Accordingly, we will have to look to language and to the body for the basis of an ethics capable of dealing with the problems of a planet entirely created by humans.

The body delineates the limits of nature within us and without: the great rhythms of birth and death, the permanent link to the cycles of day and night, the seasons, growth and aging. In a world built by technology, equilibrium and change depend on our choices; rhythm and respect for limits no longer exist, if ever they did, through primal human contact with nature's imperatives. Instead they are the product of a conscious morality that assumes responsibility for nature while responding to it.

Indeed, it is precisely this twofold meaning of the word "responsibility" that roots ethics in language. Culture is the space in which every moral choice is bound to take form. In the planetary society of information, to name things is to bring them into existence. What should be done with language? This is the new frontier of the ethics of complexity. How and to what end should we use the *power of naming*, which enables us to create the world and force it to conform to the signs with which we give it (or neglect to give it) voice? It is language that meets the challenge of meaning or its reduction to signs. It is through language that, today, even nature can be named or erased.

In Praise of Wonder

Changing our form requires a fluidity of process, the capacity to maintain and to give up, the courage to risk and the prudence of respect for limits. The cold, calculating rationalism that has guided contemporary experience in the West is ill-suited to these requirements. New qualities are needed, about which we are just beginning to learn.

To pass from one form to another without exploding, to hold together the fragments of the unpredictable, requires the intuition and imagination that have always been segregated from "rational" action, and to which access was granted only on special occasions or by exception: dreams, play, artistic creation, love.

There can be no metamorphosis without loss and without vision: to change form one must be prepared to lose oneself, to wonder, and to imagine. The fairy tales demanded by the inhabitants of a disenchanted world no longer feature elves and witches, but they still have to teach us to wonder.

We have lost the language of wonder. To be able to wonder requires clear vision and an open mind. This is a rare state for the heirs to the technological creed: We are still the offspring of an industrial culture that has lost its utopian passion. The great mainspring of progress no longer moves the clock of history and leaves us the orphans of hope. Thus we are weighted down by the past and anxious about the future, without, however, the solace of faith. The broken spell quickly begins to resemble certain *terrains vagues* that surround our metropolitan areas: arid deserts cluttered with the remains and waste of civilization.

Wonder, on the other hand, needs space in which to take root. The territories of the internal planet are enormous, and we have barely begun to explore them. During the next few years we will probably discover new continents. Greedy and barbarous *hidalgos* are already preparing their *armadas* to search for El Dorado. But instead it should be possible for these lands, so unique and so intimate, to be explored and governed by each individual for herself or himself and to be opened to friends and guests when the person is willing. To assume responsibility, to protect them from the dangers by which they are threatened, to cultivate them with respect and without violence, is a duty that calls those who are concerned with the future of our planet—a duty that individuals must undertake, but which we cannot consider merely an individual task: it is today a collective cultural goal.

An ecology of economic, political, and technological choices cannot live without an ecology of everyday life, of the words and gestures with which we create or destroy the internal planet. Forms of awareness and communication are the areas in which we can apply what we have learned about ourselves and our environment, in a second-degree learning process that is already beginning to take the place of a culture based exclusively on content, values, goals. The *forms* and *processes* of human action become extremely important when the pace of change makes content ephemeral. The *how* of our action acquires value and meaning: it is a message as much as or more than the *what*.

To bring bodily, cognitive, and relation-based processes into the field of conscious intervention and responsibility means transforming behavior into message, in a meaningful signifier that is able to bear witness to deep ties between interior and exterior, between our inner nature and the nature that surrounds us. The challenge that lies before us is that of living within the continuity and discontinuity between nature and culture, within the paradox that occurs when *consciously* (that is to say, *culturally*) we seek to *become nature.* The internal planet, nexus between body and language, behavior and reflection, is the link in the chain that joins "heaven and earth."

As I have said, we have so far only explored the nearest margins of the internal landscape. Everything that we discover there will not necessarily belong to the realm of the rational, as defined by modern Western culture. In that definition, profound spiritual needs and human qualities were often mortified. Today, new mysticisms are being reborn to remind us of our unsatisfied thirst for the sacred. Like all preachings of salvation, these are violent. The *conquistadores* count on their firepower, but the missionaries accompany them with the violence of the word. The task of colonizing the internal planet may be divided between the two.

Facing these risks means following the paradoxical road of the *profane experience of the sacred:* opening up to what continually eludes us, accepting silence, being present, ready to wonder. It is a difficult road, and even words seem taxed to describe it. Yet it precisely toward this research that the internal planet calls those who have crossed the desert of disenchantment and are no longer afraid to wonder.

Contemporary social movements, those of women, youth, environmentalists, peace movements, and the like, have been among the first announcement of the enormous cultural change that is already taking place. To reduce them only to their political outcomes is like believing that our shadow could exist without our person. The politics of the new social movements are eminently personal politics, rooted in a profound need to exist as autonomous individuals, capable of respect and communication.

Contemporary social movements remind us by their *forms* of action that we can work more on processes than on contents to face the challenges and the dilemmas of a complex world. By including care for the internal planet as an important part of present collective tasks, people who are today willing to contribute to a more democratic, more just and compassionate society on a world scale would be able to redefine their collective action. Instead of expressing frustration and despair over the ineffectiveness of the movements in the last decades, we should recognize instead their "success" in changing our minds and cognitive frameworks and our view of the future. The collective action portended by the new movements expresses the fact that we are able to take responsibility for both the global planet *and* the internal planet—that is to say, that we are concerned with meaning.

NOTES

1. Jean L. Cohen, "Strategy or Identity: New Theoretical Paradigms and Contemporary Social Movements," *Social Research* 52 (1985): 663–716: Bert Klandermans, Hanspeter Kriesi, and Sidney Tarrow, eds., *From Structure to Action* (Greenwich, Conn.: JAI Press, 1988); Claus Offe, "New Social Movements: Challenging the Boundaries of Institutional Politics," *Social Research* 52 (1985): 817–68; Sidney Tarrow, *Democracy and Disorder* (Oxford: Clarendon, 1989).
2. Alberto Melucci, *Nomads of the Present* (London: Hutchinson Radius; Philadelphia: Temple University Press, 1989).
3. Gregory Bateson, *Steps to an Ecology of Mind* (New York: Ballantine, 1972); and *Mind and Nature* (New York: Dutton, 1979).
4. John Keane, ed., *Civil Society and the State* (London: Verso, 1988).
5. Carol Gilligan, *In a Different Voice* (Cambridge: Harvard University Press, 1981).
6. Jürgen Habermas, *Theory of Communicative Action* (Boston: Beacon Press, 1984); Anthony Giddens, *The Constitution of Society* (Berkeley: University of California Press, 1984).

CHAPTER 20

New Social Movements and the Transformation to Post-Fordist Society

Margit Mayer and Roland Roth

□   □   □   □   □   □   □   □   □   □   □   □

This chapter examines some recent social movement theories to see what insights they might offer into the current contradictory situation of social movements in the advanced Western nations. We use Germany as a case in point, but many Western European and North American new social movements share this paradoxical situation: While they have managed to find recognition and support in broad sectors of society and while many of their demands have been incorporated into governmental policies and institutions, social dispossession and political disenfranchisement have been spreading, and political systems have in many respects become more intransigent to demands for civility and peace than ever. We find that recently formulated theories of social movements succeed in accounting for the specific attributes and meanings of the movements characteristic of the 1970s and 1980s but fall short of explaining their current ambiguities and transformations. We reach toward a different theoretical framework—regulation theory—which allows us to place these developments in their specific social and political context and thus to understand the contradictory effects and achievements of the new social movements.

Social Movement Theories

Even though the United States has a rich history of expressive movements oriented toward cultural change, the theoretical approach dominating the field of social movement research in the United States privileges a different type of movement, one that is interested in strategic effectiveness, tangible goals, and a (larger) share of the distributional pie. This approach is concerned with the internal development of movements, their ability to mobilize resources, their practical accomplishments, and their immediate impact on policy.[1] It is less concerned with the sources of discontent, the motives for participation, or the collective identity or ideology of the movement. Resource mobilization (RM) theory regarded deficiencies in political institutions as the source of the movements of the 1960s and 1970s. This approach has thus been most fruitful in analyzing the process of mobilization and in emphasizing the role of existing organizations and networks. But certain radical movements, such as SDS or the Weathermen, do not quite fit into its horizon; and of the contemporary movements, certain segments (such as the radical ecology strand of the environmental movement, civil disobedience, or direct-action movements) disappear behind environmental public-interest liberalism or other, "normalized" forms of political action.[2]

This theory of social movements refrains from placing one social conflict on a higher order than another, and does not attribute to one social movement a more fundamentally challenging character than another. This restraint may reflect the fact that U.S. society has been more obviously shaped by the coexistence and overlapping of different systems of domination than Western European societies, where the "central conflict" discourse has a long tradition mirroring the prevalence of class conflict. While the American approach does not make claims about one central conflict or one "most radical" movement, this reticence leads it to be systematically silent on the (possible) link between social movements and social change.

In contrast to this theory of social movements (it might more adequately be called theory of mobilization), the theoretical perspectives recently developed in Western Europe reserve the term "new social movement" for social protest that aims at a fundamental or emancipatory transformation of society.[3] When European new social movement (NSM) theory is contrasted with American paradigms, it is usually presented as "structural," in contradistinction to the attitudinal and organizational studies of the resource mobilization perspective, because it links social movements to large-scale structural or cultural change and because it focuses more on the "why" than the "how" of social movements.[4] But besides their shared focus on the structural causes of social movements, their ideologies, and their relation to the culture of advanced capitalist society, there are more specific commonalities to these NSM paradigms regarding the claims made about the changes in late-twentieth-century society and about the role new social movements play within them.

Contrary to the timeless and unstructured conception of social organization that the RM approach holds, European approaches place social movements within the broader parameters of class relations and the specific logics of production and reproduction. Due to the tensions and antagonisms in those relations, societies periodically undergo a fundamental restructuring. While there is much dispute over the nature of the current restructuring of capitalist societies—whether they are in transition from industrial to postindustrial or programmed society, from industrial to information society, from modernity to postmodernity, or from Fordism to post-Fordism—European sociological theories all reserve a special place in this transition to (some of) the contemporary social movements. This broader conception of societal change allows these theories to investigate conceptual links between social movements and social change. Depending on what they see replacing the era of industrial conflict, the role of the new social movements is seen in rather divergent ways.

In an effort to capture what seems novel and distinctive about the social movements active in the current transition, various authors have emphasized a variety of different characteristics and identified emergent cultural and political currents that have been undervalued in traditional accounts. Some see these movements as new because their concerns no longer revolve around legal and political equality or economic demands, issues that used to characterize the important movements in Western Europe's past. The fact that they are about lifestyles, cultural politics, identity, and the politics of everyday life, and only secondarily interested in state policy or state power, is made out to be the shared and defining feature. Others see them as new because their organizational forms appear more informal and egalitarian than those in other movements. Yet others emphasize the fact that a shared class base does not seem to be common to those active in the movements.

All of these definitions of novelty can, however, be empirically challenged: research has identified cases where these qualifications do not apply. In the debate about the "new" forms of collective action, three positions or schools deserve to be highlighted because they attempt to go beyond empirical generalizations and help us recognize, instead, the plurality of meanings and forms of action of new social movements in the context of a transitional society.[5] The perspectives we present here are significant because they developed theories in conjunction with empirical studies of social movements. The teams involved in Touraine's studies of various movements, Melucci's study of Milan, Roth's study of movement milieus in Germany, as well as other scholars inspired and influenced by their approaches, all place the movements under study within theoretical frameworks of societal transition and develop models for interpreting the new social movements.

Programmed Society and the Struggle against Technocracy

Beginning in the mid-seventies, Touraine and his research group have worked on an elaborate research program on contemporary social movements, producing the most comprehensive study on this subject worldwide to date. Its unique contributions lie not only in the rich data on new social movements that they have made available but also in their method of sociological intervention and in the fact that it is grounded in a theory of societal change, both of which we will sketch briefly.[6]

Touraine's assumption is that all eras have been shaped by one principal conflict; in programmed society,[7] this conflict is between technology and the bureaucratic control of everyday life and the people who challenge it.[8] Reading the social movements since the 1960s in those terms, Touraine developed a radical departure from system-theory approaches (in which structures matter more than actors), pursuing instead a "sociology of action," which attributes central importance to the impact of conflicting social actors on society. In analyzing various social movements since the 1960s, Touraine and his group developed a set of analytical categories and applied a research design that allowed them both to account for the different actors of a social protest and their diverging goals, as well as to conceive of their own research consciously as intervention into social struggles.[9] This approach of "sociological intervention" or "permanent sociology" implies that the practice of the group researched is to be "lifted up" to the highest level conceptually possible. This means the researchers help the activists to identify the central conflict and to act effectively to challenge it. Touraine arrives at that conceptual level by diagnosing contemporary society as in a phase of mutation from the industrial to a new type of society, a postindustrial or programmed one. While in previous eras social movements always referred to some metasocial principle in order to justify their struggle against domination (divine rule, natural law, or progress), emergent postindustrial society is seen as characterized by the capacity for self-production and self-transformation. This means that all metasocial principles are now suspect.

Touraine originally placed high expectations in the oppositional identity of a force capable of shaping society,[10] but by 1984 Touraine conceded that neither the grand adversary (technocracy) against which the various social movements were supposed to coalesce nor the anticipated "programmed" postcrisis society had materialized in as clearcut a fashion as he had predicted. He now says that even if the researchers were to discover a "central" social movement in a given collective action, this does not mean that this "highest" analytical meaning will determine the most important effect of a collective action. For example, in the antinuclear movement that the group studied, an antitechnocratic component existed and did challenge nuclear power, but this "highest" meaning of the protest movement was less important politically and practically than the crisis of industrial culture that was finding many expressions at that time (1976). In most cases, the highest possible meaning of a collective action does *not* coincide with its main political and social effects (just as class-oriented political action did not lead to revolution but to market economy and redistribution by the state of a large part of the national income).

While the group's studies of individual movements could not demonstrate the formation of a new social movement articulating the central contradiction,[11] they did find the movements freeing themselves from the control of political parties and ideologies and thus gaining in autonomy. They also observed that cultural problems take on increasing significance in societies where "cultural industries" play a rapidly growing role, and that the movements responded to these.

Compared to Habermas or Luhmann, whose social theories assign mere residual status to social movements, Touraine has reserved for them a space in his sociological thinking that does not require him to expand the theory with every new wave of protest. This concern with mediating the categories of structure with those of action has been a very positive and productive influence on social movement research. The fact, however, that this theory of social movements is constructed in analogy with the historical labor movement and its Marxist analysis is more problematic. It conjures up a certainty of social change and of the emerging cohesive antitechnocratic movement that could not be demonstrated. In this "provisional findings"[12] Touraine blames regressive societal developments for the fact that social movements in France (as well as their social scientist researcher-participants) have so far remained "prophets without power."[13] This inconclusive finding also reflects the problematic aspects of his concept of action research, which is primarily concerned with generating and strengthening social movements.

Very recently, Touraine has acknowledged these problems and moved closer to the "new social movements" concept by recognizing the plural character of contemporary social movements and connecting the concept with that of a strengthened democracy centering on "the rights of the individual over against encroaching political power."[14]

Complex Society and the Control over Actions

While Touraine's research program was designed for manifest social conflicts and action groups, the research team around Alberto Melucci concentrated on the analysis of "movement spheres."[15] With Touraine, Melucci's group shared the emphatic analytical concept of social movement—that is, social movements are understood as shaping society—locating new forms of collective action in "complex societies" that open up new grounds for struggles over citizenship, social and cultural issues, and codes of life.[16] These new roles of shaping society, as Touraine found, are not immediately visible in the specific object of research. While Touraine's method of making them visible was "conversion," that is, lifting the groups to the highest conceptually possible level of historical actors, Melucci's research design is more modest. Over a few years, the team worked with the alternative community of Milan, a movement milieu that was seen as either the result of past visible movements or a potential actor in future such movements. In a comprehensive stock-taking they produced a "map" of movement spheres; then they chose central affinity groups from each grouping (women's, ecology, youth, and spiritual groups), and contracted with them for a laboratory phase of a few months, during which the definition of the group, by both its members and the outside environment, was clarified. In-depth interviews and feedback phases were supposed to control for the distortion produced by the artificial laboratory situation and also generate more information about the movement spheres.

While Touraine's team sought a power-oriented social movement producing fundamental political alternatives, the Milan study discovered a movement essentially focused on the reproduction of its *cultural identity*. This movement is composed of loosely connected and frequently unstable groups, infrastructures of communication, and manifold personal networks. Oppositional identity (a crucial element in the definition of a social movement for Melucci) is developed primarily through lifestyles, behavioral norms, and ethical claims, which the movement groups perceive as self-defined alternatives against the norms of the majoritarian culture. Out of this conscious daily reproduction of cultural identities only occasional visible actions arise. The focus of Melucci's movement spheres is not so much political action and the claim to transform society but rather the *altri codici,* the alternative patterns of behavior and messages, the latent processes of trying out new forms of life in movement networks held together less through organizations than through a cultural identity.

Melucci's is not a "structural approach" in the sense that European NSM theory is always presented in the comparative literature[17] but rather an attempt to produce an analysis that captures both agency and structure at the same time. Melucci's focus is on actors rather than structures, but on actors within the limits and possibilities thrown up by structures. By asking how and why heterogeneous elements form a collective actor, and how this unity is maintained, collective action is understood to be the product and the accomplishment of a variety of individual actors (their choices, strategies, and assumptions). This constructivist approach led Melucci to develop a research methodology that could focus on "the underlying structure of action"[18] or the "submerged reality of the movements." It seeks to account for three questions: How do individuals become involved? How do collective actors construct their unity and collective action? How do we understand the meaning that is produced out of heterogeneity?

To answer the first question, Melucci focuses on the relationship between motivations to participate and the construction of a collective identity as a way to bridge the gap between structural conditions for action and collective action itself. He does not assume interests to be preconstituted or already present, ready to be mobilized merely by being appealed to (as in resource mobilization and "consensus mobilization" concepts).[19] Rather, he sees collective identity as the result of a process of constructing an "action system," the construction of a "we," in which common cognitive frameworks are developed and relationships are entered through which individuals can recognize themselves as part of a collectivity. In answering the second question, collective action is also not understood as a given but rather as a product of continual tensions and negotiations within a "multipolar action system."[20] Here the constructivist approach helps us to reveal and analyze the fragile and conflictual character of contemporary movements, which continually need to (re)produce unity in the face of diversity and tension. These processes of negotiating unity are detectable only at the subterranean organizational level.[21] Therefore, Melucci's research methodology directs him to the networks that constitute "the submerged reality of the movements before, during and after the events."[22] Here, the process by which movements (re)formulate and construct identity can be assessed: whether they succeed or fail to do so, whether they do so in weak or in strong ways.

In addressing the third question, he describes these latent movement areas as the place where "alternative frameworks of meaning" are produced.[23] They are "networks of meaning"[24] that put into practice the alternative meanings that they produce and reproduce. Through them, contemporary movements translate their action into "symbolic challenges that overturn the dominant cultural codes.[25] Their effect—often more important than that of overt political action—is to render power visible and to show that difference is possible.

While Melucci's project corrects some of the problematic aspects of Touraine's research design (by discarding the action research approach and by cooperating with "natural" instead of artificial groups formed by the researchers), it raises some problems of its own. Based on the movement communities in Milan at the beginning of the 1980s, it exhibits all the limits of a case study: the movement sectors studied and their lack of political involvement may be a result of the particularities of the Italian metropolis, where the "new topics" could gain hold only by breaking with the revolutionary, class-struggle versions of political militance. In other Western European countries, traditional leftist groups have been far more open to the issues of the "new politics." Melucci's finding of a split between cultural and political orientations, however, is generalized as a characteristic of all new social movements.[26] Furthermore, due to the research period, when only a few visible movement activities and dealings with the state occurred, the relationship between visibility and latency remains unclear. A mobilizing capacity of these movement sectors is not demonstrated, hence it is not clear what the distinguishing factor between social movements and subcultures might be.

While Melucci's notion of complex society is helpful in that it points to the paradoxes of control and emancipation (and thus to the social space for action and agency), we find it too unspecific to provide a foil for the increasingly observable ambiguity of collective identity, cultural codes, and symbolic challenges. "Complex society" is too vague to account for the changes the state, the ruling institutions, and the hegemonic cultural codes are undergoing, incorporating some of the innovations of movements in the process and thereby continually shifting the line of conflict. Movements are not unambiguously opposed to dominant cultural codes, nor are these codes monolithic, but the concept of complex society does not allow us to capture differences within contemporary social movements over time and space.[27]

Social Movements within a Regulation Theory Framework

Regulation theory is not a theory of social movements but a framework to account for the socioeconomic development of capitalism. Originally developed by French economists, over the last few years it has attracted international interest. The first international conference on regulation theory (held in Barcelona in 1988) drew not merely scholars in economics, labor-market analysis, and industrial sociology (which might be regarded as the core fields of regulation theory) but also many social scientists and students of social change interested in a framework to understand the restructuring processes currently affecting different levels of capitalist societies. This broad interest is due to the French authors' promise of a theory of capitalist development *after* late capitalism without assuming a lessened role of material production, as do concepts of the communication society (Jürgen Habermas) or of postmodern society (Scott Lash). Regulation theory has developed a periodization concept of capitalist development based not just on technological or strictly economic developments but rather on the varied societal institutions, social movements, and political struggles that allow specific historical formations to cohere and reproduce in a somewhat stable manner, in spite of class contradictions and antagonisms that tend toward instability and disintegration.[28]

The period most thoroughly studied by the regulationists is the post-war years, which were experienced by most advanced capitalist countries of the West as a "golden era." The development model prevalent in these societies has been called "Fordism."[29] Its central characteristic is the historically novel, tight relationship between mass production and mass consumption, which has allowed broad strata of the population unique participation in prosperity. Keynesian economic policy and the political goal of balanced living conditions across a national economy enforced the trend toward relative equality and security. Regulation theory has highlighted the role of particular institutional practices, norms, and behaviors (called "modes of regulation")[30] which contributed to the stability and reproduction of this model for a certain period of capitalist history—as well as to its crisis.

The societal changes of the last twenty years have been marked by the crisis of Fordism and efforts to overcome it.[31] In studying different experiments and ways out of the crisis (their effects, their potential generalizability), regulationists look less for the blessings or dangers of new technologies and more to the *forms of regulation* that might supplement the more flexible productive structures with compatible wage relations, consumption patterns, and welfare regulations.

This explicitly antifunctionalist perspective (which does not assume that reproduction must occur but looks instead at the mechanisms that contributed to the coherence of past regimes) offers a promising framework for analyzing the role and agency of social movements. In Aglietta's analysis of the phases of U.S. capitalism, for example, social movements matter: Workers' resistance against Taylorism and proactive movements such as the progressive movement are seen as relevant factors in the rise of Fordism in the United States, and workers' resistance against the further deepening of the division of labor is of central importance for the crisis of Fordism. Similarly, in the current debate about a post-Fordist society, the regulationist authors emphasize that ways out of the crisis will result from social struggles and political concepts.

At the beginning of the 1980s, it seemed as if a neoliberal model (emphasizing deregulation and austerity politics) might prevail in the competition for solutions, but ten years later its achievements no longer appear convincing. In spite of differences among authors, some elements are accepted as characteristic of a post-Fordist regime, such as flexibility of production and labor organization on the basis of new technologies, flexible wage forms and labor markets, internationalization of production and a global financial market, deregulation in some political institutions, a polarization of the social structure, and so on. Regulation theorists consider it their task to analyze not only the restrictions thrown up by these developments but also to increase social movements' options in shaping a possible future regime of accumulation and its modes of regulation.

Since the middle-range level of institutions and political conflict play such a central role in this theory of society (as opposed to the macro level of analysis of society as a whole, or to the micro analysis of risk society), it is more amenable to "downsizing," to bringing its concepts closer to empirical description, which makes it more useful in developing verifiable hypotheses than Touraine's mutation to programmed society or Melucci's concept of complex society, in which social movements are assumed to play an essential and unambiguous role, on one side of the central conflict.[32] If viewed from a regulationist perspective, contemporary social movements appear as more ambivalent and their contradictory effects can be described more precisely than by the other theoretical models we have discussed. We will use the recent developments of new social movements in Germany as a case to demonstrate this.

New Social Movements in the Federal Republic

Contrary to premature assessments pronouncing the demise or end of the new social movement cycle,[33] social movement activities and topics have acquired a stable place in the German political culture, where they initially had been a novel phenomenon.[34]

Visible protest activities during the eighties and early nineties, beyond the ebb and flow of large mobilization waves over such issues as the NATO double-track decision or abortion legislation, have become a stable feature of German life, increasing even in the course of the decade.[35] The remarkable mobilizations against the Gulf War in 1991 confirmed this trend. The movement themes have also resonated with the public: according to survey research, the number of followers and those expressing willingness to participate have not been declining but rather slightly increasing. Supporters of the ecology movement rose from 7.8 percent in 1982 to 17.3 percent in 1989, while supporters of the peace movement increased from 15.8 percent to 23.2 percent in the same period.[36] Furthermore, studies of contemporary youth show that movement activities are not a generational phenomenon: "A significant majority of the young sympathizes with the new social movements and fundamentally agrees with their goals and forms of action. . . . More than 5 percent up to 25 percent of the young are personally mobilized."[37] The massive participation of high-school students in the 1991 antiwar actions supports these findings.

Important as causes for this new "normalcy" are the manifold forms of institutionalization in the new social movements, which have led to an overall institutionalization of this type of movement politics. Movement networks have emerged on local, regional, and issue-specific levels, stabilized by a variety of institutions, initiatives, and projects ranging from the daily newspaper *die tageszeitung* all the way to the Green Party. Another form of institutionalization are local movement communities and alternative public spheres, which keep cultural motives of opposition alive and guarantee their presence in everyday life. Furthermore, in all the different movements, the establishment of projects has contributed to developing and sustaining professionalism as well as to the institutionalization of the challenge. This trend has been furthered by the differentiation of individual movements; for example, in the area of ecology, garbage initiatives have formed, nuclear waste initiatives produce their own media, there are recycling newsletters, and so on. There are also groups and initiatives that guarantee solidarity and support for movement activities involving a certain amount of risk, such as civil disobedience ("Red Help" organizations and similar ones). Finally, there are movement organizations that help to bridge phases of latency—that is, phases of relatively little visible activity. For example, the Network Peace Cooperative, founded in 1989 after the dissolution of the central coordinating committee of the pace movement, aided the rapid mobilization of peace activists during the Gulf War.

These new movement institutions do not seem headed in the direction of hierarchy, bureaucracy, and formal organization. Rather, a host of different organizational patterns coexist simultaneously, ranging from informal grassroots groups to professional enterprises such as Greenpeace. So far, neither party politics (via the Greens or the Social Democrats) nor associational politics (via groups formed to protect the environment) have become exclusive heirs to these institutionalizations. Evidence seems to point, rather, in the direction of a relatively independent sector having emerged next to or underneath the other institutions of political interest mediation (parties, associations, unions); both sectors are, however, competing with each other to mediate political interests. Assessments of the consequences of this competition vary. Some observers perceive cooperation more than opposition, seeing the existence of both sectors as contributing to the expansion of people's repertoire of political action.[38] Others call attention to the negative effects for the established institutions, such as the decrease in party membership rates and a decline of party activism during the 1980s.[39] But nobody claims any more that the traditional political institutions will absorb the social movement activities.

Increasing Heterogeneity of the New Social Movements

The picture we have just sketched of the institutionalization of the German movement sector is, however, misleading in suggesting a stability that exists only in the aggregate. Besides the expansion of movement politics and the growing resonance that their issues have been finding, social movements during the 1980s also produced contrary tendencies. First of all, while from the beginning new social movements have been rather heterogeneous, contrary to widespread expectations of increasing convergence we must note their increasing social and political heterogeneity. On one end of the spectrum we have the so-called autonomous (clandestine action groups with anarchist orientations) and punks, characterized by existential radicalism; on the other end, church-oriented peace groups distinguish themselves with demonstrative civility. While on site they may deal cordially with each other,[40] they rarely support each other. (They did come together to protect those threatened by the violent attacks of right-wing gangs.)

Secondly, we need to be aware that the impression of movement continuity is partly due to the fact that protest practice has spread to include more population groups and issues. Steelworkers in Rheinhausen have taken to civil disobedience, and the Gray Panthers introduced old people to the tactics of demonstrations and sit-ins. While social movement practices and discourse have spread, protest activity in "core" sectors of the new social movements (for example, the new women's movement) has probably declined.

With the institutionalization of the new social movements, their boundaries seem to become more blurry. It is no longer clear whether certain self-managed projects and collectives are still part of the movement milieu or not.

The green-alternative movements have been startled in recent years by countermovements that also use the action repertoire of the new social movements. For example, an organized opposition to policies of the Social Democrat–Green dominated Senate in Berlin that strove to reduce automobile traffic in the city captured the public's attention for months with noisy car demonstrations protesting the 100 km/h speed limit on one of the city's highways.

Finally, there are remarkable local differences in patterns of politics and the composition of movement milieus. In a research project on local movement networks,[41] we found that project-oriented decentralized networks,[42] which are often cited as characteristic of the new social movements, existed only in one of the three localities under study. While in one place the movement milieus were found to be declining and drifting apart, in another movement politics were stabilized through a regional movement organization. Groups that once had determining influence had completely withdrawn in one place. And such differing constructions of movement milieus have themselves significantly contributed to these divergent developments.

In trying to account for the contradictory development of these movement scenes, Melucci's conception of "alternative codes" obviously goes along way to explain their oppositional yet changing identity as it unfolds primarily at the level of behavioral norms and ethical claims, which are perceived by Melucci as self-defined alternatives against the norms of the majoritarian culture. However, these movement milieus exist in a political context whose dynamics have affected the career of German social movements. Melucci's sharp dichotomy between political action and collective identity formation tends to neglect analysis of these dynamics. Similarly, we can find confirmation for Touraine's approach, which focuses on collective actors challenging the dominant technocratic model. But this thesis, that out of these challenges a unified central actor will emerge, obviously has to be rejected. Such a development did not occur in Germany, where the new social movements have developed more vigorously than in other advanced Western nations, and it is unlikely elsewhere: the movements remain heterogeneous actors and do not homogeneize into one cohesive antitechnocratic movement. German new social movements' development from fundamental opposition to their current contradictory manifestations and functions can better be explained within a regulationist perspective.

New Social Movements in Germany Seen through the Regulation Approach

The regulationist perspective would suggest connecting the rise of new social movements to the specific conditions of German Fordism and explaining their subsequent development and significance in terms of the crisis of Fordism and the search for a new regime of accumulation.

The antiauthoritarian protest of the 1960s developed its themes, its critique of consumption and mainstream culture, against the normative power of the "Fordist compromise"—that is, the growth-oriented compromise between unions and capital, flanked by welfare-stated security systems and the expansion of consumer credit. The "modern" way of life and work that developed on this basis was not without contradictions: The "performance principle" shaping people's work lives on the one hand, and the hedonistic pleasures appealed to by consumptive norms on the other, provided motives for protest movements emerging during the 1960s. These movements challenged the achievement ethic, the nuclear family, and sexual self-discipline as well as planned obsolescence and the standardized norms of cultural consumption. The cultural hegemony of the Fordist project was contested for the first time, and as the critique spread it contributed to Fordism's crisis.

Next, while reviving the traditions of the labor movement, the New Left also broke with the "productivity pact" still adhered to by the Old Left. Contrary to the Old Left's hopes of a gradual transformation of society brought by the development of productive forces, the New Left challenged that such growth necessarily leads to improvements for oppressed groups. They saw that in spite of the incredible productivity of capitalism, aggression, alienation, and wars in the Third World persisted. These perceptions spawned an opposition movement that, because of widespread prosperity and security, could not hope to gain broad support. Thus it developed a particularly radical and utopian critique of capitalism. Since the system seemed to function so well for so many, the movement's hopes focused on the modest symptoms of crisis and emergent opposition visible at the time, such as the September strikes of 1969, the struggles of labor immigrants and other marginal groups, and liberation movements in the Third World. Beyond these currents of fundamental opposition, the new social movements springing up in the 1970s gradually politicized the neglected interests and externalized costs of the Fordist compromise: ecological devastation, the destruction of cities for the sake of the automobile, forced mobility, infrastructure deficits, patriarchal family structures, and the gendered division of labor. These movements participated in triggering the crisis of Fordism by delegitimating existing political forms and cultural models and by creating a heightened awareness of the costs of Fordism.

With the crisis of Fordism the conditions for protest were transformed. As crisis symptoms spread, they broadened the appeal of various protest movements: ecological and feminist protest and the critique of technocracy and culture were no longer solely the province of small oppositional minorities. As the movements gained more widespread support, however, they also lost their radical and utopian vigor, and they assumed a more pragmatic character with the entry of movement entrepreneurs as well as political parties. At the same time, so-called "old" issues came back on the agenda: demands for full employment, welfare-state programs, and redistributive measures (once guaranteed by growth) found their way onto the agendas of some of the new social movements. During the initial stages of the prolonged crisis, the new movements were blamed for the difficulties with crisis management in the Federal Republic. For example, they were held responsible for stagnating investments (slowing down nuclear plant construction and similar such developments). Unions organized counter-mobilizations,[43] and the state led an intense campaign to stigmatize the movements. This antagonism served, however, to reinforce the movements' efforts to build their own countercultures and institutions. Thus, while their political influence was at a low, their internal strength and autonomy were growing.

During the 1980s, the relationship between the movements and the state took a new turn. The crisis of the bureaucratic welfare state had become obvious, and reformers in all political parties were busy searching for new forms of regulation to replace the Fordist ones (productivity-oriented wage gains, welfare-state provisions) that had become dysfunctional with the productivity slowdown. Increasingly they turned to the innovations of some of the new social movements. Local governments began to co-opt self-help programs, discovered the usefulness of alternative employment relations such as coops and collectives, began to accept new lifestyles, and incorporated new (more client-based) social services as well as elements of alternative culture into their newly entrepreneurial urban management, which is concerned with developing endogenous potentials.[44] For example, some cities established self-help rehabilitation programs after squatters had saved historic housing stock, and they funded unemployed and immigrant youth in rehabbing houses that have subsequently become magnets for gentrification. Cooperative relationships have frequently emerged from these efforts, but the old state-movement antagonism also reappeared with a vengeance (as in the boycott of the 1987 census or the massive protest against the Wackersdorf reprocessing plant). Meanwhile, broad segments within the social movement sectors took a stance of Realpolitik, one of aiding a more flexible capitalist future.

If we view this amazing trajectory from fundamental opposition and sociopolitical marginalization, all the way to acceptance as an innovative resource, in the context of regulation theory it becomes clear that we are not merely witnessing a normal movement cycle from protest to reform[45] or from protest to institutionalization (following Roberto Michels' iron law of oligardry). Instead, we can delineate how this development is encouraged by a specific social and political opportunity structure that has emerged out of the crisis of an accumulation regime.[46]

The profile of the German new social movements up to 1980 is a direct result of the relatively closed input structures and of the state's strategies of exclusion and marginalization of critical voices. (Since the prohibition of the German Communist Party in 1956 no protest-absorbing left party existed on the national level until the emergence of the Greens in 1980.) This led the movements to develop orientations of fundamental opposition and strongly articulated countercultures, which were simultaneously encouraged by the federal state's weak capacity to implement its policies. (Courts allow citizens in many cases to block or slow down implementation of centrally decided policies.) In comparison to other nations, state repression was intense, provoking additional countercultural and terrorist tendencies.

During the 1980s, the facilitated by the Greens, the state and the established parties began to open somewhat; even the conservative turn following the fall of the Social Democratic–led government in 1982–83 did not stop this opening. A continuing high level of state repression of the more radical currents in the movements as well as of civil disobedience actions in the new peace movement contributed to stabilizing the movement sector as an oppositional force. At the same time, the different levels of local and regional governments, the federal organization of the state, as well as state financing of the political parties provided diverse opportunities for certain movement sectors to make their influence felt. This is especially true for green-alternative local politics and the red-green governing coalitions that have formed on local and state levels.[47]

A "politics of a medium path"[48]—between Scandinavian welfare capitalism and the British and American strategies of economic liberalism—has kept the speed of transformation and the scope of institutional restructuring moderate. (This is true for the entire system of interest mediation.) On the other hand, it provided space for a relatively successful adaptation to increasingly competitive world market conditions, to new production structures, and—certainly not least—to the challenges of the new social movements. A U.S. observer has described the politics of the 1980s as "hidden flexibility within stable institutions."[49]

Effects and Achievements of the New Social Movements

This comparatively smooth and gradual transition toward post-Fordism is in no small measure also a result of the new social movements.[50] Their strong positions on environmental issues and their veto power on expanding nuclear energy have prevented investment ruins in West Germany, turned industrial environmental protection into a growth industry, and encouraged more ecologically safe production and consumption.[51] Movement impulses have been co-opted in similar ways in many different areas. The new social movements have not intended this result. The more flexible model of accumulation, which they unwittingly helped create, does not resolve any of the fundamental problems the movements have been articulating; rather, it externalizes, represses, and disguises them.

These processes of co-optation take various forms. Sometimes individuals are co-opted, such as environmental movement activists who have been appointed to cabinet posts (Leinen in Saarland, Griefan in Lower Saxony); most frequently movement themes get co-opted, as when the then minister of economics Jürgen Möllemann, in starting his position in 1990, defined his task as the "reconciliation of ecology and economy." In some policy areas, social movement projects are directly co-opted—for example, when Christian Democrats support the official recognition of houses for battered women (as occurred in Odenwald County, where the Christian Democratic Union is in the opposition).

Co-optation is in fact the appropriate term for these processes precisely because they were able to prevent decisive change in the way the institutions function and avert actual shifts of power. New institutions have been established in reaction to the new social movements and their agenda, such as environmental ministeries or posts for women's affairs. These are a means of offering small concessions and reforms and creeping changes in institutional politics. On first sight, the dominant politics of the Federal Republic in the early 1990s would thus appear to be responsive: everybody is displaying the movement colors of green and purple. But what in fact reigns is merely symbolic politics: everyone is expected to pay "ecological lip-service."[52] The reality of weapons export during times of intense peace rhetoric, the participation of German firms in selling weapons to Sadam Hussein, has been a particularly spectacular example of symbolic politics.

The legitimation problems raised by the new competition from the social movement sector are, finally, processed in yet another form, and that is that established politics increasingly violates its own rules for the sake of power. Over the last twenty years, manipulation and corruption have become more widespread and gained in political significance—and not adherence by the elite to the democratic rules of the game. A further reaction to the decline in voluntary party work and to the "participatory revolution" of the new social movements has been the increasing commercialization and stratification of the political parties.[53]

These examples illustrate that there are not just slight openings toward movement issues but also strong institutional reactions in opposite directions. What is decisive from the perspective of new social movements is that no institutional concessions have been made to their demands for more democracy (such as procedures for direct democracy or control of administration), which are central to the practice of citizens initiatives and new social movements.

The contradictory situation in which contemporary social movements find themselves in the 1990s can best be explained through research based in regulation theory, which suggests that social movements should be examined in terms of their contribution and challenge to the new forms of regulation and their role in shaping the new regime of accumulation. Regulation theory helps us to see them act and be affected by the new terrain of post-Fordist capitalism and the post-Fordist state, which, while fraying at the margins (that is, admitting some representation of the new movements' demands), is concentrating increasingly authoritarian and militaristic power at the center, more protected from citizen participation than ever.

NOTES

1. While resource mobilization theorists generally adhere to Charles Tilly's definition of a social movement as constituted by an aggrieved, mobilized mass opinion aimed at the authorities (see, for example, Sidney Tarrow, *Struggle, Politics, and Reform: Collective Action, Social Movements, and Cycles of Protest,* Western Societies Program Occasional Paper no. 21 [Ithaca, N.Y.: Center for International Studies, Cornell University, 1989], 11; and Tilly's elaboration of

his definition in *From Mobilization to Revolution* [Reading, Mass.: Addison-Wesley, 1978]), this definition has not prevented an inflationary usage of the term in the North American context. It comprises practically every form of noninstitutional political action including protest, interest-group politics, and collective episodes.

2. See Frances Piven and Richard Cloward, "Normalizing Collective Protest," *International Journal of Politics, Culture and Society* 4, no. 4, (1991).

3. Other contemporary protests and mobilizations are excluded from this definition of new social movements. Populist, religious, right-wing or countermovements, as well as the "old" working class movement, although alive and active in contemporary society, are not included in this concept.

4. See Bert Klandermans, "New Social Movements and Resource Mobilization: The European and the American Approaches Revisited," in Dieter Rucht, ed., *Research on Social Movements: The State of the Art* (Frankfurt/Boulder, Colo.: Campus/Westview Press, 1991), 22ff; Sidney Tarrow, "National Politics and Collective Action: Recent Theory and Research in Western Europe and the United States," *Annual Review of Sociology* 14 (1988):421–40; Hanspeter Kriesi, "The Interdependence of Structure and Action: Some Reflections on the State of the Art," in Bert Klandermans et al., eds., *From Structure to Action* (Greenwich, Conn.: JAI Press, 1988).

5. The body of literature concerning NSMs is, of course, much broader. Once new social movements became the preferred umbrella concept for the sundry protest movements that emerged in the aftermath of the 1960s, and the academic disciplines began to reflect the rise of this topic in the early 1980s, a broad spectrum of work began to take shape. A wave of empirical studies were undertaken by people in or close to the movements, producing a wealth of data—most of it to feed immediate political interests or to confirm speculations about how modern, postmodern, antimodern, or neoromantic the movements were. This phenomenon occurred because the debate was strongly framed by the larger philosophical and social science literature, where grand macrosociological and cultural paradigms struggled with each other. New social movements figure very prominently in this philosophical discourse (for example, Jürgen Habermas, "New Social Movements," *Telos* 49 (1981):33–37; Habermas, *The Theory of Communicative Action*, vol. 2 (Cambridge: Polity, 1987); Niklas Luhmann, *Soziale systeme* (Social systems) (Frankfurt: Suhrkamp, 1984); Ernesto Laclau and Chantal Mouffe, *Hegemony and Socialist Strategy: Toward a Radical Democratic Politics* (London: Verso, 1985). However, these theoretical propositions present such encompassing general theories of society that they are not verifiable or translatable into empirical research. While much is being said about how the movements should be interpreted, they are themselves treated as a black box: how movements mobilize, how they organize their collective political will, how they manage continuity and unity—that is, all the factors that make them into a collective actor—remain unaddressed in this literature.

6. The group presented major studies on the student movement of 1976 (Alain

Touraine et al., *Lutte etudiante* [Student struggles] [Paris: Editions du Seuil, 1978]), on the antinuclear protest (Touraine et al., *La Prophétie anti-nucleaire* [the antinuclear prophecy] [Paris: Editions due Seuil, 1980]), on the workers' movement (Touraine et al., *Le Mouvement ouvrier* [Paris: Fayard, 1984]), the new peace movement in France, Solidarity in Poland, and others. All of these studies provide a differentiated analysis of the respective movement discourse and of the various protest milieus involved.

7. "In postindustrial society all of the economic system is the object of intervention of society upon itself. That is why we can call it the *programmed society*, because this phrase captures its capacity to create models of management, production, organization, distribution, and consumption, so that such a society appears, in all its functional levels, as the product of an action exercised by the society itself, and not as the outcome of natural laws or cultural specificities" (Touraine, *Return of the Actor: Social Theory in Post-Industrial Society* [Minneapolis: University of Minnesota Press, 1988], 104). "Programmed society is necessarily also a society of protest, of imagination, and of utopia, because it is wholly traversed by the social conflict between apparatuses with the capacity and the power to program, and the appeal to a creativity and a happiness constantly threatened by the logic of these apparatuses" (ibid., 115). See also Touraine, *The Voice and the Eye: An Analysis of Social Movements* (Cambridge: Cambridge University Press, 1981), 6ff.

8. Touraine, *Return of the Actor*, 110.

9. Touraine, *The Voice and the Eye.*

10. Alain Touraine, *Self-Production of Society* (Chicago: University of Chicago Press, 1977).

11. "[They] expressed more clearly the crisis either of an institution or of a political ideology than the formation of a new social movement, and were rapidly destroyed by internal contradictions" (Alain Touraine, "Commentary on Dieter Rucht's Critique," in Dieter Rucht, ed., *Research on Social Movements: The State of the Art* [Frankfurt and Boulder, Colo.: Campus/Westview Press, 1991], 303).

12. See Touraine, *Return of the Actor.*

13. Claus Leggewie, "Propheten ohne Macht: Die neuen sozialen Bewegungen in Frankreich zwischen Resignation und Fremdbestimmung" (Prophets without power: The new social movements in France between resignation and heteronomy), in Karl-Werner Brand, ed., *Neue soziale Bewegungen in Westeuropa und den USA* (New social movements in Western Europe and the United States) (Frankfurt and New York: Campus, 1985), 83–139.

14. Alain Touraine, "Beyond Social Movements?" *Theory, Culture and Society* 9, no. 1 (1992): 143.

15. Alberto Melucci, *Altri Codici: Aree di movimento nella metropoli* (Different codes: Movement spheres in the metropolis) (Bologna: Il Mulino, 1984).

16. These are societies where material production is increasingly replaced by the production of signs and social relations. Society's capacity to intervene in the

production of meaning extends to areas that previously escaped control and regulation: areas of self-definition, emotional relationships, sexuality, and "biological" needs. See Alberto Melucci, *Nomads of the Present: Social Movement and Individual Needs in Contemporary Society* (Philadelphia: Temple University Press, 1989), and Amy Bartholomew and Margit Mayer, "Nomads of the Present: Melucci's Contribution to New Social Movement Theories," *Theory, Culture and Society 9*, no. 4 (1992):141–59.

17. See, for example, Bert Klandermans and Sidney Tarrow, "Mobilization into Social Movements: Synthesizing European and American Approaches," *International Social Movement Research* 1 (1988):1–38; Sidney Tarrow, "National Politics and Collective Action: Recent Theory and Research in Western Europe and the United States," *Annual Review of Sociology* 14 (1988):421–40.

18. Melucci, *Nomads of the Present*, 338.

19. See, for example, Klandermans and Tarrow, "Mobilization into Social Movements," 12–13.

20. Melucci, *Nomads of the Present*, 332.

21. Ibid., 333.

22. Ibid., 338.

23. Ibid., 70.

24. Ibid., 58.

25. Ibid., 75.

26. For example: "Contemporary social movements, more than others in the past, have shifted towards a non-political terrain: the need for self-realization in everyday life. In this respect social movements have a conflictual and antagonistic, but not a political orientation, because they challenge the logic of complex systems on cultural grounds" (Melucci, *Nomads of the Present*, 23).

27. See Amy Bartholomew and Margit Mayer, "Nomads of the Present: Melucci's Contribution," 141–59.

28. See Michel Aglietta, *A Theory of Capitalist Regulation: The U.S. Experience* (London: New Left Books, 1979), 15ff.

29. The concept of "Fordism" had already emerged during the interwar years; it derived from the remarkable success of the automobile manufacturer Henry Ford. (See Robert Lacey, *Ford—The Men and the Machine* [London: Heineman, 1986].) We use the term as shorthand, as it has come to be used among regulationists, to characterize the shared features of the particular developmental phase of capitalist societies from the 1950s to the 1970s. See Robert Boyer, *The Regulation School: A Critical Introduction* (New York: Columbia University Press, 1990); Joachim Hirsch, *Kapitalismus ohne Alternative?* (Hamburg: VSA, 1990); Alain Lipietz, *Towards a New Economic Order: Postfordism, Ecology and Democracy* (New York: Oxford University Press, 1992).

30. The mode of regulation connotes that "totality of forms, networks, explicit and implicit norms, which secure the compatibility of behaviors within the framework of a given accumulation regime" (Alain Lipietz, "Accumulation, Crisis, and Ways out of the Crisis: Some Methodological Reflections on the Concept

of 'Regulation,' " *Prokla,* no. 58 [1985]: 121). Generally speaking, regulation of a social relations means "the way in which this relation reproduces itself in spite of and because of its conflictual and contradictory character" (Lipietz, "Accumulation, Crisis, and Ways out of the Crisis," 109).

31. Central to the crisis of Fordism is a leveling off of productivity stemming from the exhaustion of the productivity enhancements of the Fordist/Taylorist organization of labor. Not just technically limits (such as the rigidities of mass production) but also social limits (saturation of markets, inverse effects) and growing externalization costs and their politicization (ecology) play a role in constituting the crisis.

32. However, at this stage most regulationist research has focused on the politics of labor and of consumption: political-cultural areas have not been central to the regulationist research agenda, and no theoretical concepts have as yet been developed to analyze social and political institutions. Another problem is that authors differ remarkably in their description of the causes, definitions, and ways out of the current crisis. Thus, we still do not have "the" regulation theory as a fully elaborated, empirically substantiated social theory. Despite these shortcomings, we argue that the approach can be developed further in that direction.

33. Such as Bernd Ulrich, "Keine Experimente!? 11 Schnapsideen zum Torkeln der Bewegungen" (No experiments!? Eleven silly ideas about the staggering of social movements), *Kommune* 6, no. 11 (1988): 6–11; Helmut Wiesenthal, "Die Grünen im Bewegungsherbst" (The Greens in the movement autumn), *Gewerkschaftliche Monatshefte* 5 (1988): 289–99.

34. Grassroots activity outside the traditional institutions of representative democracy was initially perceived as quite abnormal in the German context, where class and interest group struggles have always been mediated through a partisan political system. When citizens' initiatives first emerged in the early 1970s, they were regarded as highly suspect by both politicians and mainstream social scientists.

35. Rudd Koopmans, "Democracy from Below: New Social Movements and the Political System in West Germany" (Ph.D. diss., Free University, Amsterdam, 1992).

36. Dieter Fuchs and Dieter Rucht, "Support for New Social Movements in Five European Countries," discussion paper, Science Center for Social Research, Berlin, 1992).

37. Klaus-Jürgen Scherer, *Jugend und soziale Bewegung* (Youth and social movements) (Opladen: Leske & Budrich, 1988), 197.

38. Jürgen Hofrichter and Hermann Schmitt, "Eher mit-als gegeneinander; Zum Verhältnis von neuen sozialen Bewegungen und politischen Parteien" (Rather with each other than against each other: On the relation between new social movements and political parties), in Roland Roth and Dieter Rucht, eds., *Neue soziale Bewegungen in der Bundesrepublik Deutschland* (Bonn: Bundeszentrale für politische Bildung, 1991), 469–88.

39. Elmar Wiesendahl, "Der Marsch aus den Institutionen" (The march out of the institutions), *Aus Politik und Zeitgeschichte*, no. 21 (1990): 3–14.

40. See Helmut Berking and Sieghart Neckel, "Die Politik der Lebensstile in einem Berliner Bezirk" (The politics of lifestyle in a Berlin district), in Peter A. Berger and Stefan Hradil, eds., *Lebenslagen, Lebensläufe, Lebensstile* (Life courses and lifestyles) (Göttingen: O. Schwartz, 1990), 481–500.

41. Regina Dackweiler et al., *Struktur und Entwicklungsdynamik lokaler Bewegungsnetzwerke in der Bundesrepublik* (Structure and dynamic of local movement networks in the Federal Republic) (Berlin: Freie Universität, 1990).

42. Joachim Raschke, *Soziale Bewegungen* (Frankfurt and New York: Campus, 1985).

43. See Heinrich Siegmann, *The Conflicts between Labor and Environmentalism in the FRG and the US* (New York: St. Martin's Press, 1985).

44. See Margit Mayer, "Politics in the Post-Fordist City," *Socialist Review* 21, no. 1 (1991): 105–24.

45. Sidney Tarrow, *Struggle, Politics, and Reform*, 41–56.

46. On the concept of political opportunity structures, see Sidney Tarrow, *Democracy and Disorder: Protest and Politics in Italy, 1965–1975* (Oxford: Clarendon Press, 1989), and Hanspeter Kriesi, "The Interdependence of Structure and Action," Bert Klandermans et al., *From Structure to Action* (Greenwich, Conn.: JAI Press, 1988), 349–68.

47. See Roland Roth, "Local Green Politics in West German Cities," *International Journal of Urban and Regional Research* 15, no. 1 (1991): 75–89.

48. Rüdiger Schmidt, *Die Friedensbewegung in der Bundesrepublik Deutschland* (The peace movement in the Federal Republic of Germany) (Opladen: Westdeutscher Verlag, 1990).

49. Peter Katzenstein, ed., *Industry and Politics in West Germany* (Ithaca: Cornell University Press, 1989), 9.

50. At least it was smooth until the unification of Germany. Since then a new political formation has emerged, the contours of which are only gradually taking shape. At this point it appears the unification process has brought about a weakening of the new issues in two respects. The high costs associated with unification slowed down the structural adaptation process toward post-Fordism and reduced the political significance of the new social movements. "Old" topics and conflicts are once again in the foreground.

51. However, these improvements have been accompanied by exporting more toxic and risky production facilities and the domestic waste abroad, especially to Third World countries. Movement criticisms of these exports have not been addressed.

52. Ulrich Beck, "Der ökologische Gesellschaftskonflikt" (The ecological conflict in society), *WSI-Mitteilungen* 12 (1990): 753.

53. Christine Landfried, *Parteifinanzen und politische Macht* (Party finances and political power) (Baden-Baden: Nomos, 1990).

CHAPTER 21

Rethinking Revolution in Light of the New Social Movements

Allen Hunter

□   □   □   □   □   □   □   □   □   □   □   □

Few radicals call for revolution today, many considering it a dangerous chimera. The writer George Steiner has summarized the fear well: "When [Marx] urged a kingdom of social justice, of classless fraternity on earth, he was translating into secular terms the sunburst of the messianic. . . . Human egotism, the competitive pulse, the lust for waste and display can be suffocated only by tyrannical violence. And, in turn, those who practice such violence themselves wither into corruption. Ineluctably, collectivist-socialist ideals seem to lead to one or another form of the Gulag."[1] Analytic Marxists and critical theorists alike reject the Hegelian, teleological elements in Marxist versions of revolutionary theory.[2] Radical democratics subsume socialism within democracy and stress the continued expansion of democratic rights and not a structural break with capitalism.[3] Emphasis on the potential of civil society is joined to a rejection of revolution.[4] New social movements portrayed as uninterested in seizing state power have also been invoked to legitimate the rejection of revolution.[5]

Today's critics of revolution take issue with three main aspects of revolutionary theory: the strategic focus on seizing power, the transformation of social structures, and utopian longings.

First, the political moment in revolutions has been classically defined as a decisive rupture of the political order when oppressed people—generally operating outside established political rules, often resorting to violence—seize power from their oppressors to establish new forms of political rule that promise a more just social order. There are several reasons why this chiliastic view of revolution as a total break with the past is no longer analytically or emotionally compelling for many people until recently attracted to it: despair about the possibility of fundamental change; fear that such seizures of power can only lead to authoritarianism; worry that seizing state power and the commanding heights of the economy are inadequate to realize the goals set by many contemporary social movements because power and politics are not uniquely defined by the state, but help constitute all social relations; and hostility to classic revolutionary parties, viewed as elitist and charged with reducing qualitatively different goals to a homogenized universalism.

Second, in classical definitions revolution entails the quantitative transformation of the whole social structure and not only the leading political institutions. In this view revolution is necessary to overcome systemic, structural impediments to desired change. This aspect of revolution is also in disrepute. Revolutionary theories have focused on supposedly core features of a society and have assumed that destroying those structures would bring the dawn of a new era as secondary patterns of oppression and domination also crumbled. The main theoretical culprit here is Marxism, which is criticized for class reductionism and an exaggerated emphasis on capitalism. Few radicals today believe that all social inequities can be explained solely in terms of class relations or that capitalism is a unified field of domination uniquely responsible for all the problems against which social movements struggle. Indeed many radicals today argue that unified explanations are elitist myths enunciated to legitimate positions of privilege and that they result in authoritarian politics.

Third, is the utopian moment in which revolutions are intended to create a new social order. Revolutionaries seek power to fracture the structural constraints on social change because they envision a more just and liberatory society. This is the emancipatory moment of revolution; it has posited redemption, transcendence, and even human perfectability. For instance, in the *Economic and Philosophical Manuscripts* Marx wrote: "communism . . . is the genuine resolution of the conflict between man and nature and between man and man—the true resolution of the strife between existence and essence, between objectification and self-confirmation, between freedom and necessity, between individual and species. Communism is the riddle of history solved, and it knows itself to be this solution."[6]

Today this aspect of revolution seems too utopian, apocalyptic, and unidimensional: New social movement activists and theorists view the expectation (especially prominent in Hegelian and populist strands of Marxism) that the separation between the particular and universal, self and other, subject and object can be overcome as not only unrealistic but dangerous, because attempting to transcend all such divisions may suppress cultural difference, individual rights, freedom, and tolerance.[7] Most utopian visions have proceeded from criticisms of some basic form of oppression or alienation—be it destruction of community, distance from the divine or the natural, exploitation of labor, or loss of authenticity— that revolution could overcome. Thus today's radicals view yesterday's utopias as not only potentially dangerous but distant from the diverse political projects in which they are engaged.[8]

This fulsome rejection of revolution is both a cause and a consequence of the crisis of modernity. Central aspects of the revolutionary socialist tradition—the violence of revolution, the authoritarianism of socialist regimes, and the inability of socialist movements and parties in the West to forge compelling alternatives to their own societies or socialist regimes—have contributed to the crisis of modernity. In turn, doubts about Enlightenment reason, worries about the destructive domination embedded in science and technology, and enthusiasm for particularist identities have undermined commitment to revolution by challenging the modernist assumptions upon which those commitments were based.[9]

□ □ □

A variety of of political positions are being put forward today that are meant to stand as realistic alternatives to revolutionary politics. They include the embrace of civil society, democracy, human rights, particularist identity politics, new social movements, romantic pre- and postmodern rejections of the Enlightenment tradition. These are not strictly parallel: some are more grounded in intellectual critique and others in political practice. Nor are they mutually exclusive; many theorists and activists alike favor enriching and expanding the domain of civil society by strengthening social movement activism, for instance. Other movements pursue broad goals across several domains. Many feminists, for example, try to reform civil society, democracy, and human rights regimes so they will contribute to the erosion and not the reproduction of gender inequality; they debate whether gender-specific or more universalist goals best advance feminist goals and seek to understand whether Western rationality is male, and if so, whether and how it can be modified. Some popular movements in the Third World reject technocratic science, invoke human rights, and seek to expand democratic features of civil society, all as necessary complements to their struggles for well-being, economic justice, and environmental sustainability.

While I believe that current rejections of revolution cumulatively register a compelling critique of received notions of revolution, they have problems of their own. Let me mention several concerns. First, it is an understandable rhetorical gambit to contrast new political impulses favorably to previous political traditions; yet is analytically inadequate to compare the ideals and potentials of political movements with brief histories still in their bloom to the troublesome outcomes of past political movements with long, faded histories. A self-deceptive feature of the current celebration of postrevolutionary politics is the tacit assumption that rejecting past practices and proclaiming fidelity to new values are sufficient to avoid problems similar to those faced in past political struggles. Second, there is a mistaken tendency to perceive the unintended consequences of revolutionary politics more than the unintended consequences of other forms of politics. The Jacobin tradition is far from alone in having produced outcomes radically degraded from the promised future. Self-proclaimed revolutionaries are far from unique in finding that their acquisition of state power has led to outcomes at odds with their initial promises. The failures of Reagan's supply-side economic policies in the United States in the 1980s and the devolution of Polish Solidarity from a "self-limiting" oppositional movement to a fractured set of political tendencies and state functionaries are but two recent examples. That is, problems that critics ascribe to revolutionary politics may be much more endemic in the general process of historical change. Third, such obdurate, troubling issues as the mean-ends relation, the use of violence in politics, and the role of hostile conflict and naming other groups as the "enemy" in political identity formation are not solely the province of revolutionary politics. Finally, there is a mistaken tendency to collapse all aspects of revolutionary politics into a unity. For better or worse there is no simple correlation between the personal qualities of political activists, the ideology or political style of political organizations, a movement's or organization's historical significance while contesting for power, and the outcomes of its rule should it govern.

At times it seems as though critics of revolution believe that critique is sufficient; yet the consequence is that they deflect attention from crucial theoretical, strategic, and normative issues raised by the very alternatives they offer in place of revolution. In brief, they give insufficient attention to the questions of how much and what kind of change is necessary to realize their goals, of what it means to speak of fundamental change, of how thoroughly existing social structures and political institutions have to be modified so that changes they desire can be realized. Because it was first presented at a conference on social movements, this chapter focuses on the ambiguities of the stress on new social movements as a basis for and response to the rejection of revolution, but I believe that all the varied responses of radicals and former radicals to the collapse of revolutionary politics are open to similar criticisms, and I will argue that we need to rethink revolution before we reject it.[10]

Indeed, the goals of the new social movements, when woven into a compatible, complex vision, are radically subversive of present social orders and demand transformative political change at the social-structural, institutional, and inter- and intrapersonal levels. These changes may not eventuate in anything like previous revolutions; but their goals, even when couched in the languages of democracy and rights, can only be realized through vast changes. My criticisms are not with the expansive goals raised by today's social movements. In brief, I do believe the contemporary social movements have the potential to contribute to radical political change and hold out the promise of finding different ways of answering dilemmas raised by revolutionary theories and traditions and of posing important questions marginal to past revolutionary thought. But currently the harsh juxtaposition between the (bad) old politics and the (good) new social movements is self-deceptive, misleading, and can inhibit the kind of critical interrogation of current prospects for radical change that is needed. Here I will touch on several features of today's new social movements that I fear are insufficiently addressed by their adherents and even more ignored in most of the academic literature about new social movements.

First, few proponents of today's social movements reckon with just how revolutionary the sum of their demands is. There are two sides to this. Some radical critics of new social movements fear that, for instance, the changes sought by gays and lesbians can be realized within "existing society." Worries that successful attacks on particular problems may leave the dominant structures standing are misplaced. From the point of view of people in their gay and lesbian identities, what is wrong with that? If different axes of domination are (relatively) distinct, then, whatever "existing society" may mean, life becomes dramatically improved if gays and lesbians can live in a world without homophobia. While I doubt that homophobia can be conclusively ended without addressing broader questions concerning gender relations, the family, and sexuality, it should be a cause for celebration and not regret that particular forms of domination could be decisively ended without "revolutionary" change. My greater worry, however, is less that Marxist or socialist critics of the new social movements may ask something of them that does not arise from the imperatives of the movements themselves as it is that many people active in or sympathetic to those movements underestimate just how broad are the changes required to achieve the goals they seek. This is especially true of movements that combine ecological concerns with feminist and/or economic-justice values. These movements often avoid questions of capitalist imperatives ether by focusing on discrete problems or by dissolving capitalism into the vaguer construct of modernity. (It may well be the case that capitalism is a variant of a more general category such as modernity, but critiques and modifications of modernity that do not address the specific qualities of capitalism at issue are inadequate.) There is a related tendency to ignore questions of power and conflict. It may be true, as poststructuralists argue, that power is pervasive and constitutive of all social relations, but the question remains of how oppressive power relations can be changed.

Second, few movements today try to clarify what it would mean for the changes they seek to become self-sustaining and not "just" goals that constantly have to be sought. I offer a provisional way of conceptualizing the incorporation of movement achievements into the social fabric of daily life, recognizing that this effort will need many refinements. Third, I think that by linking admiration for new social movements to the embrace of civil society and the attack on statism, much of the literature about new social movements misses the extent to which those movements do make demands on the state, offer testimony to state bodies, and seek to modify state-society relations. Similarly for all their emphasis on identities and not interests, most movements today do make material demands, do engage in bargaining (however implicitly) over scarce resources. Thus critiques of statism and interests need to be refined. Fourth, and more positively, I believe that today's new social movements hold out the promise of fundamental change by combining an emphasis on qualitative change, on new ways of knowing and doing, with a focus on addressing core forms of domination and I conclude with attention to that promise. Let me now turn to these concerns in more detail.

Why Transformative Politics Remains Necessary

Critiques of classic revolutionary theory entreat us to rethink visions of a better society. Yet for all our current pessimism and chastened realism about systemic change, radical changes remain implicit in the political goals enunciated by or implicit in the actions of new social movements.

Today's social movements set numerous goals that cannot be realized through modest reform. Most revolutionary theory has focused on how revolutions can be made, not on the world they would create,[11] and little agreement exists "on what constitutes movement success."[12] Still, it is possible to specify political goals enunciated by contemporary social movements and underscore the extent of economic, political, and cultural transformation their realization would entail. Economic goals include reducing and then ending hunger, physical deprivation, gross economic inequality, and undemocratic, elite control of material and financial resources.[13] Green social movements focus on stopping environmental degradation and pursuing sustainable development grounded in an ecological critique of industrializing modernity. Identity-based new social movements seek the end of domination and marginality defined by racism, national chauvinism, sexism and homophobia. Peasant-based popular movements fight for land and water and against monoculture agribusiness. Indigenous people seek rights, autonomy, and the preservation of their lands and resources. In addition to these substantive goals, social movements and organizations are struggling for a dramatic invigoration and expansion of democracy, enrichment of civil society and public spheres, extensions of human rights globally, and firm commitments to individual freedom from state domination and repressive cultural norms.

This brief list indicates the need for the transformation of broad phenomena—undemocratic political institutions, economic, racial, and gender inequities, and industrialism's threats to humans and nature—not "just" the amelioration of particular problems. There is no end to the particular issues activists address today: homelessness and inadequate housing, unemployment, poor education, lousy medical care, racial violence, antigay violence, AIDS, domestic violence, street crime, drugs, toxic waste, runaway shops, nuclear proliferation. But many of these specific problems would not arise, or would be much less serious, in a world not structured by racism, sexism, class inequality, and homophobia. Movements focused on particular issues generally have assumptions, explicit or implicit, about the broader dynamics that create or enlarge the particular problems. It may be impossible to achieve a world in which, for instance, diseases like AIDS do not emerge; but its epidemiology would have been very different and much less deadly if Africa were less impoverished, if billions of dollars were redirected from arms purchases to infrastructural development, if women had more power globally, if homosexuals were not discriminated against, and if sexually repressive ethics did not structure most public discourse about AIDS prevention. That is, particular problems will still arise, but to the degree the general goals noted above are realized, specific problems will have less impact on fewer people and be more easily addressed with less drain on resources.

It could be argued that I exaggerate the range and depth of changes implied by the demands of today's social movements; indeed many people active in today's movements do seek only modest reforms and actively reject revolutionary visions. Thus let me clarify the normative and analytic assumptions that underlie my argument. Normatively I assume that the broad, inclusive goals of progressive social movements globally merit support and prefer those strands of movements that embrace the goals of numerous movements rather than defining their goals narrowly. Analytically I assume that as the goals of numerous movements are joined together (in ways that are at times mutually sustaining and at times in tension) the more completely current social arrangements have to be challenged.

The current goals of contemporary social movements are more radical, complex, and inclusive than those propounded by liberals, anarchists, or socialists who assumed that social transformation could be achieved by attacking a core source of domination. They are radical because their realization requires transformative social change across broad ranges of human experience (from such intimate aspects of daily life as sexuality and child rearing to the organization of the global economy and its impact on the natural environment) so that domination would become a nonexistent or marginal attribute, not a core element, of the reproductive logics of social relations that had sustained, inter alia, class, race, and gender inequities.[14] Radical social movements seek social changes that will end domination, not only political reforms that will ameliorate the worst aspects of domination. Political reforms can be routes to those more basic changes or interim remedies when the more basic changes cannot be realized.

The goals are not only radical but also complex. There is no Gordian knot that can be rent asunder so that all forms of domination unravel. The changes sought by radical social movements require changing multiple social logics so they cease reproducing, for example, racial oppression and environmental destruction; modifying the interactions between social logics so their interplay contributes to the realization, not frustration, of movement goals; and adapting institutional cultures and practices to the new, more egalitarian social logics. Finally these goals are more inclusive than modern utopian visions because they reject uncritical enthusiasm for economic growth without foresaking equity and they recognize and celebrate diversity without foresaking equality or liberty.

Yet, radical as they are, these goals are not grounded in utopian longings for ultimate redemption, human perfectability, or an historical end of all conflict and tension. The goals neither call for nor depend on a radical communitarian transcendance of the difference between self and other, nor the subsumption of the realm of necessity within the realm of freedom. The social order will not become transparent and directly negotiable by all, and the political articulation of many social relations will still be necessary. Moreover, these goals do not rest on a privileged social agent, historical teleology, or totalizing social theory; they are normatively grounded in broadly shared values promulgated and refined by various social movements but are not ontologically guaranteed. It follows that the list is neither exhaustive nor the content fixed. Many more goals could be added: children's rights, democratizing global governance, increasing the domains of pleasure and desire, overcoming discrimination against the handicapped, and autonomy for peoples currently dominated by nation-states, to list just a few. The open-ended, participatory manner in which goals are generated means that any particular set of goals does not articulate a radical "end to history," a pure communism, or any other state of pacific equilibrium. It does not assume that tensions between goals are ultimately surmountable, but neither does it start with views of human nature or institutional determinism that preclude radical transformation. Finally, just because these goals are not grounded in chiliastic impulses is no guarantee that attempts to realize them are immune to devolution.

There is no guarantee that because these goals are feasible, humane, and morally necessary they will be achieved. Indeed, today's social movements face many impediments to their realization: the movements are contested, tremendously burdened by the past, and sometimes represent retreats from previous movements.

First, radical new social movements are not the sole or most powerful political forces today; they compete with and are opposed by other movements. Even as anticommunism has collapsed along with communism, new demonologies are being forged to delegitimate diverse democratic movements. Anticommunism was only marginally a reasoned critique of authoritarianism; it was mainly mobilized to defend material and symbolic interests. Indeed, demonologies attacking antiracists, feminists, and environmentalists are being constructed by backlash movements and elites tenaciously clinging to their positions of dominance. In addition, new social movements are not alone in responding to the contemporary crises of modernity. Currently more powerful and much more violent than the new social movements are the many movements cohering around restorationist versions of national, ethnic, and fundamentalist religious identities. Visions of a meaningful and culturally coherent social order are among the attractions of these movements, and new social movements that reject utopian longings as outmoded, without fashioning new visions consonant with their goals, are likely to find themselves at an ideological and cultural disadvantage.

Second, radical goals are burdened by environmental damage caused by two centuries of industrialism and half a century of the nuclear arms race. While hazardous waste, the loss of species diversity, and threats to the biosphere may not resent humanity with insurmountable dilemmas, they are likely to force radical movements, as well as hard-headed policy analysts, to face trade-offs between unsatisfactory alternatives. For instance, there may not be absolutely safe ways of disposing of the millions of tons of hazardous crud seeping through untold numbers of barrels around the globe. The same dangers are likely to impose limits on libertarian and antistatist impulses; weapons-grade nuclear material has to be guarded, and toxic dumps need to be monitored carefully and indefinitely. The worse these conditions become before they are addressed, the greater will be the demands—from above and below—for statist and even authoritarian solutions.

Third, the crises of socialism and Marxism not only clear the ground for an exuberant explosion of new forms of movement activism; they also influence the political content of those movements, especially perspectives on the macroeconomy and on class. At the macroeconomic level, critiques of command economies and Marxism cut two ways, toward moderation and reformism, and toward deeper, more radical critiques of modern economies. Having lost a conception of socialism as a decisive break with capitalism, few radicals have clear conceptualizations of alternative ways of organizing complex economies. While socialists have historically focused on economics, today there "is little evidence that the socialist tradition is on the verge of reviving its economic project. Indeed, it is precisely in this domain that it now lacks confidence and originality."[15] Many radical economists and other social theorists now believe, with Adam Przeworski, that "[t]he socialist critique of the irrationality of capitalism is valid, but the socialist alternative is unfeasible."[16] This line of analysis leads to reforms within capitalism, with unclarity about how much political and economic space exists for greater economic democracy and equity. Many adherents to this view pride themselves on their rigor and realism, on their willingness to jettison dreams when confronted by economic imperatives.

At the same time, other critics of socialism and Marxism are not moving toward a more moderate view of capitalism, but are subsuming capitalism within a deeper critique of modernity, industrialism, and developmentalism, whether capitalist or state socialist. Rather than finding new virtues in capitalism because of hostility toward socialist regimes, they are evolving green or ecological critiques of the present that are different from but no less subversive than Marxism, focusing less on the exploitation and alienation of labor than on the impact of the global economy on physical and biological environments and the culturally diverse peoples of the world.[17]

Around issues of class the new social movements, at least in the advanced capitalist democracies, have retreated from the more libertarian moments in Marxist class politics. For instance, more attention has been given the professional class base of the new social movements than the influence of that class base on the goals and methods of the movements. More importantly, the politically correct triplet of race, class, and gender notwithstanding, challenging the full range of manifestations of class division is seldom a serious concern on the left. Racial and gender justice require not only correcting racially and sexually generated material inequality; they include changing the racial and gender divisions of labor, overcoming the marginalization of cultural expressions by minorities and women, and correcting imbalances of power between the races and sexes. But class justice has been narrowed to distributive justice, which treats neither the structural and institutional patterns that produce and reproduce material inequality nor social issues not reducible to inequality. Class justice not only requires distributive equity but also thoroughly challenges the social relations of production that contribute to patterns of domination and subordination, especially the social division of labor between the planning and execution of work. At first inattention to class might seem to make it easier to succeed in realizing other goals, given how radical the new social movements already are; yet preserving class positions—not only the benefits that derive from owning capital, but also those that accrue to people with cultural capital and positions of authority and expertise—can subvert democratic impulses and create destructive divisions within many social movements as well as influence visions of ultimate goals. One challenge movements today face is to clarify a class politics that is not grounded in teleologies that posit socialism as a total break with capitalism and that incorporate ecological critiques of developmentalism.

The new social movements will find the realization of their goals difficult not only because of competition from other political actors and the burden of historical legacies, but because of central qualities of the social movements themselves. In both liberal and Marxist theories of revolution, popular majorities sought to overthrow minority elites. Liberals assumed that absolutism could be ended by overthrowing kings and replacing them with bourgeois forms of representation. Marxists assumed that capitalists had to be overthrown to achieve socialism. The goal of class struggle was the end of capital's domination of labor, the transcendence of proletarian existence, and the end of class society.

Crucial aspects of new social movements, identity movements in particular, differ from both liberalism and Marxism in ways that complicate their goals. Consider the question of what social bases support political goals. Whereas nascent citizens and working classes formed (ideally, at least) the social bases of liberalism and socialism, the constituencies of many social movements are harder to grasp. Social movements against militarism, nuclear proliferation, acid rain, the greenhouse effect, commodified popular culture, religious intolerance, or government invasions of privacy do not have clear, stable constituencies. General problems like the threat of war, environmental destruction, and varied macroeconomic issues lack "natural" constituencies.[18]

Moreover, although identity groups often draw upon essentialist metaphors (of race, sex, or nationality, for example) to underscore a "natural" basis of their coherence, identity-based social movements do not have stable social bases either, and the political constitution of identities is not fixed. While some identity-based movements do enter into political coalitions with other movements around common goals, an equally strong tendency is toward ever more narrowly refined bases of affective unity, thereby fragmenting rather than unifying identity movements. The ways in which identities are socially constructed and historically variable can have a profound impact on political means and goals. Consider the importance for racial politics in the United States whether Spanish speakers are politically united as Hispanics or divided, say, between Puerto Ricans, Chicanos, and recent immigrants affiliated by country of origin. In addition, identity groups are heterogenous; differences exist within as well as between them; they can be riven by ideological fissures, such as the pornography debate among feminists, or by sociological differences such as gender, race, class, and ethnicity.

The problematic nature of constituencies for identity politics and new social movements complicates questions of representation, a crucial issue for democratic theory and practice. Even though many social movement radicals are impatient with representative forms of governance, they can only avoid, not transcend, questions about who does and can claim to speak for whom. Questions of voice and representation are involved not only when elite white men invoke a royal "we." Few identity movements claim only to speak for their active members: They also claim to speak for, to represent, others "like" themselves such as other women, other indigenous people, other gays or lesbians, other people of color.

The goals of many contemporary movements, especially those formed around identity politics, are also more complicated than those of liberalism and Marxism. Women, blacks, lesbians and gays, and American Indians, inter alia, neither refuse their identities nor seek only greater material rewards in their existing identities. They seek to transform their identities to end the oppression and marginality embedded in them. Several dilemmas arise from this complex project. First, for activists in identity movements to change themselves they also have to change others. As women, people of color, or gays and lesbians empower themselves and expand democracy and liberty, men, whites, and heterosexuals have to be disempowered as the kinds of men, whites, and heterosexuals who had oppressed them. Marxists did not seek to change capitalists but to defeat them as a class; liberal politicians do not seek to change interest groups but to set the terms for compromise. Identity politics, however, demands much more of both subordinate and dominant groups: It asks for major and subtle changes in definitions of ego and other, self and community, difference and hierarchy, and conceptions of the good life. Second, although identities are often narrowly defined, they are constructed through the articulation of many structural, institutional, and cultural practices. Women are not only oppressed by sexist men with whom they are in direct contact, but by institutional practices carried out by women as well as men, by broadly shared and deeply held traditional beliefs, and by economic dynamics not reducible to gender relations. Indigenous peoples are not only denied their rights and liberties by national and racial oppression but by powerful economic interests seeking access to natural resources.

These qualities of new social movements provoke a series of questions. How much change do identity groups demand from whom? What is entailed when oppressed people transform their identities so thoroughly that they are no longer constituted through patterns of hierarchy, marginalization, and silence? How much of the material rewards, services, patterns of deference, daily routines, traditions, cultural values, habits, and other aspects of the identities of dominant and subordinated groups have to be modified to erode the social logics that have reproduced racial, gender, and national hierarchies? Which aspects of the routines and even comforts of daily life will stay the same for whom, which will be only slightly modified for whom, and which will have to be drastically transformed for whom? How can individual autonomy and integrity be respected as people are encouraged and forced to change? Can people disempowered in their existing identities find meaning and satisfaction through empowerment and freedom in new identities not based on the oppression of others? Do the goals of the identity movements demand the creation of a whole new world, or can modest shifts in the cultural patterns of whiteness and maleness, for instance, fully accommodate antiracist and feminist goals? How do answers to these questions vary across modes of domination and marginalization?

Thus, today's social movements face formidable obstacles even as their goals necessitate more transformative change than most utopians have envisioned. It is precisely in this context that the very radicalism of the social movements could prove beneficial. Radical new social movements seek to change the rules of the game, "not just the distribution of relative advantages in a given organization."[19] Indeed, only by changing those rules can their ends be achieved. It is instructive to contrast social-movement goals with those of interest groups. Liberal pluralism assumes that interest-group competition takes place within existing structural and institutional boundaries. Economic growth is the main base upon which competing interest groups compromise and new groups are incorporated into the competitive game, because growth means that trade-offs do not take place within a zero-sum game. Economic growth can ease, if not erase, tensions and conflicts. Affirmative action is more readily accepted when the number of jobs is expanding; environmental regulations are easier to pass when they do not entail job loss and the tax base is expanding.

Interest-group politics demands very little cultural or personal change, especially of dominant or elite groups. They do not have to modify their sense of entitlement or understanding of how the basic institutional rules should work. They only have to modify their short-term expectations based on rational calculations of the balance of forces. In this model, capitalists and managers do not have to integrate into their vision of a productive enterprise a concern for job quality or health and safety; all they have to do is accede to shifts in power. Not having modified their individual or collective impulses to maximize profits, they will seek opportune moments to regain lost advantages.

Even though analysts who favor this approach to politics often consider themselves realists, the only way it is realistic is that it acknowledges the overwhelming power that economic, social, and political elites have to set the parameters within which politics is engaged. In the economic crisis of the 1970s, there was validity to the trilateralist and neoconservative argument that the proliferation of interest groups raising material demands was an "excess of democracy" threatening systemic overload. The realism of the argument rests on recognition of the tenacity with which elites, including themselves, hold onto power. Such "realists" turn the interests of elites into objective limits.

Fortunately many social movements not only want more; they want things to be different. They seek equality and respect, autonomy, and the right to participate in decision making, as well as higher wages. These goals may well involve economic growth and redistribution, but they even more demand changing the social context within which the economy is embedded and the rules of the game. These kinds of change can only be consolidated by changes in the very social logics that sustain domination, marginality, and environmental destruction. Thus Joan Cocks stresses that lasting political and social change takes place as people "supplant one 'moral-intellectual' universe with another."[20]

Defining Transformative Political Change

We need an updated, social-movement version of Andre Gorz's concept of "revolutionary reform," by which he meant "reforms which advance toward a radical transformation of society."[21] Revolutionary reforms transform basic structures by subverting the "rationality and practicality of a given system."[22] When he wrote *Strategy for Labor* (1967) Gorz viewed the working class as *the* agent of social change and capitalism as *the* source of systematic exploitation and domination, and he sought a form of struggle that "does not base its validity and its right to exist on capitalist needs, criteria, and rationales."[23] Today social movements challenge the "needs, criteria, and rationales" of many axes of domination by proposing radicalized forms of democracy to increase empowerment of more people across many domains of social life: extensions of human rights and other concepts of justice to broaden and deepen the normative grounds upon which substantive and procedural changes are based:

and substantive changes that erode persistent patterns of domination and marginality.

In *Beyond Revolution* Foss and Larkin propose a social-movement correlate to Gorz's revolutionary reforms. Successful social movements shift "the political and cultural reproduction of society."[24] They further create "changes in the locus of motivation of social movement participants, which diffuse into the larger population."[25] This emphasis on changing basic motivations is important but needs to be considered carefully. They use the term "sociocharacterological revolution," implying that all aspects of individual and collective identities are tightly and necessarily bound together. The social and psychic unity they assume has to be questioned in several ways.

First, social change is not an all-or-nothing proposition, as their phrase implies. For instance, women do not have to completely remake themselves to challenge male supremacy successfully. They have to change the relative importance of some behaviors, thoughts, and practices so that forms of sociality most in accord with their feminist ideals play an ever greater role in their lives while practices that had sustained their subordination fall away. These changes become structural as they become the basis of new individual and collective routines, are affirmed in the hegemonic culture, and are embodied in relevant institutional practices. This does not imply a complete transcendence of previous social character, although it is not clear how much change is necessary.

Second, the "we" implied by the phrase "social movement participants" needs to be questioned. As much as I wish it were the case, challenging domination within a given identity does not necessarily translate into identifying with the dominated in other identity groups, nor does it even guarantee expressions of solidarity with all people in one's own identity group. Challenges to particular experiences of domination do not necessarily lead people to oppose all forms of domination. Even more analytically challenging is the fact that individuals and small homogeneous groups are constituted via multiple axes of domination and subordination that interact with one another in complex ways. Sometimes they strengthen each other; other times they work at cross purposes. Race and gender are tightly interwoven and mutually constituting, but the actual weave will vary. There are times when racist politics heightens gender domination, yet racist organizing also can empower women of the dominant race, and antiracist activism by subordinated groups can be predicated upon and can result in the reassertion of male power within that group.

Third, patterns of diffusion of change "into the larger population" not only enlarge the social base supportive of change, but trigger resistance. The larger population not only contains people who will benefit from the change but people who have benefitted from prevailing patterns. The diffusion of political impulses or the extension of "logics of equivalence"[26] have different trajectories and political implications when they are extending a majority's liberatory impulses into new realms, when they are crossing from one social movement or identity group to another, and when they provoke yet other groups to react. Patterns of diffusion can help forge cohesive movements or coalitions, but they are also a basis of backlash politics. Hence successful movements promoting "sociocharacterological revolution" will not only produce allies but enemies.

Fourth, critiques of reductionism and essentialism within Marxism have revealed problems with postulating that certain forms of domination are primary or originary. But social movements still face analytic and strategic considerations that demand setting priorities. Are there some areas in which egalitarian practices are more readily incorporated into the repertoires of men and women? Are the areas in which women can most forcefully challenge male dominance the same areas in which men will most easily accommodate to women's demands for change? What challenges to economic inequality can best address racial and gender inequality as well? How can comprehensive challenges to economic, gender, and racial inequity be framed so they are compatible with environmental sustainability? Answers to these kinds of questions can not only provide theoretical insight into social systems but can also suggest strategic priorities to social movements, provide criteria for movement resource allocation, and identify more and less fruitful kinds of coalitions.

To return to Gorz, his stress on democratic mobilization in all spheres of society foreshadowed the current stress on the virtues of democratic practices, but it also reveals the limits of the new social movements' stress on the virtues of constant democratic mobilization.[27] He held that "[s]tructural reform is by definition a reform implemented or controlled by those who demand it . . . . a structural reform always requires the creation of new centers of democratic power."[28] He further insisted that "this power can only be exercised at the price of constant mobilization."[29] This is not quite right. In grounding structural reform in democratic mobilization, Gorz confused democratic means and substantive ends. Reforms are not structural if they have to be maintained through permanent extraordinary mobilization of the subordinate; they are structural when the "new centers of democratic power" become embodied in new daily routines not requiring constant vigilance. Let me give an example. In the United States today the rich can expect as a matter of routine that they and their children will receive good medical care. Poor people have to fight to receive good medical care at all, let alone receive it routinely. Achieving that goal will require persistent democratic struggles for reform of health care, and long-term solutions *may* involve the creation of (and provision of resources to) consultative bodies of women, minorities, the handicapped, gays and lesbians, and workers in industries with particular hazards to monitor the delivery of health care. But even here, ideally, we would want to advance to a situation in which the composition of the medical profession, the training of medical personnel, the culture of the medical profession, and the interactions of health-care provision and the broader economy were guided by an egalitarian ethos and democratic practices so that these consulting groups could work to strengthen and not resist dominant patterns in health care.

Clearly, progressive reform cannot be realized without empowerment of those currently subordinated; but neither can transformative change be realized across the vast numbers of society's inequities if in each area every subordinate group has to remain constantly mobilized. Sustainable empowerment requires overcoming the status quo through democratic mobilization *and* consolidating a new status quo. Reforms are structural to the extent that mobilization successfully produces a new social logic based on changed power relations between conflicting groups. Structural reforms modify social patterns to decrease inequity, cut down on the production of poisonous externalities, and give presence and voice to marginalized and silenced groups and individuals. To the extent that subordinated groups are able to transform the social logics that have sustained their domination, then in subsequent rounds of democratic participation they will be stronger and better able to demand further improvements in their lives.

Thus, democratic theory needs to be complemented by a theory of change attentive to how new patterns become routinized, and it needs to establish new expectations about what the world will be like on the morrow. For instance, what changes would it take for women to feel as comfortable as men walking alone at night in public spaces? Feelings of oppression and the experiences that have created them are, after all, not invariant, acontextual, or beyond change. Social movement activism like "take back the night" marches, self-help groups that offer transportation to women at night, ideological campaigns that raise the issue of women's rights, feminist-inspired reforms of police practices, and other (not gender specific) changes like sensitivity to pedestrians in urban planning can decrease women's fear. But when the march is over, energy and funds are exhausted for transport, a major developer withholds capital until he can dictate the refashioning of urban space, or some men lash out because they are enraged that women are "taking over," then advances in women's safety dissipate. Only when these "new centers of democratic power" become routinized and reinforced by other feminist advances and changes in male behavior will women regularly feel as safe as men in public. The empowerment of women has to become so thorough that it is neither counterintuitive nor counterhegemonic but constitutes the ordinary, mundane horizon of daily life, is constitutive of the practices that form and maintain institutions, and is reproduced via the many social structures in which gender is instantiated.

Structural reforms are a form of internalization; successful radical mobilizations forge a new status quo, new patterns of daily life, new routines, a new common sense. For Jean Piaget, as exogenous disruptions of a system overcome internal resistances, they become internalized, thereby creating a variation of the original system that in turn becomes the new equilibrium.[30]

While organic metaphors are not strictly applicable to political processes, Piaget's is illuminating. It helps distinguish changes that become the new equilibrium from those in which the basic reproductive logic does not change except when pressure is continually applied from external sources, be it intervention by foreign powers, state action, or nonroutine forms of mobilization. The internalization of a new social logic does not imply a static model; equilibria (old or new) can be dynamic. In dynamic systems internalization means that the trajectory of change becomes different than it would have been without the structural reform.

If structural reforms involve internalization, then Gorz's spatial metaphor—"new centers of democratic power"—is a bit misleading. New relations of power may initially take hold in particular sites, but they will only become self-reproducing, lasting "structural reforms" as they are realized as the micro- and macrolevels and across their mediations. Most feminists want their mates (generally male, but female as well) to internalize less gender-based divisions of labor, new ways of thinking about the value of housework, comprehension of the need for planning in the domestic economy, and not merely a (grudging) willingness to do specific tasks when reminded by a constantly vigilant mate. As feminists have noted, the need for constant vigilance (an individual correlate to constant collective mobilization) can be exhausting; forcing others to maintain that vigilance is itself a form of resistance to change. Feminists also seek to modify macroeconomic structures, practices, and policies so they are no longer actively male-biased or gender neutral (and hence responsive to gender-biased signals from other social relations) but instead contribute to gender equality. Of course, in early phases of such mobilization, prior to internalization, local centers of power might well exist as elements of the state, inroads in the dominant ideology, or particular institutional settings. But if those inroads are the extent of movement success, then the reproductive logic has not been changed.

There is no single correct, or even best, route to successfully achieving internalization, and a brief consideration of different ways in which successes can be realized indicates the need for a supple understanding of power. Social movements are internally complex and often embody divergent tactics. For instance, both militant mobilization and bringing expertise to bear on an issue are both prominent strategies among environmentalists. Structural reform can result from militant oppositional mobilization. The anti–toxic waste "not in my backyard" (NIMBY) movements of the 1980s led some corporations to modify their production processes as that practice became cheaper than externalizing their costs through hazardous dumping.[31] But there are other possible outcomes; successful NIMBY actions that do not simultaneously succeed in reforming production processes can increase the costs of safe waste disposal, thereby increasing taxpayer resistance.[32] Yet another corporate response is to dump waste in communities with the least organizational capacity to resist and the most economic need to receive waste; hence impoverished communities and nations can end up with it. NIMBY politics in this case enables some communities to do what powerful economic elites already do—displace costs onto others. The outcomes of militancy are thus indeterminate; the question then arises whether there are some issues over which insurgents could more positively contribute to structural reforms by offering ideologically compelling and practically viable alternatives than through resistance to the given. Militant opposition and providing expert testimony are not mutually exclusive tactics, of course; oppositional mobilization can force elites to listen to, consult with, and include insurgents in decision making. NIMBY movements, for instance, draw upon testimony of experts. In the politics of AIDS, ACT UP's acting out has been crucial; but that pressure has been applied in concert with ACT UP's capacity to intervene into scientific and medical debates and locate allies in various professions.[33] In the area of controlling biotechnology Jack Kloppenburg argues that "oppositionalist strategies are necessary, [but] they are not sufficient to achieve true economic democracy in techno-science. . . . The real challenge facing us is not to figure out how best to oppose particular biotechnologies, but to put institutions and mechanisms in place that—ideally—would preclude the need for opposition in the first place."[34]

There are dangers as well as attractions to internalizing reforms. Three particular dangers are worth noting. First, internalization is not an all-or-nothing affair. It can take place in some areas but not others, and imbalances can undercut the extent of the reforms achieved. For instance, even if it is cheaper at the aggregate level to internalize changes in production, it will often be economically rational for individual enterprises to continue to externalize costs. Different paces of internalization in a particular industry in different regions or polities in a global economy can well lead to resistance because mangers of firms that begin to internalize costs of production may fear that they will be at a disadvantage relative to corporations that continue to externalize those costs. Enterprise owners can more readily adapt to changes that slightly decrease their control over investment decisions and the disposition of surpluses when all relevant owners face the same constraints; they are much less likely to bear transition costs when others do not. This is one reason why strategies stressing internalization can seldom completely avoid state involvement; regulatory regimes that impose costs across all relevant economic actors can undermine resistance to change and help set new rules for engaging in production and other economic transactions.[35] This does not mean, of course, that elites welcome regulations that diminish their power and autonomy; they will search for ways to avoid regulation and regain their advantages, privileges, and command over resources.

Second, a similar phenomenon exists for issues raised by identity movements. Even as some groups of men, for example, begin partially to internalize feminist norms, that process does not take place evenly across all groups and regions. Thus the conflict between subordinate and dominant groups—

women and men—can become overlaid by, or even recast as, conflict based on other identities such as region, religion, or class. Successful reactive movements can create political and cultural cleavages that cut against those shaped by radical social movements, thereby forging coalitions that undercut the power of insurgent movements.

Third, and perhaps the most troublesome issue ethically, is that the internalization of new outlooks on life—not merely new structures of action—is potentially personally coercive or freedom inhibiting. It is one thing to deprive economic elites of their control over resources by anchoring property relations and economic transactions in egalitarian and ecologically sound social practices. It is one thing to demand that homophobic religious fundamentalists act with a modicum of tolerance toward homosexuals in public. Both of these changes inhibit the freedom of some (economic elites and homophobes) to enhance the freedom of others (economic majorities and gays, lesbians, and heterosexuals committed to diversity and tolerance) by changing the structures of incentives for self-interested action. However, it is more invasive to require that people not only conform to new standards of behavior but reject deeply held cultural values for themselves and their children. It smacks of social engineering to demand that people (whose culture and mores legitimate privileges) reject their own values and welcome into schools, churches, and families a cultural politics designed to instill the very values they oppose. Ultimately it is preferable that economic inequality and homophobic violence decline because people are no longer inclined to engage in behaviors that perpetuate them than because of (statistically significant levels of) rational adjustment to new regulatory regimes that discourage intolerant acts. Internalization of such new "moral-intellectual outlooks" involves changing the reproductive logics of personal values as well as macroinstitutional dynamics. Some critics of such change argue that it is an inexorable, slippery slope from, for instance, encouraging tolerance for gays to the totalitarian gulag. Yet many of these same critics believe that schools, churches, and families should teach manners and "family values," or inculcate patriotism. As is often the case, substantive and procedural commitments get confused. There are no universally valid rules for determining what kinds of attitudinal changes should be encouraged for whom and by whom in what ways.

At the same time, there are many benefits that follow when transformative change is internalized institutionally and culturally. The worry that cultural change is coercive too often marginalizes attention to the hurt felt by people who are daily confronted by intolerance, humiliation, and violence, and does not take the prevention of further wrongs seriously. If there are psychic costs for economic elites, men, and heterosexuals to shed the attitudes and privileges of their positions, there are surely greater psychic costs for the poor, women, and gays and lesbians who continue to experience domination. Homosexuals would rather not be assaulted than know they have recourse in the judicial system. Workers would rather not be maimed on the job even knowing they can sue from their hospital beds. Most indigenous peoples would rather save their lands and forests than have post facto recourse to the World Court.

There are other benefits from changing reproductive logics. The more change has to be actively regulated by the state and the more formal rationality extends over broad domains, the more complex institutional arrangements will be and the more reform will cost. Critics of bureaucracy and institutional complexity and libertarians committed to freedom from coercive states have a stake in directly transforming the basic patterns that reproduce domination and environmental destruction. It will not be possible to get rid of all complexity, but in many ways modest reforms are more costly and complex than radical ones. Modest reforms can either be a route to or retreat from radical reforms. Take, again, the issue of violence against gays. For the economy as a whole it is cheaper for heterosexuals to stop beating gays than for gays to succeed in expanding police patrols, calling upon therapeutic services, taking court time to prosecute their assailants, and possibly even jailing some of their abusers. Successful demands for these partial responses will increase taxes, create more public sector jobs, and shift the patterns by which the state acts relative to sexual preference. Depending on one's perspective the costly inflation of the state can be blamed on homosexuals with the temerity to insist on their rights and bodily integrity, or on those who resist change.

As gays and lesbians, feminists, environmentalists, and others succeed in achieving the internalization of their goals, or even some of their goals, then democratic activism takes place on a qualitatively different social terrain, the nature of necessary trade-offs will change, and the ways in which civil society functions will be more democratic and liberatory. Successful social movement activism then also means that the kinds of complementarities and tensions that exist between social movements and more routine forms of politics will also take place in different ways. Less political energy and fewer economic resources will have to go into forestalling disaster and compensating for domination. Internalizing changes in many social formations so the trajectory of change is dramatically modified toward environmental balance, equality, and respect for diversity is less dramatic than revolutionary moments that cataclysmically divide the past from the future; but the goals remain revolutionary.

□ □ □

There are many reasons for pessimism today; but these reasons are not given by nature or human nature, nor are different goals so at odds with one another they create insurmountable blocks to progress. Dominant as well as subordinate groups are increasingly riven by many competing identities which create opportunities for progressive coalitions; identities are not only given but chosen, and democratic ideology remains strong. Social changes of revolutionary proportions are essential to realize the goals already considered legitimate by many millions of people. Derrick Bells' fictive interlocutor Geneva Crenshaw was right to insist that "the goal of a just society for all is morally correct, strategically necessary, and tactically sound."[36]

NOTES

Acknowledgment: I would like to acknowledge the helpful suggestions and critical comments of Barbara Epstein.

1. George Steiner, "Books," *New Yorker,* September 10, 1990, 113.
2. Jon Elster, *Making Sense of Marx* (New York: Cambridge University Press, 1985), and Seyla Benhabib, *Critique, Norm, and Utopia: A Study of the Foundations of Critical Theory* (New York: Columbia University Press, 1986).
3. This perspective is taken by a number of commentators today. See, for instance, Samuel Bowles and Herbert Gintis, *Democracy and Capitalism: Property, Community, and the Contradictions of Modern Social Thought* (New York: Basic Books, 1986); Ernesto Laclau and Chantal Mouffe, *Hegemony and Socialist Strategy: Towards a Radical Democratic Politics* (London: Verso, 1985); Chantal Mouffe, "Preface: Democratic Politics Today," in Chantal Mouffe, ed., *Dimensions of Radical Democracy: Pluralism, Citizenship, Community* (London: Verso, 1992), 1–14; Jürgen Habermas and Adam Michnik, "Overcoming the Past," *New Left Review* no. 203 (January–February 1994): 3–16.
4. Andrew Arato and Jean L. Cohen, *Civil Society and Political Theory* (Cambridge: MIT Press, 1992).
5. See Jean L. Cohen, "Strategies of Identity: New Theoretical Paradigms and Contemporary Social Movements," *Social Research,* special issue on social movements, vol. 52, no. 4 (Winter 1985): 663–716; and Alain Touraine, "The Idea of Revolution," *Theory, Culture & Society* 7 (1990): 121–41.
6. In Robert C. Tucker, ed, *The Marx-Engels Reader* (New York: W. W. Norton, 1978), 84.
7. For conservatives this fear conveniently legitimates anti-elitist *and* antipopulist fears: totalizing visions do not arise from liberal democratic politics but spring full-blown from the heady idealism of arrogant elitists, and / or they are the unleashing of uncontrolled, visceral populist movements. But conservatives are not alone in criticizing emancipatory visions. For a useful compendium of post-Marxist worries about and criticisms of emancipation as a political goal see Ernesto Laclau, "Beyond Emancipation," *Development and Change* 23, no. 3 (July 1992): 121–37.
8. L. A. Kauffman, "Socialism, No," *The Progressive,* April 1993, 27–29.
9. Both Goren Therborn (who still finds value in modernist projects) and Zygmunt Bauman (who embraces postmodernity) link the fates of socialism and communism to modernity. See Goren Therborn, "The Life and Times of Socialism," *New Left Review* no. 194 (July / August 1992): 17–32; and Zygmunt Bauman, *Modernity and Ambivalence* (New York: Routledge, 1991). Indeed Bau-

man states that "people who celebrate the collapse of communism, as I do, celebrate more than that without always knowing it. They celebrate the end of modernity actually, because what collapsed was the most decisive attempt to make modernity work; and it failed. It failed as blatantly as the attempt was blatant" (Zygmunt Bauman, *Intimations of Modernity* [New York: Routledge, 1992], 222).

10. While in a minority, I am not alone in taking this position. For instance, the authors of *Transforming the Revolution* argue that today's social movements are "transforming the revolutionary process itself" (Samir Amin, Giovanni Arrighi, Andre Gunder Frank, and Immanuel Wallerstein, *Transforming the Revolution* [New York: Monthly Review Press, 1990], 11); see as well Barbara Epstein, *Political Protest and Cultural Revolution: Nonviolent Direct Action in the 1970s and 1980s* (Berkeley: University of California Press, 1991).

11. Michael Walzer, "A Theory of Revolution," *Marxist Perspectives* 2, no. 1 (Spring 1979): 30–44.

12. Sidney Tarrow, *Struggle, Politics and Reform: Collective Action, Social Movements, and Cycles of Protest* (Ithaca, N.Y.: Western Societies Program Occasional Paper no. 21, Center for International Studies, Cornell University, 1989).

13. Even though most of the literature about the new social movements argues that they are framed by cultural politics, not distributive concerns, I note the continuing importance of economic demands for three reasons. First, the scholarly literature underplays the economic component of many new social movement issues—for instance, race and gender issues like affirmative action or comparable worth have clear economic dimensions. Second, in the United States new social movements do not have a monopoly on progressive activism. Many organizations with working class and poor constitutencies constantly organize around economic issues as well as issues associated with the new social movements. For a recent overview of community organizing projects attentive to identity politics as well as classic community-organizing concerns see Gary Delgado, *Beyond the Politics of Place: New Directions in Community Organizing in the 1990s* (Oakland: Applied Research Center, 1993). Third, popular social movements in the third world are often based among peasants, urban and rural workers, and the poor, for whom economic demands alone, or economic demands fused with environmental or other concerns, are central. A small sample of this literature includes: David Slater, ed., *New Social Movements and the State in Latin America* (Amsterdam: FORIS Publications, 1985); Susan Eckstein, ed., *Power and Popular Protest: Latin American Social Movements* (Berkeley: University of California Press, 1989); Arturo Escobar and Sonia E. Alvarez, eds., *The Making of Social Movements in Latin America: Identity, Strategy and Democracy* (Boulder: Westview Press, 1992); Elizabeth Jelin, ed., *Women and Social Change in Latin America* (London: Zed Books, 1990); Robin Broad with John Cavanagh, *Plundering Paradise: The Struggle for the Environment in the Philippines* (Berkeley: University of California Press, 1993);

Ponna Wignaraja, ed., *New Social Movements in the South: Empowering the People* (London: Zed Books, 1993).

14. I know the term "transformation" is vague; it gestures to something more than minor reforms within the existing rules of the game; it is something other than an apocalpytic revolutionary "moment." In using the term I mean, as I indicate below, changing the social logics that have reproduced domination so the direction of change is toward the diminuation of domination, the enhancement of equality and democracy. I recognize that this remains vague. For a consideration of uses of the term in the context of South Africa in transition from apartheid, see Mala Singh, "Transformation Time!" *Transformation* no. 17 (1992): 48–60.

15. Martin Jacques, "After Capitalism, What Now?" *Social Policy* 21, no. 2 (Fall 1990): 14.

16. Adam Przeworski, *Democracy and the Market: Political and Economic Reforms in Eastern Europe and Latin America* (New York: Cambridge University Press, 1991), 133.

17. See, for instance, the essays in two recent volumes edited by Wolfgang Sachs, *The Development Dictionary: A Guide to Knowledge as Power* (London: Zed Books, 1992), and *Global Ecology: A New Arena of Political Conflict* (London: Zed Books, 1993).

18. See Barbara Epstein, *Political Protest and Cultural Revolution,* and Ellen Meiksins Wood, "Capitalism and Human Emancipation," *New Left Review* no. 167 (January/February 1988): 3–20.

19. Alain Touraine, "An Introduction to the Study of Social Movements," *Social Research* 52, no. 4 (Winter 1985): 753.

20. Joan Cocks, *The Oppositional Imagination* (New York: Routledge, 1989), 78.

21. Andre Gorz, *Strategy for Labor: A Radical Proposal* (Boston: Beacon Press, 1967), 6

22. Gorz, *Strategy for Labor,* 7.

23. Ibid.

24. Daniel A. Foss and Ralph Larkin, *Beyond Revolution: A New Theory of Social Movements* (South Hadley, Mass.: Bergin and Garvey Publishers, 1986), 2.

25. Foss and Larkin, *Beyond Revolution,* 90.

26. The phrase is Laclau and Mouffe's from *Hegemony and Socialist Strategy.*

27. It also prefigured the New Left's civilizational critique of daily life by moving beyond an economist version of class politics.

28. Gorz, *Strategy for Labor,* 8, footnote.

29. Gorz, *Strategy for Labor,* 10.

30. Jean Piaget, *The Equilibration of Cognitive Structures: The Central Problem in Intellectual Development* (Chicago: University of Chicago Press, 1985). Thanks to Jeremy Brecher for mentioning Piaget to me in this context.

31. Andrew Szasz, "In Praise of Policy Luddism: Strategic Lessons from the Hazardous Waste Wars," *Capitalism, Nature and Socialism* 2, no. 1 (February 1991):

17–43; also see his *EcoPopulism: Toxic Waste and the Movement for Environmental Justice* (Minneapolis: University of Minnesota Press, 1994).

32. Wally Seccombe, "Changing Our Relationship with Nature: Elements of a Transitional Program for a Green Economy" (1990).

33. Steven Epstein, "Democratic Science? AIDS Activism and the Contested Construction of Knowledge," *Socialist Review* 21, no. 2 (April–June 1991): 35–64.

34. Jack Kloppenburg, Jr., "Alternative Agriculture and the New Biotechnologies," *Science as Culture* 2, no. 4 (1991): 496–97.

35. The tendency to view new social movements as uninterested in the state is too simple. It may be that they do not have a vocation for achieving state power as liberal and socialist movements did; but they do often seek to modify state-society interactions in profound ways, to demand that the state intervene into economic or social practices.

36. Derrick Bell, *And We Shall Not Be Saved: The Elusive Quest for Racial Justice* (New York: Basic Books, 1986), 256.

ABOUT THE CONTRIBUTORS
AND INDEX

□

About the Contributors

□   □   □   □   □   □   □   □   □   □   □   □

RICHARD A. CLOWARD is Professor of Sociology at the Columbia University School of Social Work. He and Frances Fox Piven updated their co-authored classic, *Regulating the Poor: The Functions of Social Welfare*, in 1993. He and Piven have also co-authored a series of books on popular struggles and state responses, including *Poor People's Movements* and *The Mean Season*.

MARCY DARNOVSKY, a Ph.D. candidate in the History of Consciousness program at the University of California, Santa Cruz, is writing a dissertation titled "The Greens Go to Market: U.S. Environmentalists Confront Consumer Culture." Her recent publications include articles on gender and advertising and on the history of the U.S. environmental movement. She was a co-organizer of the conference from which this volume emerged.

ALICE ECHOLS is the author of *Daring to be Bad: Radical Feminism in America, 1967–1975*. She lives and teaches in Los Angeles and is currently working on a book manuscript titled "Nobody's Girl: The Life and Times of Janis Joplin."

BARBARA EPSTEIN teaches in the History of Consciousness program at the University of California, Santa Cruz. Her most recent book is *Political Protest and Cultural Revolution: Nonviolent Direct Action in the 1970s and 1980s*. She was a co-organizer of the conference from which this volume emerged.

JEFFREY ESCOFFIER is a freelance editor and writer living in New York City. He is the author of *John Maynard Keynes*, a biography in a series about notable lesbians and gay men. He is former editor of the *Socialist Review* and former publisher of *OUT/LOOK: National Lesbian and Gay Quarterly*.

ILENE ROSE FEINMAN is currently writing her dissertation in the History of Consciousness program at the University of California, Santa Cruz. Her fields of interest are twentieth-century history and politics of U.S. militarism and the anti-militarist movements therein. She was a co-organizer of the conference from which this volume emerged.

RICHARD FLACKS teaches sociology at the University of California, Santa Barbara. His recent books include *Beyond the Barricades: The Sixties Generation Grows*

Up (with Jack Whalen) and *Making History: The American Left and the American Mind.* He is currently developing a project on the uses of music by social movements.

CYNTHIA HAMILTON is director of African and African American Studies at the University of Rhode Island. She is a long-time community activist.

ALLEN HUNTER, a sociologist, is the Administrative Director of the A. E. Havens Center for the Study of Social Structure and Social Change in the Sociology Department at the University of Wisconsin, Madison.

L. A. KAUFFMAN, the former executive editor of *Socialist Review,* is writing a book on radical activism since the 1960s.

REBECCA E. KLATCH is Associate Professor of Sociology at the University of California, San Diego. She is the author of *Women of the New Right* and is currently working on a manuscript titled "A Generation Divided: The New Right, the New Left, and the 1960s."

MARGIT MAYER is a professor of politics at the Free University of Berlin. She has written on urban social movements and state responses in the USA and West Germany, on the genesis of the American nation-state, on the German Green Party, and on post-Fordist cities. She is currently editing a book, "Theories of New Social Movements in Europe and the USA."

ALBERTO MELUCCI is Professor of Sociology at the University of Milan. He is the author of many books on social movements and sociocultural change. His *Nomads of the Present: Social Movements and Individual Needs in Contemporary Society* is available in English.

BRONISLAW MISZTAL is Professor of Sociology at Indiana University, Fort Wayne. He has edited and co-authored three books on social movements: *Poland after Solidarity: Social Movements vs. the State; Social Movements as a Factor of Change in the Contemporary World;* and *Religion and Politics in Comparative Perspective: Revival of Religious Fundamentalism in East and West.* He is currently working on a volume about religion in the twenty-first century and two other book projects on social movements and social change.

OSHA NEUMANN is an attorney in private practice in Berkeley, California, specializing in police misconduct and the rights of the homeless. He also paints, draws, and agitates on a regular basis.

FRANCES FOX PIVEN is Distinguished Professor of Political Science and Sociology at the Graduate Center, City University of New York. She and Richard

Cloward updated their co-authored classic, *Regulating the Poor: The Functions of Social Welfare*, in 1993. She and Cloward have also co-authored a series of books on popular struggles and state responses, including *Poor People's Movements* and *The Mean Season*. Piven recently edited *Labor Parties in Post-Industrial Societies*.

CRAIG REINARMAN is Professor of Sociology at the University of California, Santa Cruz. He is the author of *American States of Mind*, co-author of *Cocaine Changes*, and co-editor of *Crack in Context: Demon Drugs and Social Justice*. He is currently engaged in a cross-cultural project on drugs and social policy.

ROLAND ROTH is a professor of politics at Magdeburg. His writing focuses on social movements, local politics, regulation theory, and political corruption. His most recent book is *Democracy from Below: New Social Movements on the Way to Becoming a Political Institution*.

MINDY SPATT received her J.D. degree in 1979 from the Antioch School of Law and is a freelance writer and political activist in San Francisco.

ARLENE STEIN teaches sociology at the University of Oregon. Her articles on sexuality, culture, and social movements have been widely anthologized. She is the editor of *Sisters, Sexperts and Queers: Beyond the Lesbian Nation*.

NOËL STURGEON is Assistant Professor of Women's Studies at Washington State University and has written on the direct-action movement and the ecofeminist movement. She is presently working on a book entitled *Ecofeminist Nature: Race, Gender, and Environmental Politics* (forthcoming).

ANDREW SZASZ is Associate Professor of Sociology at the University of California at Santa Cruz, where he teaches courses in environmental sociology and sociological theory. He is the author of *Ecopopulism: Toxic Waste and the Movement for Environmental Justice*.

HOWARD WINANT teaches sociology and Latin American Studies at Temple University in Philadelphia. He is the co-author (with Michael Omi) of *Racial Formation in the United States: From the 1960s to the 1990s*. He has also written *Racial Conditions: Politics, Theory, Comparisons* and *Stalemate: Political Economic Origins of Supply-Side Policy*.

Index

□ □ □ □ □ □ □ □ □ □ □ □

128497